Refiguring American Music
A series edited by Ronald Radano and Josh Kun
Charles McGovern, contributing editor

The Political Force
of Musical Beauty

BARRY SHANK

DUKE UNIVERSITY PRESS | DURHAM AND LONDON | 2014

Designed by Amy Ruth Buchanan
Typeset in Chaparral Pro and Avenir
by Tseng Information Systems, Inc.

Library of Congress Cataloging-in-Publication Data
Shank, Barry
The political force of musical beauty / Barry Shank.
p. cm — (Refiguring american music)
ISBN 978-0-8223-5646-2 (cloth : alk. paper)
ISBN 978-0-8223-5658-5 (pbk. : alk. paper)
1. Music—Social aspects. 2. Music—Political
aspects. 3. Group identity in the performing arts.
I. Title. II. Series: Refiguring American music.
ML3916.S53 2014
781.1′1—dc23
2013042799

Contents

Acknowledgments

||||

The first lie in every book can be found on the cover and the title page. Although the concept of social authorship is widespread and everyone knows that no author works alone, only a single name appears on the publishing contract. The name of the book graces only one CV. When the work is cited, algorithms accumulate the total for only one career. I sincerely apologize for this first lie. The second lie in every book is most often found in the acknowledgments, where the credited author tries to make up for the first lie by thanking all those who made the work possible. Where the first lie is one of commission, the second is most often one of omission. It is nearly impossible to thank all who contributed to the creation and publication of this book. If your name is not here, you know you helped. And you may berate me for my lying ways the next time you see me. I'll buy you a drink.

I am grateful for the institutional support of the division of Arts and Humanities at The Ohio State University, who provided me with a two-quarter leave that resulted in drafts of three chapters of this book as well as helping support trips to the United Kingdom in 2011 and to Germany in 2010 and 2012. Considerably more gratitude is owed to the Department of Comparative Studies, especially the two chairs, David Horn and Eugene Holland, who recognized the value of yet another book on popular music. Many colleagues at OSU helped both intellectually and emotionally, including especially Hugh Urban, Philip Armstrong, Ruby Tapia, Arved Ashby, Graeme Boone, Brian Rotman, Dorry Noyes, Joe Panzner, Ricky Crano, Lindsay Bernhagen, RaShelle Peck, and Brian Murphy. Arguments and materials that ended up in this book were presented to sharp critical auditors in departmental colloquia for Comparative Studies and the Musicology Lecture Series, at various meetings of the American Studies Association, the U.S. branch of the International

Association for the Study of Popular Music, the EMP Pop Conference, the Annenberg Research Series at the University of Southern California, and the Post-45 group. Many colleagues in those organizations helped me to sharpen my arguments, but I want to give special thanks to Jason Toynbee, Charles McGovern, Eric Weisbard, Josh Kun, Bernard Gendron, Ronald Radano, Cotton Seiler, Caroline Polk O'Meara, Karl Hagstrom Miller, Kevin Gaines, David Suisman, Steve Waksman, Diane Pecknold, Alejandro Madrid, Keir Keightley, Kevin Fellezs, Penny Von Eschen, Alice Echols, David Hesmondhalgh, Shana Redmond, and Roshy Kheshti. My dear friend Jason Toynbee helped to organize a trip to the United Kingdom in 2011, during which parts of this book were presented to frighteningly astute audiences at the University of Leeds and the University of East London, and to an excellent conference the following year titled "Music, Methods and the Social" at the University of Leicester. With the help of the Fulbright Commission and the unequaled organizational skills of Udo Hebel, I enjoyed the opportunity to present some of this material to groups at the University of Regensburg; the Ludwig Maximilian University, Munich; the University of Rostock; the Martin Luther University of Halle-Wittenberg; and the University of Leipzig. Early versions of arguments from chapters 1 and 3 appeared as "The Political Agency of Musical Beauty," *American Quarterly* 63, no. 3 (September 2011); "Productive Orientalisms: Imagining Noise and Silence Across the Pacific, 1957–1967," in Alejandro Madrid and Ignacio Corona, eds., *Postnational Musical Identities: Cultural Production, Distribution and Consumption in a Globalized Scenario* (Lanham, MD: Lexington Books, 2007); and "Abstraction and Embodiment: Yoko Ono and the Weaving of Global Musical Networks," *Journal of Popular Music Studies* (Winter 2006). Portions are reprinted with the permission of the publishers.

I would like to thank the editorial staff at Duke University Press, particularly Ken Wissoker and Elizabeth Ault. Ken found two incredibly helpful readers who provided immense aid, Bernie Gendron and Ron Radano. Although I did not always take their advice, this book is much better for their having offered it. Sara Leone helped guide this book through production, and Rebecca Fowler contributed an immense amount of copyediting advice. Out of nothing but their own good will, many friends also read and commented on drafts of several chapters. Big thanks to Jason Toynbee, Cotton Seiler, Philip Armstrong, Benjamin Piekut, Eric Weisbard, and Ricky Crano. Ricky also contributed yeoman work at two different stages of this project. He tracked down many of the sources that helped structure the earliest drafts of many chapters. More recently, he helped me find photographs and obtain permissions for the use of these photographs. He even drove to Cincinnati to take photographs of Tinariwen for the book's coda. Glen Friedman and Charles Peterson allowed the use of their amazing photographs. I am most grateful for the time and sincerity with which members of Alarm Will Sound patiently answered my questions and for the grace with which they allowed me to watch their rehearsals: Alan Pierson, Gavin Chuck, Stefan Freund, Jacqueline Leclair, Payton MacDonald, Courtney Orlando, Jason Price, and John Richards. Special thanks to Michael Harley, who introduced me to his friends and convinced them that this project had some value.

Most important, Shari Speer and Claire Shank put up with a house endlessly echoing with the sounds of Vera Hall, Pete Seeger, Sam Cooke, Yoko Ono, Takemitsu, the Velvets, Patti Smith, Bad Brains, Beat Happening, Bikini Kill, Alarm Will Sound, and Tinariwen. Shari and Claire's patience and love make everything else possible.

| | | | |

The Political Force of Musical Beauty describes the relationship between a set of powerful musical experiences and the incoherence of political belonging. The book's basic argument is that the act of musical listening enables us to confront complex and mobile structures of impermanent relationships—the sonic interweaving of tones and beats, upper harmonics, and contrasting timbres—that model the experience of belonging to a community not of unity but of difference. The pleasures that derive from this experience are both aesthetic and political. The task of this book is to explore that experience in search of the abstract connections between those two realms. Its key terms are: *music, musical listening, political community*, and *beauty*. Through an analysis of these terms and a series of close readings of a group of musical texts, I try to demonstrate the intricate and incalculable relation of mutual determination between the experience of musical beauty and the feeling of political belonging.

We all know this feeling: the joy of mutual recognition that leaps within us during moments of dance-floor communion, when the DJ or the musicians *hit it*. We also know this feeling: the profound disappointment that comes over us when later conversation with our dance-floor compatriots reveals vast gulfs of mutual incomprehension. I am interested in both of those feelings. Why is it that we feel as though those with whom we share brief moments of musical bliss must be like us in some important ways? Why do we feel so frustrated when they turn out to be unlike us in matters of equal significance? What is it about this combination of communion and disappointment, of joy and frustration that captures the sense of both shared musical pleasure and political struggle?

||||

Many scholars, musicians, and activists have written and sung about the entanglement of music and politics. In most cases their attention has been focused on the political use of music. In most cases, even in high-quality studies such as Craig Werner's *A Change Is Gonna Come*, Marc Anthony Neal's *What the Music Said*, and Robert Cantwell's *When We Were Good*, the central topic is the ways in which political actors used music to forward their goals.[1] These books and others like them have documented the importance of music in social movements. Nearly anonymous Civil Rights marchers sang together to keep their spirits up and to remind each other of their shared purpose. The drive for social justice and the continuity of black community was a central topic in songs written by and sung by Stevie Wonder, Marvin Gaye, Nina Simone, and countless others. The right to sexual autonomy has been carried atop melodies sung by Patti Labelle, Gloria Gaynor, Frank Ocean, and so many more. But in almost every discussion of the convergence between music and politics, the music has simply served as a vehicle, conveying already shared political sentiments back and forth among singers and listeners.

The Political Force of Musical Beauty tries to do something else. In this book, I show how music, mostly popular music but also some religious and some postclassical music, enacts its own force, creating shared senses of the world. The experience of musical beauty confirms within its listeners the sense that this moment of listening has within it the promise of things being right, of pieces fitting together, of wholes emerging out of so much more than assembled riffs and rhythms. That affect is powerful. It can overwhelm the most cautious and sober rationalist. Just think of Theodor Adorno trying to explain the power of Beethoven, reaching for precision yet achieving only delicate metaphor.[2] When we hear the exquisite combination of right sonic relations, of auditory sensations of tension and release, of concentrated effects of sounding pressure and muscular response, we sense a commonality that feels right, that announces that this *we* that we are at this moment is the right *we*, the *we* that we are meant to be. Dave Hickey describes it this way: "The experience of . . . beauty is inextricable from its optimal social consequence: our membership in a happy coalition of citizens who agree on what is beautiful, valuable, and just."[3]

Of course, this is not literally true. Even when sharing experiences of beauty, we do not agree on all that is beautiful or valuable or just. It simply feels as if we do. This contradiction, the coexistence of a feeling of unity and shared beauty with the knowledge that those with whom we are sharing that feeling can and do disagree with us deeply on funda- mentally important matters, has defeated many attempts to understand the force of musical beauty. How can both of those conditions be true? If we belong to a group forged from musical beauty, not a group brought together by an already existing shared political sensibility, then most often we contain multitudes characterized by difference, not unity. If this is a group formed in the late twentieth or early twenty-first century in the United States, this *we* could include free-market absolutists with proponents of economic redistribution. It could blend Young Earthers with Darwinists, advocates of marriage equality with antihomosexual activists.

In what sense, then, can this be a political community? Simple: political community is not characterized by sameness. A political community does not consist of those who agree on the matters at hand, but instead is made up of those who recognize each other as speaking with legitimate political voices. It is precisely that group which is characterized by the existence of meaningful difference among its members. A political community is one that disagrees. It is one where agonistic struggles for power constitute its daily activities. But not all difference. A political community embraces only some differences, only those differences that are felt to be legitimate. This is the understanding that Jacques Rancière brings to the intersection of aesthetics and politics. The aesthetic and the political converge on what he calls "the distribution of the sensible."[4] A truly aesthetic musical act is one that reveals the political significance of sounds previously heard as nothing but noise. In this way, an aesthetic musical act changes the shape of the political. It can render previously inarticulate voices in such a manner that their beauty cannot be denied and, in so doing, extend the range of the political to include these voices in its incoherent communion.

This is why I insist on beauty as the locus of music's power. The experience of beauty is the recognition of the way things could be, the way things should be. The ability to produce beauty, therefore, is an index of the ability to imagine a better future. It is important not to confuse musical beauty with prettiness or quickly achieved consonance. Many of the examples of musical beauty that I analyze delay resolution, refuse traditional harmonic progressions, and avoid melodies that end where they began. They largely eschew clean timbres, replacing them with rasping voices, scraped strings, and electronically enhanced distortion. It is also necessary not to link musical beauty too quickly with an assumed teleology of musical advance. Although some of the music I discuss was initially heard as avant-garde, other examples were aimed at commercial success and some were deliberate throwbacks to previous forms of musicking. Sometimes the music I analyze is out of tune and out of time. Nonetheless, each of these examples creates a particular set of terms whereby the sounds within them emerge as beautiful. They all produce a sonic image of right relations, an audible constellation of mobile forms shifting in time, performing and occasionally transforming one's sense of the world.

Let me rephrase that last sentence. To be honest, every one of the musical examples I analyze transformed my sense of the world. From "A Change Is Gonna Come" to "The Star-Spangled Banner," from "Revolution 9" to "Philosophy of the World," from "November Steps" to "Heroin," from "Rebel Girl" to "Pay to Cum" to Patti Smith's versions of "Gloria" and "Hey Joe," every one of these and the other examples I discuss hailed me instantly, and in so doing, changed me and changed the world that I had been living in, making it somehow new. In this book I insist that those changes were brought about musically, through the "tonally moving forms" that made up the substance of their sounds.[5] I spend a considerable amount of time, therefore, explaining how those sounds worked. The articulation of particular sonic forms is a necessary condition of possibility for the beautiful power of these songs. These forms were combined at the moment of the music's production, capturing an emergent sense of the world. They are historically specific both in terms of the musical conventions they engage (including the social ground of those conventions) and in terms of the political effects they generated. The forms' effects, however, are not frozen at the time of production. They resonate anew with each hearing. Against music absolutists, I argue that the real moment of musical beauty comes in the time of listening. That is when the effects spread, when sounding sources meet musical listening.

Musical listening transforms our auditory attention just when we decide that the sounds we are hearing are music. Musical listening carries the expectation that a set of sounds can be apprehended as formal relations interacting with each other. As awareness shifts, attention focuses. I am not talking about rarified "structural listening" here.[6] Instead I am talking about an everyday occurrence. Everyone listens to music in this way. Even those who have no musical training at all hear some sounds as music and others as noise. The capacity to make that judgment is incumbent upon the phenomenon of musical listening. Musical listening brings together the distributed sensible of the world of the listener and musical beauty's potential to transform that world.

The Political Force of Musical Beauty examines several cases of the musical redistribution of the sensible. It begins with an analysis of the layering of misplaced intentions upon the golden voice of Vera Hall. In 1999 the electronica artist Moby released his version of Hall singing "Trouble So Hard," retitled "Natural Blues." While some heard this re-contextualization of her voice as little more than theft, I argue for hearing Moby's work as a means of working through the history of multiple thefts of her voice. The second chapter discusses anthems, the music most commonly thought of as political. It traces the development of anthems from their religious origins through the rise of the nation-state to Civil Rights songs and eventually the pop anthem. Traditional anthems reinforce already existing political communities. Pop anthems are more momentary in their effects. But they have the potential to evoke a new sense of the world. In so doing, pop anthems help to produce the mass-culture phenomenon that Lauren Berlant has named "intimate publics." An intimate public is an achievement. Participants in an intimate public, one created by a pop anthem, for example, feel as if they "*already* share a worldview and emotional knowledge that they have derived from a broadly common historical experience."[7] This moment of commonality is both deeply felt and recognized as tenuous and fragile. A song such as Sam Cooke's "A Change Is Gonna Come" precisely captures that blend of vulnerable intimate commonality.

Following the analysis of the anthem comes a discussion of two Japanese musicians' attempts to escape the constricting effects of historical experience. In the first half of the twentieth century, traditional and Western forms of music were both mobilized in service of the imperial state. Western "classical" music became strongly associated with the Japanese state's modernizing efforts, while traditional court music retained its associations with the cultural elite. Japanese composers took a variety of stances in response to these conditions, but found it very difficult to escape the widely shared sense that the state was the proper organizing frame for thought and musical expression. In the 1960s, two young musicians paradoxically chose to dive deeper into traditional Japanese musical sounds and strategies as part of an effort to escape that organization of the sensible. Takemitsu Toru and Yoko Ono took up the sounds of ancient Japanese instruments and traditional singing styles in an effort to forge new connections with Western music and to wrest those sounds from their subservience to the Japanese sphere of influence.

The next two chapters address similar cases. In both, a critical re-evaluation of inherited forms enabled a reformation of the beautiful and a transformation of the musically sensible. Theoretically, these chapters rely on the concept of musical beauty to link Pierre Bourdieu's concept of a field of cultural production to the world of power, a linkage that Bourdieu leaves only at the level of homology.[8] In the mid-1960s, a manufactured pop group that had formed in order to promote a hastily written and recorded single was recruited for an art project funded by Andy Warhol. With that endorsement, the Velvet Underground was able to reorganize the concept of the hit. As a rock 'n' roll band, the Velvets were driven by a desire to attract a large audience. But they were also freed to rethink the combination of sounds and approaches that could combine into a hit. Making the most of that freedom, the Velvets created a distillation of the longing within the pop commodity. Despite its length, topic, and droning sound, "Heroin," their first single, was truly intended for the pop charts; because of its length, topic, and droning sound, "Heroin" achieved a level of conceptual purity that exposed the empty hunger at the heart of the popular. In its beautiful sound, this emptiness was shown to be constitutive of the most normative of desires, linking those desires to the secret longings of the marginal.

In the middle of the seventies, rock developed a self-consciousness that built on the conceptual purity of the Velvets. Artistic amateurism, coded as authenticity, applied a critical attention to rock's conventions as artistic amateurism linked those conventions to the extramusical. Rock was an impure style that borrowed, indeed stole, from R&B, soul, jazz, country, folk, and even music-hall pop. Rock's conventions were not rooted in a coherent musical tradition, but instead were revised and reformed with irregular passion. Patti Smith's highly reflexive reconfiguration of the poet–rock star audaciously revealed the racialized and gendered requirements of the role first inhabited by Bob Dylan. Through her studied performativity, Smith revealed the limits of rock's comprehension of the world. A rethinking of musical authority resulted. Bad Brains emphasized the virtuosity required from marginalized groups. Their focus on speed and precision invigorated the DC scene, challenging (but not defeating) rock's racialized limits even though it reinforced the individualist masculine competitiveness that quickly dominated American hardcore. This competitiveness turned inward as the form of authenticity it generated demanded an ever-greater purity from each person. Following on the dominance of this approach, a rethinking of musical authority resulted. Beat Happening refused virtuosity with an equally focused intensity. The authority of this band grew from its attention to emotional honesty. By rigorously performing imperfection, Beat Happening shifted attention away from the means of performance to its end. Where hardcore's authenticity retained a vigorous individualism and an insistent personal equals political equals personal equation, indie instilled incompleteness, contradiction, and an insatiable hunger for constantly deferred meaning. Riot grrrl's musical genius was to reforge the connection between those two approaches. "Rebel Girl" was an ambivalent anthem that claimed legitimate authority in a world of power to which it did not wish to belong.

Both of these chapters proceed through close readings of recordings. One of the main points of this approach is to draw attention to the specificity of rock's generic conventions. I use a listening method attuned to the antisystematic means whereby great rock recordings create their aesthetic intervention into the political. In each of the recordings that I analyze, a particular performative imprecision becomes an audible hook, a quality of sound that demands the listener's attention. Lacking conscious intention, these musical gestures are nonetheless the key to rock's beauty. They mark the gaps in the capacity of the inherited understanding of the world to generate meaning and value. Again, many of these songs do not fit into traditional understandings of the beautiful. Their beauty and, therefore, their power come from their ability to produce sonic images of a sense of the world just beyond what already is. *Beyond* is the key word here because rock's impulse was never fully utopian; instead it creatively imagined a more intensely responsive world of greater satisfaction but not one where satisfaction itself was thought anew. Rock's beauty derived from a teasing alertness to an inwardly directed formal innovation even as it denied formalism, insisting instead on a direct relationship to the extramusical, which in turn was nothing more than a generic convention. Rock's formal inversion of itself continues to drive its cycle of critical transformation (as we shall see in the concluding chapter).

A sense of lost possibilities, of a kind of melancholy that comes from recognizing the limits of musical beauty's political force, is the subject of the penultimate chapter. Alarm Will Sound is a postclassical new music ensemble that initially formed at the Eastman School of Music. Their concert collage, *1969*, imagines a musical collaboration between Karlheinz Stockhausen and John Lennon, setting this musical association between two of the most highly regarded musicians of the time in the year after 1968's global challenge to the political status quo. *1969* registers the sense of loss felt by cultural elites as efforts to form a meaningfully broad-based political alliance through musical beauty fail. But *1969* also reminds us of the centrality of musical listening, of the true political force that musical beauty generates. While the melancholy of lost possibilities saturates the piece, the beauty of its own performance in our time is highlighted by Alarm Will Sound's acoustic version of the Beatles' "Revolution 9." By changing the sounding sources from tape collage to strings, winds, pianos, handclaps, and shouts, Alarm Will Sound encourages its audience to listen musically. In the process, the longing for an emergent and decentered collective spreads throughout the performance space.

|| || |

The concluding coda recollects a number of themes that wound their way through the preceding chapters, returning in particular to the first chapter's development of the book's central theoretical framework. The coda also foregrounds a particular problem of listening. Phrased in one way as the Alan Lomax problem and in another way as the "aural imaginary," this problem emerges from the inescapable limits that listening places on the political force of musical beauty. Even if one truly reaches out for new sonic combinations, the listener cannot escape the structuring effects that previous listenings have had on one's ability to hear the new. In fact, innocent listening, a listening that hears only the newness, is impossible. We always listen through previous listening. We always encounter the music of others through our imaginary relation to that otherness. These limits are not debilitating, however. They simply mark the ground on which musical listening takes place. The encounter between the indie rock band TV on the Radio and Tinariwen, a band of Tuareg musicians, figures the practice of musical listening across commonly recognized borders and differences, not as a utopia of commonality but as a leaning gesture, a practice that continues, over time, to recognize the beauty of new sounds, the force of that beauty, and the extension of the political community of difference.

Musical listening requires listeners, socially located listeners with their own specific aural imaginaries, to shift the resonance of the tonalities they hear. The purpose of this book is to call attention to that process, not to document its spreading multiplicity and certainly not to account for each individual listening act. *The Political Force of Musical Beauty* draws the bulk of its evidence from readily available sources, from sounds recorded on tape and transferred to wax or encoded into digits and bonded onto plastic and metal. The book describes acts of listening that cannot be replicated completely but from which echoes emerge, mapping aural pathways that you can trace with your own ears and your own leaning capacities. Real moments of musical beauty capture the infinite specificity of that listening. When you and I hit the dance floor together, listening to the elegant dynamism of a perfect beat, we will feel a community that will never be exactly the same for either of us. The force of that difference is what propels us.

Chapter One

Listening to the Political

| | | | |

In 1999 Moby released his multiplatinum-selling album *Play*. Most of this album consists of a blend of sampled gospel and blues with electronica-dance instrumentation and beats, exemplifying through its mixture of racially coded genres one of the most common strains of crossover success in American popular music, the recasting of black musical traditions for the profit of white musicians. Initial critical response was mixed, with quite a bit of commentary focusing on Moby's use of the older material. At *Pitchfork*, Brent DiCrescenzo wrote, "The sampling and processing of passionate folk and blues roots music drains whatever emotional ballast kept the music so spiritually afloat. . . . A performance loses raw magnetism after being chopped up in ProTools, cut from its atmosphere, cleaned, and gutted from its accompanying guitar." In the *Village Voice*, Frank Owen was slightly more positive, misdescribing Alan Lomax's source recordings as "field recordings from the '20s, '30s and '40s," but also noting that the "weary but hopeful '40s gospel singer Vera Hall in 'Natural Blues' . . . wouldn't sound out of place at the old Paradise Garage, a dancehall where space-age Baptists regularly congregated in the '80s." Writing for *Salon*, Scott Marc Becker noted, "She's [Hall] as potent in Moby's hands as she was a cappella, the ghost of her voice resonating as if she were still alive." But "luxnigra," writing as recently as 2007 for a blog titled *The Last Angel of History*, declares that Moby is just another in a long line of white appropriators of black music: "Moby is the Elvis or Benny Goodman or Beastie Boys of his genre and generation. He directly appropriates African-American music, such that he is the white mediator through which the blues records he samples are 'brought to life,' as one critic, in 'The Big Takeover,' commented. In fashioning a career while seemingly unaware of how his whiteness functioned and functions at every point in his career, he is fully complicit with white supremacy in the US."[1] Well, yes. And no. Not fully. To racially code technology as white and heartfelt emotion as black is complicit with the history of white supremacy. Although Moby cannot be held uniquely responsible for that—the critical response to the album indicates that the racial coding of its musical signs preceded the album itself and structured its reception for many listeners—it is clear that *Play* does not resist that reading. What is also clear is that *Play*—one song in particular, "Natural Blues"—is a way of working through that history.

Throughout the twentieth century, white musicians drew heavily from black musical traditions in an effort to achieve major commercial success. A continual strain of critical debate accompanied this phenomenon, arguing the merits and the crimes of such cultural borrowing. The market success of such acts as the Original Dixieland Jazz Band, Paul Whiteman's Orchestra, Elvis Presley, Eminem, and so many others has been challenged by critics asserting the superior musical and social value of musicians like Sidney Bechet, Fletcher Henderson, Chuck Berry, and Tupac. Karl Hagstrom Miller has recently shown, however, that the very idea of racially separated music traditions was an invention of the music industry who sought to streamline the distribution of particular musical commodities to specific audiences.[2] Scholars from Ronald Radano to Marybeth Hamilton have uncovered the deep white investment in the very category of black music even as the aural consistency and political significance of genres identified as black has been demonstrated by generations of scholars and critics, from W. E. B. Du Bois to Portia Maultsby, Samuel Floyd, and Mark Anthony Neal.[3] The racial coding of particular sounds and specific genres has varied historically. Before the twentieth century, the sounds of a banjo evoked blackness; after the invention of "old-timey music," the same sounds indexed an image of white communities. In the past ten years, scholars such as Maureen Mahon, Greg Tate, and Kandia Crazy Horse have insisted that black rock musicians be returned to the discussion of this presumably white form.[4] Further complicating the racialization of musical genres, George Lipsitz, Rafael Pérez-Torres, Frances Aparicio, and Josh Kun have reminded us of the interweaving of black and Latino styles, while Deborah Wong and E. Taylor Atkins have explored the convergence of East Asian and African American musics.[5] The ever-more intricate and self-reflexive nature of this struggle over musical traditions and cultural borrowing was captured by Roshanak Kheshti in her discussion of Sasha Frere-Jones's use of *miscegenation* to describe the white use of black-identified sounds in rock. Kheshti neatly uncovers the homosocial nature of the white-male use of the musical signs of black passion for cultural reproduction.[6]

Throughout this critical history, musical traditions and their political significance have been linked to racialized populations whose boundaries have been momentarily stabilized in part through the very processes of musical performance and reception that form the heart of the debate. This is the truth that ethnomusicology explores. Ethnomusicology establishes the expressive connection between the social real of an ethnos and the songs that both move and solidify the identity of that group. Within the operating assumptions of ethnomusicology, it is not too difficult to comprehend the musical resonance of social belonging, or the longing to belong. It is not a stretch to imagine the pleasure of identification or the warmth of a social connection that ensures fellow feeling—even where the feeling is in response to a threat. In traditional country blues, a constantly humming minor third is played by a guitarist alternating a down-tuned D with an F natural, bumping that bass line twice a second with the right thumb while the fingers of the left hand map a descending array of sevenths, fifths, and thirds across the fretboard, and a male voice sketches the outlines of a cypress grove within which he sings the insecurity of love; this pattern of harmony and rhythm not only enacts a solidarity of masculine vulnerability, a vulnerability made more palpable by the history of slavery and Jim Crow, but also evokes the work of the hands that counter that vulnerability through the sheer fluid ability to sound and resound again the irrepressible presence of desire. That unending movement back and forth from the D to the F structures the ineluctable. A voice maps a melodic arc that immediately falls upon its rise, that breaks itself in two and then four, and then recombines its wholeness through a downward slope that returns to a home that simply cannot feel safe. Listening to this, it is not difficult to feel the bonds of the community that chases itself into and through that musical metaphorical space. The social formation that produced these sounds might no longer exist, but its musical pleasures, the beauty of the political struggles that defined that social formation, remain. Skip James's "Cypress Grove Blues" exemplifies the quiet power of ethnomusical politics—the construction of an ethnicized community through song. Country blues no longer actively shapes the boundary of a people. Nevertheless, the continued experience of its beauty reaches beyond the historical moment of the song's conception, responding to changing historical circumstances with appeals rooted in its ethnomusical heritage but branching outward to grasp the attention of differently attuned listeners. The music's meaning grows organically and politically.[7]

In a turn of events that would probably have surprised Theodor Adorno, the most-productive efforts to link the musical and the political have taken shape not in European aesthetic theory or traditional musicology but inside the discipline of ethnomusicology—traditionally understood as the study of the folk and popular musics of the non-Western world. As early as 1973, John Blacking could assert that "because music is humanly organized sound, there ought to be a relationship between patterns of human organization and the patterns of sound produced as a result of human interaction."[8] This relationship between patterns of sound and human organization was not merely homological and covarying, according to Blacking. Speaking of the Venda, the particular people whose music Blacking studied, he claimed that their music was political "in the sense that it may involve people in a powerful shared experience within the framework of their cultural experience and thereby make them more aware of themselves and of their responsibilities toward each other."[9] The politics of Venda music consisted of the reaffirmation and reinforcement of the human organization named the Venda people. Through expressing an already existing social real, music could reproduce the boundaries of that community. But that was all it could do. Here is Blacking again: "Music cannot change societies. . . . If it can do anything to people, the best that it can do is to confirm situations that already exist. It cannot in itself generate thoughts that may benefit or harm mankind[,] . . . but it can make people more aware of feelings that they have experienced, or partly experienced, by reinforcing, narrowing or expanding their consciousness in a variety of ways."[10] Insofar as the music of the Venda could heighten awareness of their feelings, it could act in the world; the music could provide an arena for the contestation over cultural values. But these values were the values of the Venda that could only be expressed by Venda music when performed by the Venda people.

Throughout most of the history of ethnomusicology, even the most thoughtful and careful scholars have found themselves working within this frame. When Steven Feld wrote about the music of the Kaluli, the linkage he found between musical style and extramusical meaning was based in a concept of group identity that had to remain stable for the linkage to function. While Kaluli music might be characterized by "lift-up-over sounding" and that quality might also characterize the cooperative nature of Kaluli social organization, the music was an expression of the basic value hierarchy that marked one as Kaluli. If one is Kaluli, one cannot sound otherwise. Social organization and musical style that is not "lift-up-over sounding" cannot be Kaluli.[11]

Despite its success at demonstrating linkages between music and politics, the fundamental assumption of traditional ethnomusicology is hampered by an inherent circularity. The idea that groups make music that identifies the group and thereby expresses the values of that group relies on a static concept of identity and a relatively firmly bounded notion of the group that frustrates any effort to think about the political force of music. If all music can do politically is to reinforce the already existent values of an already defined group, then music acts more as a conveyor of values constructed elsewhere than as an agent itself. In its traditional formulation, ethnomusicology can conceptualize only the political uses of music, wherein a particular group promulgates its interests through the musical performance of identity.

This problem—the tendency to reduce music's political force to an expression of a group's already existing and stable identity—is exacerbated by an accompanying tendency toward essentialism (since essentialism extends an enclosed ethnos indefinitely into the future). In his classic study of racial formation, *The Black Atlantic*, Paul Gilroy asks, "What special analytical problems arise if a style, genre, or particular performance of music is identified as being expressive of the absolute essence of the group that produced it?"[12] The special analytical problems are many. But for my immediate purposes, the chief problem is this: linking the relationship between the political and the musical through identity often solidifies that identity. When that occurs, that identity becomes a reified object rather than a subjective set of processes. Identity becomes susceptible to essentialist concepts, and the linkage between music and identity loses its dynamism. Music's political role is reduced to the advance, or the defense, of this identity, and music loses its capacity for productive action in the world.

In the introduction to their superb collection *Music and the Racial Imagination*, Ronald Radano and Philip Bohlman acknowledge the traps of traditional ethnomusicology, rooting the field's reliance on a fixed identity in its area-studies origins. Radano and Bohlman go on to argue for replacing the centrality of ethnic identity with a focus on the racializing practices that are entwined with the production of musical meaning. Rather than following traditional ethnomusicology's tendency to accept "differences as if they were givens," they argue that "'race' defines not a fixity, but a signification saturated with profound cultural meaning and whose discursive instability heightens its affective power." Race should be understood as a subjectifying practice, not an object, they rightly insist. The difficulty of following through on this editorial intention can be traced through many of the articles in the collection. Even Christopher Waterman's otherwise sterling analysis of the crossover hit "Corrine Corrina" by Bo Chatmon depends on a posited hybrid "mulatto" identity for Chatmon as the experiential ground out of which the song's political significance could grow. It is as though the laudable effort to identify racializing tendencies in musical performance can only be understood as the expression of a preexisting and stable identity.[13]

The tendency to think the political through the limits of a fixed identity haunts not only ethnomusicology but also popular-music studies. In her compelling ethnography of the production and consumption of banda music in Los Angeles, Helena Simonett identifies moments when young Mexican Americans, inspired by hearing banda on the radio, begin a more visible and audible relationship to Mexican culture. In her analysis, this moment of musical identification becomes a reconnection to already existing roots, a reaffirmation of a belonging that was always already there rather than a productive connection that generates new experiences of subjectivity.[14] Aaron Fox's sensitive ethnography of white working-class culture introduces a degree of collective agency to the performance of "real" country music, seeing this performance practice as a means of maintaining a social identity that is threatened by increasing complexities in the world of work and by the sentimental evacuation of that identity through Nashville-style production and commodification practices. But even here, the musical qualities that distinguish "real country" from its blander competitors can only be identified through these qualities' capacity to enable members of this social group to recognize each other as real-country people.[15] These are important examples of music's political action. The musical confirmation of already existing political groups helps to consolidate them as self-aware communities. But I am mainly interested in a different direction that music's political power can take.

For example, Louise Meintjes's stunning *Sound of Africa!* reports an informal discussion among a group of musicians about a complex of musical sounds—a musical form. Her analysis of this conversation uses the concept of "the figure" as a doubled formal structure that combines the social notion of a "socially constituted type, or icon, presented and recognized through style" with the musical concept of a figure as a "repeating motive or pattern." Meintjes fuses these two ideas into a socio-musical concept that becomes "a process of arguing musically, by means of repeated and varied motives, over ideas about social relations."[16] She describes a moment in a recording studio when a particular timbre associated with East Africa is imbricated with an approach to guitar playing that is already identified as South African (using an existent socio-musical link). This timbral resonance, echoing East Africa, shifts the sociocultural reference of the guitar style. The new sound is intended to reference "Africa," an impossible semiotic object in itself, but a meaningful auditory symbol in the market for world music, particularly when contrasted with "white pop." Each of these terms, each of these figures, each of these references are relatively fluid concepts that are at play in the conversation among the musicians who are working to create this sound. Their conversation is made up of a set of strategies for marketplace success. But the musicians' goal is to create a sound that can solidify a musico-cultural reference to Africa that will carry an affective charge beyond the reference's value as a commodity marker in the world music marketplace. The musicians want to create what could be really felt to be the "sound of Africa." This analysis reintroduces an element of dynamism into the linkage between music and identity, demonstrating the imbrication of extramusical thinking with formal musical creativity. The analysis is deeply contextualized in terms of the meanings carried by the musical form and the historical moment out of which this element of musical beauty can be heard. My argument will build on Meintjes's discussion to suggest that this affective charge, if successful, could consolidate an emergent identity with real political force. The affective power of musico-cultural figures can change the relationship of the ethnos to the demos, shifting the relations of those who are legitimately included inside the political community. The fundamental assertion of this book is that music is one of the central cultural processes through which the abstract concept of the polis comes into bodily experience. Music's ability to effect this experience must have already taken place before any of the debates about genres and peoples, of sounds and identities, can begin. Simply put, the political force of music derives from its capacity to combine relations of difference into experiences of beauty.

The experience of musical beauty can reinforce already existing political communities with familiar sounds and a seemingly coherent and regular resolution of tension. This musical conservation of existing community is the work of anthems, and it is the object of much traditional ethnomusicological and popular-music study.[17] More interesting for me, however, is the work that musical beauty performs when it moves beyond the intentions of its creators and outside the preformed identities of its fans. I am interested in the ways in which the experience of musical beauty complicates the experience of group identity as well as confirming it. Further, I want to understand music's ability to consolidate an entirely new sense of the self and its relation to others. I am looking to explore the ways that music both constitutes and disrupts the political, where *the political* is understood as that arena within which diverse collectivities of people come together to explore and define themselves as a group. I am interested in music's capacity (in the words of Georgina Born) not only to "*reproduce*, reinforce, actualize, or memorialize *extant* sociocultural identities . . . [but also to] prefigure, crystallize, or potentialize *emergent, real* forms of sociocultural identity or alliance."[18] The experience of musical beauty, when it emerges from unfamiliar sounds or surprising combinations of sounds quite common, has the capacity to redistribute an auditory sensible and to change, thereby, the sonic *sens*[19] of the political.

MUSICAL BEAUTY

My thesis builds on the observation that the affective power of music produces in listeners a capacity for taking pleasure in difference and in the organization of difference. Even to experience music is to make a judgment about sound. From the moment of John Cage's "4′33″" on, it has been clear that sounds enter into a special category of perception once they have been deemed to count as music.[20] To categorize an auditory experience as music is to make the decision that what is heard is coherent: an architectonic combinations of timbres, rhythms, competing and overlapping structures, auditory pressures of tension and release. The political force of music derives from its capacity to entrain subjects to feel pleasure in particular combinations of auditory difference and to reject other combinations as noise. The pleasure taken in the experience of musical beauty is a consequence of formal musical attributes that build affective attractors from abstract relations of sonic difference. Musical beauty is a subset of the larger category of sonic beauty. To perceive sonic beauty as musical beauty is to hear a set of sounds as a coherent whole, the coherence and continuity of which enables a felt connection between the sounds themselves and the social world from which they emerge. Whereas sonic beauty can come from attentiveness to the natural or even the mechanical world, musical beauty always emerges from the social.[21] This is not to say that musical beauty can be purely and totally reduced to social concerns. Music is commonly said to be non-referential. But the pleasures produced through the experience of musical beauty affectively bind our sensibilities into patterns of engagement with the social world. The semantic emptiness of musical structures begs to be filled in with social content even while musical beauty escapes any final concrete social articulation. The experience of musical beauty is a compelled but willing acquiescence to what are felt to be right relations of difference. When the sonic relations that construct this experience are familiar and comforting, they reinforce existing political relations. But when music redistributes the auditory sensible, the experience of musical beauty generates a sonic reshaping of the experience of relations of difference. New possibilities for political community can emerge from the pleasurable experience of new formations of difference. This suggests that the emergence of political community is, in part, an aesthetic experience. It cannot, therefore, be understood as a singular historical event. Instead the political force of musical beauty repeats as and when necessary, changing the shape of any community it reproduces. In setting forth these propositions, I do not mean to suggest that there is a one-to-one relationship between musical taste and particular political positions. The political force of music does not act at the level of policy or program. Instead the experience of musical beauty, the instant judgment that a set of differences is in proper relation with one another, should be understood as an experienced emergence of political community.

We all experience the political force of music. Yet it is a force that operates most powerfully when we are not quite aware of it. Music's political power does not result in easily measurable direct effects; instead, it operates indirectly, obliquely. Wherever we find musical beauty, it results from an attentive (even when not fully conscious) engagement with sound—the flow of rhythms; the assonance of harmonies; the resolution of pitch-based tensions; the surprising splashes of color, tone, timbre; and even the disturbing clashes of chaos, dissonance and silence, all of the coordinated violence and peace shaped by the ludic synchronization of sound. The undeniable physicality of sound vibrates the eardrums, sends pulses down the synapses, snaps muscle fibers into action, and stimulates interpretation machines. Hairs inside the auditory canal, hairs on the back of the neck, hairs that line folds of skin, and skin that crinkles and stretches, all respond to air pressure, tripping us into a choreography of meaning. Music, the most fully embodied symbol, revels in the physical experience of subjectivity. Embraced by the experience of musical beauty, our most private feelings become recognizable in their social fullness. Music is the absolutely undeniable evidence of the sociality of human feeling. Music confirms the belief that we feel as collective beings. The experience of musical beauty is the experience of the collective nature of subjectivity. As Jacques Attali puts it, "All music, any organization of sounds[,] is then a tool for the creation or consolidation of a community, of a totality."[22]

Traditionally, the production of musical beauty has been studied by musicologists who focus on the internal relation of parts in a practice of articulating a purely musical meaning, purified of political and social constraints.[23] Countering that tradition, the cultural musicologist Lawrence Kramer has argued that extramusical meaning accompanies every act of music making and is the paradoxical result of the oft-remarked nonreferentiality of music. Rather than reducing the potential meaning of music to a self-referential engagement with its own processes, Kramer understands that the lack of ostensive indexing sets music up to function precisely as the object of projective subjective desire. In Kramer's words, "In music . . . the structure of prejudgment," by which he means the set of predispositions necessary for the production and comprehension of any meaningful utterance, "becomes lived experience more plainly, palpably, and dramatically than virtually anywhere else," as a result of the apparent absence of purely musical meaning.[24] As Kramer insists, this projective aspect of meaning, filtered through subjectivity, is an ineradicable aspect of all meaning making. Music, by virtue of its abstract formality, simply renders that aspect more palpable. The attentive engagement with musical beauty necessarily builds from a subjective positioning, but its allure pulls the listening subject out from that position in an effort to understand the beauty that escapes the mere repetition of the known. The projective production of extramusical meaning works through the subject, but it is instigated by an experienced gap (of seeming meaninglessness) between the musicality of the musical object and the position of the listener. In a cyclical process that presages recognition, the experience of musical beauty engages the listener in a search for the extramusical. But even as the listener enfolds sound and world in the moment of audition, the world rebounds as the sound echoes away. A gap between the listener and the world remains, despite our efforts to fill it.

For the philosopher Jean-Luc Nancy, it is precisely the interaction of the desire for meaning with this unbridgeable gap that results in musical listening: "Musical listening seems, then, to be . . . a relationship to meaning, a tension toward it: but toward it completely ahead of signification, meaning in its nascent state, in the state of return for which the end of this return is not given (the concept, the idea, the information). . . . To be listening is to be inclined toward a reserve that is anterior and posterior to any signifying punctuation."[25] According to Nancy, musical listening is an attentive relationship to meaning that reveals the gaps in symbolizing while it revels in the social and embodied sensuousness of its reflexive processes. Musical vibrations themselves are a repetition of difference that can be perceived as a unity of pitch, timbre, and rhythm. That simple translation represents a nearly instantaneous leap from the physical sensations to a subjective judgment of musicality. When we listen, we find ourselves drawn to those gaps between sensation and music, wanting to fill them with something like meaning. Our attention is drawn to what lies just beyond our ability to understand it, those sounds that seem musical. A great song on the radio, or spat through our computer by Pandora or Spotify, forces us to ask: what was that? A set of vibrations overlapping in innovative waveforms forces reflection: Is this reggaeton? Drum and bass? Electro-minimalism? Just another pop song? Nancy refers to this appealing quality of engagement with the musical as *sens*: "To be listening is always to be on the edge of meaning, or in an edgy meaning of extremity, and as if the sound were precisely nothing else than this edge, this fringe, this margin—at least the sound that is musically listened to, that is gathered and scrutinized for itself, not, however as an acoustic phenomenon (or not merely as one) but as a resonant meaning, a meaning whose *sense* is supposed to be found in resonance, and only in resonance."[26] Repeating, resounding, resonance presents the possibility of musical sens. It is an effect of our attentive listening, one form of the insistence that the world be feelingful and intelligible. Nancy uses the French word *sens* to represent the general form of this longing for shared meaning. The lure of sens pulls us toward a world of meaning in a recursive set of ongoing judgments that demand new configurations of the sensible and the material. As we work to make sense out of the sens of music's musicality, we attune ourselves to music's formal characteristics—even if we know "nothing about music." Music is a field of relations made audible and meaningful through its form. These relations are what we hear the moment we decide that what we are hearing is music. Even when listening to noise music, once we decide that this noise is music, our attention has been turned to the formal relations entrained in and emergent from those sounds. This process happens so immediately that even when we do not have the official musicological language to label these relations, we feel them and apprehend them as we listen. These formal qualities extend beyond music's syntax (i.e., metrical and pitch relations) to include such properties as sound quality (timbre/noise) and intensity (volume/tempo), among other factors. These formal qualities of music carry no necessary narrative; they are nonindexical. Instead they are first experienced bodily as a series of regularized pulsations and tones. But those pulses and tones are immediately transformed in a process that is both abstract and embodied. Through our irrepressible insistence on the meaningfulness of those sounds, through our ability to construct a form from those pulsations and tones, embedded and enfolded with our subjective placement in the world, music makes sensuous and audible the material, social, and political relations of its time. This is why Adorno insists on a formalist method for his materialist aesthetics. "The unsolved antagonisms of reality return in artworks as immanent problems of form," he says. "This, not the insertion of objective elements, defines the relation of art to society."[27]

Filtered through the discursive structuration of subjectivity, the experience of musical beauty is an instantaneous judgment about the right form of relations of difference. That is what we hear; that is what we feel; that is what we talk about when we long to make meaning out of music. The pleasure of musical beauty is the harmony of what we know and what we feel. But this pleasure is also the intriguing beckoning of what we don't quite know toward what we might feel. It is in this beckoning, in its ability to produce feelings of coherence from nearly boundless waves of incomplete repetition, that music renders the political.

DEMOCRACY'S IDENTITY PROBLEM

This luring, inclining, yearning quality of musical sound is the basis of music's political force. The desire generated through sens intervenes in one of the key problems in democratic theory. Although this problem can be stated in a number of ways, it ultimately reduces down to the question of difference within a pluralist democracy. How does a state legitimate itself with respect to an internally divided populace? How does the state, and indeed the political community itself, determine the borders between those differences included within itself and those excluded from its reach? What relations of difference constitute the political community and which ones must stand outside? Who should be of the polis?

These are not questions that can be answered rationally. They are always judgments made on the basis of a felt sense of right relations of difference. Traditionally, the recognition of political partners as equal participants in the democratic community has been mediated through a process of mutual identification with the nation, imagined as a site not only of formal equality but also of substantive commonality. As the political theorist Clarissa Hayward articulates it: "Democracy requires . . . democratic citizens . . . who regard one another as political equals, who are motivated to engage one another in collective deliberation, and who are willing to accept as legitimate the laws that democratic processes yield." This equality requirement most typically devolves into some ver-sion of group identity. Hayward writes, "Democracy needs some form of citizen-identity for purposes of integration. Individual citizens can be motivated to look beyond what they understand to be in their self-interest and what they understand to be in the interest of their familiars, and to do so for the good of their fellow citizens, who remain to them *strangers*, only if they feel some sense of identification with those strangers: some sense of solidarity with them, some sense of sharing with them in a collective purpose or a collective project."[28] Citizenship is a recursive political category. It is formally awarded only after the sense of belonging to the polis can be recognized by others. This suggests that the formal category of citizenship must come after the recognition of a shared substantive identity. But democracy's identity problem is not easily solved. This desire for a shared identity is constantly haunted by an insistent demand for the same, a sufficiently constrained identity that can be quickly recognized and easily confirmed. The cost of following this temptation is well known, resulting in the violent monotonal roar of fascism, or the smug Muzak of white supremacy.[29]

Perhaps, then, one ought to abandon the search for a shared identity of the polis that can be rationally described and accept in its place not only the affective but also the fundamentally irrational aspects of the political and its identifications. Perhaps it would be best to recognize that every politically salient group is constituted by and of difference and that political identification requires neither the suppression nor the transcendence of those differences. This discordance of the polis is one of the basic assumptions of what Chantall Mouffe calls "agonistic pluralism." For Mouffe, difference must not be understood as a problem to be managed, but seen instead as the very energy and force of the political. Building on the conceptual foundation that underlay her collaboration with Ernesto Laclau in *Hegemony and Socialist Strategy*, Mouffe argues that the contradictory and indeterminate nature of political alliances is the productive outgrowth of the irresolvable contradictions at the heart of democracies. The generative contradiction, the irreducible conflict between ideals of liberty and equality, that constitutes democracies results in "nonachievement, incompleteness, and openness," guaranteeing continual struggle. As she puts it, the "common good can never be actualized, it . . . cannot have a real existence." It can only ever be an ideal—of which there will always be competing visions. Ongoing conflict is central to life in a democracy—at its periphery and at its core.[30] Democracies require *something more* than rational procedures and *something other* than substantive identity to hold them together in the face of this fundamental conflict and the inescapable fact of difference. Rather than attempting to eradicate or even mediate difference so that reason can shape political relations, perhaps it may be best to recognize the role of aesthetic judgments in the acts of recognition that constitute a political community.[31]

Political judgments can be understood as aesthetic judgments insofar as they are based upon a felt sense of right relations that cohere in the form of the political community. Like musical sound, the political community is constructed of difference. The complexity of the political community is built out of architectonically arranged power relations that emerge from, even as they shape, struggles on the ground. The judgment of the legitimacy of the political community is nothing other than a judgment that the set of relations of difference inherent in the community results in a sense of balance or well-formedness. The sense of the political community is always a judgment about the proportional relations of difference, about the beauty of an object constructed from difference.

THE AESTHETICALLY EMERGENT POLITICAL COMMUNITY

Political judgment and musical judgment are based upon the extrarational capacity to evaluate the harmony, the sense of balance and the legitimacy, of a set of relations of difference. But the judgment of this harmony requires a particular approach, a specific attitude toward listening and the political. Earlier I borrowed Nancy's idea that musical listening is a relationship to meaning, a kind of leaning toward the sound that provides the opportunity to reflect on the immediacy of the aesthetic perception that transforms pulsations and tones into music—an attunement to sens. I want to turn now to a different aspect of Nancy's work to buttress my argument about the aesthetic component of political judgment.

Instead of having a primary reputation as an aesthetician or a music theorist, Nancy is better known as a political philosopher. In particular, he has developed some important ideas about the formation of political communities that can help illuminate the aesthetic aspect of political judgment. Alert to the problems of essentialism and arbitrary exclusion that result from traditional communitarian thought with its dependence on a preexisting commonality, Nancy has worked out an approach to the concept of community that does not require a shared element around which the community must form. For Nancy, community is a process, not an object. Community is also not an experience that we have. Instead it is best described as a leaning toward each other, a *clinamen*, that "makes us be." Part of what it means to be a person, in other words, is this clining, this leaning toward others. Part of what enables our very existence as individuals is what Nancy calls "being-in-common," where the common is both an effect of the actions of individuals and the ground out of which those actions emerge. Communities do not exist on their own—they are not immediately apprehensible objects. That is what makes it so difficult to talk about communities. The effort to talk about *a* community, as a thing, often leads to errors of essentialism in the search for the common factor that all members share. When people try to solidify a community, to reify it into a *thing* that has its own existence, they must restrict its constitutive operations. They must stop the unpredictable but continually productive and transformative qualities of being-in-common in order to create a set of rigid social limits. The boundaries that result are produced at the cost of stopping the productivity of the relationships among persons, the ever-continuing production of being-in-common. This stabilization of community produces the illusion of a center, an essence that all members must have in common. This freezing of human relationships is the opposite of community. Rather than thinking of a community as a thing—as a society that "must be defended"—community should be understood as the productive, active, and unending process of creating being-in-common.[32]

This active productive concept of community provides a way of understanding how the polis forms. Even though Nancy describes a process of being-in-common that is never completely stopped and that has potentially infinite expansion, it is evident that humans sort themselves into groups that they understand to be different from each other, with competing goals and interests. The agon that Mouffe describes is not dissipated by the clinamen that Nancy posits, for there is no single center toward which all persons lean in any community. Instead these two concepts must be thought together in order to map the relations within a polis constituted by difference. Communities in process overlap and disrupt each other in changing patterns of allure and attraction, calling and responding, echoing and resonance. The common does not preexist the agonistic struggle to create it. Nor does the momentary appearance of a recognizable common halt the process. Instead, a felt harmony of the political (which includes its dissonant moments of tension) indicates a temporary being-in-common, a kind of musicality of different feelings and tones that creates a temporary sens of a tonal center. The felt illusion of a center is the momentary product of the necessity of human being-in-common and the leaning toward each other that results. This leaning is similar to the inclining toward meaning that, for Nancy, constitutes musical listening. To be attentive to the emergence of a being-in-common requires the same posture of response as does listening for the musical in sound. Assonance and dissonance can only be understood in relation to each other. Only through the effort to comprehend the contributions of difference can a sense of the whole emerge. The sens of music co-responds with the sens of the political.

It is important to emphasize that the community that Nancy describes need not produce a cultural commonality. It is not just that being-in-common does not precede the clining that brings people together. Just as important, no identity at all need be produced as a result of that coming together. No cultural character or unifying habit must exist to hold together the community. The being-in-common can arise from historical concerns, strictly political issues, or aspirations for the future. For example, Tommie Shelby describes a form of black solidarity that requires no cultural commonality whatsoever. According to Shelby, the force that inclines persons toward black solidarity is constructed out of historical memory and ongoing conditions of inequality that are based on characteristics ascribed *by others* to black persons. In Shelby's words, "a collective identity is not a necessary condition for cultivating effective bonds among African Americans, and in fact[,] . . . attempting to forge one would be self-defeating." Instead, he posits "a conception of solidarity based strictly on the shared experience of racial oppression and a joint commitment to resist it."[33] As Shelby explains, a black political community can even produce a momentary being-in-common that is the desire for its own ceasing-to-be. James Baldwin pointed out decades ago that whiteness also has no center; whiteness's commonality is founded instead through acts of exclusion amid a longing for innocence.[34] These examples show that there is not necessarily an identity or a group of shared cultural practices, habits, or beliefs around which persons must incline in the production of a political community. Put in this way, the formation of community sounds instrumental, abstract, and coldly calculating, a matter of strategic thinking only. Of course, it is not that at all. Instead, the formation, maintenance, and destruction of community are dense with affect and tense with meaning. But the lure that pulls people together cannot be cognized. Or rather, it refuses to be cognized in a stable, rational fashion. Just as musicality shifts around the production of particular tones, beats, and other relations of difference, the formation of political community proceeds by the lure of sensing an almost constructed being-in-common.

AESTHETIC SENSIBILITY AND POLITICAL JUDGMENT

Music enacts its political force through its entrainment of sensibilities attuned to form, sense, and relations of difference. By leaning in we find ourselves caught in the resonance of the common, which is produced as an experience in the event of listening, not as a referent to an already preexisting substantive community. This musically produced common is a felt sens, not an empirical set of resources or power relations. While the core of that experience is the musical sound that attracts the listener, and while that sound is produced and heard as beautiful primarily as a consequence of the way in which the structured sonic relations function, the being-in-common that is generated through those vibrations always includes more than the music. In fact, the experience of the common generated by music constitutes a sensibility that enables other sorts of experience to come to awareness. This sensibility consists of an alertness not only to particular sounds but also to the relationships among those sounds, with the sensibility generated through that experience extending beyond sound to other bodily capacities. The perception of sound itself is the perception of relationships of difference, but when the sound is judged to be musical, it is then heard as an architectonic structure of interlocking relationships whose complexity models the complexity of the common. Without needing to fill in any social content, the experience of musical beauty can confirm the ability of a particular sensibility to recognize ever-more complex structural relationships within the common and the meaningfulness of specific moments of deviation from those structural relationships. In addition to this purely musical effect, the experience of musical beauty can carry with it the secondary associations that accompany the musical sound. Social content can be filled in—through lyrics, images, associations of a genre with a particular group, and other means. But there is an important difference between the way in which the musical sound functions and the way in which the associations function. The experience of musical beauty never enforces a particular social attitude or belief. The musically produced common instead establishes the sensibility within which social associations or political positions can be perceptible and, therefore, become a matter for debate. This is why partisans of the same music can be political adversaries. In order to debate, they must be able to acknowledge their opposition as potentially legitimate opponents. The experience of musical beauty establishes the structure of relations of difference that can be felt as legitimate.

This language of sensibilities follows from the work of Jacques Rancière and particularly his idea of the distribution of the sensible. Rancière uses this idea to demonstrate the functional link between the realms of aesthetics and politics. He defines it slightly differently in different locations, but one influential statement defines the distribution of the sensible as "the system of self-evident facts of sense perception that simultaneously discloses the existence of something in common and the delimitations that define the respective parts and positions within it."[35] Rancière is at pains to show that this idea carries with it not only a concept of inclusion and exclusion but also the means whereby specific parts of the common are attached to specific included groups. For Rancière, the common is divided—so much so, in fact, that there is always a "part that has no part," a group that cannot be recognized as part of the political at all. The concept builds from the fact that the very ability for a group to engage in politics has two fundamental requirements. A political subject must be able to symbolize meaningfully, and those symbols have to be recognized as more than howls of pain or animalistic expressions of desire; the subject's articulations have to be recognized as complex and multilayered statements that display conscious intention and a nuanced grasp of the world. They cannot be simply private comments about the domestic sphere; they must have public resonance. This relationship of speaking and hearing requires a framework within which utterances can rise to the level of political engagement. Rancière is not talking about something as simple as a shared language. He uses the examples of women and workers who spoke the same language as men and factory owners but who were operating in a distribution of the sensible that determined that their speech was nothing more than guttural demands. Demands can be answered or not. They involve private affairs, not concerns of the polis. For a subject to be political, its utterances must become sensible as political statements. The real work of politics, for Rancière, is the work of changing the sensible and thereby the transformation of what had previously been merely a private issue into a matter of public concern: "Politics invents new forms of collective enunciation; it re-frames the given by inventing new ways of making sense of the sensible, new configurations between the visible and the invisible, and between the audible and the inaudible, new distributions of space and time—in short, new bodily capacities."[36] In this way, politics affects aesthetics, demanding new forms of the sensible.

Conversely, the political role of aesthetics, or the heteronymous function of aesthetic production, derives from its ability to change the sensible. The experience of musical beauty is one of the means whereby the distribution of the sensible can be transformed. In changing the sensible, musical beauty does not produce social justice, equality, or any other political value. Musical beauty itself takes no political stance. It simply or not so simply affects the shape of the common, changing the qualities of feeling and the possible elements that can be included in the debate by shifting the sensibility toward relations that can forge together into a meaningful (if divided) whole, creating thereby "a new form . . . of dissensual 'commonsense.'"[37]

The political agency of music works by distributing the sensible in such a way that it transforms the experience of the common. This felt difference in the common then prompts the leaning in described by Nancy as a clinamen. With tilted heads, with ears alert, we hear new sounds as music, and this sense of musical beauty demands to be filled with a social that is consistent with its ensemble of relations.

THE FORCE OF MUSICAL SENS:
THE PERSISTENT POWER OF VERA HALL

On March 3, 2005, Gabriel Greenberg gave a speech at Judson College in Marion, Alabama, honoring the induction of the folk singer and domestic servant Vera Hall into the Alabama Women's Hall of Fame. Greenberg began his speech by acknowledging the evident differences between him and the woman being honored.

By looking at me, you can tell that I am not African-American. From my accent and rapid speech, you know that I can't be from the South. And you'll see from the programs you are holding that my last name is not a Christian one. What, then, you might wonder, am I doing here? What is a White, Northern, Jewish boy doing here talking about a Black, Southern, Christian woman who live[d] nearly half a century ago? For Vera Hall and I exist in worlds that differ not only along the fundamental dimensions of race, region and religion but also those of sex, class and time.[38]

Greenberg was chosen to introduce Hall to the audience at the ceremony because of the work he had done to promote Hall's work as a singer. Greenberg established the Vera Hall Project after first hearing her voice coming through his car radio in the summer of 2000. In his words, Greenberg was "electrified: riveted by the swell of the woman's chilling, mournful tone and delighted at the precision of her phrasing, the surprising shifts of her rhythm."[39] What Greenberg had heard, however, was not a broadcast of one of Hall's folksinging performances, but her voice sampled and mixed into the fifth single that had been released from the album *Play* by the white techno artist Moby. Captured by the resonance of that sample of Hall's tone and timing, Greenberg spent the next five years searching out her story and working to publicize what he had discovered. But Greenberg was not the first white Northern man to be caught by the power of Hall's voice. He was, rather, only one in a line of such devotees that stretched back more than sixty years. Many of those in that line documented their opinions of her voice. Although few articulated so clearly the power of this voice to compel an inclination to listen, what stood out for all of them was its ability to cross the boundaries of identity that were so salient to each of them. For decades Hall's voice enacted a political force that demanded an attentive listening and a corresponding leaning, a clinamen, toward a community that is still not built but is occasionally experienced.

It is almost certain that Hall was first recorded by John and Ruby Lomax on the front porch of Ruby Pickens Tartt's home in Livingston, Alabama, in the spring or summer of 1937.[40] Tartt was John Lomax's connection to the black community in Sumter County, Alabama. Although she came from a well-to-do family, the Depression had wiped out both her and her husband's families, and she had been forced to work for the Works Progress Administration. Tartt was an educated, liberal, white Southerner of her time. This meant that although she accepted her privileged racial position as part of the natural order of things and her responsibility toward the local black population as a burden she must carry, she also found some of the practice of white supremacy to be abhorrent. Refusing to follow the strict dictates of Jim Crow segregation, Tartt would play with local black children, enter their homes when invited, and invite their parents to her own house. On the other hand, she remained the "boss lady" and expected to be treated with the deference that she considered proper. Her familiarity with black singing styles was a consequence of her attendance at black churches and her willingness to roam black neighborhoods, habits that scandalized her white neighbors. The Works Progress Administration hired her as a folklorist, which provided an official governmental justification for her wandering inquisitiveness. Her sensibilities and her connections made her an ideal informant for Lomax's work for the Archive of American Folk Song.[41]

This fit was in part because John Lomax's relationships to white privilege and black culture were equally complicated, if not quite so contradictory. Lomax's paternalism and sense of white superiority is well known. As Norman Porterfield points out, "Lomax was constantly banging his head on the matter of race, and he never understood why."[42] Lomax was quick to insist on his appreciation of black songs despite his firm belief in the inferiority of black people. And as he remarked later in his autobiography, Tartt was "Fond of her Negroes," and "she could laugh at them, too."[43] It should not be surprising, then, that when Tartt arranged for Lomax to record Hall and her cousin Dock Reed, the two singers at first felt awkward and quite unsure of how they were supposed to act. According to the story, first published in Lomax's autobiography and then repeated in biographies of Tartt and Lomax, it was only after Lomax played his recording of prisoners at Parchman Farm singing "I Don't Mind the Weather," a song that both Hall and Reed knew, that the two informants relaxed, smiled, and were ready to sing themselves. The display of power—not simply the mechanical power to reproduce sound but the institutional and political power that enabled Lomax to enter prisons, record black prisoners' voices, and take them away with him— clearly demonstrated the facts of the relationship that their singing was meant to enact. Hall and Reed were to sing; their voices were to be recorded; Lomax was to take those voices to use as he wished. They complied, with the deferential affect they could produce so well. Lomax responded powerfully to their performances. For the remainder of his life, he repeated his opinion that Hall and Reed were among the best singers he had ever heard. Something about their voices made him lean closer.

During that session and three others, one later that year, and one more each in 1939 and 1940, Hall and Reed gave dozens of performances to Lomax for the Archive of American Folk Song. Among those performances was a version of "Trouble So Hard," recorded in July 1937. Reed took the lead on this song, as it was considered a spiritual, the category of song for which he was best known. On this recording, Hall follows Reed's lead, slightly behind his notes, always an octave higher, always precisely in tune. When the classic "blue third" comes at the end of the phrase—the pitch that falls between a minor and a major third—their rhythms line up with each other exactly. The chorus lines out the title of the song—"Oh, Lord," sung on the fifth (A over the tonic D), "Trouble so hard," rising from the tonic up to that not-quite-major, not-quite-minor third (D to F~)—as it maps out a classic blues tonality. In his role as leader, Reed chooses the words; in this version he includes verses associated with the classic "Scandalize My Name." Although Reed's voice is deep and strong, with a power akin to that of Son House at his best, Hall's voice seems to cut across that deep strength, thinner but more finely honed—a head voice contrasting with Reed's chest voice. She's not accompanying him. Hers is also a leading voice, layered on top of his. It is a voice that cuts through every barrier, that demands not only to be heard but to be listened to.[44]

"Trouble So Hard" was not John Lomax's favorite of those that Hall sang for him that summer. He preferred her version of "Another Man Done Gone," which he chose to play at a ceremony honoring the seventy-fifth anniversary of the Emancipation Proclamation at the Library of Congress. It was his son Alan Lomax who identified "Trouble So Hard" as a particularly good performance and selected it for release on the first commercially available recordings from the Archive of American Folk Song, released in 1942. Alan also arranged for Hall to perform at Columbia University's Festival of Contemporary American Music in May 1948. This festival, mostly noted for its championing of art music from the European tradition, devoted one night to the performance of contemporary folk music.[45] Titled "Ballads, Hoe-Downs, Spirituals (Black and White) and Blues," the night featured performances by Texas Gladden, Hobart Smith, Jean Ritchie, Brownie McGhee, Vera Hall, Dan Burley, and Pete Seeger. Alan Lomax narrated the proceedings.[46]

While Hall was in New York for this concert, she sat for several hours of interviews with Alan Lomax that he later transformed into a "folk novel" and published as part of the book *The Rainbow Sign* in 1959. Listening to the tapes of these interviews, you can hear a casual intimacy flowing between Hall and Lomax. Something very important was different about her relationship with the younger Lomax. The interviews took place in the Lomax family apartment. At times the phone rings, and Lomax's daughter interrupts the two adults. Lomax asks Hall to sing many of the same songs she had recorded for his father, and she speaks openly and forthrightly not only about her own life and the songs but also about the crimes that forcefully punctuated race relations in Alabama. One of the stories Hall tells is about the Boyds, a white family who, in a vengeful rage, murdered every member of the Robertsons, a black family, following a fatal fight between two young boys. This mass murder prompted Hall's father to give one of the few overt lectures he ever delivered to his daughters on race relations. Lomax gives the story and the lecture considerable space in *Rainbow Sign*, quoting Hall quoting her father. "Don't think you can fight a white child back," she remembered him telling her.

> Don't make nary one of those little-bitty ones cry, because the old boss might come out there and kill you, just shoot you down like you was a rabbit. So try not to have nothing to do with them. If they bother you, just let them do anything they want with you. [He] Say, "I love you just as hard as they do their children, but I don't have the privilege of showin' it. If they was to walk up here and shoot one of you-all, I'd just stand and look at him. That's all I could do. I couldn't even say anything."[47]

It is a dramatic moment in the transcription of the interviews and in the book based on those interviews. Here is a precise articulation of the threat of violence that had hung over Hall's head all of her life. She could not more clearly state the extreme power difference between white families and black families in Sumter County. After years of thinking about this passage in the context of Hall's long relationship with the Lomaxes, I still can't quite decide if Hall was doing more here than simply repeating a story from her youth, describing conditions that only pertained to the families that lived together in Sumter County in the first decades of the twentieth century. Is it possible that she was describing the conditions that continued to structure her relationships to whites? Was she giving Lomax a clue about why she had been such a good informant for his father? Was she perhaps even framing her ongoing relationship with the younger Lomax as well? If so, Lomax could not have been more oblivious to the message. He narrates this story as though Hall had retained the same calm quiet matter-of-fact tone in telling it that she had used throughout the interviews. In Lomax's writing, Hall's demeanor seems transcendent, capable of almost spiritually rising above these episodes of white rage.

In the opening pages of the section of *Rainbow Sign* devoted to Hall's story, Alan Lomax introduces her as a natural, calm woman, comfortable with her position in life and "gifted to sing":

> Nora [the pseudonym he gave to Hall] is a large, handsome, brown-skinned woman . . . whose manners are so serene and so gentle that she quickly puts one at ease. . . . Her singing is like a deep-voiced shepherd's flute, mellow and pure in tone, yet always with hints of the lips and the pleasure-loving flesh. . . . The sound comes from deep within her when she sings, from a source of gold and light, otherwise hidden, and falls directly upon your ear like sunlight. . . . This is the voice that lent wings to American Negro music, for it combines the subtle rhythm and the playful sensuality of Africa with the ringing, bell-like fullness of the best European singing.[48]

There is nothing political, nothing assertive, nothing agentive at all in Hall's singing, so far as Lomax is concerned. Her voice is a natural outgrowth of playful sensuality and clear tone. Her voice's source must be in sunlight, even if the direct line toward that light is blocked. He seems to have completely missed the darkness and the clear-eyed perception of injustice that drives her expressive power. But at another moment, concerning an entirely different topic, Lomax asks her if she has to be sad to sing the blues; he says, "You don't seem so sad. Or do you have reasons for feeling sad even though you look happy?" Hall responds, "I don't have any reason to be sad except like I told you when my mother was real sick. I never had any trouble with no man or anything like that." Lomax then probes a bit: "What about if you get treated bad on a job or someone speaks very rudely to you or something like that?" To which Hall replies: "Well, I just always asks why that? Well how come you said so and so to me in such and such a way? Did I do something wrong or what?" She goes on to explain that she was well known in Tuscaloosa as an excellent worker and she did not have to put up with bad treatment from any boss.[49] Was she implying that Lomax was, like Ruby Pickens Tartt, a good boss? Or was Lomax not really asking her questions that she did not want to answer, slipping the yoke just enough to allow the conversation to continue?[50]

Lomax and Hall seem to have collaborated on a story that placed the most horrific experiences of racial violence deep in Hall's past. What remained were simply the incoherencies of racism. Whites were odd, Hall noted. In the book, Lomax quotes her:

> Blues puts your mind all in a wonder. You gets to studying over different things, wonderin how they come out to be so sad and so funny like. Now one thing I never could understand and I'm gonna ask this question—all my life those white people, they didn't even want you to sit in a chair they had in their house, didn't want you to have nothing to do, we Negroes, with nothing they had. But in their kitchen, they would want us to make um up a pan of biscuits, and make um with our hands—and I said, "Well, I declare, that's funny. Look like I'd be more scared of that than I would be somebody sittin in a chair."[51]

"To this day" white folks are crazy like this, she says. That seems to be what Lomax and Hall can agree on. That craziness, the continuing incoherence of racism, is what powers blues singing. Hall's voice conveys that power, telling a story deeper, richer, more evidently attuned to the painful realities of inequality than her calm demeanor would suggest or than Lomax's narration can describe directly.

In 1959 Alan Lomax again traveled through the South, recording singers and musicians for a trip sponsored by Atlantic Records. By the late-fifties, Atlantic was one of the most successful independent record companies in the United States. The company was run by Ahmet Ertegun, a son of a Turkish ambassador to the United States, who had fallen in love with R&B. Atlantic had already produced major hits by Ray Charles, Big Joe Turner, Ruth Brown, and a number of other artists.[52] Ertegun was committed to the commercial exploitation of black Southern musical styles. But he also had a scholar's streak to him. Lomax had originally approached Columbia Records, asking them to sponsor the trip. But Columbia insisted that Lomax employ a union recording engineer. Ertegun, perhaps more familiar with the special requirements of Southern recording conditions, made no such demand and so Atlantic Records earned the rights to release its choice of the recordings.[53] The results of Lomax's trip were never aimed at any of *Billboard*'s charts, but were instead released as a seven-LP series titled the Southern Folk Heritage Series in 1960. Accompanied by a young English folksinger, Shirley Collins, Lomax began the Southern journey intending to revisit familiar singers as well as discover new ones. The series of recordings was documentary in its frame, but aesthetic in its approach to its object. On the afternoon of October 10, 1959, Lomax and Collins recorded Hall singing fourteen different songs, some with multiple takes. Over halfway through the session, Hall sang a new version of "Trouble So Hard."[54] By this time, Hall was a well-known local gospel singer. She did not earn a living from singing—although she might have, had she chosen to take advantage of the opportunities that were offered to her. In addition to her work with the Lomaxes, the folksong collector and record producer Harold Courlander had produced recordings of her singing. Should she have been willing to tour, she could have tried to profit from the folk and blues revival. Instead, she remained in Tuscaloosa, working as a domestic servant and singing in her church.

For this 1959 recording, produced more than twenty years after that first version of "Trouble So Hard," Hall's voice sounds professional, assured, confident, and solemn. This time she is singing solo, no longer required to follow her cousin's lead. She raises the pitch a half step and chooses different lyrics, dropping the words borrowed from "Scandalize My Name" and adding a more chilling verse that was not present on the first version:

Went in the room
didn't stay long.
Looked on the bed,
brother was dead.

A lot might have changed in Alabama between 1937 and 1959. But one thing that had not changed was white violence in the service of policing the boundaries of the political. In 1937 this gospel song spoke of scandal and family betrayal. By 1959 Hall sang of death with a certain resignation, giving off the sense that there was no reason to linger on this death of a brother, for another death would come again too soon. By 1959 Hall could insert this direct evocation of a political moment into an old spiritual that she had sung hundreds of times. This time she used new lyrics to render irrepressible the sociopolitical grounding of the aesthetic power of her singing. This time, for a recording produced by her old friend Alan Lomax for a collection to be released not by the Library of Congress or Folkways Records but by the commercial company Atlantic, she cut through the surface gentility and golden light that had blocked the ears of her previous producers and created a haunting beauty that no one could bury.

That new verse is the musical moment that Moby highlights in his version, which he titled "Natural Blues." This track appears on *Play*, his album from 1999, which remains his largest commercial success, with more than nine million copies sold. Before releasing *Play*, Moby was an established rave DJ with a few electronica subhits to his name. He enjoyed a much larger following in the United Kingdom than he did in the United States. Moby found the Lomax recording while sifting through the "folk" racks at the old Tower Records store that is no longer in Greenwich Village. While he might have been initially struck by the same voice of gold and light that hit Lomax, his focus on dancing pleasure emphasizes the political highlights of the a cappella version. Although Moby does even out the verses, forcing them each to adhere to the same eight-bar length, his attention to structure draws the audience's awareness to the shape of the political made palpable in "Trouble So Hard." It resonates fully—gesturing, beckoning, luring. The basic beat that drives most of the techno version of the song is an electronic hi-hat that precisely mimics the hand-clap rhythms of church gospel. He locates the crucial verse right in the middle of the track, just before a change in the chord progression that melodically intensifies the minor key that guides the song. The intensity of the verse is highlighted by a drone of synthesized strings that enters just at the moment when Hall lyrically enters the room— these artificial strings sounding and resounding the tonic B♭ that marks the home of the song and anchors Hall's range. Just before the repeat of "brother was dead," everything stops but Hall's golden voice, which now sounds darkly matter-of-fact: "Brother was dead." The sens of the song is opened up by this gap—the sudden silence that embraces that line and forces the listener to ask, "what?" This sens that drew listeners to lean ever closer toward a community still to be built is not simply the appropriation of a racially coded naturalness; the sens beckons instead from a well-worn, indeed polished, assertion of the centrality of difference for the imagined community that it almost constructs.

A lot changed between Tuscaloosa, Alabama, in 1959 and New York City in 1999. But the resonance of "brother was dead" had not faded. The pleasure of "Natural Blues" requires the listener to consider its production, to ask himself or herself why Moby, a descendant of Herman Melville, chose to blend the most current synthesized sounds with these echoes of the costs of white supremacy. That requirement will not allow the listener to dismiss that song as mere entertainment or as musical deracination or theft of one people's tradition by another group. Vera Hall's voice was taken from her by Alan Lomax and Ahmet Ertegun for the purposes of documentation and scholarship. But it was Moby's focus on pleasure that brought out for his listeners the intensity of the song's articulation of the political. Reviewing a Moby concert for the *New York Times* soon after *Play* had been released, Ann Powers described what she termed, "the best moment of Moby's show": "As the world-burdened voice of Vera Hall singing, 'Oh Lord, trouble so hard' rode like jetsam on the current of the preprogrammed rhythms, Moby quietly stood and sang along with the refrain. His performance illustrated how a song, no matter how distant its source, can become immediate again with each listener's embrace."[55] The political force of this moment in Moby's performance of "Natural Blues" cannot be contained by concepts that reduce music's power to the reproduction of the values of an ethnos. This force cannot be captured by an analysis of lyrics. It cannot be canceled by claims of appropriation, no matter how historically accurate those claims might be. This moment in Moby's recording is dependent on the power of Hall's voice and may also be equally dependent on the collecting work of Tartt, the paternalistic recording strategies of John Lomax, the careful coaxing of Alan Lomax, and the commercial as well as historical motives of Ertegun. The power of Hall's voice singing "brother was dead," set off by a quick silence, followed by a set of synthesized strings, demonstrates the ongoing political salience of racial difference in the cultures of the United States. And this musical moment demonstrates the power of musical beauty to continually draw our attention to the work that still must be done to build political community with the knowledge of that divide, a political community of difference, with agon at its core, and an ever-more complex edge, drawn inward by music.

Chapter Two

The Anthem and the Condensation of Context

| | | | |

Traditionally, the discussion of music and politics focuses on stirring songs that bring together like-minded individuals eager to work together for a cause. Songs such as "We Shall Overcome" and "Blowin' in the Wind," or nationalist patriotic music such as "God Save the King" and "America the Beautiful," are among the first to come to mind when the conversation turns to overtly political music. Whether identified as official national songs, protest songs, or those of social movements, these songs can all be described as anthems. Anthems rouse groups of people, transforming crowds into mobs, mobs into movements, movements into parties, parties into nations. With each higher level of organization, however, the work of the anthem becomes more tenuous, the political community it resonates with becomes less solid, and the potential for anthemic music to fall into cliché and propaganda grows higher.

Most political music (understood in this way) is simple, easy to sing, and lacking in ambiguity or complexity with respect to either its musical or lyrical message. Not all anthems are wrought from cliché, however. The trick of the anthem is to combine a clear lyrical message with an unchallenging musical form that uses a rhythmic and melodic flow to reinforce the sense that the lyrical sentiment expressed is natural, normal, and equally felt by all hearing or (preferably) singing along with it. It is possible for songs that do not obey these rules to be taken up as anthems. "The Star-Spangled Banner" defies the musical requirements, prompting regular criticism about its extended melodic range. The lyrics of "Born in the USA" challenge the visceral response prompted by the song's punchy chorus. Such incidents always result in controversy; complex music and ambiguous lyrics prove challenging for the purposes of anthemic political organization.[1]

While the first job of an anthem is to use music and words to define the group whose political desires the song manifests, its success in doing so is often constrained or enabled by the context in which the anthem is performed. Anthems began as religious songs, where their affective power was reinforced by all the ritual and majesty of sacred service. With the rise of the modern nation, the political function of anthems began an incremental move out of the church, trailing along as the sovereign slowly lost divine right. The first true national anthem, "God Save the King," marks this procession, carrying with it the traces of sacred pomp in its performance of political unity. In mass democracies, the sense of national unity becomes ever more abstract. National anthems tend to arise at moments of crisis when unity is both a question and a necessity. Aside from such critical periods, the unity of mass democracies often relies on the mediating function of an *intimate public*. Intimate publics, Lauren Berlant's term for groups formed in and through a sense of shared and ordinary feeling, are energized through the infusion of an almost religious sense of ordained purpose, and they create a sense of equality among their members through that shared sense of their ordinariness.[2]

These traces of religious setting and feeling resurrect from time to time in the modern use of the anthem; they became particularly salient in the Civil Rights Movement. The convergence of religious singing practice, secular political purpose, and popular song in this historical moment was so effective that it has set the terms for most scholarly discussions of politics and music. Indeed, the musical experiences of the Civil Rights Movement, which brought together folk songs, work songs, spirituals, and the most pure pop with an expansive sense of the political community, established the modern sense that popular music could be a political force and that the direction of this force could be toward justice.[3] The congregational singing style that unified the marchers and the jailed throughout the South confirmed the sense of unity across difference that characterized the Movement. The style lent a sense of purpose and meaning to the songs themselves, to the genres and performers associated with the songs, and to those who inherited and worked with those styles and songs. Soul music elaborated the style and the sense of political purpose that adhered to movement songs and introduced that combination of possibilities into the popular-music marketplace.[4] Musicians working in this genre then established the conventions of the popular anthem, the most abstract, attenuated, and momentary example of the political force of musical beauty. The popular anthem works best when it approaches the conditions and settings of the traditional anthem. But the popular anthem's power can be felt, however briefly, however disturbingly, even when it exceeds or escapes those limits and conditions. Lasting maybe no longer than a single night, the clining political community built by pop anthems such as "I Will Survive" and "Empire State of Mind" entrains bodies otherwise stifled toward an awareness of the shared, the mutual, the collective that extends beyond the ordinary and the same.

The concept of the political is central to the class of songs that we call anthems. The anthem's traditional function is to delineate political bodies, to define human groups by their fealty to an object that unites them. When this function builds upon a preexisting object of unity, anthems reinforce Carl Schmitt's understanding of the political. Traditional anthems function most effectively when the central object of unity is clear, the boundaries of loyalty are easily perceptible, and the friend-enemy distinction is in dominance. Traditional anthems fare not so well when the sense of the community is still to come. If the polis is emergent, or nascent, as discussed in the thinking of Jean-Luc Nancy, an anthem can support that emergence through its ability to prompt an embodied experience of an almost-felt collective. Pop anthems can reinforce already existing political communities, but these anthems can also do more. The social experience of the simultaneous comprehension of relations of timbre, rhythm, and organized waves of tonal exploration and resolution can force a recognition of mutual predicament and mutual pleasure. This recognition can permeate the boundaries of the ordinary, slipping through and across intimate publics and knotting together their distinctive threads of difference, rendering nearly palpable the texture of a new political fabric.

FROM RELIGIONS TO NATIONS: THE EMERGENCE OF THE ANTHEM

Anthems began as a form of religious song called an antiphon.[5] Antiphons were a subcategory of hymns that were sung in a Latin Mass before psalms. As musical moments that responded to particular religious passages, antiphons wove a thread of theological consistency through the service that helped to intensify religious feeling. According to Joseph Otten, the antiphon "gives the key to the liturgical and mystical meaning of the psalm."[6] With the Reformation in England, the name of this type of song was anglicized into *anthem*; its function changed as well. English-language anthems began to be sung in the Anglican Church by

1549, and in her Injunctions of 1559, Queen Elizabeth I decreed that anthems could become part of the regular church service: "In the beginning, or in the end of common prayers, either at morning or evening, there may be sung an hymn, or such-like song, to the praise of Almighty God, in the best sort of melody and music that may be conveniently devised, having respect that the sentence of the hymn may be understood and perceived."[7] Beyond declaring the queen's acceptance of the practice in the regular Anglican service, the significance of this decree is twofold. First, it allows the anthem to mark the temporal edges of the service, the beginning or the end. In this way, the anthem called together the congregation, separating them off from all those outside the service. From this early moment then, the anthem's function was to define a human group—a specific body of worshipers at a time when religious choice carried ultimate political significance, precisely the distinction between friend and enemy. Elizabeth's Injunctions were additions to the Uniformity Act and confirmed many of the liturgical practices that distinguished the Church of England from the Roman Catholic Church. Anthems musically marked this distinction. Second, the sense of the words was supposed to remain clear; they were not to be obscured by musical decoration. According to Nicholas Temperley, English anthems were characterized by the singing of a "choir leading, guiding, and intensifying, by means of music, the unspoken religious feelings of a listening congregation."[8] The music of an anthem was intended to do nothing more than express and, perhaps, intensify the already present feelings, conveyed by the song's words, that united a clearly demarcated group. Both the group and the feelings that defined the group were oriented around a central nodal point. The worship of God centered the congregation, and anthems were both praise songs to God and the musical construction of the community of worshipers. In the Church of England after the Reformation, anthems were explicitly contrasted with the compositions featured in Roman Catholic services. This older form of religious music had become not only too difficult for most congregants to sing but also so ornate that the sense of the words was no longer communicated. The point of Elizabeth's authorization of anthems was to clarify the purpose of religious song and to describe the means whereby these purposes could best be served. Contrived to be simple songs, with direct and clear lyrical meaning, anthems soon became "the most powerful of devotional forces in the Protestant churches."[9]

Yet the constraints that defined the anthem did not preclude musical development. Early religious anthems provided an opportunity for composers to create four- and five-part vocal compositions, displaying their ability to weave together a wider range of voices, to create more-complex patterns, while still maintaining singable lines and the lyrical emphasis. Among the more-celebrated anthems were those of William Byrd, whose later Anglican choral works follow Elizabeth's injunctions for musical clarity while creating works of intricate beauty.[10] Byrd, who had been raised Catholic and who seems to have retained a fealty to that congregation his entire life, was adept at carefully signaling his conflicted loyalties, reflecting his need to retain his position as gentleman of the Royal Chapel while composing works that gestured beyond the bounds of the Anglican Church. Scholars such as John Harley have suggested that much of Byrd's greatness derives from his intensive efforts to resolve in his music this political contradiction. Harley argues that Byrd's ability to write intricate yet singable music was an effect of his personal emotional growth born of this political friction. His anthems included as many as six voices, often setting words of particular import for Catholics to an arrangement that fit the needs of his Anglican employers. Byrd's efforts demonstrate the ways in which the theological/liturgical and the political were woven together in the anthem, and his efforts illuminate the aesthetic possibilities that anthems retained. In Byrd's hands, anthems intended to define political difference could become works of musical beauty with ambiguous, indeed fuzzy, political boundaries.[11]

With the development of the European Enlightenment and the corresponding rise of European nationalism, the political function of anthems slowly began to take precedence over their liturgical significance. Their political meaning was solidified when George Frideric Handel's coronation anthems for George II were first performed. This set of compositions included a piece titled *Zadok the Priest*, which "has been sung at every English coronation service since its original appearance in 1727."[12] Early political anthems were the equivalent of praise songs to the sovereign. They relied on a religiously sanctioned form to reinforce loyalty to the king or queen. The anthem's particular blend of theological and political practice enabled this musical representation of the commitment to the sovereign to aid in the construction of a new feeling of national unity.

The musical projection of national unity in and through the monarch's body became ritualized in September 1745, when Thomas Arne's arrangement of "God Save the King" simultaneously premiered at the two leading music houses in London. Arne is not considered the author of this song. The words had appeared in print before this date, and Arne never claimed to have written them. But his musical arrangement of the already common tune closely followed the injunction to not over-decorate the sense of the words. With an almost military precision, the tune moves only slightly away from the tonic just to return as quickly as its short steps allow. In the words of Paul Nettl: "It is an optimistic and very well-balanced phrase which expresses confidence but keeps aloof from exaggerated emotionalism."[13] Generally recognized as the first true national anthem, "God Save the King" represents a significant shift in the trajectory of the national song. In "God Save the King," the king's two bodies have musically merged into the central object uniting the nation. No aspect of this song's music stands in the way of its lyrics: it is almost monotonous in its rhythmic regularity and nearly pedantic in its tonal clarity.

As it unites an "imaginary community," a politically effective anthem must manifest two key qualities. First, there must be a central object of identification that is clearly articulated. Anthems began as hymns, with God at their center. Slowly, this object was secularized to the monarch and then abstracted to the nation itself. But whether the central object is the monarch, a claim to bloodlines, a set of geographic boundaries, or even a specific history or a set of vague ideals, this object must clearly be capable of uniting its audience in identification with its centrality. To be truly a national anthem, a song must produce identification with an object that specifies the distinction between those who belong to the nation and those who do not. There must be no doubt about the object's significance; the nation has to be sufficiently powerful to inspire the feelings of uniqueness that membership in this national body confers. Second, for the anthem to function as effectively as possible, it should be sung together. As Benedict Anderson puts it, "No matter how banal the words and mediocre the tunes, there is in this singing an experience of simultaneity. At precisely such moments, people wholly unknown to each other utter the same verses to the same melody. The image: uniso-nance[,] . . . the echoed physical realization of the imagined community. . . . How selfless this unisonance feels! . . . Nothing connects us all but imagined sound."[14]

In its simplicity, "God Save the King" encourages group singing. Within decades, the easily sung melody, with its equally familiar, almost too-regular rhythms, was adapted for a variety of purposes, including the political solidarity of the rebelling North American colonies. Songs titled "God Save America," "God Save Our Thirteen States," and "God Save George Washington" were sung during the revolutionary era. With additional words, the same tune accompanied Washington's entry into New York for his inauguration as president. In its first years as a patriotic song in the new United States, this familiar melody encouraged identification not simply with Washington as sovereign but also with the president as a signifier for the nation, and even the nation itself apart from the body of the leader. In less than fifty years of performance in North America, the object of political identification for songs based on the melody Arne made famous shifted away from the individual head of state to the nation itself through the song's adaptation by an alternate concept of sovereignty. Robert Branham points out: "By the time that Rev. Samuel Francis Smith composed the lyrics to 'America' in the winter of 1831, its melody had been extensively and variously employed in the assertion of national character and accomplishment for decades."[15] The song's didactic melody could be used to identify a wide—indeed, conflicting—variety of political communities. This was not the work of the melody alone. Decades of singing practice, within which this melody signified and enacted political unity, buttressed the effects of the tune and allowed its central object of identification to shift.

Samuel Smith's verses directly replaced the image of the king as sovereign with an idealized nation, a "sweet land of liberty." Building on the familiarity of the tune as well as its ease of singing, Smith set up an abstract vision of the nation's identity, descended from pilgrims but grounded in the land, as the central object. Robert Branham quotes Oliver Wendell Holmes, who located the effectiveness of the lyrics in the use of the first-person singular: "If he had said 'Our Country,' the hymn would not have become immortal, but that 'My' was a masterstroke."[16] With that gesture, the lyric emphasized the individual felt experience of identification; the line grounded the abstraction of liberty in the everyday connection to the land. Since it was sung in a group, the multiple mentions of "I" reinforced the connection between the individual and the collective that lies at the center of national unity.[17] In addition, the focus on individual experience helped make up for the increasingly abstract nature of the object of identification. With the removal of the sovereign as the central object of identification and loyalty, anthems had to develop alternate means of producing the sense of a political community. A common experience of the land (my country) identified with a set of values (liberty) could become the central object of a sung community, but only if a particularly powerful process of citizenship formation had developed to support this singing.

In the period from the middle of the sixteenth century to the beginning of the nineteenth century, then, the anthem was transformed from a choral incitement to proper religious feeling, whose political significance was an outgrowth of its functional delineation of a religious community, to a collectively sung reinforcement of civic engagement and identification with a modern nation-state. This movement traced an underlying shift in the felt commitments of sovereignty. As the political theorist Carl Schmitt has argued, it was no accident that the modern nation-state developed contemporaneously with the European Enlightenment. The intellectual project of the Enlightenment concentrated on the identification and exploration of the rational rules that governed the operations of the universe. Similarly, the modern nation-state sought to establish the rules whereby people would consent to be governed. For Schmitt, the rational effort to expunge the universe of miracles was equivalent to the effort to purge the nation-state of the exception—that moment of strife and chaos that cannot be predicted by rational rules nor governed by them. In Schmitt's analysis, the fundamental role of the sovereign is to decide on those moments of exception: when they have begun, when they have ended, and what must be done during them. This ability to pronounce upon the exception logically precedes the rule of law, for no legal system can account for events that obey no rules. Only after the exception has ended can laws begin to be effective. Schmitt famously understood this and all "significant concepts of the modern theory of the state" to be "secularized theological concepts." Changes in the operation of the anthem marched in step with this process of secularized sovereignty. And the eternal return of the exception haunts the secularization of the anthem.[18]

The abstraction of the central object of the anthem co-occurred with the spread of mass democracy. Historians have shown that the democratizing process in the United States was regionally varied and anything but linear. Democracy took different forms in different locales, but the spread of the franchise to more inclusive groups of white men was consistently accompanied by the removal of voting rights from women and from property-owning African Americans. According to Sean Wilentz, there were two very different versions of American democracy by the 1840s: a "southern democracy" that "enshrined slavery as the basis for white men's political equality" and "northern democrats" who saw slavery as "a moral abomination that denied the basic humanity of blacks and whose expansion threatened white men's political equality."[19] (Indeed, Robert Branham has pointed out that "America" became the object of many parodic revisions by abolitionists who found the claim to a "sweet land of liberty" ludicrous.[20]) The intense localism of most democratic processes across the country had structured the national political parties that were increasingly consumed by the sectional crisis. While this crisis grew in intensity, it remained a struggle over the future of a single nation up until the point where the Confederacy formed. While "America" was certainly a popular and powerful anthem for the nation in the 1850s, it was not sung with "unisonance" across the country. The overall increase in the number of voters and the increasingly mediated system of representation simultaneously produced a more abstract understanding of the nation and a more intensely personalized sense of the relationship between individual citizens and the national community. Note that musically, the song continued to function anthemically. It forged individuals into political communities, but not a single national one.

As the sectional crisis heated into conflict, one other song was as widely sung across the United States as "America," albeit with as equally divided a set of local meanings. First performed as part of the blackface minstrel routine of Bryant's Minstrels in 1859, "Dixie" also relies on both the first-person singular and the longing for a particular place as a means of producing identification. The song begins by proclaiming a desire for the South imaged through its agriculture: "I wish I was in the land of cotton." But the object that centers the process of identification in this song is not a simple one; it implodes with all the weighty complexities of the blackface tradition. The song's authorship is disputed, but whether solely authored by Dan Emmett, in collaboration with a pair of black songwriters, or by a pair of white Southern writers, "Dixie" cannot escape its provenance as a signifier of cross-racial fantasy during the ever-heightening sectional tensions of the immediate antebellum period. This origin in the permanent ambiguity of blackface renders "Dixie" a complex and indirect anthem. At first glance, it seems to defy all the rules that have been established so far. Its range of feeling is shaped by its commercial context; the song does not suggest identification with the labor of cotton picking, or even with agrarian pastoral values, but instead relies on the image of cotton to suggest nostalgia for a land and a time where slaves—precisely the group with which most nationalist singers would *not* identify—were happy. The central human figures in the song are not the citizens of the political community that "Dixie" constructs. In fact, they are explicitly excluded from this community. Initially sung by white men in blackface for Northern audiences who shared no abolitionist sympathies, the song became an unofficial anthem for the Confederate States when it was sped up and performed during Jefferson Davis's inauguration as the president of the Confederacy in 1861. The song's nearly instant popularity across the South seemed to suggest a celebration of the peculiar institution as the precise sign of the South's uniqueness. "Dixie" was perhaps the most popular published commodity in the South as "the production of songbooks and sheet music outstripped every other area of southern publishing during the war." Minstrelsy itself spread across the South during the early years of the war, and "Dixie," voiced through its blacked-up characters, appeared to offer "unassailable proof of the essential righteousness of the system."[21] But according to Coleman Hutchison, the song's popularity exceeded the regional nationalism that was associated with it. While "Dixie" became an unofficial national anthem for the Confederacy, the song continued to be played in the North during the war. According to Hutchison, the power of the tune might have outweighed the specificity of the lyrics. The snappy rhythms of its verses, balancing dotted eighths and sixteenths against the underlying march beat, and the determined if indirect tromp up and down the scale in the chorus, give "Dixie" an easily recalled and eminently singable quality.[22] Musically, "Dixie" did not challenge the constraints placed on anthems. But its popularity across the Mason-Dixon Line does not mean that the song served an anthemic function everywhere it was sung. "Dixie" performed ambiguous cultural work that was enabled by its sentimental openness. Like mass-market literature, "Dixie" invited an identification not with any particular character or set of people but instead with a sense of belonging to a group identified by its shared feelings. "Dixie" created a common sense of belonging to a community and, in so doing, provided support for an imagined genteel plantation society. Although Hutchison makes much of the fact that the song was initially popular in the North and that Abraham Lincoln used "Dixie" as a campaign song during his initial presidential run, there is no indication that the song retained broad anthemic power in the North after secession. The unity constructed by "Dixie" may have crossed the Mason-Dixon Line, but it was still a unity based on the centrality of slave labor.

THE INTIMATE PUBLIC OF "THE STAR-SPANGLED BANNER"

Quite possibly what anthems of the mid-nineteenth century, including "America" and "Dixie," had in common with each other was not a purely unmediated effect of their melodies or lyrics. National political unity could be imagined, but it was nearly impossible to bring into felt experience. Political unity in mass democracies requires an imaginary component that can be experienced through a kind of sentimental yearning. In her analyses of sentimental culture, Lauren Berlant has developed the concept of the intimate public to articulate the work of this yearning. Intimate publics simultaneously emerged with mass democracies. As Berlant demonstrates, intimate publics first developed in women's culture in the mid-nineteenth century around texts such as *Uncle Tom's Cabin* and *The Lamplighter*. Intimate publics came together through the reading of popular novels and built their conditions of belonging on the basis of vague identification—not necessarily with any characters or subject positions elaborated in those texts but instead with the feelings produced by the texts. These feelings were believed to be shared by all those who read these novels. The belief in shared feeling made this public intimate, and the difficulty of speaking clearly and directly about those feelings rendered the structure of the public vague and open. "The offer of the simplicity of the feeling of rich continuity with a vague defined set of like others is often the central affective magnet of an intimate public," asserts Berlant.[23] The bonds that link together intimate publics are more affectively based than those operating among the newspaper-reading market-linked imagined communities of Anderson. Participants in an intimate public feel as though they belong, Berlant argues, because it "seems to confirm the sense that even before there was a market addressed to them, there existed a world of strangers who would be emotionally literate in each other's experience of power, intimacy, desire, and discontent, with all that entails."[24] Intimate public spheres operate via recognition. They validate the feelings of their participants through the mass-mediated echoing of those feelings in the experience of consuming mass culture. Most important, "a public is intimate when it foregrounds affective and emotional attachments located in fantasies of the common, the everyday, and a sense of ordinariness," says Berlant.[25] This sense of the ordinary is crucial; it confirms the state of belonging. The feelings that bind together an intimate public cannot be idiosyncratic; they cannot even be too finely tuned or too tightly focused. They must remain general, ordinary, and, therefore, vague. Participants have a *sense* that their emotional world is shared, and this vague sense is what holds them together. Through a particularly effective hegemonic maneuver, intimate publics circulate the reciprocal recognition of ordinary feeling.

Although Berlant calls intimate publics "juxtapolitical" to indicate their avoidance of focused political discourse, intimate publics can take on social causes and can stimulate political action—they are juxtapolitical, not antipolitical. The sentimental attachment to the equality of ordinary feelings produces a soft but necessary commitment to all who feel this way. In the process, the ordinary becomes normative—just. Thus, a sense of justice can become part of the affective glue that holds together the intimate public. This sense is what confirms the legitimacy and the ordinariness of the members' private feelings. The binding affect of intimate publics is a sentimental assertion of the equality of feelings, so long as those feelings are ordinary. In this circular fashion, then, the normative becomes normal. It becomes part of the assumptive world of the intimate public. In this world, the sung anthem became the musical form that could most equally demarcate a sense of mutual belonging. Through their ambiguous power, anthems unite subjects into intimate publics with a belief in common feelings at their core. While this feeling of sung unisonance does little to solve the problem of difference in a political community, it does suggest an ameliorative response as the sense of unisonance presumes a sentimental quality of unity underlying those differences, a unity achieved through a sung simplicity of shared feeling.

Intimate publics link their sense of justice to this validation of the sentimental ordinary. Those who challenge the legitimacy of the ordinary are not simply mistaken, therefore; they are violating common sense and promoting injustice. The boundaries of an intimate public are often charged with affective intensity, where different values or ways of being that can't be ignored can spark a struggle between the ordinary and the unjust. This affective intensity often erupts in a sense of scandalous outrage that ordinary feelings would be challenged. So the power of intimate publics has a negative component of scandalous rejection as well as a positive appeal. Mass markets and mass democracies bind together their publics by claiming the ground of the ordinary as normative, asserting the value of that ordinary through sentimental appeals to the equality of feeling shared by all participants, and by excluding and scandalizing all who challenge the powerful attractive force of this sentimental equality. Intimate publics use sentiment to suppress difference in the name of inclusion and acceptance. Hence, the friend-enemy distinction necessary to the political body can be affectively affirmed through the equalization of sentimental relationships and the sense of the ordinary normative that binds together the intimate public. Anthems have the capacity to heighten the political function of the juxtapolitical intimate public. By focusing the attention of the singing members on their common object of identification, anthems can increase the intensity of the boundary marking beyond the needs of the intimate public and toward what is necessary for true political formation. While its ultimate character may be sentimental and its ostensible aims juxta-political, the singing intimate public can be a powerful instance of the political, with as clear a sense of its boundaries as any republic. "Dixie" operated in just this way. It confirmed the everyday ordinariness of a world built by slave labor. Under conditions of war, the song confirmed the political unity of the Confederacy.

While some nations build their unity on a shared ethnos, ethnic commonality has come to characterize fewer and fewer modern nation-states. As a consequence, national anthems have taken on the task of catalyzing an intimate public into the legitimating body for a nation, in an era when the nation feels increasingly abstract.[26] Anthems musically catalyze intimate publics to the extent that they produce a sense of belonging among a community of sentimental equals. Each member of the group formed by an anthem holds an equal relationship to the central object of unity. That sense of equality and the ordinariness of that relationship can be affirmed through collective singing. The collective formed through group singing of a simple tune is powerfully normative. A report of the Boston School Committee in 1838 linked communal singing to civic virtue: "Through vocal music you set in motion a mighty power which silently, but surely, in the end will humanize, refine, and elevate a whole community."[27] The ordinary normative of the intimate public is reinforced by the unisonance of the sung anthem. Anthems can articulate and render audible the norm of feeling that holds together an intimate public—whether that feeling be loyalty to a nation or a sense of purpose.

Difficult to sing and lyrically obscure, "The Star-Spangled Banner" does not easily fit into the standard category of an anthem. It was not even declared the national anthem until 1931 with an act by President Hoover. Before that, "The Star-Spangled Banner" was one of many patriotic songs performed by marching bands and military groups who relied on its underlying rhythmic drive to push along its musical complications. The tune began as a drinking song originally associated with the Anacreontic Society (a group of English musicians). The melody spread across the American colonies and eventually the new nation via the networks of the Masonic Society. (I guess one should not be surprised that the tune of the national anthem was made popular by drunken Masons.) After Francis Scott Key put words to the tune in 1814, the piece was rapidly promoted as an American patriotic song. Both sides of the Civil War claimed the song. Lyrically, the song depicts a hard-fought battle. It is often heard as militaristic, and the connection with marching bands reinforces this association. In 1889 it was selected by the U.S. Navy as the song to be played whenever the flag was raised. In 1916 President Wilson decreed that the song be played during official military occasions. From the military "The Star-Spangled Banner" crept into sports. It had been performed at some baseball games from the 1880s on and with greater regularity after 1918. However, it was not until after World War II that the song became a regular feature of Major League Baseball games. In his still authoritative discussion, Paul Nettl notes that the desire for an official national anthem is often prompted by war or major social unrest.[28] The slow movement of "The Star-Spangled Banner" from one of many patriotic songs to the national anthem maps onto moments of disruption. Wilson's promotion of the song occurred alongside World War I; Hoover's official declaration took place during the Great Depression. From its promotion by marching bands to its adoption by the military and promotion by one of the nation's more imperial presidents, "The Star-Spangled Banner" has become increasingly performed as part of a spectacle of imperial military power, not as a sung anthem of national unity. It is curious that this most militaristic of patriotic songs is also among the least singable, with more musical interest than most anthems. The relative musical complexity adds to the song's spectacular nature and detracts from its ability to bind an intimate public. Instead of producing unity through collective singing, instead of constructing a union of shared feeling, the song seems to demand recognition, rather similar to an old-fashioned sovereign watching over a military parade.

Or else it operates by a different principle. Perhaps "The Star-Spangled Banner" does not work like the normal anthem. Its musical structure, while relatively straightforward, is significantly more complex than that of "God Save the King." The melodic leaps of "The Star-Spangled Banner," those startling and commanding arpeggios, that disturbing sharp fourth (F♯ in the key of C major), and the final leap up to the fifth in the next octave (often embellished by professional singers with a slide to the next highest tonic) all demand an attentive listening and, perhaps, an aspirational approach to singing. This sense of aspiration, of the song being just beyond the reach of most of those who attempt it, may just be the source of the anthem's effectiveness. Perhaps the difficulty of that melodic span of an octave and a half presents a musical parallel to the aspirational nature of the nation the song represents. The highest note is, of course, sung to the word *free* in the only verse most people know. The phoneme itself, the sound of that *eee*, increases the difficulty of the piece, because the mouth must be stretched wide apart in the front, closing the throat in the back and constricting the airflow required to hit the note. Very few can sing it well. But there is an upside to this difficulty. It is almost as if every failure to sing the song well is a reminder of the work still to be done to achieve the promise of the nation. By thwarting the rules of the anthem, "The Star-Spangled Banner" produces in its singers a sense of the promise of freedom, a promise not easily kept, a promise that must continually be worked toward. But all of that possibility, all of that reminder of the aspirational nature of the union, disappears when the uniquely talented sing and the song's potential for spectacle dominates. When Whitney Houston displays all her melismatic skill, as she did prior to the Super Bowl in 1991, or when Robert Merrill's classic baritone is echoed with crashing cymbals before the New York Yankees take the field, attendant listeners are no longer impressed with the difficulty of achieving freedom. Instead, the work of the anthem and the work of the nation seem best left to others. Rather than producing an intimate public, "The Star-Spangled Banner" most often constructs a docile one, one normalized not by an equality of singing but rather by the consuming equality of spectatorship. This is the double-edged effect of complex anthems. They require a particular context of mutual effort to counter the difficulty of achieving their beauty.

LIFT EVERY VOICE AND SING

When James Weldon Johnson and J. Rosamond Johnson composed "Lift Every Voice and Sing," it was explicitly designed for group singing. In his autobiography, *Along the Way*, James Weldon Johnson tells the story of its moment of authorship. In early 1900, a group of young men in Jacksonville, Florida, began to organize a celebration of Lincoln's birthday. Johnson had been thinking for some time of an epic poem that would describe Lincoln's achievement from the perspective of black Americans. But the task seemed too hard for him. One afternoon, while working out material for the birthday celebration with his brother, Johnson was caught up with inspiration. It is worth quoting his telling of the story at length, for his narrative strategy in the autobiography shares an important quality with the lyric of his most famous song:

I got my first line: — Lift ev'ry voice and sing. Not a startling line but I worked along grinding out the next five. When, near the end of the first stanza, there came to me the lines:

Sing a song full of the faith that the dark past has taught us.
Sing a song full of the hope that the present has brought us

The spirit of the poem had taken hold of me. . . . As I worked through the opening and middle lines of the last stanza:

God of our weary years
God of our silent tears
Thou who has brought us thus far on our way
Thus who has by Thy might
Let us into the light,
Keep us forever in the path, we pray;
Lest our feet stray from the places, our God, where we met Thee.
Lest, our hearts drunk with the wine of the world, we forget Thee . . .

I could not keep back the tears, and made no effort to do so . . . I knew that in the stanza the American Negro was, historically and spiritually, immanent.[29]

Johnson has made a beautiful claim here. A community is historically and spiritually immanent in this lyric. Where? On the surface, the words are simply a hymn that asks God to keep his people on the right path. If an anthem unites a people through intensifying feelings of identification with a central object, these lyrics seem to reinforce the traditional religious function of centering a people on their God, returning the anthem to its liturgical origins. Indeed, Johnson always claimed that this song was a hymn, not an anthem. Nevertheless, the song has functioned as a political anthem for decades. At least since the early years of the Civil Rights Movement, "Lift Every Voice and Sing" has been referred to as the "Negro National Anthem," regardless of Johnson's authorial intent. Edward Brooke, a former senator from Massachusetts says, "The National Anthem was for all Americans, black, white, red, brown and yellow. But 'Lift Every Voice and Sing,' which later became known as the Negro National Anthem, was uniquely for us. To me it spoke of black life in white America. It spoke of where we had been and where we were. It spoke of what we had learned and what we could not forget. It spoke of lingering pains of slavery and the continuing evil of segregation and discrimination."[30] Amiri Baraka finds in this song "a feeling of some still not completely identified 'We-ness.' . . . [It is] a lyric whose aesthetic dialectic uncovers and releases deep historic and ennobling experience from within itself, swinging joyously into ourselves, trigged by our singing."[31] Clearly, for at least fifty years and probably for its entire life, this song has functioned as a political anthem—triggered by the collective singing of a well-defined group.

But, for a political anthem, these words are amazingly indirect. There are no references to heroic individuals. No references to a specific land that has been bravely defended. No reminders of military victory. None of this is present on the surface of Johnson's lyrics. How, then, has the song musically constructed a political community? There are several factors. First is the indirect line taken by the political function itself. By rooting the political struggle of African Americans in a pledge to be true to God's will, Johnson plugged into a powerful tradition in black life. As Eddie Glaude has shown, even before the Civil War, black churches mediated between the racialized state and the black community: "The church stood not only as the institutional organization of the community's resources and a kind of ideological and cultural common ground for everyday interaction or association among antebellum blacks." Glaude continues, "Black religious institutions were, to a large extent, the consequences of the efforts of members of the community to address their common ills."[32] Black churches were a key site for the formation of a black public sphere. Evelyn Brooks Higginbotham has demonstrated the continuation of this political function into the twentieth century, showing that the Baptist Women's Convention enabled black women to assert "agency in the construction and representation of themselves as new subjectivities—as Americans as well as blacks and women." Armed with this new sense of themselves, black women worked in and through religious organizations to change America's racial hierarchy, "for the sake of America's soul."[33] Higginbotham's research focuses on the period between 1880 and 1920, covering the era when Johnson's song was composed and first found its national audience. She makes evident the overlapping religious and political context for the recognition of a black political community, a condition quite similar to the original context within which the anthem emerged as a distinct musical form. With the political function of this song anchored in a religious setting, "Lift Every Voice and Sing" could take advantage of the public sphere already formed in and through black churches. In this context, the political community formed by this anthem organized itself around the historic struggle of African Americans. Around that struggle the song's lyrics could build an intimate public defined by the equal status of all affected by antiblack racism. "Lift Every Voice and Sing" was and remains crucial to the reproduction of black political solidarity as Tommie Shelby defines it.[34]

The second major factor that supports the anthemic status of "Lift Every Voice and Sing" is its music. Most of the commentary on this song focuses on its lyrics. But as the opera star Jessye Norman acknowledges, "It is a mighty anthem, highly singable, stirring and satisfying."[35] While not simple, it features only one significant melodic leap, and it is not terribly difficult to sing. Set in 6/8 time—that perfect metrical expression of the African diasporic tendency toward overlapping rhythms—the opening phrases are relatively straightforward. Following a pick up note on the seventh (G in the original key of A♭), the melody marches up to the third and then back down to the tonic—nearly as direct and purposeful a melody as "God Save the King." The completion of the initial phrase is satisfying if somewhat musically commonplace. But the "B" section of the melody turns inward on itself in a surprisingly dark fashion. Not only do the harmonies move to the relative minor, but the melody moves down from the initial tonic in repeating steps that suggest not just a dark journey but an unending one, filled with numbing repetitions of the same darkness over and over. In the second half of this section, Rosamond Johnson inserts a minor second (a B♭♭ in the original key) that takes some practice to learn to sing properly. When mastered, however, this half step up from the tonic becomes the pivot note that lifts the melody out of the darkness of this section and back into what becomes an undeniably stirring return to the first section and the reward of enduring the struggle.

Finally, "Lift Every Voice and Sing" functions as a political anthem because it is sung like one. Originally written for a choir of five hundred children, the song has been traditionally sung in what Anderson would call unisonance at public gatherings, marking the coming together of a public that is organized by its shared and equal relationship to the struggle and the history conveyed both subtly and directly by this song. Juan Williams has described the experience of singing this song in an interracial audience: "When the piano begins that simple, easily recognizable melody and the first few black people stand, soon joined by every other black adult in the room as an expression of solidarity and black consciousness, there is a clear divide."[36] It becomes evident who is brought together as a political community by this anthem and who is not. "Lift Every Voice and Sing" musically confirms the political fact that, as Shelby puts it, "black Americans are a people—an intergenerational community of descent" linked by "the shared experience of racial oppression and a joint commitment to resist it."[37]

In 1919 the political significance of "Lift Every Voice and Sing" was confirmed when it was adopted by the NAACP (National Association for the Advancement of Colored People) as its official song. The intimate public that received, circulated, and extended its solidarity in relationship to "Lift Every Voice and Sing" was sustained and supported by a tradition of singing that reached forward to the freedom songs of the Civil Rights Movement as well as back to the spirituals of the antebellum period. I do not mean to reduce the full cultural force of this tradition of singing to a purely political function. Rather, I want to bring out the political force of this singing tradition, a force that wove together a struggle for survival and dignity with a religious faith in a God of meaning and grace. Even as the lyrics present evidence of the tradition that the song came from, its spreading popularity was both an effect and a reinforcement of that ongoing linkage between singing in church and the political movement.

Among the most significant chroniclers of that linkage is Bernice Johnson Reagon. Reagon's work, both as a singer and activist in the Civil Rights Movement and as a historian of black culture and political movements, documents the real political power of anthem singing and helps to specify the conditions under which music can enact its anthemic political force. In multiple essays and lectures, Reagon has repeatedly emphasized that the power that so many have located in the songs of the Movement was much more directly an effect of this tradition of singing. It is not that the songs themselves were unimportant. To the contrary, it was no accident that many spirituals became the basis of freedom songs. But the political power of these songs came from the traditional practice of group singing—drawn largely from congregational singing style—that helped to transform these songs of everyday life and struggle into movement anthems.

CONGREGATIONAL SINGING STYLE AND
THE CIVIL RIGHTS MOVEMENT

Congregational singing style is group singing that relies on songleaders to begin the song. Songleaders are not soloists, nor are they necessarily the best singers in the group. As Reagon puts it, "African American congregational singing . . . is the tradition in which singing for a gathering comes from those who fill the pews. Songs are raised by a songleader and survive and fill the air and the hearts of those souls who with their voices, hands, and feet, give it life."[38] If a song is not taken up by the group, it dies away to be replaced by another. Once a song, in its totality as words and music, has been chosen by the group, it becomes the audible manifestation of the group's felt cohesion. Simultaneously, singing together reinforces the group's solidarity as an intimate public, organized as a set of equal relations to the anthem which becomes the public's audible form. Congregational-style singing does not consist of every individual singing exactly the same pitches for exactly the same duration. Instead, multiple entry points, multiple approaches to time, and multiple ways of approaching the pitch constitute what Charles Keil has called "participatory discrepancies." Through this embrace of difference, in Keil's terms being "out of time" and "out of tune," congregational singing style produces sung unisonance.[39] Within the Civil Rights Movement, the political force of anthems resulted from a specific confluence of particular musical texts with congregational singing practice.

The singing of freedom songs helped to solidify the community of activists in the Movement as early as the Montgomery Bus Boycott of 1955–56. The Montgomery Gospel Trio, three high school girls, contributed their voices as songleaders "soon after the first mass meeting." One of those young women, Jamilla Jones, remembered the power of traditional hymns like "Onward Christian Soldiers," songs that explicitly merged religion and the force of social determination. But she also recalled that among the most successful anthems they sang was "This Little Light of Mine."[40] Indeed, this old spiritual was the favorite song of the Student Nonviolent Coordinating Committee (SNCC) leader Fannie Lou Hamer. The fact that this old spiritual could be raised, taken up, and affirmed as a civil rights anthem demonstrates the power this singing tradition had to invigorate a song with social purpose. For Hamer, the song seemed to symbolize the collective significance of her own and each individual's efforts to build a movement.[41] At a reunion of SNCC activists held in 1986, Reagon affirmed the song's significance: "This song was sung more than 'We Shall Overcome.' Many times it went several times a night, and I think it went several times a night because it was very important to understand that you don't get a group if you don't get some individuals."[42] Reagon insists that "singing is an organizing experience."[43] The singing of anthems enables an embodied experience of the abstraction of a collective. In most circumstances, that collective already exists — as a church or a movement. But the organizing power of group singing transforms that idea of a collective, its abstract name, into a felt and lived reality. "This Little Light of Mine" produced a political community centered on the individual's capacity to contribute to, indeed to create, the collective. The song shares the easy singability that characterizes all effective anthems, from "God Save the King" to "Lift Every Voice and Sing." But "This Little Light of Mine" also demonstrates another key contribution from the singing practices of the black church. The unisonance that comes from singing "This Little Light of Mine," or any other song from the spiritual tradition, foregrounds the rhythmic participatory discrepancies that Keil characterized as "processual."[44] Each vocalist can enter the phrase at a moment of his or her choosing. Freed from the ponderous simultaneity of many traditional anthems, "This Little Light of Mine" produces through its rhythmic openness the audible contribution of multiple different voices in the construction of the political.

Within the conditions of confrontation and bravery that framed the actions of the Civil Rights Movement, a song from almost any genre, if it were sung properly, could function as an anthem. Candie Carawan, an activist with SNCC, remembers nights locked in segregated jail cells where the collective solidarity of the group could only be maintained through singing. The group sang to each other for hours at a time, maintaining contact with each other even though they were physically separated: "We sang a good part of our 8 hour confinement that first time. . . . Never had I heard such singing. Spirituals, pop tunes, hymns and even slurpy old love songs all became so powerful. The men sang to the women and the girls down the hall answered them."[45] Guy Carawan, Candie's husband and the director of the Highlander Folk School, affirms the power of singing: "Those students who have faced the angry mobs, suffered the beatings and jailings, and gone through so many other trials . . . have found from experience that singing these songs has inspired them and given them sustenance for the continuing struggle. Singing has become one of the chief forms of group expression in the movement."[46] Although specific songs are often remembered as particularly successful, the political purpose of these anthems, their most important function of solidifying the group, was an effect of singing in the dangerous circumstances of struggle (see figure 2.1). The music critic Robert Shelton noted in a piece he wrote for the *New York Times* in 1962 that "this use of folk music has to be heard in context to be fully understood." Heard in the North, in concert settings, the songs may seem cliché-ridden and full of empty slogans. Instead, Shelton advised, "imagine 1,000 voices at a mass meeting in Albany's Mount Zion Baptist Church [in Georgia], singing the universal theme song of the movement, 'We Shall Overcome.'"[47] Reagon sum-

FIG. 2.1 Singing the cross-racial alliance of the civil rights movement. Mississippi Freedom Summer, 1964. Photo © Steve Schapiro; courtesy of Corbis.

marized this point: "Out of the pressures and needs involved in maintaining group unity while working under conditions of intense hostility and physical threat, student organizers of sit-in campaigns developed their own supportive activist culture—and music was its mainstay."[48]

Congregational singing style connected the political work of the spirituals in the time of slavery to that of the freedom songs in the Civil Rights Movement. This style of singing materialized an intimate public as more than a juxtapolitical group. It became instead a solidified collective organized around a central object of identification that demarcated a clear difference between those who belonged to the group and those who did not. The political force of this distinction could not be missed when the force was reinforced by jail cells, water hoses, billy clubs, and attack dogs. During the early sixties, however, the membership of this public changed. While the political centrality of singing in styles drawn from black churches remained, the changing membership of the movement meant that the central object of identification at the center of the intimate public had to change as well. With the infusion of white college students and other activists from the North, the solidarity of the movement could no longer be constructed as an equality of relationship to the struggle for black freedom. That is, for all the intensity of commitment and purpose evinced by the young whites joining the struggle, most of them were operating at two removes from this musicalized object of political unity. First, most new activists simply could not bring with them a personal, familial, and religious history of singing that had musicalized the political unity of the groups to which they belonged. Second, the political collective that these activists transformed by joining was not simply and solely unified behind the goal of black political freedom. The cross-racial unity of the Civil Rights Movement was more complicated and more specific. It was not possible for an intimate public to be constructed out of singing freedom songs that would unite black Southerners and white Northerners in relationships of equality to anything other than the Movement itself. This is one way of understanding what Julius Lester meant when he asked, "What did they [whites] know of these songs we would sing in church and in the field, songs the old folks sang when they were ironing or just settin' on the porch in the evening as the sun went down and the frogs came out? Nobody had ever hated them."[49] It was, therefore, quite difficult for white Northerners to have the same relationship to the songs or to the traditions within which the songs took on their political significance. However powerful "This Little Light of Mine," "Onward, Christian Soldiers," or other Baptist hymns might have been during the earliest years of the movement, once the larger coalition began to draw ever-increasing numbers of those not raised in Southern black culture, the movement needed a new anthem to center its intimate public. This was the function of "We Shall Overcome."

WE SHALL OVERCOME

"We Shall Overcome" is probably the most frequently discussed "political" song of the second half of the twentieth century. Analyses of that song form the center of numerous discussions of music's political effect. Ron Eyerman and Andrew Jamison introduce their book *Music and Social Movements* with a discussion of the song's derivation and use in the Civil Rights Movement.[50] Nancy Love centers her analysis of "freedom songs" on this tune.[51] Indeed, the song was centrally featured in the "integrated socialist education system of the G.D.R. [East Germany]" in the 1970s.[52] Of course, any discussion of the link between the folk revival and the Civil Rights Movement, any discussion of the impact of Pete Seeger, Joan Baez, or even Bob Dylan on the social movements of the period, must come to terms with this song.[53] Every discussion cites the song's origins as a spiritual, its various appropriations for labor struggles, and its lyrical transformation from first-person singular to plural and from *will* to *shall*. Throughout these discussions, the song's publication history is traced through two gospel songs. The first song, "I'll Be Alright," is the source of the tune. The second gospel song was authored by Charles Tindley and titled "I'll Overcome Some Day." Tobacco workers who were organizing for a strike sang a blend of these two songs as they marched, using phrases from "I'll Overcome Some Day" with the older tune. Zilphia Horton heard this at the Highlander Folk School in the late forties. She taught the song to Pete Seeger in 1947 (see figure 2.2). Over the following decade, the song was refined and expanded with some new words added by Seeger and some by others in the classic folk process. Over the course of this process, the lyrics underwent two significant changes. The first-person pronoun became *we*, and the future subjunctive form of *shall* was inserted in place of *will*.

As part of Seeger's regular repertoire, the song, now "We Shall Overcome," was heard in many different contexts. Seeger sang it at the twenty-fifth reunion of the Highlander Folk School in 1958, after Horton's death. According to Seeger, both Ralph Abernathy and Martin Luther King Jr. heard the song at that performance. But Seeger insists that it was only after Guy Carawan took over the Highlander School and began singing "We Shall Overcome" regularly at events connected with the Freedom Rides and the sit-ins that the song became a regular feature of the Civil Rights Movement.[54] The tune stayed relatively stable from the time that Horton first heard it through Carawan's move to the South. Like most anthems, the melody is simple, characterized by single steps with only one movement of a fifth in the chorus. The final line, "we shall overcome some day," leaps from the fifth (G in the key of C) down to the tonic and then back up a third only to walk back down, reinforcing the certainty of the lyric with the steadiness of the melody's return to home. It is quite singable, with no ambiguity about either its tonal or lyrical center.

But the shift of "We Shall Overcome" to anthemic status needs to be examined carefully. The song was not the unifying anthem of the original intimate public that made up the Civil Rights Movement in its early years. However frequently the song might have been sung before 1960, "We Shall Overcome" did not become central to the movement until after the point where large numbers of whites began to participate. This change in the makeup of the activists required a whole new sense of the political community involved. The key word in the song quickly became

FIG. 2.2 Pete Seeger's universalist dream. His banjo surrounds hate and forces it to surrender. Photo by Megan Westerby.

the plural pronoun with which it began: *we*. "The most important word is 'We,'" said Seeger. "And when I sing it, I think of the whole human race, which must stick together if we are going to solve crucial problems that face us all."[55] Reagon understands the implications of that word differently: "I always worry about that word 'we.' I don't know what 'we' means. When somebody tells me 'we,' I want to know, 'Well where are you going to be?' 'We' is a way to avoid testifying your personal stance. Now, if I say where I'm going to be, you say where you're going to be, then the 'we' is understood and we will all know what's going to happen. Progressive White people in the Movement changed 'I'll Overcome' to 'We Shall Overcome,' to correct it grammatically, also because they believed 'I'll Overcome' to be an individualistic statement."[56] Whether or not Reagon is correct that the use of *we* allows one to avoid taking a personal stand, it is clear that she is more wary of the plural than is Seeger. Where both singer-activists understand the profound political significance of the first-person plural, they differ on its solidity. In "We Shall Overcome," the *we* makes a claim about a political community, a union of participants in the movement. Although it was sung at movement actions before 1960, the value of the particular *we* the Movement constructed—the *we* that could simultaneously and ambiguously suggest all of humanity even in the absence of the spoken commitment of each participant—was not salient before the moment when participants might have had motives other than achieving the political autonomy of African Americans. When the solidarity that shaped the boundaries of the participants could not be equated with black solidarity, when the movement began to be as much about the moral value of the nation as a whole, an ambiguous and fluid *we* became a more central sign of the movement's coherence. At that point, the core of the movement could be better performed anthemically with "We Shall Overcome" than it could be with "This Little Light of Mine" or "Onward, Christian Soldiers." Singing "We Shall Overcome" with arms crossed over the front of the body and holding hands with the people standing beside you became a way of solidifying the movement itself as the object of identification for those in the Civil Rights Movement. With all of its sing-along power, "We Shall Overcome" became precisely the anthem of the Movement, not an anthem for black political autonomy.

In its immediate context of struggle, "We Shall Overcome" produced a clear sense of the political with unmistakable distinctions between friend and enemy. When sung in the context of the Civil Rights Movement, the song was a powerful reinforcement of an already present political community. Singing "We Shall Overcome" produced a source of energy that could renew the purpose of those included inside its circle of swaying, singing bodies. As those bodies sang together, they experienced a resonating political body that centered around a clear object, forming an intimate public with equal relations to the movement itself. The political force of "We Shall Overcome" was an effect of the song's firm grounding in the anthem tradition, which worked best within such a solidifying context. The combination of a clear object, an immediately evident friend-enemy distinction, and a long tradition of harmonizing one's sense of belonging collaborated in this peak moment. But the ambiguity at the heart of the song, its wonderful ability to suggest a community that it could not promise, added another element to its success while marking the song as a transition piece to a new anthem form.

Seeger's insistence that the song's *we* must mean all of humanity, because only all of humanity could solve the big problems in which he was interested, weakens the sense of the political as a firmly bounded entity. Imagining a community of all necessarily abstracts from the specificity that is needed to distinguish a polis. This is the essential work of the sentimental in the juxtapolitical formation of an intimate public. Not even Nancy's community-to-come is all-inclusive: to participate in the community to come, one must incline toward that undefined collective; some will not. The hopeful vagueness that Seeger attached to "We Shall Overcome" certainly allowed many thousands of Americans to sing along, at movement actions as well as in concert halls across the country. But this openness has its defects too. Reagon's understanding that *we* allows a slippage for the singing *I*, freeing *we* from the forthright declaration of one's own risk-filled stance, raises an important concern. Traditional anthems work best when the political community has definite and clear boundaries, functioning to reinforce political groups that already exist. Anthems' musical agency consists of the force needed to reproduce and reinforce those already present distinctions. "We Shall Overcome" clearly grew out of the anthem tradition as this tradition cycled back through religious practices and the convergence of religious and political groups. But to the extent that the song reached out, with its vague and sentimental yearning, beyond the historical moment of the Civil Rights Movement, it pointed the way toward something new, an anthem for an intimate public that would last only as long as the tenuous sentimental feelings that bound it together. "We Shall Overcome," with all its ambitious ambiguity, set the terms and established the conceptual possibility for a new song category, the pop anthem.

The pop anthem is a juxtapolitical sentimental anthem, fully in line with the demands of the intimate public and, if not thoroughly comfortable in, at least not fundamentally antagonistic to the commercial setting of the popular-music industry. The pop anthem can be sung along to, but when that happens, that singing is just as likely to take place in private, in a car or the shower, or at a commercial performance, in a night-club or a concert hall, than in church, at a demonstration, or with fellow prisoners in a county jail. The pop anthem's intimate public is perhaps more likely to dance along as it is to sing along. Absent the traditional anthem's preexisting political community, the pop anthem constructs a new tentative *we,* centered around affectively charged objects whose power is musically suggested rather than contextually and extramusically confirmed. The pop anthem stretches the reach of the traditional anthem by embracing the affective potential and the semantic emptiness of musical sound as the anthem risks a quick ephemeral decay when it spreads itself too far. The pop anthem shares with William Byrd's six-part voicings the power and the ambiguity of musical beauty built from simple lines. Byrd's music was anchored in the performance practice and reception context of the Church of England; this music was shaped and limited by the political tensions that agitated religious belonging. But the beauty his music produced was able to reach out beyond the political community that provided the generative context for the initial power of his anthems and, with tentative and ambivalent reach, embrace for a moment those not yet aware that they belonged.

One of the most fruitful grounds for the development of pop anthems was the genre of soul music, which emerged coterminously with the Civil Rights Movement. This historical coincidence has spawned numerous studies that have tried to specify the relationship between these two developments. For many observers, soul music seemed to carry more of the feeling of the Civil Rights Movement than the folk revival conveyed. At the very least, the musical force of soul grew out of the characteristics it shared with black gospel.[57] Some scholars have challenged the political significance of soul music, basing their arguments somewhat precariously on the racially mixed nature of many of the Southern studio bands that helped to create this genre, and the relative absence of overt political activism on the part of some of the main stars.[58] Every serious discussion of soul, however, regardless of the relative weight given to its direct political effects, emphasizes that a major source of its musical power derived from the singing styles found in black churches. In 1968, Amiri Baraka, writing as Leroi Jones, articulated it this way: "Even today a great many of the best R&B groups, quartets, etc. have church backgrounds, and the music itself is as churchified as it has ever been."[59]

For many, soul is simply secularized gospel. The musical boundaries between sacred and secular music are rarely clear. Gospel and blues shared musical characteristics from the earliest days of Thomas Dorsey, often referred to as the "father of gospel music," who began his career as the blues singer Georgia Tom.[60] Sister Rosetta Tharpe, who continued to score hits on the spiritual chart after poking fun at self-righteous church folk with the boogie romp "Strange Things Happening Everyday" in 1945, relied on the same guitar riffs and vocal techniques regardless of the genre her music was slotted into or the venues where she performed.[61] As Albert Murray famously described it, the songs sung during the Saturday night function may sound like those sung during the Sunday morning service, but they carry completely different meanings.[62] The need to keep those meanings distinct ensured that the production and marketing for gospel and R&B records remained mostly separate until 1954. That year Specialty Records, which up to that point had been almost exclusively a gospel label, scored a number 1 R&B hit with Guitar Slim's "The Things I Used to Do." And Roy Hamilton had a hit with a gospel-style version of "You'll Never Walk Alone." The commercial potential for sacred-secular crossover was confirmed later that year when Ray Charles added secular lyrics to an established gospel song, "There's a Man Going 'Round, Taking Names," sped it up, and created the R&B hit "I Got a Woman."

This commercial success sparked a series of tendentious negotiations among musicians, fans, and recording companies. While the gospel audience was stable and consistent, usually allowing for hit sales of around forty thousand or so, the R&B audience was more finicky but also significantly larger, generating sales of more than a hundred thousand for major hits. In search of those larger sales, record-company owners such as Art Rupe and Syd Nathan began urging major gospel singers to record secular songs. But the path to crossing over from gospel to R&B was fraught. Throughout the fifties, an artist's shift from sacred to secular music was felt as a betrayal by large portions of the gospel audience.[63] This sense of betrayal was exacerbated by the ways in which these crossovers transgressed the boundaries of the intimate public. Inside the church, the intimate public of believers was firmly grounded in an equality of feeling oriented toward God and salvation. Outside the church, there could be no presumed equality of feeling. When singers began to use the sounds of gospel outside of their orienting context, the singers revealed these sounds' formal properties—vocal techniques and rhythmic power—as simply sounds made musical. Soul music was the result of performers transforming the constraining context of gospel into a set of musical sounds that carried the potential for creating an intimate public from the church and moved it into the secular world.

Sam Cooke's "A Change Is Gonna Come" marks an early apotheosis of soul's efforts to textualize gospel's intimate public, to forge a pop anthem that, through its beauty, could produce a longing to belong among a body of listeners that would otherwise never incline together. This shared longing was in part an effect of Cooke's vocal sound, his smooth blend of gospel techniques with the relaxed tone of the crooner, which enforced a redistribution of the sensible. Certainly Nat Cole and other jazz vocalists had already approached a similar vocal tone, but the political force of Cooke's particular sound resulted from his performance of graceful striving, his seemingly effortless mastery.[64] This calm accomplishment enabled a felt awareness of black political self-determination. His famous vocal signature, of seeming to exert no effort as he reached for clear tones just at the edge of his range, rendered audible and, therefore, sensible the transformation in political relations of the Civil Rights Movement. In so doing, the force of the song reached beyond the intimate public that had provided the Movement's affective ground and created a temporary and tentative *we* bound together by the beauty of his song.

By the early sixties, Cooke was already a crossover star, with a well-established cross-racial audience. "You Send Me" had hit number 1 on *Billboard*'s pop chart in 1957. In the years after this success, Cooke toured the Southern R&B circuit, occasionally performing on gospel bills and occasionally playing in white-oriented supper clubs. Working in a recording industry that was organized by racial categories as well as genre labels, Cooke found himself, as so many other black artists before him, having to carefully balance his desires for large sales and the mainstream recognition that his talent deserved with the need to stay connected to the intimate public out of which his art grew. As a major pop artist in 1958, Cooke was booked as part of a package called The Biggest Show of Stars, with the performers Paul Anka and the Everly Brothers, among others. But that tour had to be rerouted out of Southern cities such as Columbus, Georgia, and Birmingham, Alabama, because white and black performers were not allowed to share the same stage. A year later, when touring on his own, Cooke refused to perform separate shows for black and white audiences in Little Rock, Arkansas, and settled for a rope down the center of the floor separating his crossover audience. By 1960, as the sit-in movement spread across the South, Cooke toured the South as part of the Supersonic Attractions tour. The musicians on this tour could not ignore the rising racial tensions that surrounded their appearances. After Jackie Wilson refused to play a second show for whites only in Little Rock, the tires were slashed on one of the tour's cars. Scheduled to play in Memphis in May 1961, Cooke and Clyde McPhatter refused to go on when they found out that the audience for their show was not only segregated but that blacks were forced into the back and sides of the hall. The constant pressure of dealing with segregated shows and seg-regated hotels, of having to carry with them food cooked by fans and friends of the local bookers in order to be able to eat when restaurants refused service, of confronting white police officers who saw the musi-cians' popularity as a threat to their authority, grew more intense as the music performed by Cooke, Wilson, McPhatter, Hank Ballard and the Midnighters, and a very young Aretha Franklin, along with other R&B acts, drew ever larger audiences from both sides of the color line. Under these conditions, the everyday contradictions of show business became inescapably politicized. Faced with the undeniable evidence that their music crossed the color line and that some whites were determined to maintain racial privilege in the face of this shared experience of musical pleasure, Cooke had to confront the fact that shared musical taste did not directly lead to shared values.[65] He responded to this conundrum in the best way a musician can.

As Peter Guralnick tells the story, it was the Christmas season of 1963 when Cooke put together the chords, melody, and lyrics for "A Change Is Gonna Come." The fundamental ambiguity that is characteristic of the pop anthem is present in the song's basic structure. Ostensibly in the key of B♭ (as both the highest and lowest notes in the melody), the vocal line works its way down, around, and through a G-minor blues scale. Using the same time signature as "Lift Every Voice and Sing," the song suggests both a double and a triple meter. The basic feel of the song is simultaneously melancholy and earnestly determined as the harmonies reinforce the minor-key tendency while resolving on B♭ major. This basic structure is both simple and complex, perhaps signifying the straight-forward sincerity required to respond to a violently insane world. The theme of simple complexity carries the lyrics as well: "I was born by a river, in a little tent." The double meaning of that opening line could not have been lost on Cooke's gospel audience. But Cooke piles on the multiple meanings by following the trope of rivers and (re)birth with the classic connection between rivers and time and eternity, knowing that the significance of rivers in the history of slavery would conjure dreams of escape and hopes for salvation—hopes and dreams that had often been pushed into the future as the river of history continued to only run by. In an astonishing move for a pop song, however, the second verse presents a harsh contrast to the hope of eternity. Where a gospel number might have followed the trope of the river with a promise of salvation, this verse instead leads us to a direct confrontation with mortality. Salvation is not guaranteed in the next world; heaven is not assured. No one, certainly not the singer, really knows what is up beyond the sky. The third verse is even more concrete: "I go to the movies and I go downtown. Somebody keep tellin' me, don't hang around." There is no overt effort at poetry here. These words are not gussied up. They are not made pretty in any way. Nor is this evocation of segregation intensified with images of violence. The not-quite-present violence quietly hides behind the authority of the voice that simply says, don't hang around. Like the second verse's refusal of guarantees, this verse states the real conditions that confronted musicians like Cooke. Threats did not have to be spoken aloud. They were part of the social order. The bridge marks a turn, though, as violence does appear, this time in response to a direct plea for help. After being knocked back on his knees, the singer reaches up for that high B♭ that opens each verse and, through the beauty of the descending twists of the melody, assures all listeners that he will carry on. No wonder that his business partner, J. W. Alexander, thought "A Change Is Gonna Come" might be the best song Cooke had ever written.[66]

"A Change Is Gonna Come" demonstrates both the strengths and the weaknesses of the pop anthem. Unlike anthems anchored in the full political or religious context, pop anthems have to construct and present the object of feeling that can center the equality of the juxtapolitical intimate public they call into being. They have to work with simple musical forms while creating moments of intense beauty capable of inspiring the desire to belong while eschewing any sign of propaganda or enforced authority. Pop anthems must, even if only for a moment, shift the way the world is heard. They work through an appeal that does sentimentalize, that does suggest, perhaps even propose, a larger equality of feeling than they can really produce. For the only equality a pop anthem can truly construct is an equality of relation to itself. "A Change Is Gonna Come" is not just a pop anthem, however. It is an anthem created with the tools of the emergent genre of soul music. The timbre of Cooke's voice carries with it the authority and power of the great male gospel singers. His trick of allowing you to hear him reach for the highest note in the melody while still seeming to exert no effort at all reinforces that power and authority. The arrangement, by Cooke's musical partner, Rene Hall, layers simple lines of strings and horns that convey a sense of independent motives coming together for a collective purpose, each in its own time, each with its own specific contribution to make. "A Change Is Gonna Come" demonstrates the potential that a specific anthemic tradition can carry in its generic markers. As the genre of gospel secularized into soul, the musical sounds that had confirmed the already existing unity of a political community confirmed by its congregational context were transformed into musical agents capable of generating new and expansive inclining communities united for a moment by a song. It is highly doubtful that this song directly changed the attitudes toward civil rights of anyone listening in 1964. But its beauty, once apprehended, did produce in each listener the awareness that the Civil Rights Movement was a political struggle that involved all of them. In so doing, the song produced an intimate public that embraced more people than those who had already known that they belonged as "A Change Is Gonna Come" redistributed the sensible.

I want to be clear here about the claims that I'm making for the pop anthem. "A Change Is Gonna Come" internalizes and textualizes the context out of which it developed. The intensity of Sam Cooke's performance and the clarity of the song's musical and lyrical rhetoric ensure that no one listening could misunderstand the force the song carries. One might shrug it off, but no listener is unaffected. Yet the very act of distilling this complex context into a recorded song that could be experienced apart from its historical moment requires an act of abstraction that brings with it an element of openness and ambivalence. A masterful recorded song such as this one carries with it the history that brought it into existence. In the absence of the living, breathing, swaying, dancing, and singing collective, however, the song's specific power risks being diluted by the sentimentality that an intimate public requires. Even a song this strong can become little more than the pleasant background to a contentious community, unwilling to stand by the mutual equality that the song asserts. This is the limit of the political force of musical beauty. It cannot enforce a relation of equality among its listeners. It can only make those listeners aware of that demand while it implicates its auditors as its mutually responsible recipients. That is what a great pop anthem can achieve, and it is no small thing. It shifts the way the world is heard. This achievement, this ability to reconstruct in a moment of listening the struggles of history and to command the attentive awareness of its audience is the quality shared by pop anthems such as "I Will Survive," "I Am Woman," and "Courtesy of the Red, White, and Blue," to name only a few.[67] These songs do not summon us into subject positions, and they do not force us to agree with any policies the songs support. Ever ambivalent, ever haunted by clichés, these songs work instead, simply and directly, through the power that music has to catch our ear, fix us in place, and get us to listen.

Chapter Three

Turning Inward, Inside Out:
Two Japanese Musicians Confront
the Limits of Tradition

| | | | |

A well-constructed anthem that is sung together in an embodied rever-
beration of unisonance can present to shared feeling the abstraction of
a political community. The pulsing in and out of a vibratory not-quite-
there can link together chains of agonistic difference in the mutual recognition of their interrelationship. When that unison is complemented
by a sense of antagonism toward those outside, however, the political
community can become hardened, inflexible, defensive, and vigilant,
constantly examining itself and its borders, looking for challenges to its
imagined consistency. The same act of reflection that promotes a longing for undefined unity can transform from a seeking for connection to a
fierce interrogation, suspicious of any variation from common practice.
The difference between those two intentions makes itself felt in tone and
in rhythm: not by the implementation of specific beats or harmonies but
always as a consequence of layers of sound interacting with each other,
shifting the relations of power within the sound. This chapter focuses on
the work of two musicians born in Japan in the 1930s, both of whom performed in the United States in the late sixties and early seventies. In the
process of developing their singular sounds, Takemitsu Toru and Yoko
Ono confronted traditions of music making and musical meaning that
had consolidated around techniques such as *hetai* singing and instrumental timbres and performance styles, and around distinctive musical
concepts such as *ma* and *sawari*. Both Ono and Takemitsu dove deeply
into the traditional approaches to these sounds and styles, finding that
a thorough investigation into their vibratory potential allowed for an escape from the constraints of Japanese musical histories and the political
connotations of those sounds. In the years leading up to World War II,
political philosophy and musical possibility had been forced into a collaborative reinforcement of the state. In the postwar context, ancient

Japanese instruments, singing styles, and performance practice became an invigorating resource, capable of refusing the already known and re-distributing the musically sensible.

Takemitsu was born in 1930 in Tokyo. His early days were marked by the expanding Japanese Empire, as he lived for a number of years in Manchuria where his father was serving as part of the colonial elite. His parents enjoyed listening to early jazz recordings, and much later Take-mitsu recalled having heard the music of Kid Ory in the family home. After Takemitsu's father died (when Takemitsu was seven), the boy went to live with his aunt and uncle in Tokyo. His aunt gave lessons on the *koto*, one of the oldest and most traditional of Japanese instruments.[1] Ono was born in 1933, also in Tokyo, to one of the most elite families in Japan. Her father worked as an investment banker for a large firm. Her mother's family was from a lineage even higher in Japan's intensely hier-archical social world. She was trained in the elite traditional arts, includ-ing calligraphy, flower arranging, and traditional music. When Ono was three, she traveled with her mother to San Francisco, where her father had been assigned by his bank, to meet him for the first time. In his youth, Ono's father had harbored dreams of becoming a professional piano player and had supported himself for a while by playing the songs and rhapsodies of George Gershwin along with pleasant melodies from Western classics at society parties.[2] The early lives of both Takemitsu and Ono were marked, then, by the reach of empire into their families. The families of both musicians evinced a love of music, including tradi-tional Japanese and Western styles. The lives of both were completely disrupted by the events of World War II. And each found ways to make use of Japanese philosophical and musical traditions while eschewing the tightly wound political associations that had been so powerfully at-tached to them by earlier generations. In so doing, Takemitsu and Ono demonstrated the ability of music to escape constricting contexts and to render present the possibility of new forms of political community.

MODERNIZING JAPAN AND WESTERN "CLASSICAL" MUSIC

During the first few decades of the twentieth century, Japanese leaders worked to contain and channel an influx of cultural forms, values, and habits that had been one of the consequences of the Meiji-period deci-sion to open the island nation to trading with the West. One response to the turmoil that developed was a heightened emphasis on traditional notions of Japanese superiority and unity, refigured and brought up-

to-date as modern nationalism. If Japan were to become a modern nation, this modernity would have to be based on an essential element
that linked together all Japanese, despite the new tensions. Perhaps
Japan could become modern through conceptualizing "the ever new
in the ever same." As Harry Harootunian describes it, this desire "resulted in an immense effort to recall older cultural practices (religious,
aesthetic, literary, linguistic) that derived from a remote past before the
establishment of modern, capitalist society, and that were believed to be
still capable of communicating an authentic experience of the people—
race or folk that historical change could not disturb."[3] Consequently, a
preoccupation with what was truly Japanese haunted the nation's encounter with Western philosophy and Western musical forms even as
post-Enlightenment philosophy emerged as a model for modernity itself
and Western music became the focus of the relatively recent advent of
music education across the nation.

During the Meiji restoration, Western music became a key part of the
nation's educational curriculum. In 1879 a plan for broadly introducing
Western music through the schools was put forth. There is some disagreement about the exact reasons for this. But the ethnomusicologist
Bonnie Wade offers a compelling explanation. Previous to the restoration, she argues,

> each genre of music was clearly associated with some particular group
> of people and performance context; who made the music, for whom,
> and where really mattered, with implications of social status and
> morality. *Gagaku* . . . was the music of the imperial court and of Bud-
> dhist temple and Shinto shrine ceremonies; *koto* . . . was the instru-
> ment of elite and upper middle-class citizens; the *no* drama . . . was
> the special purview of the elite and especially the *samurai* class; *syami-
> sen* (samisen)-accompanied songs were particularly associated with
> the popular theater and adult entertainment world. None of them
> was appropriate for primary school education for the entire popula-
> tion of children.[4]

For each of these styles and instruments, the historical context of performance limited their use even for modern concerns. Consequently,
Western music, particularly folk songs based on pentatonic scales, became the basis for elementary music education. These five-note songs
were free of the cultural associations connected to indigenous genres,
yet the songs easily meshed with traditional Japanese modes (which

also relied on five-note scales). Fundamental characteristics of Japanese pop—pentatonic scales, easy-to-sing choruses, heavy sentimentality—have been traced to this syncretic moment.[5]

In art music, Western styles were overtly treated as ideological tools that could contribute prestige to the modernization of Japan. Initially adopted because of the sense of modern power associated with these sounds—that is, they carried with them the sense of economic and political modernity that Japanese leaders were trying to create—Western art music also brought with it ideas and concepts that were completely alien to traditional music making. As Luciana Galliano points out, when "Japanese art music began to imitate and adopt some European musical ideas and practices," it also encountered the nineteenth-century model of the composer along with the accompanying concepts of "personal expression and creative subjectivity."[6] Japan's historical ability to absorb elements of other cultures had led to the common practice of adopting the technical aspects of artistic practice, with confidence that fundamental Japanese values would sufficiently ground any imported technique in a familiar approach to the world. But the Western ideas of personal expression and creative subjectivity were foreign to Japanese aesthetics in general, not just to music making. It would be incorrect to suggest that traditional Japanese aesthetics had no sense of the self or of subjectivity. It is more accurate, instead, to acknowledge that the traditional concept of the Japanese self was "constructed intersubjectively." It was understood to be part of an intertwined network of selves, each of which understood its work as contributing to the core of tradition.[7] This relationship among creative subjects, each oriented toward a coherent tradition, significantly varies from the Western idea of agonistic achievement described in Harold Bloom's *The Anxiety of Influence*.[8] When Japanese composers began to study European compositional techniques, they confronted a creative practice that was organized around individual accomplishment. Instead of a home being built by a collective of musicians, the grand tradition of European music was a mountain to climb.

Japanese composers also encountered an entirely different relationship between music and meaning. Writing in 1959 for the Asiatic Society of Japan, Dan Ikuma proposed that Western music was a process of "thinking in sound." In contrast, Japanese music was "thinking accompanied by sound." For Dan, this was the most significant factor in the "influence of Japanese traditional music on the development of Western music in Japan." Whether or not his larger claim is true, if we understand his distinction, we can grasp something of the difficulty that faced the first few generations of Japanese composers who grappled with this new form of music. As Dan explains, Western composers thought in musical structures. Putting aside whether or not *thought* is the best word to describe this phenomenon, it is clear that Dan means that the import of Western music is conveyed by the interrelationships of sounding structures. In contrast, the "thought" of Japanese music takes place not in and through the sounds of the music but in the spaces opened up within and between sounds—in the ma. "Our traditional music is thinking accompanied by sound, or thinking in the silences known as *ma*," Dan writes. "*Ma* is the term for the interval between sounds in Japanese music and is not to be confused with the rest in western music," he explains. I discuss *ma* in more detail, but for now, the significance of the concept lies in its *khora*-like function. Ma is not silence or nonsounding so much as it is a site that is shaped by the sounds around it so as to enable certain qualities of feelingful response. All aspects of the sounds that surround the site contribute to the shape of ma. Shape, of course, is a metaphor, as is khora. But the importance of the concept is its centrality to music's meaning making in Japan.[9]

Although ma is a moment of no sound, it is the opposite of a rest. Ma is not only shaped by the sounds around it but the experience of ma orients the listener toward the surrounding music. Ma is the central location in the experience of music, the moment when meaning is produced. One important consequence of ma's special function is that meaning is not conveyed in Japanese music; meaning is produced in the experience of music. In the dominant Western tradition, musical meaning reflects the intentions of the composer as realized in performance by the musicians for the audience to attend to. In the Japanese tradition, meaning is an effect of the coming together of the listeners and the musicians in a particular experience of ma. For Dan, "the music of the East differs so radically in its very concept from that of the West that the two cannot properly be compared or even studied in the same terms." And for the first generation of Western-oriented Japanese composers, the encounter between the two traditions produced severe conceptual difficulties that no mere mastery of technique could overcome.[10] Consequently, years of struggle and experimentation produced some quality work and much that simply explored approaches that had already been nearly exhausted by German and French composers. Galliano narrates this period with compelling detail and suggests that it was not until the mid-1930s that a productive engagement between the two traditions developed.[11]

At the same time, Japan's growing imperial ambitions, supported by its occupation of China, produced nationalist pressures that founded Japanese regional superiority in the country's ability to master and subsume Western concepts within its own traditions. Philosophers such as Nishida Kitaro and Watsuji Tetsuro synthesized post-Enlightenment thought with the expanded and fully interrelated concept of the subject derived from Buddhism. Both of these thinkers grounded their interventions in compelling and powerful revisions of such concepts as unity, wholeness, particularity, and universality. For both Watsuji and Nishida, the differences between the Western and Eastern understandings of the subject could be rectified by means of rethinking the different relations of those fundamental concepts.

There were significant political consequences to this project of rethinking the subject, because neither philosopher considered the isolated fully individual subject to have any substantive reality. Watsuji rooted his ethics in a recognition of the multiple and fundamental interconnections among all humans. When thought spatially, these interconnections argued for a disbursed understanding of human being, partially located in each person but more importantly constructed through and by the networked linkages among them. Humans are always born into social networks and carry the effects of those networks with them even when they are alone. *Ningen*, Watsuji's term for "human being," was characterized more by emptiness and a capacity for connection than it was by any universally shared content. One of the political consequences of Watsuji's concept of interconnectedness was the prescription that human beings ought to subsume their individual desires to the needs of the state. This prescription was deeply rooted in Japanese history, wherein the nation, geographically bounded as an island and culturally bounded by the long-standing concern with the essence of Japaneseness, became the legitimate political unit, the best means of conceptualizing the fundamental interconnectedness of human being.[12] Watsuji's thought, therefore, became useful to the imperial throne as it worked to justify its military dominance of the East.

The individual plays a more crucial role in Nishida's thought than it does for Watsuji. But in Nishida's thinking too, the nation functions as the primary political unity that enables the realization of the individual self. Human being is developed through the fulfillment of the individual personality, but this personality cannot be known in isolation. Individual consciousness is not an expression of a "separate unifying self," but is part of a "social consciousness." Nishida develops this concept this way: "Social consciousness consists of various levels. The smallest and most immediate is the family." However, "at the next level beyond the family, the nation unifies the entirety of our conscious activity and expresses a single personality." The nation is the site where the full development of personality best emerges: "The essence of the nation is the expression of the communal consciousness that constitutes the foundation of our minds. In the context of the nation, we can accomplish a great deal of personality; the nation is a unified personality, and the systems and laws of the nation are expressions of the will of this communal consciousness." Nishida argued further that the nation was not the final full expression of this consciousness, for that would "require a social union that includes all humankind."[13] While it remains theoretically possible that Nishida's universalism could found a progressive politics, his gesture toward the universal development of social consciousness beyond the nation instead became an important philosophical cornerstone of the Empire of Japan.[14]

PHILOSOPHICAL AND MUSICAL
CONSOLIDATION IN IMPERIAL JAPAN

In 1935 Nishida and Watsuji were invited to join the Committee for the Renewal of Education and Scholarship. This committee met for the first time in December of that year, with the purpose of clarifying the Meiji-period document "Kyōiku ni Kansuru Chokugo (Imperial Rescript on Education)." This earlier brief, one-page statement, written as a letter from the emperor to his subjects, prescribed that all Japanese must be loyal to their parents and family, be modest and moderate, pursue learning and cultivate the arts, develop intellectual and moral powers, advance the public good and promote common interests, respect the constitution, and observe the laws. Finally, the document required that all subjects "offer [themselves] courageously to the State; and thus guard and maintain the prosperity of Our Imperial Throne coeval with heaven and earth."[15] This statement of fundamental purpose became the founding document for Japan's system of modern public education. The document established that the primary goal of modern public education in Japan was to produce moral citizens loyal above all to the emperor; the document centered public education as the primary ideological state apparatus. By the mid-1930s, however, following the individualizing influence of consumer culture, this directive no longer seemed clear enough to ensure the level of obedience that the emperor required.

Consequently, the renewal committee was formed, and it consisted of university professors and researchers employed by the National Spirit Cultural Research Institute. They were charged with producing a document that would unify philosophy, culture, and education in support of the Japanese emperor and his nation. Invited to help author the statement, Nishida attended only the first meeting.[16] Watsuji, on the other hand, was active throughout the work of the committee, which labored for more than a year to draft an official state document. Titled *Kokutai no Hongi* (Cardinal Principles of the National Body), the pamphlet that the committee produced declared that "the various ideological and social evils of present-day Japan" were the result of a too-rapid importation of European and American ideas and values. The pamphlet continued, "The views of the world and of life that form the basis of these ideologies are a rationalism and a positivism, lacking in historical views, which on the one hand lay the highest value on, and assert the liberty and equality of, individuals, and on the other hand lay value on a world by nature abstract, transcending nations and races."[17]

According to the statement, where Euro-American culture had gone wrong was to abstract the concept of the individual and consequent ideas such as rights and liberties out of the proper historical context of nations. Nations, with their deep history and fully developed self-awareness, provided the only frames within which one could comprehend the appropriate duties of human beings. The people of Japan should look to their nation for their purpose. This meant, of course, that they should honor their special relationship to their emperor, which wholly consisted of loyalty on the part of the people: "Indeed, loyalty is our fundamental Way as subjects, and is the basis of our national morality."[18] Fully supported by its subjects, Japan's proper national role was to function as the leading force in the Asian resistance to Western encroachment. This destiny was rooted in the country's divine origins and its uninterrupted line of descent from those origins. Japan's history as one of the few true and whole nations in the world provided it with the legitimation it needed to pursue its empire. Or so said the authors of *Kokutai no Hongi*.

The publication of this document in 1937 contributed to and consolidated ongoing efforts to circumscribe the world of music in Japan. The year before, musicians had been the objects of a directive from the state that commanded that they write in a Japanese style in order to keep "social morale high" and follow "the government's precepts in all matters." The mandate for artistic works in support of the imperial state was philosophically grounded in a widely shared understanding of the dialectical method of another of Japan's leading philosophers, Tanabe Hajime. Tanabe's efforts to think about Japanese and Western philosophical concepts together had produced a "logic of species" that seemed to subsume the proper activities of all individuals to the final will of the state. In such writings as "The Logic of National Existence," the state appeared as the "realization of the universal," and the dialectical process found its primary purpose in the continued reproduction of the polity. The demand to bring sensuous experience under the control of a determinate intending will tainted musical composition in Japan between the wars with the inescapable connotations of nationalist fervor.[19]

Over the course of the 1930s, organizations of musicians were disbanded and replaced by a succession of official state groups. Among these new organizations were the League for Japanese Culture, the Central Union for Japanese Culture, and eventually the ominously named Association for the Advancement of the Imperial Way. A subgroup within this last organization was the Association for Japanese Musical Culture. Some musicians complied with the command to produce uplifting music in the service of the state while others, such as Matsudaira Yoritune, wrote nothing at all.[20] As war pressures increased, the government set up a licensing procedure to control musicians. The Association for Japanese Musical Culture coordinated the licenses and recruited musicians willing to create morale-boosting music. The musical result of these efforts, in Galliano's words, combined "the glamorous, bombastic aspects of the European orchestra spiced up with a touch of Japanese folk music" and "a huge number of lengthy and relatively worthless pieces that used the symphony orchestra to reproduce the solemn sounds of ancient Japanese court music."[21] Once again, overtly political motives resulted in bad music.

RETHINKING MUSICAL MEANING AFTER WORLD WAR II

Immediately after the war, many of the authors of *Kokutai no Hongi* were removed from their official positions. But the U.S. occupation forces allowed most musicians to continue their work. In fact, Yamada Kosaku, who had been the president of the Association for Musical Culture, was chosen by the U.S. occupation to organize music and theater offerings throughout Japan.²² The musical world was not calm, however. After the utter destruction of three major cities, the surrender of the army, and the astonishing experience of hearing the emperor's voice announcing defeat on the radio, the prewar associations that had grounded the meaning of music were overturned. It would not be accurate to say that musical sound had been freed from associative meaning, leaving an open field of sounding possibility. The memory of the earlier associations that had linked aspects of Western art music and Japanese indigenous sounds to the upholding of social morale combined with the collapse of the social scaffolding that held up those associations meant not that music was free but that all possible associations were in doubt. As Judith Herd puts it, a "fragile juxtaposition of cultural self-awareness and ideological reassessment of alien musical forms was the prime motivation for the development of new musical styles in Japan."²³

After the war, occupation rules condemned overt nationalism in any form, rendering problematic any direct musical reference to Japanese traditions. Although instrumental music was largely exempt from occupation censorship, a simple adoption of established Western musical forms was not a compelling option either. The prewar generation of Japanese composers had been trained in nineteenth-century compositional techniques, mostly derived from German examples, and that set of sounds was doubly tainted—by its association with Germany's military ambition and by its prewar adoption as a sign of prestige by Japan's defeated elites. Beethoven's Symphony no. 9 had become a popular sonic image of hope and renewal, performed and sung at the end of each year. But by virtue of this endless regularity, the symphony's techniques had taken on the aura of cliché. French styles, in particular those connected to Claude Debussy and the group of composers dubbed Les Six, offered two advantages—one political and one musical. The obvious political advantage of not being associated with the losers of World War II combined with an almost nonclimactic dynamic flow, a timbral palette that emphasized wind sounds and lush rising string sections, and a harmonic language that avoided harshness while it expanded the range of possible intervals on which harmonic relations could be built. Each of these stylistic options offered elements that could be merged with traditional Japanese musical conventions with more grace than had been achieved before. Of course, many aspects of the French style had derived from Debussy's fascination with Japanese art, so the influence went both ways.²⁴ Both styles shared a fondness for intervals of seconds and sixths, along with an almost tidal dynamic organization punctuated by occasional explosions of sonic force. Both styles resisted martial connotations and strident sonorities.[25]

In the mid-1950s, a number of groups of composers and artists formed in an effort to forge new relations of tradition and innovation in search of authentically postwar Japanese musical culture. Certain groups decided to combine some of the oldest Japanese traditional styles with twentieth-century innovations, believing that the combination of these approaches would yield a music that could resound as Japanese and new simultaneously. Judith Herd has grouped these musicians together under the heading of "neo-nationalists" and argues that their compositions laid the groundwork for the new directions followed by Japanese musicians in the following decades. What seems striking is the apparent need for the major composers of this era to provide overt and easily recognizable auditory sounds of Japaneseness throughout their work. This concern with maintaining a recognizable Japanese style remained dominant across a range of composers who were influenced by styles from France as well as Germany, including those who understood their work as challenging nationalism as well as others who were supporting it. It seemed important to musically maintain the coherence of the political community as a grounding reference point for musical meaning.[26]

Under these conditions, it is not surprising that ancient Japanese music would become an appealing source from which composers could draw. But as we saw, specific forms of indigenous music had been closely connected with particular strata of Japanese society. Samisen-accompanied songs (like much Japanese folk music) were associated with the pleasure quarters of large cities and were, therefore, not an obvious choice for the revival of Japaneseness in art music. *Gagaku* was the traditional court music of Japan and was, perhaps, the oldest indigenous musical style. This music, the instruments typically used to perform it, and Buddhist chants had been very closely tied to elite tastes. After the war, well-paying audiences displayed a marked preference for Beethoven over any traditional Japanese sounds, which had the perhaps not surprising effect of making gagaku more intriguing for those looking for a new way. For one group of composers in particular, Sannin no Kai, (Association of Three) which included Mayuzumi Toshio, Akutagawa Yasushi, and Dan, the move to incorporate the instruments and techniques of gagaku and the sounds of the Buddhist temple was a daring rejection of the current market as well as a potential resource for the renewal of Japanese musical traditions. Even more daring, however, was the assertion by this group that these sounds could be used to create a Pan-Asian style that would reach out beyond the islands. The idea of a Pan-Asian unity had been the basis for the coprosperity sphere, the concept that had legitimated Japanese imperial aggression. And according to Judith Herd, Sannin no Kai produced some of the more overtly neoimperialist music of the era, fully in line with prewar concepts of an Asian sphere centered around Japan.[27]

Of this group, Mayuzumi's work came the closest to achieving a Pan-Asian musical synthesis with Western forms. In 1959 Dan expressed his own frustration with efforts to combine Western and Japanese music. His most successful works are operas that borrow small bits of Japanese folk songs and story lines. Akutagawa's work tended toward Russian styles and really did little to create an innovative blend. But Mayuzumi's 1958 work, the *Nirvana Symphony*, is a truly remarkable piece. It refuses to rely on the rather obvious and somewhat simplistic strategies that had been used before to blend Japanese and Western musical styles. It does not use traditional Japanese instruments, nor does it build on the structures of gagaku. Instead, the symphony interweaves patterns of tension and release that echo such Western composers as Maurice Ravel and Igor Stravinsky as it builds its sonorous intensity from a set of timbres that were commonly used in Buddhist rituals. The sonic identity of the piece draws on an overtone series that imitates the sound of the bells in many Buddhist temples. Each partial in this set of overtones is identified and separated out in order to be performed as individual pitches on different instruments—mainly piano and selected percussion (along with woodwind and brass sections). In the liner notes for a recording of this piece by the NHK Symphony Orchestra, Mayuzumi writes that he was drawn not only to the fact that the overtones have the peculiar quality that they cannot be represented by integral relations (i.e., as a multiple of the fundamental frequency) but also to the fact that the overtones themselves changed as the ringing bells echoed and decayed. By identifying the individual overtones and isolating them, Mayuzumi was able to manipulate the floating transformations that characterized these sounds. When performed by a large orchestra, these pitches create a massive sound—not simply replicating the tonal resonance of ritualistic bells but producing those tones with great intensity, apparently saturating the performance hall with an undeniable amplification of the sacred transience of things.[28]

A second sonic characteristic that the *Nirvana Symphony* draws from Buddhist rituals is that of a chorus of monks chanting. This sound is much less sonorous; at first listen it seems not so very musical at all.[29] But with repeated listening, the effect of multiple male voices creating that creakingly open-throated sound, spread out across the chromatic scale, contributes to the sonic saturation that is one of the dominant effects of the piece. Finally, the chant itself is of a sutra commonly referenced by the Tendai sect. In the aforementioned liner notes, Mayuzumi claims, "It was my idea to create my own music through clarification of the secret of a strong attachment I had for temple bells and Sutras. This I tried with my Oriental musical instinct separate from my musical training based on Western tradition. In other words, I composed this symphony with the idea of creating my own musical Nirvana."[30] The force of the piece grows out of the blended flows of the different tonalities of the standard Western orchestral instruments, the combined pitches that create the bell tones, and the almost-aching voices. The piece is not precisely serial, but it is twelve tone and borrows its organizational structure largely from twentieth-century European innovations, building to climaxes that strike dissonant intervals and clusters before quietly residing. Nevertheless, it is hard to hear the *Nirvana Symphony* as an abstract piece of pure music. Instead, a powerful religiosity is as present here as it is in any William Byrd hymn. And as with Byrd's music, the symphony conjures a sense of complex political community, a coprosperity sphere with Japan at the core of its conceptual organization.[31]

Matsudaira Yoritsune took a different approach to blending Eastern and Western music. A self-proclaimed antinationalist, Matsudaira consistently asserted that his method for blending Eastern and Western forms was an abstract one, purely based on almost accidental musical similarities. His work is most often composed strictly for Western instruments, but he constructs the lines composed for these instruments and their architectonic organization from gagaku forms.[32] In "Sa-Mai" (1958) and "U-Mai" (1957) (two "movements" of the suite *Bugaku, pour orchestre*), the pitches were determined by tone-row manipulations, but the row itself was generated by analyzing the pitches in two common gagaku melodies. The combination of the two melodies creates twelve-tone possibilities that Matsudaira uses in ways that can seem both non-Western and thoroughly modern. For example, a flute line rises up by a tritone and then glides to a minor second while overblown to emphasize the breath of the performer. In some of the fragments (sections of these pieces are titled "Fragment 1" and so on), drums do not establish a beat, nor do they accompany dynamic crescendos. Instead, drums mark the end of short solo lines and, through their emphatic percussive nowness,

drums open up an empty space that follows each quick melodic fragment. Although this space is suggestive of ma, in that a gap is created
between the end of the previous line and the beginning of the next one,
Matsudaira discourages this interpretation. In fact, most of the fragments balance the Japanese-leaning line structures with a fullness of
sound that does not leave room for ma, and, in some cases, the fragments even go so far as to suggest an elegant dance movement with clear
four-beat measures.[33]

Matsudaira claims not to have had any overtly nationalist or "Japanese" expressive goals for his music. He not only eschewed the common
strategies for integrating Japanese content into Western forms but he
also decried the overt sentimentality that characterized so much of the
music made in his country.[34] He says, "It has never been my intention
to create a kind of 'nationalistic' school that takes Japanese traditional
music as one basic ingredient. If I use *gagaku* and serialism, it is only to
foster my own 'individual' style. What is 'Japanese' in my music has not
been intended as such, it is only a byproduct of my search for individuality."[35] He has further insisted that gagaku's formalism distances it from
any nonmusical associations and is used by him purely for aesthetic purposes.[36] Despite these intentions, Matsudaira's work is often discussed
in the context of Japanese nationalism. His blend of gagaku and serialism results in a set of sounds that are heard as Japanese, over and
above their equal rooting in serialist techniques.[37] His expressed desire
to be taken as an individual and not as a representative Japanese is over-
ridden by two factors. The first is that the sounds of gagaku diverge so
powerfully from Western musical sounds and are, therefore, so easily
identified—even when they are performed by Western instruments in
a European-developed form—that these sounds have difficulty escaping
the centuries of meaning attached to them. Second, those meanings are
so profoundly interwoven into the history of Japanese political community that an overblown *shakuhachi* (a flute) or the vigorously plucked
loose strings of a *biwa* (a type of lute), or even the particular shape of a
solo melodic line played on a modern flute, conjures not only an imagined Japaneseness but also the history of Japanese political struggle.[38]

Bonnie Wade argues that the Japanese concern with defining indigenous qualities in music produced by all Japanese musicians results from their history of borrowing styles and elements from other
cultures.[39] Considered in this fashion, the Japanese case appears to be
unique. But I believe that the Japanese case is only a more extreme and
clear-cut example of the problems that arise from a too-quick confla-

tion of music and identity. Regardless of the political positions of the composers and regardless of the meanings that they choose to emphasize when they discuss their work, the tightly interwoven textures of Japanese music and identity conjure a polis that is inwardly focused and centered on commonality. It is true that the difficulty for any composer escaping this constraining environment was heightened by the island's long premodern isolation followed by the political history of Japan in the twentieth century. The rapid rise to regional power followed by the destruction caused by World War II intensified the volatility of political struggle and reinforced the long tendency in Japanese culture to look inward for sources of stability. But it must be recognized that the group of composers often termed the postwar neonationalists were also postwar modernists. The critical discourse equally stimulated by the music of Mayuzumi (an explicit nationalist) and Matsudaira (an avowed cosmopolitan) demonstrates the difficulty of escaping this restricting context. Thus the trap of identity plays out here in full view. Japanese musicians using Japanese sounds could apparently only create Japanese music.

This was the trap that both Takemitsu and Ono struggled with for much of their careers. Both of these musicians came of age in the immediate postwar era. Both found initial common ground with antiacademic, antiformalist, and conceptually oriented artist collectives (Fluxus for Ono, Jikken Kobo [Experimental Workshop] for Takemitsu). Both found ways in their more mature works to identify, isolate, and exaggerate musical sounds familiar from their earliest musical experiences in order to break with the constraining context of identity—not by denying its effects but by calling attention to it directly and showing it to be a resource that can be intelligently manipulated by the creative musician. In so doing, both Ono and Takemitsu created music of great beauty that beckoned outward, expanding the listening polis while refusing to be reduced to exotic Orientalist tokens.

TAKEMITSU AND THE PRODUCTIVITY OF ORIENTALISM

On November 9, 1967, the New York Philharmonic debuted *November Steps*, by Takemitsu. This work had been commissioned along with seventeen others for a celebration of the orchestra's 125th anniversary. New pieces by twelve American composers (among them Roy Harris, Milton Babbitt, Elliott Carter, and Aaron Copland) joined with works by one composer each from England, Italy, Spain, the Soviet Union, Germany, and Japan. Representing the largest commissioning project undertaken by the organization up to that time, the music that resulted was explicitly modern and often quite difficult. Clearly the goal of the project was to demonstrate the global mastery of the orchestra. Seiji Ozawa, at the time the music director of the Toronto Symphony and a regular guest conductor for the New York Philharmonic, recommended that Takemitsu be commissioned to represent Japan's contribution to modern music. Ozawa had been deeply impressed by a short piece that Takemitsu had written in 1966 for two traditional Japanese instruments, the biwa and the shakuhachi. After hearing these traditional instruments for the first time in Takemitsu's piece *Eclipse*, Ozawa was convinced that Takemitsu could produce a work that would simultaneously look backward and forward, that could combine Japanese traditional high-court sounds with modern Western musical form. Note that Ozawa was unfamiliar with the traditional instruments that he found so compelling in *Eclipse*. Note also that the point of the commission was precisely to produce a blend of West and East, the task that seemed only to produce recognizable sounds of Japaneseness in the neonationalists. Although Takemitsu was best known in Japan for his film scores and, to the extent that he was known in the United States, he was most recognized for his Western avant-garde compositions, he was nominated by Ozawa above Matsudaira and Mayuzumi (and, of course, all other candidates) to compose a piece scored for orchestra and the two traditional Japanese instruments. In a review of the premiere performance, the *New York Times* found the passages for biwa and shakuhachi to be "without meaning to these western ears." Although the piece as a whole was "often beautiful, always fascinating," *November Steps* was described as "an exotic piece indeed," "static," and even "passive."[40]

It should not be surprising that the *New York Times* review of *November Steps* displayed such overt Orientalism.[41] After all, the purpose of the commission was to create a piece that would represent Japan for Western listeners, an Orientalist goal in itself. Furthermore, an Orientalist frame reflected the paper's opinion of Takemitsu's work more generally. A review of the American Symphony Orchestra's performance of Takemitsu's *Music of Trees* from 1965 said that it had a "gentle personality of its own." The Philadelphia Orchestra's performance of another orchestral piece by Takemitsu, *Green*, struck the reviewer as "pleasant but rather weak tea." In each of these reviews, Takemitsu's work was contrasted with music by Western composers. Arnold Schoenberg's *Five Pieces* had apparently provided the original model for *Green*. Works by Beethoven and Paul Hindemith were heard as considerably more "active" than

November Steps. Takemitsu's work, regardless of whether it was complex avant-garde music scored for Western instruments or orchestral pieces incorporating instruments and tonalities from the Japanese gagaku tradition, was heard as music of the East and was described therefore as less masculine—less active, more gentle, and weak—in comparison to the Western musical canon. The response to *November Steps* did not indicate an escape from the trap of identity. Indeed, Takemitsu's music seemed to be encountering constraints similar to the reductive listening that limited the resonance of Matsudaira's and Mayuzumi's work.[42]

However, I am not interested in chastising the reviewers of the *New York Times* for their kneejerk Orientalism or for their inability to step outside the historical moment of their writing. Rather, I want to demonstrate the ways in which this Orientalism can be understood as the basis of Takemitsu's syncretic construction of a new musical polis. Matsudaira's and Mayuzumi's efforts to synthesize purely formal aspects of twelve-tone music, Western instrumentation, and Eastern timbral and melodic structures—work that was highly abstract and musical at its core—could still be reduced by listeners to functional expressions of Japaneseness. Takemitsu's response to the challenge offered by the New York Philharmonic's commission was not to attempt so complete a synthesis but instead to foreground difference in the musical matter he brought together.[43] In so doing, he extended Orientalist representations of Eastern musical practices and Asian philosophy produced and circulated by avant-garde American composers like John Cage.

As early as 1948, Takemitsu was using found sounds, chance processes, and tape manipulations in an effort to bring music closer to the physical rhythmic experience of life as he knew it. With the founding of the Jikken Kobo, an experimental crossmedia performance group formed by nine young Japanese composers in 1951, Takemitsu and his colleagues committed themselves to an antiacademic, anti-Japanese artistic stance. Between 1951 and 1957, the Jikken Kobo performed a number of concerts that introduced performance ideas influenced by the works of Cage to the avant-garde audience in Japan. During this period, Takemitsu was writing largely atonal music using only Western instruments. His first work to receive international attention was *Requiem for Strings* (1957), which caught the ear of Stravinsky. This piece rigorously avoided any possible Japanese connotations. Speaking later about this time in his life, Takemitsu said: "For a long period I struggled to avoid being 'Japanese,' to avoid 'Japanese' qualities. It was largely through my contact with John Cage that I came to recognize the value of my own tradition."[44]

Throughout his career, in multiple interviews and published writings, Cage located the source of many of his most startling innovations—the escape from the prison of harmony, the significance of indeterminacy, and the focus on sound itself—in diverse elements of Asian musical and philosophical practice. His approach to Asian music and philosophy was almost classically Orientalist. This approach blurred together bits and pieces from multiple cultural traditions, selected isolated ideas, and took them out of context, and even filtered his interest in Asian cultures through the dominant stereotypes of Asian masculinity that buttressed Orientalism. In his 1958 lecture, "The History of Experimental Music in the United States," Cage likened the silence found in experimental music to the spaces in a Japanese stone garden, as equally a component of the final construction as the stones. He justified his focus on the qualities of sound itself "in order that each sound may become the Buddha." Typically for Cage, bits and pieces of Hindu concepts merged with Zen ideas, lending credence and authority to his own insistence on composition as a process requiring intensely focused aural awareness. In 1963, after Cage had actually visited Japan, he praised the young generation of Japanese composers, because "they don't use sound to push me where I don't want to listen." In other words, part of Cage's attraction to Japanese music was the perception of an absence of aggression within it. This perception, of course, mirrors the stereotypes of Asian masculinity produced in Orientalist discourse.[45] For Takemitsu, however, the perception of a lack of aggression became a positive attribute. The perception enabled him to hear past the history of Japanese dominance with which these sounds had previously been associated. The apparent absence of aggression had the effect of freeing the sounds of Japanese music from the intensely nationalist connotations that had been layered onto it before World War II. By foregrounding and highlighting the distinctive qualities of those sounds against the backdrop of the New York Philharmonic, as he did in *November Steps*, Takemitsu reconstructed Orientalism as an intervention into musical common sense.

Takemitsu's encounter with Cage accelerated when Ichiyanagi Toshi returned to Tokyo after nine years of study at Juilliard and with Cage at the New School. Soon after his return, Ichiyanagi organized the performances of many of Cage's pieces. Indeed, in 1962 Ichiyanagi helped arrange for Cage and David Tudor to tour Japan (see figure 3.1). This was the trip where Cage gained his first direct exposure to the music of Takemitsu, Yuasa, Matsudaira, and others, the music that he praised because it did not push him around. Only after Cage and Tudor's tour of Japan

FIG. 3.1 Yoko Ono and John Cage in Japan, 1962.
Photo courtesy of Yasuhiro Yoshioka.

could Takemitsu begin to consciously look back at traditional classical Japanese music and see the potential that could be found in these musical resources. "From that time on," he wrote years later, "I devoted a great deal of energy—as much as possible—to studying Japanese musical traditions, with particular attention to the differences between Japanese music and western music. With great diligence I tried to bring forth the sensibilities of Japanese music that had always been within me."[46]

Takemitsu's first attempts to use traditional Japanese instruments were for a documentary on the kimono for NHK, the Japanese television network in 1961. He soon experimented with the tonal qualities of the koto, the shakuhachi, and other traditional instruments for film scores and for a television drama series set in the past. In each of these cases, however, the use of traditional instruments could be understood as motivated by the narrative or thematic content of the program. By 1966 he apparently felt comfortable enough with the sounds produced by these traditional instruments to employ them in his concert music. *Eclipse*, written for biwa and shakuhachi, was the piece that Ozawa heard, prompting him to nominate Takemitsu to represent Japan for the 125th anniversary of the New York Philharmonic. Between the composition of *Eclipse* and *In an Autumn Garden* (1979), Takemitsu completed six concert works that featured traditional Japanese instruments. These pieces remain important not as an attempt to merge East and West, but rather as explorations in the quality of the sound event, and for rethinking the relations between sound and silence, music and noise, composer and audience, and, implicitly, between an imposed structural hierarchy and a more open social structure.[47]

Soon after accepting the commission from the New York Philharmonic, Takemitsu abandoned the idea of creating a work that would blend together Eastern and Western modes of musicality. "I came to realize that a fundamental indescribable difference existed between Western and Japanese instruments," he wrote years afterward. "The more I looked at the two worlds of sound the greater the differences loomed."[48] Traditional Japanese instruments are not designed to produce purely pitched tones. Yuasa Joji explained it this way: "In Japanese traditional music there is no clear distinction between pitched sound and noise. There is an interpenetration between sound and noise, as exemplified in performances on the *shakuhachi*." The shakuhachi is a notched flute, blown into from the end. In contrast to the objective of Western performers, which is to achieve as pure a musical tone as possible, "the *shakuhachi* master thinks it would be wonderful to create in his own performance the natural sound that emanates from wind blowing through an old bamboo grove and striking its roots."[49] Indeed, the musical character of traditional Japanese instruments derives from the ways in which the sounds the instruments produce evoke the materials from which they were made. The biwa is one of a family of stringed instruments (with the koto and the samisen). These are lute-like instruments, with strings stretched across a series of frets, but they do not resonate with deep, rich tones as we expect from Western instruments such as the lute or the guitar. Rather, they sound as though they are made of tightly wound cord and wood. The biwa is of particular importance because it has a special piece that is placed beneath the strings called the sawari. "The *sawari* is part of the neck of the instrument where four or five strings are stretched over a grooved ivory plate. . . . When a string is stretched between these grooves and plucked, it strikes the grooves and makes a noisy 'bin.'" This component of the instrument can be placed where the performer wishes in order to manipulate the quality of the noise that is contributed with each pluck or strum of the strings. The biwa, therefore, is the key instrument for discussing the important Japanese concept of sawari. Just as the wind picks up and then quietly blows away, leaving the bamboo grove silent again, the shakuhachi is the key instrument for discussing the equally important concept of ma.

Sawari and ma are both multifaceted anti-idealist concepts. This brief discussion is incapable of discussing sawari and ma in all of their complexity. But it is necessary to convey a few central ideas. One of the important meanings of *sawari* is "obstacle." Another is "touch." Insofar as it incorporates all those aspects of the materiality of the instrument, *sawari* subsumes the concept of timbre, but its philosophical meanings are much richer. All instruments have a certain amount of sawari in their sounds. The sound of fingers squeaking against new acoustic guitar strings is a Western example. Indeed, Henry Cowell insisted in 1929 "that there is a noise element in the very tone itself of all our musical instruments." But sawari is not just noise. In traditional Japanese performance style, no musical sound is complete without its element of noise. The pure pitch, the relentlessly periodic sine wave, is simply not musical. Of course, it is not particularly musical in the West either. The overtones produced by Western musical instruments are key to the musicality of the sound. Since Debussy, there have been Western composers who focused on the tonal color of various instruments, but typically the better C note on the Western flute is the one that calls the least attention to the materiality of the instrument. The finger squeak on guitar strings is considered to be an accident; it is nonmusical. There have been avant-garde experiments with noise in the West at least since the Italian futurists, but in traditional Western musical thinking, noise is opposed to music. For Japanese musical instruments, this is simply not the case. Noise is an active contributor to the musicality of sound. The term *sawari* carries with it the sense of the need to work with and through physical limitations. It is a reminder of the impossibility of transcendence, a recognition of the irreducible power of the materiality of the present. While a score for a biwa will indicate notes on a scale, it is impossible to prescribe exact pitches or to write fast passages for it. Composition for this instrument requires a certain latitude on the part of the composer. The performer will have to work with the sounds that a particular biwa can make in its particular environment at the moment of performance. Sawari defeats the will to control sound. But once sawari is accepted as a necessary component of music, it can be heard as beautiful.[50]

Ma is equally complex. Although it too is an active contribution to the quality of the musical work, it is not in itself audible. This inaudible productivity suggests that ma may be akin to silence—to the absence of sound, or at least to the very full silence that Cage speaks of. But ma is not the banal idea of silence, nor can it be reduced to the plenum of Cagean silence. Where Cage's silence encourages us to attentively listen to the inescapable ambient sounds that surround us, ma draws our attention to the range of sound between any two sounded events. Yuasa insists that ma is "substantial silence [that] has a value equivalent to sound." Takemitsu puts it this way: "To bring *ma* to life means to make the most of the infinite sounds that exist between two performed sounds. . . . Instead of communicating solely through the actual sounds that are performed, in Japanese music the space created between realized sounds plays a significant role." Indeed, the master performer of traditional instruments seeks to "enliven the *ma*," to render the moment before a note or between sound events as full of meaning as possible while not making a sound. Composition, while not irrelevant here, cannot singly determine the production of ma. The quality of ma, its aliveness, is a joint result of the work of the composer, the performer, and the listener, who must carefully attend and sensitively respond to the meanings that emerge between sounds. Taken together and understood within the context of Japanese aesthetics, sawari and ma suggest an approach to listening that equalizes the contributions of composer, performer, and audience. There is not a hierarchy of determination where the composer organizes the musical material in line with a particular concept of harmonic-melodic development that must be executed by the performer and appreciated by the audience.[51]

November Steps is written for the biwa, the shakuhachi, two oboes, three clarinets, two trumpets, three trombones, two harps, four percussionists (with gongs, bells, cymbals, and tam tams), and a large string section (forty-eight players, seated half on each side of the stage). The placement of the instruments suggests a distinction between the Japanese instruments, which are seated at the front of the stage, between the director and the audience, and the Western instruments, which are seated in a standard Western orchestral pattern (strings to each side, woodwinds and brass facing the director, and the percussionists in the back corners of the stage). The two harps sit at the front internal corners of the string sections. Lewis Cornwell suggests that the placement of the harps is one of two key mediating strategies that *November Steps* uses to bring together the Western and Eastern instruments. Placed as they are, in the center of the Western orchestral seating (instead of the more typical behind the strings position) and directly behind the Japanese instruments, the strings of the harps may function as resonating surfaces that equally respond to the vibrations caused by the biwa and shakuhachi as they would to those vibrations emitted from the Western instruments. Cornwell believes that another mediating strategy appears in the way that Takemitsu writes indeterminacy into the score. At key moments in the piece, when the focus shifts from the Japanese instruments to the orchestra (or vice versa), the score indicates that certain Western instruments—the first violins, say—play the highest note they can. This note will be different for different players with their different instruments and skill levels. Such instructions treat the violins (following our example) in the way that the score often treats the shakuhachi. Instructions for the Japanese instruments are written on a standard staff often using standard notation. But frequently that notation is supplemented by an additional set of instructions. Entire passages for the Japanese instruments are scored with no bar lines. While pitches are indicated, the approach to the pitches is modified so that slides up to or from the pitch, or jumps far away from or close to the pitch, are prescribed, but the precise notes to be played in those slides and jumps are not indicated. During the passages without bar lines, instructions are sometimes given to play rapidly or slowly—the precise meaning of rapid or slow is not determined (as it could be using, for example, a metronome marker). Rests are written into these sections with no precise determination of their length. Finally, the biwa performer is occasionally instructed to "hit the body of the instrument with the plectrum" or "hit the body of the instrument with the finger, fist or palm." The shakuhachi player is told to "tap the hole of the instrument strongly with the fingers" and to "make an accent with strong breath." As Cornwell notes, another strategy of mediation is suggested by the special instructions for the harp, which include "pluck with finger, letting the string strike against the fingernail immediately," and "make a quick and powerful glissando on the string with coin in the direction shown by the arrow." Despite the apparent accuracy and rigor of the instructions, they are simply incapable of precisely determining the sounds, the pitches, and the lengths of the notes. All of these special instructions attempt to implement these instruments' capacities for producing sawari and ma. Rather than incorporating the Japanese in-

struments into the structural organization of harmonic-melodic development, Takemitsu uses *November Steps* to show the differences between
Eastern and Western music. When the instruments from the different
traditions do come together, they tend toward implementing the musical attributes that distinguish the Japanese tradition.[52]

Takemitsu spent five months working on *November Steps*. After the
writing was completed, he hired two musicians to accompany him to
North America and perform the parts for the Japanese instruments.
Yokoyama Katsuya was a young shakuhachi master, the son of another
shakuhachi master. Tsuruta Kinshi was quickly becoming known for her
mastery of the biwa. Takemitsu had previously worked with these two
for the performances of *Eclipse*, the first concert piece he had written
for traditional instruments. In an article first published in 1971, Takemitsu describes the first rehearsal with the Japanese musicians and the
orchestra as a gradual triumph of musicianship over a fear of the Other.
Ozawa had tried to prepare Takemitsu for some of the resistance that
he might face from the orchestra, telling him that "the New York Philharmonic is hostile toward contemporary music." Still, the open antagonism displayed by the orchestra surprised Takemitsu. As Takemitsu tells
it, this antagonism did not begin to dispel until the Japanese musicians
began to play. *November Steps* is approximately twenty minutes long.
Near the end of the piece is an extended cadenza for the biwa and shakuhachi by themselves. After this opportunity for the Japanese musicians
to demonstrate how these two instruments could work together, "the
final orchestral coda was so alive that it was hard to imagine that it was
played by the same orchestra that had begun the piece." When the first
rehearsal of *November Steps* was complete, "bravos and applause broke
out from the orchestra." The evident abilities of Yokoyama and Tsuruta
to create musical meaning from ancient instruments overcame the
orchestra's resistance to direction that was vastly different from what
they were used to.[53]

A version of this cadenza was recorded by Yokoyama and Tsuruta for
Deutsche Grammaphon in 1977. On this recording, Tsuruta's biwa plays
solo for the first ninety-nine seconds. Notes are played quietly. They are
approached with bends and slurs. The plectrum slides down the strings.
Once in the opening minute, the body of the instrument is struck forcefully. There is little sense that each note leads to the other. There are
nodal points, however, places where all strings are strummed or a bent
string slowly slides back to straight. When those events happen, there
does seem to be a center, an organizing moment for that individual

sound event. But each sound event stands on its own; the sound events do not build into recognizable Western-style phrases. The shakuhachi enters with a single note, briefly held with a slight vibrato. The biwa responds to this note with a centered clearly struck note of its own. This exchange is followed by a gradual increase in intensity, a series of slides down the strings of the biwa over a set of fluttering birdlike tones on the shakuhachi. But the intensity does not build into a Western-style climax. After two longer-held tones, both instruments fall silent again for about three seconds near the three-minute mark. After a series of single-note exchanges, varying in sound quality but not in pitch, a harsh blow from the shakuhachi sends the biwa into a rapidly strummed, intensely noisy event that begins at about the four-minute-and-forty-second mark and lasts for fifteen seconds. For the next three minutes each instrument plays single notes with intervening moments of quiet, which serve to contrast the lengthy breathy sustain of the shakuhachi with the nearly instant sonic decay of the biwa. At just under eight minutes, three slides of the plectrum down the strings of the biwa lead into a fiercely strummed and harshly blown climax of noise. This climax is not led up to in any smooth fashion. Rather, there is little transition between the slides and the intense strumming and blowing. After thirty seconds of this demonstration of the inescapable presence of sawari, both instruments return to a quiet exchange of single tones interspersed with that fullness of meaning conveyed by ma until an extended passage of quiet ends the cadenza.[54]

This section was the part of the 1967 performance that the *New York Times* reviewer found "meaningless." It is difficult to imagine how it could be called passive. No more direct a confrontation with the difference of Japanese music could have been presented with these two instruments in an orchestral setting. The performance contained no recognizable harmonic-melodic development. The sounds themselves, organized into disarticulated sound events, were constituted as much by noise as they were by Western standards of pitch and rhythm. The moments of silence seemed erratic in their length, not easily counted into standard measures. The performers were not constrained by a demand for an accurate enactment of the composer's inscribed will. Although it was a display of mastery, the performance did not demand the passive acquiescence of the audience. Instead the performance required an active attitude of acceptance and attention.

I have described *November Steps* as an evident tour de force. It is a rigorous, powerful display of the differences between Eastern and Western styles of concert-based music making. But in some ways, the *New York Times* review is not inaccurate. Finding the piece "often beautiful, always fascinating," and pointing toward the skillful playing of Tsuruta and Yokoyama, the reviewer still could not avoid the judgment that the piece was, after all, exotic. And it was, for exoticism was its purpose. Takemitsu accepted the challenge of producing a piece of music that would represent modern music in Japan, that would bring together traditional classical Japanese instruments with a Western orchestra, for the American audience of the New York Philharmonic. At the time of its premiere, the performance could not have been heard as anything other than exotic. This was not simply a factor of the historically determined Orientalist frame in which the piece was necessarily received. It was also a result of the Orientalism that inspired Takemitsu to investigate the music of Japan's past. Cage's hit-and-miss appropriation of Asian philosophy enabled him to develop his concept of composition as a process that was not determinate of its performance. This version of indeterminacy helped free Japanese traditional music from its pre–World War II associations with Japanese hypernationalism. Only after this conceptual purging could Takemitsu look back at these instruments and this musical tradition for new ways to compose with rigor and with the most finely tuned intention while escaping the prison of historical determinacy. The biwa and the shakuhachi put profound obstacles in the way of the composer's will. The noise they produce is an emblem of the unrepresentable difference at the heart of any social. The silence they perform is filled with the inarticulable desires that disrupt the most carefully planned intention. Finding beauty in noise and meaning in silence is one way to combat the top-down intentions that would determine proper performance. Jacques Attali has said that composition, when fully understood, "appears as a negation of the division of roles and labor as constructed by the old codes. Therefore, in the final analysis, to listen to music in the network of composition is to rewrite it." If what is to be rewritten is to be anything other than a refinement of the same, then silence and noise, ma and sawari, must direct our listening through refusing to determine what we hear.[55]

November Steps challenges the Western relationships between performer and audience, between music and noise, between the dominant concept of the political community and the people excluded from it. The last distinction, between those who fit into the hegemonic understanding of the political community (the polis) and those who stand outside it (the demos), is a central concept in Jacques Rancière's understanding of the political. For Rancière, the only politics that matters is this effort to challenge the consensus of any political arrangement by bringing awareness to the part that has no part, those without a voice in the current arrangement. The political force of aesthetic production, then, is a consequence of changes in the distribution of the sensible. By challenging what can be sensed, felt, and heard as music; read as literature; and seen as art, aesthetic production also challenges the dominant sense of the world. By directly bringing to auditory awareness sounds that do not fit the accepted aesthetic, music shifts the relations of groups and in so doing forces open the space of political dispute. It is easy to follow Rancière too far in this direction and find oneself trapped in the classic avant-gardist dead-end. But Rancière's link between aesthetic innovation and the expansion of the polis helps to explain why Takemitsu's heightening of difference in his music, his playing to the Orientalist interpretation, could have productive results.[56]

The form and structure of a composition, its means of determining and understanding the relations between music and noise, between primary sensuous sonic material and finished composition, are an aesthetic correlate of social possibilities. When the confrontation staged in a work such as *November Steps* is first heard as beautiful, it creates a transformation in the distribution of the sensible and, therefore, in the shape of the political. Yuasa Joji, a Japanese composer and partner with Takemitsu in the Jikken Kobo, argues that "the act of composing music challenges the very nature of music and this challenge asks us to redefine ourselves as human beings." The incorporation into music of sounds previously considered to be noise represents a rethinking of the boundaries of the political. By emphasizing the noise, the Otherness, of the biwa and the shakuhachi, *November Steps* directs its listeners' attention to the musico-political boundaries between East and West. By *not* creating an effective synthesis that smoothly integrated the sounds of these instruments with those of the New York Philharmonic, Takemitsu forces listeners to consider their opposition. When they hear that opposition as beautiful, the potential for a larger polis, with more-complex relations of difference, is experienced as an objective possibility. At the most profound level, the musical beauty created by works such as Takemitsu's *November Steps* establishes the aural aesthetic possibility of a more open polis.[57]

Ono's primary strategy of sonic disarticulation was her focused fore-grounding of a rough-edged sawari, the manifestation of the physicality of any instrument—the "apparatus of an obstacle," in Takemitsu's words.[58] Throughout her career as a composer, conceptual artist, and pop singer, she consistently emphasized the physical obstacles that had to be overcome before the union of audience and performer could be achieved. Despite the shared root in the concept of sawari, however, each obstacle presented in her work took on a different physical form, appropriate to the material of the performance. In each case—compositions that take the form of instructions, art that requires the audience to perform the action that completes the work, a singing voice rooted in Kabuki—Ono's work presents an obstacle that must not be simply overcome; instead it must be integrated into the experience of the work. Where Takemitsu emphasized the sound of traditional Japanese music in order to leave behind the militaristic context of Japanese history and achieve the confrontation of difference, Ono emphasized the physicality of sound and thought in order to leave behind the equally limiting patriarchal context of Japanese philosophy and music. Sawari, a concept firmly grounded in Japanese aesthetics, became the means of Ono's escape from the constraining context of those aesthetics.

Takemitsu defines *sawari* as "an intentional inconvenience that creates a part of the expressiveness of the sound." He uses the loose bridge of the biwa to illustrate that definition. Sawari is not simply an obstacle. It is "the apparatus of an obstacle," a "deliberate obstruction." Among its many connotations is "the monthly biological function in women." Considered in this way, Takemitsu says, "the inconvenience is potentially creative."[59] Sawari arises from and references the specific physical means through which the creative act takes place. The reference to menses underscores the peculiar role that sawari has in Japanese aesthetics. Where most of the most lauded concepts in Japanese aesthetics—*wabi* (remote simplicity), *sabi* (aged beauty), and the like—refer to aspects of the apprehended object even as they bring to consciousness a sense of time, or wear, or fallibility, sawari is heard as a creative inconvenience, a means to an end that must, finally, become an active part of the end, that must not be erased from one's appreciation of the final object. If music is heard properly, one always hears the necessary sawari, the physicality of the sound, the disturbance in the air. But sawari can be ignored. And in fact it is often occluded in common discussions of music's beauty. Just as months of bleeding are forgotten at the moment a child is born. A performance that calls attention to the apparatus of its obstacle, therefore, commands an uncommon quality of listening.

To this point, the discussion in this chapter has only briefly mentioned one female musician and no female philosophers. The patriarchal character of the Japanese state had been clearly articulated by the official Meiji-period doctrine that women were banned from the political arena and should devote themselves to serving the state by being a "good wife, wise mother." A nascent feminism briefly rose up in Japan between the wars, but the basic outlines of the official policy of exclusion did not change before World War II. The *modan garu* (the modern girl who worked outside the home) who dressed in contemporary clothes, flaunted her physical appeal, and shopped for trifles was an image of threatening Western values. And the pressures of the war were enough to clamp down on any such threat, real or imagined.[60] Within the harshly militarized and masculinized world of imperial Japan, it was not surprising that the committee that authored *Kokutai no Hongi* was all men or that the composers included in the groups of neonationalists were all men. It may not be expected that the founding members of Takemitsu's Jikken Kobbo, the explicitly antitraditional group of experimental composers were all men. But they were. And when Ono told her father that she wanted to be a composer, he looked at her askance for the simple reason that it was "a field that was too hard for women."[61]

What was appropriate for his daughter, though, were lessons in Western music. It is well known that Ono's early education was of the sort only available to the most elite families in Japan. In fact, her education was extraordinary for a young girl of even her situation. Her father was also a highly skilled pianist. His taste for Bach, Beethoven, and Brahms, as well as Gershwin, was fully in line with the interests of a rapidly modernizing Japan, eager to demonstrate its ability to compete on a global scale with Western industrialized nations. Ono's mother was a descendant of one of the oldest and most elite families in the country. She displayed her elite status and her freedom from economic constraints by mastering a variety of traditional Japanese practices and was particularly skilled in the performance of traditional Japanese music. Women such as Ono's mother conspicuously resisted superficial modernism, in particular the image of the modan garu, through immersion in the traditional cultural signs of elite standing in Japan. The mastery of Western music was an almost-necessary accomplishment for young women of Ono's status. But when she told her father that she wanted to become a pianist, hoping to please him, he dismissed the desire because her hands were too small. He did agree to her taking piano and vocal lessons, however.[62]

As part of her early music training, Ono was taught Western systems of notation and melodic construction. A common exercise assigned in the musical kindergarten she attended was to notate the everyday sounds she heard around her. This translation exercise foregrounded the encounter between Japanese and Western music traditions. A central principle of Japanese musical aesthetics encourages a focus on the presentation of sounds heard in other realms of life.[63] Among the most highly prized qualities of a skilled shakuhachi player, for instance, would be the ability to produce the sounds of wind blowing through a bamboo grove. Notation, on the other hand, represents the Western method of controlling and filtering sound, of distinguishing as clearly as possible between those aspects of sound that are considered to be musical and those that constitute noise. To notate the sounds of everyday life, therefore, would be to commit oneself to a radical act of translation, forcing into contiguity entirely disparate conceptualizations of music. This exercise in notation was equally an exercise in stripping sawari from the sounds of everyday life. To turn the sounds of doors slamming and birds singing into notes on a staff is precisely to erase the physicality from those everyday events. Any trace of the material required to produce those sounds has been removed in the translation to notation.

After the war, Ono began a course in philosophy at Gakushuin University. She completed two years of study there before her family moved to New York, where her father had been sent by his bank. She soon enrolled at Sarah Lawrence University, studying both literature and music, from 1954 to 1956. But she stopped going to her classes after one of her music professors told her about the emerging performance-art and music scene that was developing around Cage's course in composition at the New School in Manhattan. Attending seminars and performances with her soon-to-be first husband, Ichiyanagi, Ono discovered a world where composition could take the form of instructions for specific behaviors. Ono had already created a few of these instruction pieces as a way of imagining her own survival.[64] The instructions for her "Secret Piece," which was published in *Grapefruit* as early as 1964 but is listed by Ono as having been originally conceived of in 1953, read as follows: "Decide on one note that you want to play. Play it with the following accompaniment: The woods from 5 a.m. to 8 a.m. in the summer." The execution of the piece inserts a specific element of creative obstacle. One must play in the early morning in the woods. The sounds of everyday life are reinserted. The notation exercises that erased sawari are precisely reversed.[65]

Instruction pieces became an important medium for the artists who attended Cage's classes and the series of performances at Ono's Chambers Street loft. This series took place during the winter of 1960–61. Co-organized with La Monte Young, performers at the loft included Terry Jennings, Henry Flynt, Jackson Mac Low, Richard Maxfield, Ichiyanagi, Young, and others. Ono's only performance in this series was a piece inspired by a Japanese ritual where she flung peas at the audience while swirling her hair around.[66] This piece was considered a composition, and its performance was to be received as music, as was Young's famous *Compositions 1960 #9*, the instructions for which read, "draw a straight line and follow it." But the differences between these two instruction pieces again bring out the significance of sawari. For Alexandra Munroe, the senior curator of Asian art at the Guggenheim Museum in New York, the central characteristic of Japanese conceptual art is that "its universe lies in the most simple somatic and everyday processes."[67] To swirl one's hair requires spinning. It is a dizzying endeavor to throw peas while spinning. During this part of her career, Ono's compositions consistently, perhaps obsessively, interrupted their performances through the apparatus of an obstacle.

As Ono's work developed over the course of the sixties and as she became more directly connected with the Fluxus group of neo-Dadaists, she began to create objects that required action on the part of the observer for their realization. They were similar to instruction pieces in that way, but some of the construction work had been done. Among the most famous of these is *Painting to Hammer a Nail*, which asks the viewer to use the hammer that hangs from the canvas to hammer a nail in and then tie to that nail a hair from the viewer's head: "The painting ends when the surface is covered with nails."[68] Most of the critical attention paid to this piece has focused on the action of hammering the nail. But it is important not to forget the hair. The hair tied around each nail is the reminder of the specificity of each individual contribution to the collective work and an unmistakable hint of sawari.

Ono's performances were also built around increasingly difficult obstacles. *AOS—For David Tudor*, first performed in 1961, requires that two performers stand back-to-back, taped together and wrapped in gauze with bottles and cans hanging from them. With the lights dimmed, the two performers must find a way to leave the stage, making as little sound

FIG. 3.2 Yoko Ono performing sawari with John Cage, Toshiro Mayuzumi, and another performer, Tokyo, 1962. Photo courtesy of Yasuhiro Yoshioka.

as possible.[69] In 1962 Ono moved back to Tokyo, where she participated in one of Cage's performances at the Sogetsu Art Center, which she had helped arrange with Ichiyanagi. One of the featured pieces was *Music Walk* (see figure 3.2). The score is notated graphically, with transparency sheets that, when placed on the score, specify directions for the performers. As they circulate around a piano, they can make particular sounds. Some of those sounds may come from the piano, and some may come from radios or other electronic devices. While Cage, Tudor, and Mayuzumi walked about the stage, reading and performing the instructions, Ono lay across the open strings of the piano. The gendered meanings of this performance (the active men, the supine woman) seem clichéd and outdated to us now, but they were typical associations in 1962. What was unexpected was the fact that as she lay across the piano strings, Ono opened her mouth and screamed. With her body inside the instrument, she escaped the restrictions on her participation. Through the metonymy of body and soundboard, Ono became the embodiment of sawari, the necessarily noisy sounding material in the heart of the creative act.[70]

Quite probably Ono's most firm insistence on a noisy obstacle, however, is her use of Kabuki vocal techniques. These skills, developed while she was still a schoolgirl, came to the foreground when she began to musically collaborate with John Lennon. Traditional Japanese singing demands "an extensive range" and "considerable breath control." Beyond that, the hetai technique, which Ono directly references when speaking of this style, requires that the singer "strain your voice a bit." Kabuki techniques, emphasizing tight control of every aspect of the vocal sound, often require that entire vocal lines take on the timbres that Westerners associate with the sound of screaming.[71] Indeed, Ono's vocal techniques have been linked by her and others to the cries of anguish emoted by the lead character in Alban Berg's *Lulu* and to the aggressive screams of protest that Abbey Lincoln contributed to Max Roach's *We Insist: Freedom Now Suite*.[72] Ono's screams are often as abrupt and disruptive as Lincoln's, but they can also be more controlled than Berg demands of his sopranos. Ono's creative use of these different vocal traditions results in a singular and immediately recognizable sound, ranging from controlled improvisations that extend the concepts of pitch and musical tone to abrupt evocations of the pleasures and pains of embodiment. In Tamara Levitz's words: "This voice is not beautiful, lyrical, or accompanimental, and thus does not easily inspire daydreaming or nostalgia. Rather, it forces an awareness of Yoko's very real existence, as it relates imaginatively with listeners' own inner sounds and the emotions attached to them."[73] And Ono's voice was an insistent apparatus of the obstacle for listeners who came to those collaborations for Lennon, listening for music made by a former Beatle.

On December 11, 1968, Ono stepped onstage with four demigods of English rock, joining Mitch Mitchell, Keith Richards, Eric Clapton, and Lennon for the performances that Lennon's jam band, the Dirty Mac, contributed to *The Rolling Stones Rock and Roll Circus*. As the band played "Yer Blues," Ono crawled into a black bag. Referencing one of her more familiar performance pieces of the period, she seemed completely divorced from the process of music making. But once the boys were done with Lennon's heroin-inspired deconstruction of the roots of rock 'n' roll, Ono climbed out of the bag and stood in front of Richards. Ivry Gitlis, a world-renowned violinist from Israel, perhaps most famous for his interpretations of the work of Berg and other modernist composers, also joined Dirty Mac for the next number. As Gitlis moved toward the center of the stage, lifting his violin, Ono met him at the single microphone. The English rock musicians kicked off a basic twelve-bar shuffle boogie in E and stepped back, leaving all the lead improvisatory room for the two classically trained musicians, Gitlis and Ono. Neither the modernist violinist nor the protopostmodernist vocalist appeared very comfortable with the unfamiliar position in front of a rock band. But after quick nodding reassurances from Lennon, both of the non-English nonrockers began making their contributions. Gitlis took the first few choruses, ripping away stinging riffs and thirty-second note runs up the neck of his instrument. Ono stood aside for the first minute and a half until Lennon whispered into her ear, encouraging her to step up to the microphone. Gitlis then moved back, and Ono began her trademark vocalizations, using her "sixteen-track voice" to disrupt without destroying the clichés of white boys playing the blues.[74] For the next four and a half minutes, Clapton, Richards, Mitchell, Gitlis, and Lennon shuffled along while Ono layered thickly scrunched atonal lines across the top of the song, displaying immense breath and tone control while completely eschewing the harmonies and timbres that characterize blues scales and rock singing. The DVD credits for *Rolling Stones Rock and Roll Circus* list this song as "Whole Lotta Yoko," as though Gitlis had not even appeared.

In 1969 Ono and Lennon took the stage in Cambridge, England, during an experimental jazz workshop. The resulting performance, released on *Life with the Lions* (1970), gives one of the finest examples of Ono's approach to Kabuki singing, emphasizing the extension of elongated notes and the production of overtones. Ono holds her first note for nearly forty seconds. Subsequent notes are held for nearly as long with frequent microtonal modulations, varying the pitch only slightly. Squeezing her vocal cords, Ono produces different overtones, changing the quality of the sound while still maintaining the same basic pitch. This emphasis on the lengthy exploration of the meaning of pitch characterizes Lennon's approach as well; his guitar part exclusively consists of long stretches of controlled feedback. Lennon's guitar and Ono's vocals respond to each other not with melodic echoes nor with blues-style call-and-response; the vocals and guitar carefully vary the different overtones that contribute to the fullness of musical sounds. The length of the piece, more than twenty-six minutes, challenges the pair's improvisatory abilities. But the manipulation of tones, both through changes in the shape of Ono's mouth and throat and through Lennon's stretching of the guitar's electronic capacities, renders audible the material obstacles that engender all music and the undeniable reminder of the ineradicable difference that grounds all communities. At its base, this musical exchange conveys the importance of opening one's ears to the utter physicality of musical sound and thereby to the richness of human embodiment. Just as the precisely modulated roars of guitar feedback and Ono's voice cannot be reduced to an easily notated pitch, Ono's insistence on the specificity of sawari—on the irreducible complexity and multiplicity of materiality—resists the reduction of human experience to well-defined categories of identity and of the political to positive insistence on the same.[75]

Ono's collaborations with Lennon could not be easily interpreted within the dominant frames of the time. Unfamiliar with the singing traditions and the performance styles that Ono referenced, critics, fans, and popular commentators throughout the late sixties and early seventies could only dismiss her work as unmusical shrieks. Neither Lennon nor Ono wanted to instigate rejection and dismissal. Both believed that their artistry would find an audience. Years later, Ono remembered receiving hate mail in response to her records. This surprised them both because they thought they had achieved a "meeting of the two minds, or the meeting of the two fields, or two countries. . . . Or the *two worlds*, that's what happened between us."[76] Over the next several years, Ono gradually reduced the influence of traditional Japanese music in her recordings and made increasing use of traditional rock-song forms and a more melodic approach to singing, as she worked to create more mainstream popular music. Occasionally, however, the Kabuki style would erupt again, with its insistent reminder of the specificity of the body that produced the sounds.

Approximately Infinite Universe is Ono's first full-scale attempt to produce an album full of recognizable rock songs. Although the music is hampered by Elephant's Memory's lead-footed plonk, it contains beautiful evocations of loneliness and fear ("Death of Samantha") as well as awkward calls for feminist action ("What a Bastard the World Is"). Snuck into the first side is a reminder of Ono's singular skills. "What Did I Do" is based on an old instruction piece from 1964. The instructions for *Closet Piece I* read: "Think of a piece you lost. Look for it in your closet." The lyrics for "What Did I Do" start with "I was looking for somethin' in the closet. I was sure it would be there. But to my surprise it wasn't there. And I had to look all over the world." What was not in her closet is never explicitly stated in the song's words. But the singing suggests an answer. In the section of the song marked "SOLO," Ono allows herself the only hetai singing that appears on this album. And it is the last example of that particular apparatus of an obstacle on any of her records for the remainder of the decade.[77]

The loud rejection of Ono's singing by Lennon's fans needs to be placed in the context of the *New York Times*'s response to *November Steps*. Where Takemitsu's music was heard as weak, imitative, and meaningless, Ono's singing was heard as noisy, aggressive screaming. In both cases, the listening public's resistance was because of the evident presence of an alternative aesthetic, an alternative with political implications. By staking a claim to the cultural authority of the New York Philharmonic and the Beatles, this alternative form of musical beauty pronounced an equality that most listeners of the time were not ready to grant. The listeners' resistance was to the sounds, of course, but also to the polis that the music figured. The musical interventions of Takemitsu and Ono were built from sounds derived from Japanese musical traditions. Fully contextualized within those traditions, those Japanese sounds would have carried associations of patriarchal dominance and military aggression. For their music to produce the aesthetic experience of what Rancière calls *dissensus*, both of these musicians had to choose specific aspects of the traditional sounds that they wanted to use in order to strip the full weight of traditional contexts from those sounds. And Ono and Takemitsu had to do this without depriving those sounds of the Otherness that they conveyed to Western audiences. The Otherness was not simply a function of identity for the musicians, because identity itself is too blunt a category and would have thwarted the subtle manipulation of sound that they wanted to achieve. Ono and Takemitsu did not work to deny the origin of their difference in the land from which they came, however. The power of the musical beauty created by the deliberate confrontation of alternative musical aesthetics was an effect of the careful choice of particular sounds and the presentation of those sounds in juxtaposition to the institutional and musical power of one of the world's greatest orchestras and one member of the world's greatest pop band. Through Ono's and Takemitsu's careful emphasis of particular qualities of the sounds that they used—for Takemitsu, the unmistakable timbres and noise of the shakuhachi and the biwa, and for Ono, the hetai-strained overtones of her sixteen-track voice—these musicians disarticulated a form of Japaneseness capable of interrupting the consensus of the West. Not initially heard as beautiful, and in fact first rejected as noisy and meaningless, their music slowly worked its way into the sensible. And the beauty became clear.

Chapter Four

"Heroin"; or, The Droning of the Commodity

Tuning is a function of time.

—La Monte Young, "Notes on the Continuous Periodic Composite Sound Waveform Environment Realizations of 'Map of 49's Dream the Two Systems of Eleven Sets of Galactic Intervals Ornamental Lightyears Tracery,'" in La Monte Young and Marian Zazeela, *Selected Writings*

I'm not sure at what point I crystallized on the idea of sustained tones as music. It's definitely true that I heard this Ali Akbar Khan recording that had a tambura on it in 1957. I heard it on the radio, and I literally jumped in my car and ran down to this place called Music City to buy it.

—La Monte Young, quoted in William Duckworth, *Talking Music: Conversations with John Cage, Philip Glass, Laurie Anderson and Five Generations of American Experimental Composers*

But the records everyone's making now are just fabulous. Everything's fabulous. Everything's absolutely better than it's ever been. Because all the people are getting so beautiful. The young people are getting beautiful, and that's why very young people like music, because the music's very beautiful and if it scares people it's because the people are that way, and they're scared anyway. But our stuff's very pretty. The show is very pretty and Andy is very beautiful, because he lets it happen.

—Lou Reed, alone and talking into a tape recorder in 1966, quoted in Victor Bockris and Gerard Malanga, *Uptight: The Velvet Underground Story*

When a pop anthem emerges as a potential object around which a momentary emergent community can circulate, the song finds itself enmeshed in the pop machinery, the chief mechanism of which is the market. It is well known that the pop market does not function well as a neutral judge of value, introducing instead an obliquely aligned set of constraints and desires that alter the trajectory of any evaluation.[1] In much the same way as the history of Japanese nationalism inhabited the sounds of traditional Japanese instruments and singing techniques, the history of market-derived distortions of the longings of the popular haunts the pop anthem. And as Takemitsu Toru and Yoko Ono dove deeper into traditions of Japanese music making in order to evacuate those sounds of their political legacies, the music of the Velvet Underground and one song in particular, "Heroin," investigated the core of the commodity form, slicing into its mysteries with the sonic power of the drone. This chapter traces the drone from one of its origin points in Hindustani musical practice to its adoption by American avant-garde composers and then finally into the hands of rock 'n' roll craftworkers, the Velvet Underground. Relying on the drone's ability to render audible the materiality of sound, the Velvets created a pop song, "Heroin," that disarticulated pop value from the operations of the market. In the process, they set the terms for a restricted field of cultural production that shaped the development of the rock genre, but even more importantly, they established the possibility of a pop form of beauty, a form capable of consolidating a polis while refusing to be reduced to a market.

The roaring drone of John Cale's viola is perhaps the most recognizable instrumental sound in the early recordings of the Velvet Underground. When their first album appeared in 1967, this sound—raw, wired, insistent—clearly marked the Velvets' difference from all other popular music then available—whether rock 'n' roll, soul, folk, pop, or the newly emerging form of rock. The power of this drone comes from its capacity to focus a listener's attention on the primary ontological ground of sound: the relationship between difference and repetition. Drones call our attention to the effort to contain the spread of difference, to stabilize it through endless repetition, even as the drone's concentrated physicality demonstrates the impossibility of this containment. As it resounds, the drone acknowledges the impossibility of pure repetition; each succeeding effort to sound the same varies from the one before. The drone commands that we pay attention to the materiality of all sound, to sound's existence as a set of repeating and differing vibrations. Every aspect of musical sound involves the recognition of patterns of difference and repetition feelingfully interpolated from vibrations in the air. Drones focus our awareness on this materialization of difference and repetition in musical time, shaping, in part, our sense of the proper form of right relations. When the Velvet Underground centered its early recordings around the sonic figure of the drone, the band created an inversion of the market imperative and a musical beauty that consolidated a new formation of the political in the field of popular music. Just as Takemitsu and Ono confronted and transformed the political force of the musical techniques they took from Japanese tradition, the Velvets disarticulated pop-song value from market success, producing a strict and strident beauty that tore apart and rearranged the audible *sens* of the popular.

This transformation was not magically immediate. As an intervention into popular-music production, the transformation had to work in and through market assumptions, playing off the tensions that Pierre Bourdieu identified in the "market for symbolic goods."[2] The music that the Velvets produced centered a "restricted field of cultural production" whose poles and tensions reshaped the sense of right relations that structured an experience of musical beauty within the larger field of popular music. In turn, that experience solidified a redistribution of the sensible, creating a dark awareness of the emptiness of the commodity relations that had long defined popular music.

A *restricted field of cultural production* is Bourdieu's term for artists who produce for other artists and the prestige they can convey, not directly for a market of consumers and the cash they provide.[3] Unlike the typical restricted field, the restricted field that the Velvets created was not the mere reproduction of an avant-garde within the popular, mimicking the efforts of so-called downtown composers to transform the means of production of music. This restricted field was instead a specific intervention into the field of popular music. Cale's viola would have meant little without Lou Reed's deep investment in the precise craftwork of the popular song. Sterling Morrison's commitment to the capital *R* of "rhythm guitar" and Moe Tucker's reversion of the bass drum back to its primary function as the keeper of all beats, not simply the downbeat, produced a rhythmic reinforcement of the drone that characterized the sound of the Velvets even after Cale was forced out of the band. The drone of the Velvet Underground reopened the question of the popular by alienating it from its dominant concretization — the market.

The Velvets' drone-infused restricted field enabled popular-music artists to claim the authority of the popular while they articulated values that ran directly counter to mainstream beliefs. I am not referring here to the simple and obvious point that the Velvets wrote and performed "pop songs" about heroin and sadomasochism. Instead I argue that the drone that is foregrounded in the band's signature sound was the central sonic technique used to establish a restricted field of popular-music production. By establishing this possibility, the music of the Velvets made audible the popular critique of the dominance of market evaluation—as a mainstream popular standpoint. This critique worked at the level of music before it was a conscious thought or desire held by the musicians. That is, their music was heard and felt as a meaningful sound before the musicians conceptualized its function. The drone was central to their music not because it was believed by the musicians or their fans to be a critique of the market definition of the popular, but because the drone was beautiful. Indeed, the power of Velvets' drone-based critique was rooted in its beauty.

The story of the Velvets' intervention into the popular begins before the individuals in the band met each other. When Terry Phillips met Cale and Tony Conrad at a party in the summer of 1965 and invited them to join Reed in the Primitives, a diverse set of influences flowed together. Most accounts of the band acknowledge the significance of Reed's study of narrative and character with the writer Delmore Schwartz at Syracuse University. These accounts typically highlight Cale's work with La Monte Young's Theatre of Eternal Music. Perhaps they mention the specific contributions of the rest of the band: Morrison, Tucker, and, for one album, Nico. The accounts all speculate on the impact of Andy Warhol. I will cover those events and influences. But most previous accounts ascribe the impact of the Velvets to a merger of pop and art without clearly articulating what art and pop meant and, most important, what it meant to truly combine art and pop in 1965–67. As Bernie Gendron, Simon Frith and Howard Horne have shown, it was during this period that popular music underwent a significant change, which was stimulated by the infusion of high-art values.[4] But neither of these classic studies takes into account the continuing power of the marketplace to define value, even once high-art values began to influence popular-music production. When the Beatles and the Who combined art and pop, their success was measured by their record sales. When Bob Dylan went electric, he was both championed and castigated for merging the artistic and political conventions of what was then called "folk music" and pop. But "Like a Rolling Stone" went to number 2 on the pop charts. The Beatles reached the top 10 with almost every release. Before the Velvets, chart success was the measure that mattered for popular music. Only after the Velvets was it possible for new articulations of art and pop in music to be judged by their sound and the impact that their sound had on those who made music after them. That is, after the Velvets' experiments with pop and art, it became possible to hear popular music in terms that were familiar from art, terms of influence and impact, rather than account-ings of sales figures.[5]

With the reevaluation of musical meaning that was enabled by the beauty of the drone, every other aspect of the Velvets' sonic signals took on heightened significance. Tucker's version of "African" beats was not heard as white misappropriation. Reed's lyrical precision was not judged according to the conventions of folk-descendant singer-songwriters. Morrison's mastery of rhythm guitar, where it was commented on at all, was not compared to the classic models of John Lennon, Keith Richards, and Robbie Robertson. Beneath the drone, outside of the sphere of mar-ket calculation, the Velvet Underground's sound created its own terms for critical evaluation and, in so doing, carved a new political aesthetic from the driftwood of the popular.

ENTER THE DRONE

Discussions of the Velvets' drone must trace it backward to the work of La Monte Young, for it was in collaboration with Young's Theatre of Eter-nal Music that Cale first developed his signature viola sound. While the group did not name itself the Theatre of Eternal Music until February 1965, performances by a group composed of Young, Marian Zazeela, Billy Linich, and Angus MacLise had explored the interactions of sustained tones and rapid improvisations as early as the summer of 1962. Tony Conrad attended these performances and joined the ensemble within a year. By the fall of 1963, Cale had also joined and the lineup featured Young, Zazeela, Conrad, Cale, and occasionally MacLise. The art histo-rian Branden Joseph describes the sound of this group as a mixture of iron and fire: "Conrad, Cale and Zazeela form a sort of iron triangle, a structured harmonic drone against which MacLise, on the one hand, and Young, on the other, perform incendiary permutations."[6] In effect, the Theatre of Eternal Music adopted the structure of North Indian classi-cal music, borrowing the concepts of an anchoring drone and rapidly flowing improvisations. It was only one step in Young's adventures with North Indian drones.

According to Keith Potter, Young's fascination with drones began with a walk across the UCLA campus in 1957, during which he heard a radio broadcast of a recording of a raga performed by Ali Akbar Khan, featur-ing Shirish Gor on the tamboura. Potter's version of the story is con-structed from two interviews with Young, one of which was published in 1968, the other in 1995. Even over a distance of nearly thirty years,

Young's story of this first encounter with the power of drones remains remarkably consistent. In both interviews, Young emphasizes the immediate impact that hearing this recording had on him, stimulating him to hurry as quickly as possible to purchase the recording. Young does not just tell us that he loved that sound. He tells us that he "literally" flew or jumped and ran to purchase the record. The significance of Young's first encounter with the drone is reinforced in these interviews by market exchange.[7] Conrad's first exposure to North Indian classical music was equally powerful. It also took the form of a chance encounter with Khan's long player. Conrad was on his way to visit Henry Flynt sometime before April 1960, but was stopped cold outside the door by the sound of Khan's sarod that Flynt was listening to inside his apartment. As Conrad remembered it years later, he waited, standing entranced in the hall, for the entire side to finish before knocking on the door.[8]

Considering the impact that this recording had on both Conrad and Young, it is probably worthwhile to spend some time with it and the tradition it was intended to represent. Initially titled *The Music of India*, the recording has been reissued on CD as a two-disc set titled *Ali Akbar Khan, Then and Now*. The first disc contains the material that was recorded in 1955 during Khan's first tour of the United States. This tour was organized by Yehudi Menuhin, who had been elected president of the Asian Music Circle, a London-based organization, in 1953.[9] By 1955 Menuhin had toured India twice, performing music from the Western tradition, but also seeking out expert Indian musicians. Committed to introducing these musicians to Western audiences, Menuhin leveraged his position as president of the Asian Music Circle to entice the Ford Foundation to help sponsor a tour of the United States for traditionally trained Indian musicians. Menuhin wanted to invite Ravi Shankar, with whom Menuhin had played during one of his visits to the subcontinent, but Shankar was previously committed. He recommended Khan, the son of Shankar's musical guru, to take his place. Khan was initially reluctant to take the trip, being unwilling to put aside his lucrative profession as a producer of film soundtracks. But Menuhin was persuasive, and Khan became his choice to introduce full-length performances of Indian classical music to the West. As the music historian Peter Lavezzoli points out, this tour was not the first presentation of Indian music to the United States. But it was the first case where Indian "classical" music was presented in a concert setting, with all the assumptions of prestige and cultural significance that the term *classical* carried in the West.[10] Before a concert held in the courtyard of the Museum of Modern Art, a recording session took place in one of the museum's side rooms. The result of this session was *The Music of India*.

The album was conceived pedagogically, perhaps even pedantically, as *the* first long-playing record to present Indian classical-performance practice. Everyone involved was aware of the significance of this being the first long-form recording of any ragas. The recording begins with Menuhin introducing the musicians and the sounds of the instruments. In addition to naming the two master musicians, Khan on the sarod and Chatur Lal on tabla, Menuhin introduces the tamboura player, Gor, identifying him as "a pupil of Mr. Khan's." This relationship of student or, more completely, disciple who strums the tamboura to teacher or guru who picks the notes of the raga is traditional among Indian troupes that perform classical music. The relationship is strictly hierarchical, and the hierarchy between master musician-student is precisely homological to the hierarchy between the master's solo instrument and the student's tamboura. The tamboura is considered a simple instrument, and so it is believed that no special instruction is required to play it. All that is demanded of the musician is the ability and willingness to pluck the strings of the tamboura and sound the drone for a very long time—sometimes two hours or more for a single work.[11] Musically, the tamboura establishes the key of the raga to be performed. Most typically, its strings are tuned to a perfect fifth, resting on the tonic from which the raga's scale ascends, but also reaching to the dominant and, therefore, sketching out a harmonic relationship. This drone, then, is not simply an assertion of home; it is rather the sketching of a musical space. Despite its subordinate character, the tamboura functions as a compass, mapping not only the place where musical lines begin but also the direction in which these lines must travel. The subordinate relationship of the tamboura, then, does not mean that its contributions are insignificant. Still, the instrument commands little respect.

According to Daniel Neuman, this lack of respect for the instrument makes sense within the Hindustani musical tradition insofar as the drones sounded by the instrument are fundamentally necessary for music to be performed, yet are given almost no attention by the audience. Hindustani music is conceived of as primarily melodic—*linear and horizontal*—not harmonic and therefore not both *horizontal and vertical*.[12] While the tamboura marks out the harmonic range, continually sounding multiple notes from the key within which the raga will be played, this minimal harmony remains static throughout the performance. By virtue of this unchanging and constant status, harmony does not play a powerful structural role in the conceptualization of any raga. According to A. H. Fox Strangways, a raga is simply "an arbitrary series of notes characterized as far as possible as individuals, by proximity to or remoteness from the note which marks the [general melody line], by a special order in which they are usually reinforced by a drone." The "special order" of the notes is precisely the raga itself. The selection of different "individual" notes that are more or less distant from the raga's basic structure reflects the improvisatory artistry of the musician. Although Fox Strangways was a British musicologist and likely, therefore, to highlight analogues of individualism, this definition is quoted by Anupam Mahajan in her recent study of the musical structure of ragas. Emphasizing the emotional significance of raga performance, Mahajan focuses her analysis on the melodic choices of the lead instrument. She states, "The proper sequencing, alignment, distribution and presentation of the notes is essential for creating a desired effect." In the most traditional understanding of the meaning and emotional effects of a raga, the tamboura's drone contributes the (almost but not quite insignificant) backdrop for the master's improvisations. Thus, the tamboura performs a necessary consistency: it is both required for the music to sound in the way it does, to make sense in the way it does, and yet as a result of its unvarying constancy, the tamboura can be ignored as the ear focuses on the improvisations of the lead instrument. The musical role of the tamboura maps onto the status of its player as the unmarked and unattended center around which a complex structure resounds.[13]

On *The Music of India*, the tamboura's drone immediately follows Menuhin's introduction, beginning in the first track, "Raga Bhairavi." Although the sound is immediately familiar to us now, after decades of Khan and Shankar recordings, for Young, Conrad, and other attentive Western musicians in the late fifties, the tamboura's timbre—the particularly wiry sound of its vibrating strings—would have been new and fascinating. The rather flat resonance of Khan's sarod, its startling immediate presence along with its lack of sustain, makes a sharp timbral contrast with the unending buzz of the tamboura. The two instruments also differ in their relationship to pitch. Although both are tuned to the same key, with the same basic tonic, the sarod has a much greater pitch range. If it is true that both Conrad and Young were immediately entranced by this recording, then the auditory quality that most likely caught their attention was this experience of difference: the timbral difference between the two stringed instruments—the sharp attack of the sarod against the fuzzy resonance of the drone, and the melodic difference—over the sustained constancy of the tamboura rose the furious improvisations of the lead instrument. The timbral distinction would have caught the immediate awareness of the listeners while their sustained attention would have been drawn by the relationship of lead and support mapped out by the sarod and the tamboura.

With sustained attention comes a recognition of the melodic focus of this music and the background against which that focus becomes clear. The improvisations that make up the Hindustani raga are extensive and wide-ranging in their melodic direction and rhythmic and dynamic drive. But the improvisations' pitch options are restricted to the notes demanded by the particular raga and the key that is constantly sounded by the drone. While Indian music is often said to include twenty-two notes per octave, the basic pitches that establish the scale that identifies a raga are also those twelve pitches that identify a key in Western music. The ten additional microtones are almost exclusively sounded as transition pitches, as slides between notes or as immediate pathways toward or away from the scalar pitches. These microtones—pitches between the scalar pitches—are the means whereby the master musician places his or her mark on the raga. They are expressive and individualizing. They are part of the musical repertoire of the musician but not part of the raga itself. The drone, in contrast, is constant, stabilizing, regular—in Menuhin's words, "inevitable."[14] There is no possibility of individualizing the tamboura's drone. Its sound is immediately recognizable; the instrument's thin buzzing timbre immediately brings to mind the image of three cross-legged musicians, dressed in white, ready to perform.

When Young heard *The Music of India* played on the radio, it was the drone that caught his ear. According to Young, "I noticed about 1956 that I really seemed more interested in listening to chords than in listening to melodies. In other words, I was more interested in concurrency or simultaneity than in sequence. . . . That separated me from the rest of the world. I was really interested not only in a single note, but in chords, while other musical systems have placed great emphasis on melody and line or sequence."[15] If Young's memory is correct, then the lessons he took from *The Music of India* and from the other ethnomusicological sources available at UCLA were focused on timbre and harmonic sustenance—precisely the contribution of the drone. But we also know that he continued to work with the relations between difference and repetition as a key compositional strategy. From 1957 through 1960, Young was developing his sense of composition in both formal classes (at UCLA and Berkeley) and informal collaborations with Terry Riley, Ann Halprin, and others. Over this period, Young's compositions increasingly focused not only on the exploration of long tones (notes held for a long time) but also on a more conceptual understanding of sound and composition that culminated in the series titled *Compositions 1960*. While his 1958 composition *Trio for Strings* gives evidence that Young's interest in long tones was not a leap into exotica and away from his Western training, *Compositions 1960*, first published in *An Anthology of Chance Operations*, which Young edited with Jackson Mac Low, are tightly focused on the relationship between difference and repetition as a way of thinking about sound.[16]

Perhaps this relationship is too abstract to center analyses of music. But remember that music itself consists of difference and repetition. Cycles per second and beats per minute require audible differences that are heard through this relation. Even timbre, that quality of sound that derives from the materiality of the instrument, is made audible by different harmonics ringing over the instrument's basic pitch. The relationship between difference and repetition, therefore, lies at the heart of music. The chief musical quality that Young and Conrad took from North Indian classical music was its ability to create a constrained ground of listening that would limit difference in the background to a restricted set of timbres and pitches with practically no rhythmic beats in order for the listener to focus on the linear differences produced by the lead instruments. The structure of a raga is designed to contrast the movement of the sarod or the sitar with the stasis of the tamboura. The artistry of the classical Indian musician is displayed in the manipulation of the pitches and microtones that are experienced as a set of steps away from the drone—the stretching and releasing of the tension between background and foreground. Young's structural variation on Indian music was to move the drone out of the background. Instead of the tamboura ringing behind the improvisations of lead instruments, Young began to compose for a variety of droning sounds as the sole object of audition, not only in the foreground, but unaccompanied.

We often think of drones as reductive, repetitive, and lacking in musical information—as literally the same sound going on and on. By contrast with the rapid masterful improvisations of a Khan, drones can seem boringly constant, lacking not only variation but information. Young, however, heard multiple sounds in the tamboura's drone, and over the course of the next several years, he worked to focus his own and his listeners' attention on that multiplicity. His first purely musical move was to take the background and put it in the foreground. *Trio for Strings*

(1958) consists of sustained chords that shift slowly from one harmonic relation to another serially. No fluid melody lies over the top of these chords. Instead the attention is solely focused on the slowly changing harmonies. *2 Sounds*, a composition from 1960, consists of two sounds, most usually unpitched "noises," defined as "friction sounds" (one friction sound that was often used was a tin can scraped on glass, but a bow of horsehair scraped along a string of catgut could work as well), creating a "harmonized" drone that could last any length of time and that could be made up of any two sounds. Both these compositions eliminate the flow of melody, the obvious contrast with the drone that characterizes Indian classical music. All the listener is left with is the difference internal to the drone.

The classic example from Young's oeuvre that most effectively illustrates the inescapability of difference—its inevitable presence—is *Composition 1960 #10*. The instructions for this composition are "draw a straight line and follow it." There have been a variety of realizations of this composition, but Young's own *Compositions 1961* is perhaps the most relevant for the purposes of my argument. *Compositions 1961* consists of twenty-nine iterations of *Composition 1960 #10*. For one of the series of concerts that Young organized at Ono's loft on Chambers Street, he and Robert Morris performed these twenty-nine repetitions with the aid of plumb lines and chalk. Famously, Young and Morris were never able to draw the same line twice. These lines of chalk, drawn twenty-nine times in as straight a fashion as possible, inevitably produced different enactments of the same conceptual line. Empirically, then, no two drones, even when produced as carefully as possible, result in the same object. Another of Young's 1960 Compositions, *#7*, consisted of a B♭ and an F, notated on a treble clef, with the instructions, "Hold for a very long time." Here, too, through an instruction designed to foreground sameness, Young focuses the listener's attention on a drone that in its materialization demands an encounter with difference. With *Composition 1960 #7*, the sounds are pitched, and they are sustained for an indeterminate time. While the drone depends on repetition or, better, extension for its identity, that identity is never complete, for the repeated gestures—the drawing of lines, the drawing of a violin's bow—that enact the repetition can never be totally identical. Young told Potter, "People said I was playing one note but I was trying to make it very clear that even if you try to play the same thing over and over, it will always be different." The "same sounds" are only ever repeated and necessarily variant iterations.[17]

Alongside the fact that repetition necessarily introduces variation,

Young's attention to the harmonic possibilities of the drone increased the complexity of its audible relationships. While *Composition 1960 #7,* "Fifth," does call for a standard perfect fifth, Young was also interested in the harmonics created both by extremely loud volumes and by harmonic relationships outside the standard fifths and thirds. His "dream chord," which consisted of such pitches as G♯, A, D, and G, made evident the de-centering that resulted from adding a minor second to a series of perfect fourths. This set of pitches makes it difficult to locate a constant tonal center. The cluster of minor seconds—G, G♯, and A—cannot be heard as simply a cluster because of the ringing D—both the fifth of the G and the fourth of the A. Those perfect harmonics sufficiently emphasize the D to draw the ear away from the cluster even as the cluster refuses the D as the tonal center. Following the classic Young instruction of "hold for a very long time" enables the tension between these two orientations to play out in different ways. The music performed by the Theatre of Eternal Music—Young, Zazeela, Conrad, Cale, Riley, and others—was devoted to concentrating the attention of the musicians as performers and any who would listen to them on the inescapability of difference in any real-ization of the same.

By 1962, after the earliest performances of what would become the Theatre of Eternal Music, the group was exploring as fully as possible the contrast between sustained long tones and rapid lead lines. When Conrad attended these shows at the 10-4 Gallery, he was "enraptured to find that [Young] had swerved off in an 'oriental' direction."[18] There was much to Conrad's observation, in that this version of Young's en-semble did perform long pieces with a consistent drone background and rapid improvisations over the top. Within a year, however, Conrad had joined the group, and the theoretical focus of the music tightened. In-stead of highlighting the distinction between the stable social ground of the drone and fluid individualist improvisations, the ensemble of musi-cians who organized themselves around Young produced an ever-tighter focus on the droning straight line.

With Conrad's input, the interrogation of contrast grew ever more subtle. Conrad brought with him a mathematician's interest in numeri-cal precision that found a ground in the group's study of harmony. An increased emphasis on precise intervals resulted in a turn to just into-nation. In just intonation, each ascending note in the scale can be de-rived from a calculation of ratios. That is, once the basic pitch of the scale is chosen, its cycles per second could become the basis for a system of ratios that would prescribe the notes in the scale. For example, let's choose the A below middle C as the tonic; its number of cycles per second (CPS) is 220. The interval of an octave—the A above middle C—is calculated by a ratio of 2:1. The number of CPS of that note is 440. The ratio for a perfect fifth (A below middle C to E above it) is 3:2, or a CPS of 330. Perfect fifths and octaves come out almost the same in both just intonation and equal temperament scales. The E above middle C in a well-tempered scale is 329.628 CPS. My ear and probably your ear cannot hear this difference of fewer than forty cents. But we can hear the difference when the interval is a major third (or, in this case, C♯). In just intonation, that interval is calculated by a ratio of 5:4 and results in a CPS of 275. In equal temperament, the CPS is 277.183. That difference of more than two cycles is audible to a sizeable number of listeners.[19]

What Conrad and Young discovered is that by playing in just intonation at high volume levels, the ear could experience its incredible sensitivity to ratios of vibrations. Young described the impact of volume in this way in 1968: "It happens that the audibility of harmonics can be a function of amplification—the louder a sound is, the more likely you are to hear the harmonics that sound makes, which is to say that they increase as the amplitude goes higher."[20] The ability to hear those upper partials (higher resonances of any actually sounded pitch) brings with it an increased sensitivity to slight variations of tuning. When played loudly enough, the slightest deviation from just intonation can be felt as a series of beats—the feeling of vibrations out of phase with each other wafting across eardrums. What the musicians heard, when they held intervals for a very long time, striving for just intonation at high volume, was the extended materiality of vibration, the contrasting interplay of difference and repetition. Using just intonation requires a shift in the quality of attention brought to listening. It reinforces the physicality of hearing. To the extent that the fundamental qualities of musical sound could be based on the rational relationship of integers, these qualities could be constrained as tightly as possible to match those integral relationships. When they did not match, the fluttering of audible beats literally made the deviation immediately perceptible.[21] With ratios of frequencies as the basis of harmony and timbre as well as the original pitch, Young, Conrad, Zazeela, MacLise, and, eventually, Cale, were concentrating their attention and their listeners' on the basic materiality of music and the fundamental nature of difference and repetition at the root of that materiality.

By the fall of 1963, Cale had become a regularly participating producer of what he and Conrad began to call *Dream Music*. Giving the name the

FIG. 4.1 The Theatre of Eternal Music performs in a private loft, New York, December 12, 1965. From left: Tony Conrad, La Monte Young, Marion Zazeela, and John Cale. Photo by Fred W. McDarrha; courtesy of Getty Images.

Dream Syndicate to their experiments with harmonics and long tones was a way of indicating the quality of attention and the disciplinary rigor required to hold a single pitch for up to two hours at a time. Conrad has emphasized the rigorous attention demanded by this process in his writings and interviews over the decades. In the liner notes to *Four Violins*, he describes the focused attention that evaluated each additional note: "For the first month [playing with Young], I played one drone note, then adding an open fifth for the next month or so."[22] (See figure 4.1.) In an interview with Joseph, Conrad emphasized his and Cale's attention to "the Sound!": "Returning to the sound as the substance of music; returning to the sound, sitting in the midst of it, and then manipulating it or becoming engaged actively in a discursive context in relation to the music; a group in a real time situation where the function of the score is replaced by consensus and immediate intentionality that's at the level of the fingertips and millisecond hearing relationships."[23] Cale remembers, "We created a kind of music that nobody else in the world was making and that nobody had ever heard before. . . . The concept of the group was to sustain notes for two hours at a time." Cale continues, "The members of the Dream Syndicate, motivated by a scientific and mystical fascination with sound, spent long hours in rehearsals learning to provide sustained meditative drones and chants. Their rigorous style served to discipline me and developed my knowledge of the just intonation system. I also learned to use my viola in a new amplified way which would lead to the powerful droning effect that is so strong in the first . . . Velvet Underground records."[24]

The only recording of the Theatre of Eternal Music that has surfaced commercially is a CD release by Table of Elements of a performance that took place at Young and Zazeela's studio on April 25, 1965, during a dinner party with several guests, including Henry Geldzahler and Diane Wakoski.[25] The musicians on this recording are Cale on viola, Conrad on violin, and Young and Zazeela singing. Apparently, MacLise dropped by, and he joins the performance for the first few minutes, even though he had not been a regular participant since Young had moved away from the saxophone and begun singing his parts. The performance is approximately thirty minutes of *The Tortoise, His Dreams and Journeys*, a segment titled "The Day of Niagara." Although there is much wrong with this tape—the problems are explicitly detailed on Young's website[26]— its value as a historical document is indisputable. Listened to carefully and loudly, one's attention is captured by many factors. As Young points out in his commentary on this release, MacLise has a difficult time situating his drumbeats. The absolute lack of a pulse in this music renders rhythmic interplay quite difficult. After a few efforts at quiet decoration and an almost halfhearted attempt to produce something more intricate, MacLise drops out at about the ten-minute mark. Also, one becomes aware of a profound unity of timbre. Curiously, it is not easy to disarticulate the sounds of the strings from those made by Zazeela's and Young's voices. The lowest tone throughout most of the piece seems to be Young's voice. But it has a rough timbre that sounds reedy, like the deepest note on a saxophone. That might seem as though it would be easy to pick out from the strings. But with just intonation, the strings and voices together create a set of overtones that merge together, melding their timbres. As Young says, what we hear as timbre is an effect of overtones and the relative volume of those overtones.[27] When the voices and the strings are so nearly in tune, their sound qualities blend. A second consequence of the tuning and overtone matching is the feeling of additional pitches audible above and below those notes that are actually being played. These are the difference tones. When the frequencies of the difference tones match the frequency intervals of an octave or a perfect fifth, that sound becomes audible as more than the fluttering of beats. We hear a pitch that is not being sounded on an instrument.

Evidently, the sounds of this ensemble truly are greater than the sum of its parts. The bow strokes on the strings seem to last forever. Rarely does one hear the little dip in the sound to indicate the change of the bow's direction. Cale's bow strokes achieve the greatest sustained sonority; the viola seems the most constant. Only a bit more frequently can one hear Conrad's bow change direction. But even here, in the very effort to create the same, to reduce the individuating sound of each player, comes the heard experience of difference. As those bow strokes rise on forever, the sustained sounds tremble and change. The exquisitely balanced and slowly moving harmonies surprise when they move, because the sounds that are heard are not necessarily the sounds that are played. In the second half of the piece, the pitches slowly move from a focus on E above middle C, with B, a fourth below, sounding, while the D in between and every now and then a note that must be a "blue" third—not quite a G, not quite a G♯ (sounding something like an E7 chord) can also be heard, before the focus centers on D. This movement to the D is certainly tortoise-like. At first the D over the E chord is simply a seventh. But then slowly an F♯ is heard. It wavers in and out of attention, drawing your ear away from an E tonal center, but not quite toward the D. Throughout the B stays constant, and slowly, only occasionally, an A is heard. That higher A fades back as the F♯ moves to the G again.[28] What is heard is a set of relationships. Despite the sense of stasis, these relationships are unstable. The effort to resolve them into recognizable chords traps the consciousness with an array of seconds (D-E, E-F♯, G-A, A-B)—intervals that are rare in most Western music, especially in popular music, and that are very difficult to resolve. In the end, there is no clear tonal center. There are no obvious standard chords. What the Theatre of Eternal Music created here is a sense of very slow movement with no clear direction.[29]

THE AESTHETIC SPECIFICITY OF ROCK 'N' ROLL

While Young and Zazeela became more involved in their studies of Indian classical music, Cale and Conrad began to listen more closely to popular music. As each have discussed in their writings and interviews of the past decade or more, the apartment on Ludlow Street shared by Cale and Conrad was often filled with the sounds of Hank Williams and other selections from Conrad's "huge 45 collection." Cale remembers listening to Murray the K on WINS AM and contemplating the excitement produced by the Beatles and the Rolling Stones. The impact of popular music reached an early peak at the moment that Cale and Conrad heard the Everly Brothers' "All I Have to Do Is Dream," floating over the airwaves. As Cale puts it in his autobiography: "We would listen to ["All I Have to Do Is Dream"] ad nauseam to hear the 'difference-tones' in the opening bars. We were pretty confused. How on earth could the Everly Brothers have known about theories of sound in Nashville?"[30] Of course, the Everly Brothers might not have thought anything at all about "theories of sound." They were trying to make a hit that sounded good, drawing from their years of listening to country styles of harmony singing. It is not entirely clear what Conrad and Cale learned from Hank Williams and the Everly Brothers. All that is clear is that this story has been repeated in the literature ever since its first appearance in Gerard Malanga and Victor Bockris's *Uptight: The Velvet Underground Story*, first published in 1983.[31] No other example from Conrad's collection of singles is ever named. It is almost as though Williams and the Everly Brothers are named to stand in for all of popular music. But, of course, they do not represent all of popular music. Both Williams and the Everly Brothers are recognized major artists, in fact auteurs, in country and country pop. The fiddle sounds on Williams's classic recordings are close to the tone of the strings bowed in the Theatre of Eternal Music. The Everly Brothers' harmonies, while not ambiguous as to their tonal center, created more pitches than they actually sang. Cale emphasizes this fact through his surprise at the Everly Brothers' knowledge of sound theory in Nashville. But there are no immediate and directly audible lines of influence here. The story may instead be intended to provide some ground for the musical meeting of Cale, Conrad, and Lou Reed in January 1965.

In the fall of 1964, Cale was living on Ludlow Street in New York with Conrad and devoting the bulk of his music-making energies to the production of very loud droning tones in just intonation, as part of an ensemble of musicians who were on a "mystical and scientific" journey. The mysticism derived from an association with Indian classical music. The scientific was associated, through Conrad, with the mathematics of just intonation. The journey was tortoise-like in its slow attention to the multiplicity of presence—the difference embedded within any effort to repeat the same. At the same time, Cale and Conrad were listening to pop music in the apartment they shared. Conrad remembers: "John started getting interested in rock & roll, although there was a great ambiguity in his mind about how somebody could be interested in both rock and classical music. But there was something very liberating about the whole rock thing, and in a sense 56 Ludlow Street came to stand for a lot in terms of some kind of liberating musical influence."[32] On the other hand, Cale claims no expertise in popular music prior to meeting Reed: "What I saw in Lou's musical concept was something akin to my own. There was something more than just a rock side to him, too. I recognized a tremendous literary quality about his songs which fascinated me—he had a very careful ear, he was very cautious with his words. I had no real knowledge of rock music at that time, so I focused on the literary aspect more."[33] Cale's ambiguous relationship to rock has stuck with most of the commentators, journalists, and critics who have written about the early days of the Velvet Underground. These writers seem most comfortable with the narrative that the ideas of La Monte Young met the ideas of Andy Warhol (with perhaps a little Delmore Schwartz) through the mediating minds of Cale and Reed, and voilà, the Velvets were born.[34] The complications that arise from the fact that the Velvets were a rock band interested in creating hit records are usually covered over by brief discussions of Reed's time at Pickwick and this short reference to Williams and the Everly Brothers. While it is absolutely true that the experience of performing dream music with the Theatre of Eternal Music was crucial to the development of Cale's musical ideas—that he brought to the Velvets not only an extensive experience with extended drones but also Young's "dream chord," and the concepts behind "X for Henry Flynt," "Poem," and "2 Sounds"—it is also true that the liberating musical influence of rock 'n' roll was fundamental to the beauty of the Velvets' music. The sonic power of the drone took on new meanings in the explicitly commercial context of rock 'n' roll. The clashing harmonics of the dream chord, keyboard clusters, and the scraping noise of broken glass and dragged furniture all meant something different, something strangely beautiful, on records that were produced to sell. Within the Theatre of Eternal Music, then, the production of the drone became a way of focusing the attention of listeners and musicians on the vibrational constancy of difference and repetition in a purportedly purified, isolated world. In the world of pop, however, the meaning of the drone changed. In this context, the drone exemplified the contradictory nature of the commodity by materializing the difference at the heart of every iteration of the same.

In January 1965, Conrad and Cale were at a party for Jack Gelber in Manhattan. Also in attendance was Terry Phillips, one of the A&R executives for Pickwick Records. Phillips spotted Conrad and Cale and immediately asked if they were musicians. Somewhat bemused, they assented. Phillips then asked them if they had a drummer. He was looking for rock 'n' roll musicians to form the Primitives, a not-quite-existent band who had supposedly just recorded Reed's song "The Ostrich." "The Ostrich," just one of Reed's many songs recorded for Pickwick, had received some attention from a television dance show. Musicians were needed to go "perform" the song. Cale and Conrad mentioned Walter De Maria, their neighbor, artist, and drummer, and Phillips immediately tried to hire them to join Reed in the promotion of Phillips's hoped-for hit.

Reed's employment as a staff songwriter at Pickwick had begun when Don Schupak introduced Reed to Phillips. Together, Schupak and Phillips were developing Pickwick International's burgeoning rock 'n' roll recording business. Much has been made of the somewhat dodgy nature of this business. Many of Pickwick's album releases consisted of one hit by a name star, licensed from the original label and surrounded by hastily written, sparsely arranged, and cheaply recorded original songs. Reed's job for Pickwick was to write those songs and, in some cases, to record and even sing some of them. A famous quote from Reed emphasizes the hack nature of the work: "There were four of us literally locked in a room writing songs. They would say 'Write ten California songs, ten Detroit songs,' then we'd go down into the studio for an hour or two and cut three or four albums really quickly."[35]

Reed's work for this label has been the source of some embarrassment for certain critics. For many who have discussed this period, Pickwick functions ironically as a debased site for the meeting of serious artistic minds. Phil Milstein, who in 1977 founded the Velvet Underground Appreciation Society and who still writes for the great fanzine *What Goes On*, has said: "No work Lou has done is so trivial, so prefabricated, so tossed off, as what he did at Pickwick."[36] The most common story told about the first meeting of Cale, Conrad, De Maria, and Reed details the astonishment that Conrad and Cale felt when learning that Reed had tuned all the strings on his guitar to A♯. In Conrad's words, "[This] blew our minds because that's what we were doing with La Monte in the Dream Syndicate."[37] No mention is made of the fact that alternate guitar tunings were common in blues recordings and even among the café folk scene in Greenwich Village. Stuck among Joseph's many insightful readings of the multiple scenes circulating around Conrad is Joseph's reference to "the dregs of Pickwick commercialism." Joseph can only justify the momentary existence of the Primitives (made up of esteemed artistes such as Conrad, De Maria, and Cale) through a detailed excursus through the already consecrated films of Jack Smith.[38] Only by locating the Primitives within an avant-garde trajectory through Smith's "transgressive camp aesthetic" can Joseph find any value in their work. Bockris can admit that Reed's five months of labor for Pickwick taught him something of value, but Bockris frames this value as "on-the-job training for a career in rock and roll," not as providing a valuable contribution to an aesthetic.[39] There is no question that the Primitives were a band thrown together by Pickwick Records. There is no question that Reed was hired to produce songs on demand under hackwork conditions. And there is equally no question that Pickwick would not have known how to handle the Primitives had they actually broken through with their record. But the screams and hollers that decorated the recorded version of "The Ostrich" had nothing to do with Smith. And the recordings that Reed participated in during his time at Pickwick were more than business training; they were practice in the art of rock 'n' roll.

As of this writing, much of Reed's work for Pickwick circulates among collectors, but there are two important examples more readily available on YouTube. The Roughnecks' "You're Driving Me Insane" was first released in early 1965 on Pickwick's *Soundsville!* LP. The song is credited to Reed, Phillips, Jerry Vance, and Jimmie Sims, the four who were "locked in a room" together to write songs. The song alternates between an E major–D major chord pattern, over which Reed plays a guitar solo, and an A–B pattern for the chorus. The lyrics are equally simple:

"The way you walk and carry me on,
The way you talk, you put me on,
The way that you rattle your brain,
You know you're driving me insane."

Both the structure and the lyrics put the song smack in the middle of what was then the dominant white American response to the British Invasion. "You're Driving Me Insane" would neatly fit into the Nuggets or Pebbles collections of garage bands and sixties punk. The beat is swamped with handclaps that are not always precisely in time, yet which clearly help to drive the song forward. The yells in the background also function percussively to speed the song along. These sorts of tricks had a long history in R&B recordings and helped to push rock 'n' roll hits such as "Double Shot of My Baby's Love" (1966) onto radio charts across the country. "You're Driving Me Insane" was not simply some embarrassing hack job. Reed's lead guitar sound is immediately recognizable; the tone is nearly the same as that documented on most of the Velvets' live recordings. The urgency that rises throughout the song became a standard strategy for many of Reed's later recordings, both with the Velvets and in his solo career.[40]

With "The Ostrich," also originally released in January 1965, all these techniques are intensified. The song begins with an absolutely stinging guitar that hits on and won't let go of a C♯—the minor third above the tonic—for the first six bars of the recording, while Reed hollers at the "audience" and it screams back.[41] The song proper begins with the riff made famous by "Then He Kissed Me," the dum-de-dum-dum, rising from that famous A♯ to the D–D♯–D before returning hard to the tonic. The beat here is metronomic—if there could be a drone beat, this would be it. Snare, kick, and cymbals are all bashed on each quarter note. The squeals and screams layered on top achieve a kind of ambiguous wildness, and Reed's asides, his yeah-yeahs and come ons, have all the authority and confidence of the best punk singers. You can hear why Phillips and Schupak thought they might have had a hit. This was a first-rate example of sixties punk. The Primitives were not deeply steeped in this tradition with years of playing their dues in clubs around New York. They did not have to be. That wasn't the way that sixties punk worked. The hits of the genre were most often created by young men thrown together by chance and the nearly accidental ownership of guitars. The Sonics and the 13th Floor Elevators were among the few exceptions to this rule. The Primitives were as authentic as most, and as well served by the genre as any.[42] Reed's Pickwick experience was not an anomaly that is difficult to explain away. Nor was it simply preparation for a commercial career. It was a training grounded in rock 'n' roll aesthetics. As Conrad said about meeting Reed the first time: "It was obvious that Lou really authentically loved rock & roll. . . . Lou was like a rock & roll animal and authentically turned everyone on."[43]

Reed's enthusiasm for and expertise in rock 'n' roll aesthetics comes through clearly in a piece that he wrote for *Aspen* magazine. *Aspen* was imagined to be a multimedia magazine and would include pieces from artists, musicians, and designers. The third issue was a special on Pop Art, edited by Warhol and published in December 1966. Reed contributed a piece titled "The View from the Bandstand" that began with a quote from the Crystals' "I Love You Eddie," and filled eight pages with a forceful argument for the value of popular music over and above the official culture taught in college classrooms: "Writing was dead, movies were dead. Everybody sat like an unpeeled orange. But the music was so beautiful." In this article, Reed detailed his understanding of and love for the professional artistry of popular-music production. Reed understood himself to be a songwriter and popular musician, working in the age of rock 'n' roll. His models included musicians such as Bo Diddley, Little Richard, and Screamin' Jay Hawkins. Reed proclaimed the brilliance of Brian Wilson's ability to turn the same old chords (C–Am–F–G and E–A–B) inside out and upside down. He lauded the layered drumming in Phil Spector's "Wall of Sound." Reed promoted the repeated paradiddles at the end of the Four Seasons' "Dawn." He carefully dissected the brilliance of the background singers in the Righteous Brothers' "You've Lost That Lovin' Feeling"—"the best record ever made," in Reed's judgment. Perhaps even more central to Reed's aesthetic was the work of the songwriters, teams of men and women who labored in small rooms in Motown's "Home of the Hits" and the Brill Building, struggling to churn out hit songs and succeeding more often than anyone had a right to. "The best song-writing teams in America," Reed called them: "Holland, Dozier, Holland; Jeff Barry, Wile [Ellie] Greenwich; Bachrach [Bacharach] and David; Carol King and Gerry Goffin." For Reed, the work of these songwriting professionals was more worthy of concentrated attention than the words of Robert Lowell or Richard Wilbur or even Cole Porter. Popular music was not an embarrassing secret pleasure. It was the source of lyrical and musical value, a tradition to be drawn from with respect and care. Reed's songwriting skill was not a set of displaced literary techniques. It was a meticulous cultivation of conventions specific to the popular-song tradition.[44]

THE VELVETS WERE A BAND

When the musical roots of the Velvets are traced outside of the Cale-Young connection and when Reed's contribution is understood to be more than a literary consciousness encouraged by Schwarz and focused on character development, then room is found to consider the full contributions of the rest of the band. The Velvet Underground was a rock 'n' roll band—and the sense of a *band* is very important. For Moe Tucker and Sterling Morrison, the interactions among the band members were the source of some of the band's most important qualities. As Tucker put it in an interview years after the band broke up: "I think our music sounded the way it did fifty or maybe eighty percent . . . because of the people who were in the group." The four musicians brought together into a unit a conflicting range of orientations toward music making. "Sterling had a certain style which he put into it, and Lou, and John," Tucker explained. "That's what I said before, [it was important] to have those four who were so good together, who enjoyed each other, liked each other's styles and enjoyed the music that they were playing, too."[45] Morrison remembered the productive dynamic quality of the conflicts within this unit: "We had musical differences from the first minute we were in a room together, but that made the band good. If everybody has the same ideas all the time, then you have one idea, but if you have three ideas that fight for dominance, that's a dynamic process. That's what the Velvet Underground was. . . . So that was the way the band got to work, and that's why it did work, but it's an abrasive process, not simple."[46] The process was not only abrasive. It was also fun. Describing the earliest days of the band, before the Exploding Plastic Inevitable, Morrison insisted: "We were playing Smokey Robinson and related things, some of our little ideas, too, but we were just playing for fun. If it's fun on that level, it's fun on any other level. This was music for its own sake."[47] The dynamic struggle to infuse their music with the best possible ideas resulted in music that was *fun*: music that felt good; music not only with roots in Indian classical music and the Western avant-garde but also with influences that sprang from R&B and soul; music that honored the tradition of great pop-song writing; music with a drive to sound different; but music that, above all, was beautiful—even in the early cacophonous days of the Exploding Plastic Inevitable.

While Tucker is often remembered as "very straight" and somewhat shy (apparently, she refused to type the swear words when she transcribed Warhol's novel *A*), she was also earnest, straightforward, smart, and insistent. No one could have lasted long in the Velvets without a serious intellect and a healthy suit of emotional armor. In calling her "very smart," Morrison remarked on her having won a scholarship, and Tucker told the story of almost daring her boss to fire her from a night job keypunching at a bank because of her refusal to wear a skirt. (He did fire her.)[48] Her intelligence and her lack of patience with the celebrity trappings of popular music are evident in the few interviews with her that have been published.[49] Tucker's main musical contribution to the Velvets' sound was her drum style, which refused to develop elaborate rolls and instead focused on maintaining a consistent drive that sometimes had to fight against the moving beats of the other musicians. This style derived from two main factors. First, Tucker herself says that she was not a trained nor highly experienced drummer. Prior to joining the Velvets, she had played drums with a cover band on Long Island, the Intruders. But Tucker's lack of certain select drumming skills quickly became an advantage: "I didn't learn to do a roll for five years. I was lucky, because if I was Ginger Baker, the music would not have sounded the way it did. Because I'd have been going 'tut-tut-tut-tut' all over the place, which would have changed the style of the songs, the mood of the songs."[50] Tucker turned this lack of a specific drumming skill into an advantage by drawing from an entirely different tradition of drumming: "My idea for how I wanted my drumming to sound was African drums — that's what I wanted my drumming to be like."[51]

The recording that most prominently represented African drums for U.S.-based popular musicians in the early 1960s was Babatunde Olatunji's *Drums of Passion*. Released in 1959, this album was the first effort to popularize African music in the West. It was an astonishing commercial and critical success. The album reached number 13 in *Billboard*, eventually selling more than five million copies. By 1965 Olatunji had played with most of the leading musicians in jazz, including Duke Ellington and John Coltrane, and he had formed the Olatunji Center for African Culture in Harlem. From there his influence spread beyond jazz as his center brought students together with his own work, but also with the work of figures such as Yusef Lateef and Pete Seeger. Without being called such, *Drums of Passion* was an early entry into what would become the catalogue of "world music" (joining Ali Akbar Khan's *The Music of India*). Among U.S. intellectuals who wanted to signal an awareness of African music, *Drums of Passion* became a necessary checkpoint.[52] For this recording to be mentioned as an influence on Tucker, then, is not at all surprising. Her drumming, however, does not sound anything like Olatunji's. It does not sound similar to the drums on Bo Diddley records either, although Tucker directly cites the Bo Diddley beat as one of her influences. Rather than sounding "African" or "African American," Tucker's drum style revealed a seemingly calculated reduction of rhythmic complexity to a focus on the beat that paralleled the tonal effects of the drone. For example, the funereal tone of "All Tomorrow's Parties" is reinforced by Tucker's insistent and steadfast pounding of her bass and toms precisely at the one and three beats. The only other percussion is a solitary tambourine that echoes on two and four for most of the song. By relentlessly and stubbornly refusing to add anything to the drum part for all of the song's six minutes, Tucker's drum style anchors the somber feel of the song. Her work on "Heroin" is equally precisely in time with the musicality of the song. Tom Wilson, who produced several of the songs on the first album, affirms this: "She has great time."[53] Morrison insisted that Tucker's willingness to drum in this style was the reason she was in the band: "We had one theory that said that all bands tend to sound alike because all the drumming is alike. We said our drumming is not going to be like everybody else's. . . . Maureen Tucker was willing enough to part from the usual procedures, and that was good, and that's why she was the drummer after Angus."[54] Tucker's approach to the drums equalized all beats, creating, in effect, a nonpulsating drone of beats that stabilized and collated the more frantic and diverse rhythms of the guitarists.

Even more rarely commented on than Tucker's drumming is the guitar work of Sterling Morrison. To some extent, this is probably because Morrison is the one musician of all the Velvets most firmly centered in the rock 'n' roll tradition. Like the Beatles and the Rolling Stones, Morrison's first love was "black songs, rhythm and blues, that's what we liked." Even during the early Ludlow Street period of the Velvets, much of what Morrison considered to be fun centered around the moments when they "would play 'Little Queenie' or some old favorite from days of yore." He says, "In the early days with John I remember sitting around playing a lot of Smokey Robinson stuff, just for ourselves, 'Tracks of My Tears,' or whatever."[55] For the critic Robert Mortifoglio, Morrison's guitar work provided "a steady backbeat. . . . It fell to Morrison to ground this band in some order of a rocking chordal cushion."[56] If Tucker provided a minimalist beat in keeping with the drone aesthetic of the band, Morrison performed a similar reduction in his role as rhythm guitarist. Mortifoglio reports: "Jonathan Richman once said he thoroughly 'studied' *White Light/White Heat* and concluded that Sterling Morrison was the greatest of all living rhythm guitar players."[57] Morrison's idea of great guitar playing was the "minimalist" work of Steve Cropper: "The guitar players I like are Steve Cropper and people like that, very minimal. A few well chosen notes. A good guitar riff I always thought was worth more than a good guitar solo."[58] Since the Velvet Underground was a band whose primary stylistic dictum was to place the sounds normally considered to be background directly in the front, it is not surprising that its rhythm guitarist would have made a major contribution. When Cale's bass smashes on the seventh at the end of "White Light/White Heat," fun — that is, pop-music pleasure — is produced only because of the consistency and power with which Morrison held the one chord. The power of that aggressive seventh can be felt as embodied pleasure because the song has been driven along for the previous two minutes by the minimal swing that Morrison has provided in his interplay with Reed and Tucker. Morrison's contribution to the drone is equally powerful. In what had already become a common move for the band, "Here She Comes Now" drones a tonic D throughout. That drone, however, stands in contrast to the regular I–IV and IV–VI chord changes that Morrison defines. Moving the drone to the foreground did not render the background to mere support. Instead the Velvets' drone achieved its meaning only in intricate interplay with the shifting chords against which it sounded.

As the band's most serious rock 'n' roll theorist, Morrison's aesthetic judgment consistently emphasized one of the key terms in rock 'n' roll aesthetics: *fun*. Speaking of that same early Ludlow Street moment, Morrison insisted: "This was not people practicing with a vision, mind you. We didn't say: we have a great idea and we're going to pursue it to great glory. That wasn't what we were doing. We . . . were just playing for fun. . . . This was music for its own sake."[59] Music for its own sake can be recognized by the fun that results—the embodied experience of musical beauty. Looking back, Reed confirmed the centrality of fun during those early years: "People would tell us it was violent, it was grotesque, it was perverted. We said, 'What are you talking about? It's fun, look, all these people are having fun.' . . . We were never playing to make enemies; we were playing to make music."[60] In popular music, in rock 'n' roll and in soul, aesthetic pleasure is commonly identified as fun. The word itself emphasizes the physical embodied aspect of aesthetic pleasure. *Fun* is the name given to the experience that Kant theorizes as the contingent "harmony of the object with the faculties of the subject." For Kant, the experience, because it is contingent, cannot be the result of an a priori concept. Equally, rock 'n' roll fun names more than a pure subjective moment of experience, because it is about the form of an object outside the experiencing person. It is a moment of aesthetic pleasure, the recognition of beauty.[61] What rock 'n' roll gives to Enlightenment theories of aesthetics is this renaming of aesthetic pleasure: fun. *Fun*, of course, is a polysemous word. Its meaning varies according to its context. But when musicians speak of making music only for fun, what they mean is that this making of music results in the embodied experience of aesthetic pleasure. In the context of popular music, playing for fun is the aesthetic standard that holds against the commercial imperative. As Tucker put it: "To be in a group just to make money—I wouldn't. You might do it, but you sure wouldn't enjoy it."[62] Morrison agreed: "The thoughts that filled the heads of the Velvet Underground weren't: How can we become a pop success? What do we have to do to get 45s played on the radio? We never thought about that. The thing was: What is it that we do? What are we doing now that we like?"[63] This was a radical change in popular music.

FIG. 4.2 The Velvet Underground performing at the Filmmakers' Cinematheque, New York, February 8, 1966. From left: Lou Reed, John Cale, and Sterling Morrison. Photo by Fred W. McDarrah; courtesy of Getty Images.

The Beatles aimed for "the toppermost of the poppermost." "Like a Rolling Stone" was Bob Dylan's shot at a radio hit. The Velvets eschewed all that. (See figure 4.2.) As Morrison put it: "We said, screw the marketing."[64] Nevertheless, they thought they were going to be commercially successful.

In an article originally published in *Fusion* in 1969, Robert Somma identified the peculiar charge of the rock artist. As a genre, rock was rooted in fun and pleasure, but it was also given the difficult task of producing an experience of freedom in the midst of the contradiction between commerce and culture, what Somma termed "the dilemma of American life."[65] Ten years later, Ellen Willis articulated rather clearly the paradox of anticommercial popular music, which she termed "rock-and-roll art," as worked out by the Velvets. "Rock-and-roll art came out of an obsessive commitment to the language of rock-and-roll," Willis claimed. This commitment carried with it "an equally obsessive disdain for those who rejected that language or wanted it watered down, made easier." That language she spoke of included music as well as language. For Willis, the rock 'n' roll artist had to be steeped in the traditions of the form, which was as intrinsically complex and subtly expressive as any other genre: "The Velvets were the first important rock-and-roll artists who had no real chance of attracting a mass audience. This was paradoxical. Rock-and-roll was a mass art, whose direct, immediate appeal to basic emotions subverted class and educational distinctions and whose formal canons all embodied the perception that mass art was not only possible but satisfying in new and liberating ways. . . . But the Velvets' music was too overtly intellectual, stylized, and distanced to be commercial. Like pop art, which was very much a part of the Velvets' world, it was antiart made by antielite elitists."[66] Like many first generation rock critics, Willis mistakenly assumes that her first aesthetic love is immediate and emotionally direct, despite having formal canons and a set of constraining conventions. But she did understand clearly that the Velvets inhabited the heart of the rock 'n' roll tradition and, at the same time, turned it against the commercializing processes that had been the tradition's lifeblood.

POP/ART/POP

The most powerful nonmusical stimulant for the Velvets' aesthetic intervention were the ideas and support of their "producer," Warhol. Although Warhol knew next to nothing about rock 'n' roll, he did understand mass culture. He understood the profoundly contradictory function of elitist antielitism in a world saturated by images and sounds, a world where meaning had to be reconstructed every moment because the supersaturation of the sensory environment by endlessly throbbing impulses attacked every line of tradition. Warhol sensed well before most that mass culture opened a world of possibilities, that it was not the dumbing down of fine sensibilities but rather an entirely new field within which to explore basic and contradictory human desires. Among the contradictory desires that Warhol understood and that the Velvets explored were the longing to be known by all while remaining above and aloof from the crowd; an equally powerful desire to be lost in the crowd and totally anonymous, just like everyone else and therefore free from any disciplining gaze; a longing to be lost in work while not being captured by that work; an equally strong desire to refuse the so-called nobility of work and recognize the numbingly dull repetitive nature of most all of it; an obsession with the finest details of sexuality along with a fear of the vulnerability that accompanies and amplifies sex; and finally the inescapability of death.[67]

Warhol encouraged Reed in particular to work constantly and to respect the authority of the mundane. Warhol also famously demanded that Reed not cut the dirty words from his songs.[68] *Dirty words*. What a silly, childish phrase. But, of course, its childishness is precisely the sign of the contradictory qualities of sexuality and embodiment that Warhol explored—endless kissing on a couch; the gaze of a lover on a loved one who sleeps for hours; the necessary delicacy of fellating a banana; the scorn that fails to protect from abandonment. The observation of sex quickly leads to the absurd emptiness of pornography. The awareness of being observed or, worse, the constant observation of oneself, leads to ever more frantic efforts to lose oneself in sheer physicality. Warhol's art was constructed from the simple yet precise observation of that constellation of the trivial, the obvious, and the overwhelmingly powerful possibilities of desire let loose in a world of mass production and mass media. The complexity of Warhol's vision was the result of not refusing any of the contradictions, of not straining for some version of the good or even the sensual, but of accepting the presence and the emptiness of beautiful surfaces. In Warhol's world, the longing for beauty rarely results in transcendence. Transcendence may even be the wrong goal. Whatever value art may produce could come more predictably from maintaining the proper perspective toward the dull, the stupid, and the repetitive.

Different concatenations of these concepts inhabited Warhol's art and the Velvet Underground's music. For Warhol, working in a field already constituted by the opposition of art and commerce (an opposition he never fully accepted)—a field where the authority of the artist was dependent on the singularity of the artist's vision—the incorporation of the mass image, the dull, and the superficial manufactured a break in the trajectory of artistic advance. For the Velvets, working in a field of sentiment and sound, where step melodies and simple harmonic resolutions floated endless promises over the rhythmically enforced physicality of love (Ooh wee ooh, baby), and where the quality of love's illusion found its acknowledgment in marketplace success, an equally radical transformation of the rules of the game resulted. Warhol's art and the Velvets' music were made up of relatively simple forms enlivened by a complexity of concept that neither proclaimed nor denied the value of those forms.

Concretely, Warhol's support brought the Velvets together with an audience and an entourage. By inserting the Velvet Underground as image, performer, and sound source into the Exploding Plastic Inevitable—a mixed-media assemblage of Warhol films, writhing performers, aggressive lightshows, and overdriven sound—Warhol loaned the Velvets his authority and marked them as something quite different from other rock 'n' roll bands (they were not the Young Rascals) and equally different from other avant-garde music ensembles (they were not the Theatre of Eternal Music). The Velvets received recognition, attention, and sufficient performance practice to hone their songs and their sound into precisely designed, multifaceted objects. In the studio, Warhol's authority freed the Velvets from record-label control and enabled them to capture the sounds and the songs they could imagine. This freedom from the direct control of the recording industry did not entail complete freedom from the conventions of popular-song writing or from the sounds of rock 'n' roll. But this freedom meant that the particular aural details—the harmonics that derived from droning D strings, the almost-droning rhythms that emerged from a consistent and precise attention to time, the lyrical and the musical refusal of both the dichotomy of beauty and ugliness and the concomitant ideological conflation of value with marketplace success—did not have to be toned down in any way. In fact, those details directly rose to the surface of the recording, requiring that every listener come to grips with feedback, perversion, and the aching emptiness of desire before even beginning to hear the sweet harmonic traditions buried in the mix.

"HEROIN": THE ULTIMATE COMMODITY

In February 1965, Reed quit his job at Pickwick Records. The band that would become the Velvet Underground rehearsed regularly and rigorously throughout that spring and summer in Cale's Ludlow Street apartment. Outside that apartment, Cale was still working with Young, and "The Day of Niagara" performance was recorded that April. In July Reed, Cale, and Morrison recorded a set of demos for Cale to take with him on his next trip to the United Kingdom. The hope was that these rough recordings of the group's best early songs would pique the interest of more adventurous record companies than could be found in the United States. These demos were included in the *Peel Slowly and See* box set released by Polydor in 1995 and provide significant documentation of the state of the band's material one year before they recorded their first album and five months before they met Warhol. Recorded without drums (and, in fact, before Tucker had been recruited into the band), the demo versions of "Heroin" show that the song already had in place most of its key characteristics: the basic narrative outline of the lyrics, the marvelously accurate words of the chorus—"I guess that I just don't know"—the interplay between the song's tempo and its verse-chorus structure, and the droning viola. But the song sounds young and slightly unformed when compared to the studio recording from a year later. Reed's voice quavers and whines as he struggles to sing rather than sing-speak the song; the lyrics are less bold, less certain of their metaphorical reach; the tempo shifts are subtle, perhaps even accidental with no drums to reinforce them; and the viola sounds quiet and restrained. This last point is worth emphasizing.[69]

Although the demo version of "Heroin" was recorded on a small two-track tape recorder in one room of Cale's apartment as opposed to the professional equipment of the official release, the differences in the sound of Cale's viola are considerable and cannot simply be reduced to the recording conditions. The song itself is recorded almost a half step lower, so the guitars shift from C to F rather than from D♭ to G♭ as they do on the released version.[70] Cale's main droning tone on the demo version is the C above middle C. This note sounds throughout the song. As it is the tonic, the home note of the key of the song, the note resonates neatly and clearly with both chords. It is even doubled by a calmly picked C that rings consistently through the chord changes on one of the guitars. During the chorus, however, Cale double stops an F, adding that harmony to the C. This added note emphasizes the second chord of the chorus and produces a sort of tugging effect when the C major chord is played on the guitars. The slight dissonance produced against the C chord stands out—not as an added tension that demands to be resolved so much as a distraction, a displacement of the attending ear from the central thrust of the song. Cale might have sensed this, as he plays the entire part with restraint. Not only do the notes sound clear and clean, free of the fully amplified overdriven harmonics to come, but this version of Cale's drone is even quieter and less intensely sounded than his contribution to "Day of Niagara." This drone fits into the quieter acoustic guitar arrangement; combined with Reed's less forceful singing, the song approaches folk-rock. The demo version of "Heroin" sounds like a song about heroin, ambiguous, perhaps, in its message, but not with respect to its content.

The version of "Heroin" that was released on the first album, *The Velvet Underground and Nico*, has nothing in common with folk-rock. It was recorded a year later: after Tucker joined the band, after Warhol added the singer Nico to give the band more stage presence, and after six months of steady performance practice with the Exploding Plastic Inevitable. Here the guitars are electric, which gives them more bite. One of the guitars begins with the steady plucked D while the second enters a bar later, with single strums of the two-chord cadence. Tucker's sideways bass drum comes in on the upbeat, thumping the four and leading the ear right back to the first guitar's steady eighth-note Ds. After thirty seconds of slow build, Cale's viola can be heard. This time there seems to be no need to reinforce the tonic. Instead, the viola rings out an A—the fifth of the D major chord and a curious second of the G chord. The note continues forever. Cale has apparently mastered the continuous sounding of the note demanded by the Theatre of Eternal Music, as it is very difficult to hear any breaks in his bowing. So when Reed's voice finally enters, it comes into a musical space that has already been extended beyond the normal frame of rock 'n' roll. Although the guitars are playing a quite traditional chord change, the timbre of Tucker's drums—all bass drum and toms—and her slow addition of sixteenth notes (coming first on the *second* beat) drops the bottom of the song. This happens while Cale's ceaseless high A pulls the top up and away from the pitch with which Reed begins the song; he opens with that fundamental word in pop—*I*: "I don't know / just where I'm goin.' / But I'm gonna try / for the kingdom if I can."

From this point on, this performance of "Heroin" becomes a masterful interrogation of need, desire, and the false satisfactions offered by a culture that substitutes things for people, drugs for relationships, safety for sexuality. Every element of the performance contributes to the construction of a felt sense of completion that is quickly shown to be only an illusion: "Cuz it makes me feel like I'm a man / when I put a spike into my veins. I tell ya, things ain't quite the same." What does the drug do? Exactly what the music tells you. After the beginning that proclaims the security of any ritual (those tonic Ds and the I–IV chord progression), and just after the questioning of that security by the indication of what lies outside the standard harmonies of the pop song (Tucker's low drums and Cale's high A), Reed's voice, with calm assurance, begins to narrate the luring lie of drug use, the tantalizing falseness of commodity desire, the emptiness of all promises of certain satisfaction, and the impossible, if powerful, dream that one can escape the pain, contradictions, and evils of life just through the desire to do so.

If the song had retained its folk-rock tendencies from the Ludlow Street version, it could have been heard as a paean to drug use and, by extension through the record's status as a commodity, as a celebration of the satisfaction that derives from purchasing just the right item. What is heroin, after all, but the perfect commodity? Like all commodities, heroin solves all your problems except for the problem of getting more of it. But with the new arrangement, a musical precision honed from months of focused intensity inside the Exploding Plastic Inevitable, the evisceration of this promise comes about through the precise mimicking of the drug's effects. As each line of the verse courses through the singer's throat, the number of syllables in the line increases, both guitar players' hands move more quickly, the drummer's mallets beat faster, and all the while the viola drones constantly, forever, hollow. The blood flows faster until it simply does not have to flow any more and all is (almost) still. Until the need arises again. Then the soothing thump of the bass drum picks up its accompaniment from the throbbing tom-toms, and the guitars notice each other again and wink in conspiratorial anticipation, acknowledging that they're playing just the same old chords, but insisting that this time, *no really*, this time it will be different.

It is a little bit different the second time. The crescendo is slightly more intense. After the pressure has built, Morrison's guitar adds a slide up to an A chord and back, just quickly enough to suggest that more may be possible but not long enough to really change anything. Because the result is the same. Tension, release; tension, release; tension, release (D–G again and again); faster perhaps, with the drumsticks hitting each other as well as the drumheads. But throughout it all, the viola resounds constant and hollow—electric, wired, and precise. The rush plays itself out, and the hard-earned calm returns. But for not quite so long this time. It all starts again and goes through the same motions of quiet starts and building intensity, only this time the build lasts longer and the singer seems a bit more frantic, more eager for the relief that, when it does come, is nowhere nearly so satisfying as it might have been because the memory of the last two quick releases has not faded. And so, in classic pop-song form, two-thirds of the way through the song comes the bridge: "Heroin, be the death of me / Heroin, it's my wife and it's my life." The singer chuckles during that line, indicating a bit of self-reflexive irony just before the rush comes again. Only this time the rush is different. The refrain doesn't start with a quiet beginning and it doesn't stop when it reaches its end. Instead, the overdriven pickups on the viola are driven higher and the overtones—which have been there all along, hidden just beneath the audible surface of the recording—explode. The harmonics recirculate through the speakers and back into the pick up, shrieking and screaming louder with each cycle, forcing the drug sound through every hair, every cell membrane, every bone, every nerve ending. And you can tell that it has really worked this time because the heartbeat stops. Tucker's drums, despite her best efforts, despite the desire of all of us for all the beats to pound together, to maintain some continuity through it all, have fallen behind, and, in frustration with not being able to hear anything at all but herself, she has refused to continue. A rush so strong that the heart will never need to beat again. Morrison once described the song this way: "'Heroin' is a beautiful song too, possibly Reed's greatest and a truthful one. It's easy to rationalize about a song you like, but it should be pointed out that when Reed sings he's only glamorizing heroin for people who want to die."[71] But even this promise of cessation is false. Because Tucker does pick up her mallets one more time, and the drums come back, without their confidence perhaps, but with at least something like an attempt, an approach, a struggling aching effort to keep up.

During its final seconds, the song coasts to an end. Before speaking the quietest repeat of the refrain, guessing and not knowing, Reed thanks God that he's not aware, the drums sinking back to their bare eighth notes, the guitars remaining secure in their ritual echoing of the simplest of chord changes, all the while the viola drones on and on, sounding a note that floats just out of reach of those simple guitar chords, desiring, electric, wired, constant, and hollow, always present, never ending. That drone: its vibrating intensity eviscerates the promise of the commodity, simultaneously echoing the drone's promise of the same and the specificity of difference, the oscillation between ideal repetition and the material facts of iteration. The form of the commodity promises the same in every oscillation of difference. The drone in "Heroin" rips that lie apart even as the song displays the false promise of the commodity. More. More. Again. Again.

In the context of popular music, the song's refusal of its own promise, the promise of the commodity, marks the agency of the drone. Stripped of context, isolated as a purely sonic figure, this drone is the sound that La Monte Young heard in the background of Ali Akbar Khan's pedagogical presentation of Indian classical music and moved to the foreground. This was the drone that supported the social hierarchy of Indian performance practice by enabling the rapid and expressive soloing of individual masters of the style. This was the drone that seemed to so neatly map the homology of social structure with musical structure. In Young's hands, that drone moved out of the background. Once in the front of the listener's attention, the drone's apparent sameness revealed the constant reiteration of difference. Young's fascination with the drone showed not only that no two efforts to produce the same sound could escape difference but also that the resounding qualities of any instrument produced more sounds than were intended—the so-called difference tones that even the Everly Brothers found irresistible. In Young's Theatre of Eternal Music, the drone became the source of an ever-expanding range of musical possibilities in just intonation. Taken out of the avant-garde and inserted into the heart of a pop song—and not just any pop song, but a song about the contradictions of the pop process—that drone focused the listener's attention on the impossible redemption of the promises that kept audiences coming back for more. This became the political effect of the beauty of "Heroin." The quality of the drone that most fascinated Young—the fact that no two soundings of the drone are ever the same—is the key to understanding its political force. The specific political thrust of any drone cannot be read off the sound itself. Understanding that force requires the complete comprehension of the workings of the drone within the totality of the musical field in which it is sounded.

The musical beauty of "Heroin" enabled a specific shift in positions among critics, fans, and musicians so that a restricted field of popular-music production could come into play. Drawn from the thinking of the sociologist Pierre Bourdieu, the concept of a field of cultural production can help us to understand why artists, writers, musicians, and critics can fight so adamantly over the meanings and rules that legitimate or delegitimate the value of cultural products. A field of cultural production is distinguished from a field of power by a defining *illusio*, a fundamental belief that all the participants must agree on. This illusio grounds the claim that the struggles inside a field of cultural production are about something other than sheer power: they are about cultural values or religious beliefs or the like. In the field of power, positions held and the consequences of those positions can take on brute force; value appears as economic capital, military power, and state authority. Within cultural production, actors struggle over positions that are defined by the actors. The stakes are high; actors can win or lose everything that matters to them. But the question of what matters is up to the actors themselves. The fundamental belief that motivates agents in the field of rock 'n' roll is that the fans of the music find their most authentic feelings to be produced by and reflected in this music. Rock 'n' roll establishes a world within which value accrues to those musicians and musical works that are believed to enact most directly and clearly those authentic feelings.[72] Traditionally, and predominantly in this music, the value of any work's articulation of those feelings was confirmed or disconfirmed by the marketplace. If a record sold, it was successful. It had, more or less by definition, articulated the values of its audience. Before 1966, if a recording did not achieve chart success, no one could claim that it had said something important about its audience; it had no other means of being considered significant.

In the second half of the 1960s, however, an alternative system of evaluation developed. Journals of popular-music criticism, including *Crawdaddy!, Fusion, Rolling Stone,* and *Creem,* were established and found engaged readers. As Bernie Gendron has shown, successful recordings by Bob Dylan, the Beatles, and the Beach Boys helped to substantiate the possibility of artistically meaningful recordings within rock 'n' roll, insofar as these recordings could be judged by aesthetic standards borrowed from other cultural fields.[73] These three sets of recording artists were in particular competition with each other, seeking to simultaneously create the most significant and the widest-selling recordings. Dylan's work was legitimated as poetry. "Like a Rolling Stone" reached number 2 on *Billboard*'s singles' chart. The Beatles and the Beach Boys were heard to be introducing elements of "serious" music into their recordings. The Beatles' three singles released in 1966 — "Nowhere Man," "Paperback Writer," and "Yellow Submarine" — hit numbers 3, 1, and 2, respectively. The Beach Boys' "Good Vibrations" went to number 1 in October of that year.

An independent set of standards that articulated the specific values at stake in rock 'n' roll — neither values borrowed from art music nor the values of the marketplace — would not be fully articulated for a number of years. According to Gendron, the terms of this aesthetic, the values specific to it, were not developed until the period between 1970 and 1972, in the work of critics such as Lester Bangs, Lenny Kaye, Greil Marcus, Dave Marsh, Greg Shaw, and Ellen Willis. As Gendron shows, these critics were not articulating the values that made acts such as the Beatles and the Beach Boys different from other rock 'n' roll acts. The critics were distilling the qualities that specified rock 'n' roll aesthetics, characteristics that they heard in relatively obscure recordings from the 1960s.[74] Chief among these recordings was *The Velvet Underground and Nico,* an album that never reached higher than number 177 on *Billboard*'s charts, with neither of the two singles released from it charting at all. The key song on the album was "Heroin," a track that could never be played on the radio. By 1971, when Bangs published his retrospective analysis of the Velvet Underground's recording career, he could draw from the values that had already been developed in a restricted field of cultural production by musicians, less systematically oriented critics, and several of his own recent essays. By detailing the influence of a recording that did not achieve chart success, Bangs was defining the parameters of a restricted field of cultural production in rock 'n' roll—a subset of popular music that was oriented toward the expectations and aesthetic tastes of other producers in the field.

In 1970 Bangs outlined the frame of the restricted field of rock 'n' roll production in a review of the Stooges' second album, *Fun House*. In his inimitable style, Bangs sketched the line of influence that led to the "monotonous and simplistic" but nonetheless "advanced" music of the Stooges. "The Stooges were the first young American group to acknowledge the influence of the Velvet Underground," Bangs asserted. The key to this influence was the fact that "for all the seeming crudity of their music," the Velvets "were interested in the possibility of noise right from the start." Bangs elaborated the significance of this combination.[75]

> Their music, which might at first hearing seem merely primitive, unmusicianly and chaotic, had at its best sharply drawn subtleties and outer sonances cutting across a stiff, simplistic beat that was sometimes ("Heroin") even lost, and many of the basic guitar lines were simple in the extreme.... I was finally beginning to grasp something. ... The most basic, classic rock . . . is almost idiotically simple, monotonous melodies over two or three chords and a four-four beat. What was suddenly becoming apparent was that there was no reason why you couldn't play truly free music to a basic backbeat.[76]

Crudity could blend with subtlety. Simple musical figures could provide the background for intricately imagined "outer sonances." Central among these fruitful combinations is the droning viola, electric and wired, constant and hollow, just beyond the reach of those basic guitar chords. In his 1971 review of the Velvets' career, Bangs describes "Heroin" as "a classic treatment that stares death in the face and comes back poetic if unresolved[,] . . . a resinous hymn building into a roar of agonized hostility as inescapable as one honed fingernail shrieking across a blackboard."[77] If the value of rock 'n' roll as a cultural production is to articulate the authentic feelings of its fans and musicians, and if the musical aesthetics that best enables this articulation combines both the most basic musical elements and a considered and audible freedom, then it should not be at all surprising that "Heroin" would become a central touchstone for the development of a restricted field of production that would value aesthetic strategies over, and even against, commercial goals. Nor should it be surprising that Bangs highlights the "resinous" quality of the song—the timbral effects of the materiality of the viola.

Bourdieu's conceptualization of the interplay of culture and power relies on the assertion that the struggle over the power to define value in a cultural field is homologically related to the struggle over power as it is materially enacted in modern societies. For all the sophistication of methodology and reflexive theorization that Bourdieu brings to bear on the complexities of cultural production and their interactions with political struggles, he eschews any specific role for aesthetics. And he is thereby forced to rely on the rather weak argument of homology to explain any connection between the struggles inside cultural fields and those outside, in the realm of power. "The field of cultural production produces its most important effects through the play of the *homologies* between the fundamental opposition which gives the field its structure and the oppositions structuring the field of power and the field of class relations," he says.[78] Homological reasoning is appealing in its ability to highlight a similarity in patterns of belief or behavior that suggest a deeper structural connection. But homologies are more suggestive than persuasive. Bourdieu's analytical thrust is so focused on the relations among cultural producers that he conceptualizes no direct link between the objects and positions struggled over in the field of production and the struggles over meaning and power experienced by the readers, listeners, consumers, and fans of those objects. *Why* would a song such as "Heroin" have lasting effects on the production of popular music? In what way might the struggles over symbolic capital in rock 'n' roll production have any effects in the world beyond popular music?

The gap left in Bourdieu's thought can be filled by a serious engagement with the aesthetics of music—in this case, of rock 'n' roll. The restricted field of rock 'n' roll production that came into fruition in the early seventies was enabled by the specific sense of beauty that "Heroin" (among other songs, but this song in particular) produced. This felt sense of the right relations among forms, the affective charge that accompanied the sense of beauty produced by bands such as the Velvet Underground and the Stooges, provided the energy capable of consolidating new positions in popular-music production. These positions formed around the feeling that the market that was organized by the music industry was no final arbiter of the value of popular music. In "Heroin" a droning viola captured the sense that something lay just out of reach, just beyond the standard I–IV chord change that grounded the song's lyrical tale of addiction and empty desperate longing. The fans of this music experienced that sense of beauty equally as the felt sense of the rightness of these formal relations: simplicity amid monotony, freedom amid tight generic constraints, beauty above all created out of the sheer intelligent manipulation of limited resources, and, finally, over and over the aching echoing understanding that the human production of value escapes every effort to coin it, every effort to concretize it. Thus, a redistribution of the sensible occurred. An awareness of the value of the outsider, of the marginal, of the displaced and the disgraced, the strangely queer who fit no previous models of success, became central to the polis of rock.

Chapter Five

The Conundrum of Authenticity
and the Limits of Rock

| | | | |

Authenticity is a fraught concept frequently used to link the musical with the extramusical. Typically authenticity labels music that is grounded in something more substantial than the vibrations from which it is shaped, so that the feelings that are articulated in and through its performance can be trusted. This is an issue because of the power of music, because of its ability to move us whether we want to be moved or not. In the face of this power, a set of judgments must be made in order for the listener to retain a critical autonomy in the face of music's affective power. If a performance is judged authentic, then the experience of being caught up in it is a good thing. Authentic music embraces us in something larger and greater, in a political bond for instance, that we can affirm. If, on the other hand, the performance seems to be a set of tricks and effects or if its embrace is more a tight squeeze that leaves no room to breathe, then the listener wants to shrug it off, escape its clutches, deny the group membership that the music strives to compel.

The political significance of the concept of authenticity arose with the spread of modern democracy. In his tracing of that development, Marshall Berman locates two opposed tendencies in Jean-Jacques Rousseau's formulation of the concept. Authenticity implies both the demand to be true to oneself and the need to ground the self in something larger. As Berman makes clear, Rousseau's struggles to purify the self of all falsehood leads to an anomie that can only be redressed by reference to a set of social norms.[1] Thus, the classic question of the authentic becomes fundamentally circular and profoundly political. To which group does my true self belong? Regina Bendix has shown how this romantic and circular concept of the authentic, with all of its contradictions, became a central analytical term used to legitimate the fledgling discipline of folklore studies in the nineteenth century.[2] Folklore's adoption of the authentic as a central trope locked the discipline into an almost necessarily essentialist conception of the relationship between culture and nation. And it restricted the realm of authentic culture to forms and practices untainted by the market, untouched by mechanical forms of reproduction, indeed distanced from and purified of modernity itself. Somehow, interaction with authentic culture would enable the true self to find the true community to which it belonged, but only if that culture pointed backward in history.

Despite these limitations on the concept, authenticity has been mobilized in discussions of popular music at least since the days of the folk revival, when representatives from the recording industry began searching for performers who could reliably produce the sounds that signaled to modern listeners a past "allegedly hale life . . . equated with agrarian conditions, or at least a simple commodity economy, far from all social consideration."[3] Having inherited the concept of authenticity from folklore studies, the promoters of the folk revival searched for styles and performers that were outside the mechanisms of the modern market society. So-called authentic folk artists such as Mississippi Fred McDowell and Lead Belly were preferred over commercially oriented performers such as the Kingston Trio and Barry McGuire, and myths sprang up to justify those judgments that ignored the drive for economic success shared by almost all these musicians.[4] These myths often originated in the desire for a premodern way of life, a longing that had previously helped to motivate the popularity of blackface minstrelsy.[5] These myths of a simpler time, when audiences personally knew their performers, when the social world seemed more stable, and when the pleasures of music seemed more deeply integrated into the palpable structures and rhythms of everyday life, crack open when exposed to scholarly examination. Not only were these past ways of life also riven by dissension, difference, and change but the relation of performer to audience was even then subject to mystification and deceit. From the only apparently willing-to-please slave fiddler to the weary opera diva, nineteenth-century entertainers had to become masterful performers of feelings that they did not share.[6] The key to successful performances in the nineteenth and twentieth centuries was the artful execution of conventions. Indeed, the invention and the successful execution of performance conventions formed the core practice of blackface minstrelsy, that immensely popular example of the centrality of musical disguise.

Nevertheless, the set of assumptions that supported judgments of authenticity and the structure of the myths that accompanied these judgments became part of the common sense of popular-music fans across a range of genres. In Karl Hagstrom Miller's important revision of early Southern popular-music history, the clash between folklore's concept of authenticity and the minstrels' straightforward assertion that their performances were indeed examples of genuine black music led to the development of a "musical color line" that resulted in the racialization of musical genres.[7] Blues and country music in particular became the sites for long and acrimonious arguments over the direct or indirect connections among musicians and communities, where the performances of musicians were judged by the degree to which their songs and styles accurately represented a dream vision of a past community or the values of a present one. As these arguments grew more sophisticated, focusing more and more on specific musical traditions to which performers could be linked, each with its own set of elaborated conventions and means of generating creativity, the question of musical authenticity became more evidently a matter of judgment for the listener, not a quality inherent in a particular performer, let alone an individual song. Authenticity became part of the aesthetic judgment, a question for each individual to determine based on the sense of right relations generated by the musical experience.[8]

Rock inherited these debates and the assumptions that undergirded them. Authentic performers were either individuals who wrote their own material or those who drew songs from the misty depths of anonymous time, who played the instruments on their recordings and would be making their music even if no recording industry existed to manufacture and distribute it in commodity form. They were artists whose music represented the true beliefs of a community whose wholeness could never be captured by a marketing strategy. But rock was wholly a commercial genre, developed by recording acts with fully energized commercial ambitions. From Bob Dylan to the Beatles to the Beach Boys and even the Velvet Underground, the musicians who invented rock could not be mythologized into pure representatives of an agrarian past or anticommercial artists. Consequently, the critical discourse that developed around rock, which served the need of describing, analyzing, and justifying the terms whereby the feelings generated by rock could be judged, developed an internal mythology designed to ferret out the real from the fake, the serious from the trivial.[9] Rock, however, was an impure musical form that grew and developed as it adapted stylistic conventions from other styles. The ability to judge rock's authenticity, then, could not be strictly musicological, based on the use of particular instruments, modes, phrase stylings, or rhythmic patterns. As Norma Coates suggests, rock authenticity developed through a process of exclusion, developing its authenticity against that which evidently was not—pop with all its feminine mass-culture associations. In an inescapable spiral of reasoning, rock's authenticity became strictly a matter of feeling and sensibility. In Keir Keightley's words, "Authenticity is not something in the music, though it is frequently experienced as such, believed to be actually audible, and taken to have a material form. Rather, authenticity is a value, a quality we ascribe to perceived relationships between music, socio-industrial practices, and listeners or audiences."[10] The search for authenticity in rock is a quest for a truthful and lasting connection between the musical and the extramusical, a desire that musical pleasure could mark the experience of our own proper connection both to the music that moves us and to the world in which we live.[11]

The territory here becomes tricky rather rapidly. The equivalence between the feeling of the real and the sense of the authentic also lies behind the drive for the sameness and purity that mark totalitarian political experiments and governments that base their legitimacy on practices of ethnic exclusion. Slavoj Žižek and Jacques Derrida find this tendency in Carl Schmitt's elaboration of the concept of the political. As Žižek and Derrida understand it, Schmitt's friend-enemy distinction pushes all significant difference beyond the boundary of the state. The state (or the sovereign) has the responsibility of making the decision as to whether or not existing agonistic struggles have achieved sufficient intensity to justify a declaration of war and to put people's lives at stake. Schmitt goes on to insist that by virtue of this power, the state has the obligation to enforce "total peace" within its boundaries: "To create tranquility, security, and order and thereby establish the normal situation is the prerequisite for legal norms to be valid."[12] Schmitt intended his concept of the political to be the means whereby merely cultural differences or purely economic competition could be systematically distinguished from the existential issues that truly mattered politically. But by attempting to specify the essence or purity of the political sifted from the dross of different values, Schmitt created a paranoid vision of the state, whose chief political task became the internally directed search for meaningful (and, therefore, dangerous) difference. By opposing "total peace" to the friend-enemy distinction, Schimtt hypostasizes the political community, suppressing difference within so that it could be more easily recognized without.

Rock's desire for authenticity, a consequence of the genre's emergence in the era of mass culture combined with its ambitions to achieve art status, can result in a drive for purity that mimics Schmitt's exclusionist concept of the political. More than a mere formal homology, rock's insistence on an exclusive grasp of the authentic generated a distribution of the sensible that marked all other genres as either meaningless mass entertainment or nonsensical noise—as insufficiently significant to matter politically. This chapter carefully looks at certain moments in the development of American punk rock, beginning with Patti Smith's ability to distill a rock essence from its history, an essence that justified its claims to being an art form built from the desire of amateurs. I then follow that development through the hardcore scene in Washington, DC, where an intensification of the concept of authenticity placed strict limits on the kinds of sounds and the kinds of people who would count as part of the community. I identify the ambivalence and insecurity that derived from the self-consciousness of indie rock and demonstrate the articulation of this ambivalence with hardcore's drive for purity in the music identified with the riot grrrl movement. In each of these examples, authenticity names a critical moment of judgment wherein the value of musical sounds connects to the extramusical and, in the process, undergirds an emerging orientation toward the world, a *sens* that identifies a polis.

PATTI SMITH'S ESSENCE OF ROCK

One night in the summer of 1970, Patti Smith and Robert Mapplethorpe followed Donald Lyons up the back stairs at Max's Kansas City to catch an early set of the Velvet Underground during its final residency at the club. This show was the band's first performance in New York City in three years, and the first opportunity that Smith ever had to see the group. After months of hanging out at Max's, the pair of young artists had only recently gained admission to the fabled back room, where those who seemed to be auditioning for entrance to the world of Andy Warhol's factory mixed with a spreading gaggle of music-industry professionals and rock press. The hierarchy in the back room was not rigid, but it was strict. A round table sat at the center of the action; admission to its seats was a crucial indicator of initial acceptance. Even though Warhol almost never attended nights at Max's after surviving Valerie Solanas's assassination attempt, behavior at this table seemed designed to court his favor. As Smith put it years later: "Screaming catfights erupted between frustrated actresses and indignant drag queens. They all seemed as if they were auditioning for a phantom, and that phantom was Andy Warhol."[13]

As was usual that summer, Warhol was not in attendance that night. Yet Smith and Mapplethorpe left the back room and made their way upstairs only because Lyons had insisted. Rock 'n' roll had not been a major attraction for many of the regulars at Max's. Factory denizen Brigid Berlin (Polk) claims that she almost never went upstairs at Max's and she was "never interested in rock 'n' roll music, ever." But at the end of the Velvet's residency that summer, she too found her way upstairs to a seat at a table with the poet Jim Carroll, where her cassette recorder captured the final performance of the Velvet Underground.[14] In her memoir, Smith describes the band's sound the night she heard them as having "a throbbing surfer beat." She heard the poetry in Lou Reed's songs and realized that they were "the best band in New York." But Berlin's recording of the final performance in that residency reveals no surfer beat anywhere. It would actually have been quite odd for Billy Yule, the young drummer who substituted for Moe Tucker that summer while she was pregnant, to have achieved anything close to a West Coast drum sound. If her memory is correct, then, what Smith must have heard was the anchoring of Reed's precisely observed lyrics in a classic garage-rock setting. In a small room that barely held one hundred people, a floor above the intense struggle for attention and the anguished effort to escape despair at the back room's round table, the Velvets ended their career playing songs that Reed no longer cared about to an audience ordering Pernod and barely paying attention. Except for Smith, whose ears exactly caught the core of the Velvets' sound. Despite the fact that no one else has ever described the Velvet Underground as having a surfer beat, Smith knew what she was hearing.

The link between the Velvet Underground and Smith is most commonly referenced through the choice of John Cale to produce her first album, *Horses*. Unquestionably, the selection of Cale was a confirmation of an already existing aesthetic connection—one based on a felt agreement between certain fundamental principles of rock 'n' roll performance and a romanticist sense of artistic significance. This convergence was the basis of the restricted field of cultural production that the Velvets helped to instantiate with their early performances and recordings, but that had only been consolidated and consecrated through the work of rock critics and other musicians in the early seventies. As Bernie Gendron has documented, between 1970 and 1972, rock accumulated the necessary identifying conventions and signs of value, all of which had been confirmed, consecrated, and reinforced by critics and other musicians, to be able to function as a restricted field of cultural production capable of producing cultural capital.[15] In the previous chapter, I quoted Lester Bangs's articulation of the aesthetic core of this field. After carefully listening to the Stooges and the Velvets, Bangs hit on the key point that "there was no reason why you couldn't play truly free music to a basic backbeat."[16] Smith's vocal improvisations were not free in so far as they were based on poems she had struggled over, in some cases for years. But her rhythmic associative shouting centered her voice against the garage roar of her band, in a role akin to that of Cale's viola, as the potentially explosive force inside rock's hard shell. While Smith's vocalese, Cale's instrumental inventiveness, and even Jimi Hendrix's guitar work (to echo another sounding source that was crucial to Smith's self-construction) were the result of hard work, the conventions of rock centered around a belief that pure unconstrained expression could arise from the midst of the mundane. The romanticism of rock valued an imagined freedom breaking out of a restrictive normality. The constraints of the context were as important as the escape; the escape was directed by the perimeters from which it fled. The musical beauty created by the Velvets required both four-chord structures and violent release. And that was what Smith heard the summer of 1970 as the band's "surfer beat" surrounding Reed's poetry.

In the early days of her career, Smith heightened and polished key aspects of this aesthetic. During the years between hanging at Max's and recording her first album, Smith developed a presence in New York and in the rock press as a rock 'n' roll poet. This label precisely indicated the juxtaposition of high and low, music and word, religion and sexuality, intelligence and passion that characterized her approach. For months she had been living with Mapplethorpe in lofts and small rooms, at the Chelsea Hotel and elsewhere, while both practiced their separate arts. He made constructions from found objects and photographs cut from magazines. She drew fantasy images and wrote verse that featured short lines and sharp rhythms. Both were experts at hanging out, finding their way into conversations with nodal figures such as Harry Smith and Bobby Neuwirth, both of whom encouraged Smith to keep writing. Her first major public reading was at St. Mark's Church on February 10, 1971. She read/chanted/sang seven pieces. During some of them, Lenny Kaye accompanied her on guitar. The final poem, "Ballad of a Bad Boy," was intoned over the background of Kaye's guitar imitating a car crash with the first outburst of amplified feedback ever to grace the church. Every biographer has noted the surprisingly high hipster level of the audience, which was particularly unusual for a poetry reading. Gerard Malanga was the featured poet and he brought with him the Factory crowd. Smith of course brought with her Mapplethorpe and other friends from the Chelsea Hotel. In addition, Smith's expertise at hanging out had brought her into contact not only with Neuwirth but also with Sam Shepard and Danny Fields, who ensured that a large contingent from the rock cognoscenti were present. The photographer Leee Black Childers remembered that Smith captured the audience that night with her pumping rhythm: "She hit you with it. And then, she hit you again and she hit you again and she hit you over and over and over, sometimes with the same phrases, and so it was like music."[17] Repetition and rhythmic propulsion were key aesthetic strategies that Smith took from rock 'n' roll and used in her first reading.[18]

The following year, Smith published her first poetry collection, *Seventh Heaven*, with Telegraph Books, as part of a series edited by Victor Bockris and Andrew Wylie. The book is filled with taut lines that evoke Christian symbolics of blood, thorns, pierced skin and resurrection, that describe religious figures in sexual ecstasy, historical women in flames, and current rock muses like Anita Pallenberg and Edie Sedgwick infatuated by their own power. The first poem in the book imagines Eve in the garden, shuddering while being licked by Satan's snake. The final poem describes longing as an instant opening in the ceiling above, into which flows a feeling of soaring and almost falling, like the fearsome freedom of the trapeze artist. In between are odes to Joan of Arc, Marianne Faithfull, and other heroines. These were poems of feminine desire and desire for the feminine. They were open and daring, bawdy and humorous, serious and sincere. They were not poetically innovative, however, in content, perspective, or formal structure. Instead, their power emerged out of a romanticism that was common in rock aesthetics. From the contrast against the everydayness of mirrors and hair and movies and records came the possibility of simultaneous salvation and death. With pumping rhythm.[19]

Although *Seventh Heaven* did not sell that well, it received more reviews than most poetry books. As Bockris explains, this happened "because of a carefully orchestrated campaign among Patti's rock writer contacts in *Creem*, *Crawdaddy*, and *Rolling Stone*."[20] From her first performance at St. Mark's Church through her solo poetry readings, the early series of performances with Kaye, and her work in a trio with Kaye and Richard Sohl, Smith was the darling of the crowd of writers who had grown up with rock 'n' roll, who were in the process of defining the emergent genre of rock and claiming art status for it. Her audiences were filled with writers and artists: poets, rock critics, playwrights, photographers, actors, drag queens, and other musicians. The writers published reviews of Smith's work, invited her to publish in their magazines and poetry series, and applauded her ability to legitimate rock by simply smashing it up against the romantic walls built by the Beats and the Symbolists. The artists spoke among themselves; some were jealous, some entertained. The musicians carefully calculated the effects of her work, deciding whether to align themselves with or against her poses. But the mere presence in the audience of this group of already consecrated creators functionally consecrated Smith's legitimation of rock, and the editors of rock magazines stumbled over themselves to publish her work. Dave Marsh ran her poetry in *Creem* early in 1971, and later that year he published a review by Tony Glover of *Seventh Heaven*. Glover began his review this way: "There's a new kind of poetry being made— a poetry that exists in equal partnership with the rhythm and sound of music, poetry that needs performing to make it real." He called Smith "one of the first poets of rock & roll" because her work combined "a literary background" with "the pulse and beat of the stereo and the street." When *Creem* published more of her poetry in February 1974, Bangs declared: "Above all Smith's poetry is rock 'n' roll splattered in a vibrating mosaic on the printed page." And Jan Uhelszki's introduction to three of Smith's poems stated flatly: "Patti, well she's got better things to do, magick to make, heroes to worship, demon rhythms to dance to." The main function of Smith's poetry for these writers was to legitimate rock and, by extension, the field, the community, to which they all belonged.[21]

In 1973 Smith and Kaye were performing a set called "Rock and Rimbaud," which overtly merged the romanticism of the Symbolists and the Beats with that of rock, carefully and intuitively adjusting the stylistic core of the performance (see figure 5.1). This adjustment featured two sets of qualities that Smith had in abundance. Her main asset combined a willingness to be vulnerable in public even as she performed with an aggressive attention to the traditions that her work referenced. Through the bold performative assertion of her self-education, she simultaneously affirmed the value of the literary world and the rock street. Her rapid stream of gestures toward writers such as Paul Verlaine, Jean Genet, Walt Whitman, Allen Ginsberg, and Arthur Rimbaud did not need to be completely accurate, nor did these gestures require any kind of academic nuance. Just naming the writers was enough for the bulk

FIG. 5.1 Rock and Rimbaud, Patti Smith, and Lenny Kaye, 1973. Collection of the author.

of her rock audience, most of whom knew nothing about these writers beyond their names. Even for those who were more than familiar with the work of these writers, however, Smith was forgiven for her mistakes. Her audience considered her errors to be a sign of her passion and evidence of her autodidactic self-construction. Slips, either of the tongue or the foot, were evidence of her intensity. If she forgot her own words, the gaffe was forgiven by the audience's desire to be legitimated along with her. During her second major reading, which took place in London, she dropped the flow of her first poem six minutes into it. Nevertheless, she had the audience completely enthralled as she muddled through.[22] Her combination of vulnerability and self-taught erudition was supported by every mention of rock musicians such as Dylan, Hendrix, Mick Jagger, Brian Jones, and Jim Morrison and of soul giants such as Smokey Robinson and James Brown. Dropping these names established a common sense that included her audience as part of the self-taught knowing collective. The affirmation of this audience concretized the shared and self-confirming belief that cultural value could be recognized immediately.

Apparently, her cultural authority was not dependent on traditional institutional legitimation. Smith was not the product of a writer's workshop. She had not attended one of the better schools. She had taught herself by going to museums and reading on her own and listening to records. Her example seemed to confirm that all it took to recognize the value of a performance or a work of art was an honest response to honest work. For an interview that first appeared in *Crawdaddy!* in 1975, Smith avowed: "I'd rather be a housewife and a *good* housewife, admired by all the other housewives in the area, than be a mediocre rock singer. The only crime in art is to do lousy art. I'm going to promote myself exactly as I am, with all my weak points and my strong ones. My weak points are that I'm self-conscious and often insecure, and my strong point is that I don't feel any shame about it."[23] Of course, this affirmation of intention and commitment to quality simply hid the operations of the field of cultural production within which Smith was developing her stance of self-generation.

This circle—whereby the audience saw and heard itself in Smith's work as Smith's work reinforced the knowledge and value of the audience—was the fundamental relationship that allowed performer and audience to legitimate each other as artist and art audience. The name given to this mutually confirming circular relationship was *authenticity*. Within the cultural field of rock, authenticity was constructed from the blend of vulnerability (which signified full presence) and artistry (which required both the knowledge of traditions and the ability to be innovative within them). A central value produced within the field, authenticity was also the link to outside the field, to the larger social world. The value of authenticity was an effect of the work performed inside the field, produced through the artful manipulation of conventions. But authenticity posed as and was received as a truth outside the field that anchored those conventions as natural, universal, and transparent. Throughout this cycle of legitimation, a regular pulse drove the circulation of affects and meanings, building an *illusio* of authenticity based on the invisibility of the conventions used to create it. Authenticity confirmed that the work and the value produced within the field could be transferred beyond its boundaries because the origin of the sensibility from which the work and its values developed lay outside the field.

In 1974 Smith and Kaye added Sohl on piano, who, in Smith's words, "possessed the simplicity of a truly confident musician who did not need to show off his knowledge."[24] With each performance of this trio, the band's self-effacing mastery combined with the assurance of her audience to add a kind of poetic form and increased artistic legitimacy to the restricted field of rock cultural production. Based on the musical principles developed by the Velvets and articulated by Bangs and others, Smith, her band, and her audience moved this field further toward both the status of art and the recognition of the self-determining value of rock. At the center of this field was Smith's performance style, which featured a kind of shamanistic overdrive that was self-referencing and self-reinforcing. As she chanted and sang, she would twirl and point, enacting the freely flung gestures of her lyrics. This approach, whereby she anchored her rapidly intoned, slightly out-of-control improvisatory flow of short lines of verse in a firm if not stable, familiar yet elusive, musical core, was a further development of the musical aesthetic she grasped in her hearing of the Velvets during their final summer at Max's. Her lyrical references erupted from her band's material ground, in much the same way that the quiver of Cale's viola or the quim of Reed's ostrich guitar had burst from the thumping stability of Tucker's beats and Sterling Morrison's strums.

But Smith shifted the rules of the game in several important ways. First, she began with overt and direct references to rock 'n' roll as an artistic form in its own right.[25] Her performances assumed and helped to produce an audience familiar with the nascent canon of rock. By emphasizing the dance rhythms that characterized the scansion of her lines, her readings evoked a sexualized embodied poetics. At the same time, her references to French Symbolist poets, American Abstract Expressionist painters, and Beat hipsters blended with her mastery of rock's symbolics to consolidate the genre's claim to art status. Her willingness to be vulnerable, to err in the pursuit of her image, and above all to make those errors function as signs of artistic seriousness was also important. If she dropped a line or skipped a verb or even missed an entrance or an exit as a result of her headlong drive through the material, those errors only marked the specificity of the moment. Similar to Jackson Pollock's thick, sticky blobs of paint, Jack Kerouac's maddeningly infinite sentences, and Rimbaud's adolescent admiration of delirium, Smith's mistakes and failures contributed to the beauty of her work as they affirmed a central emotional intensity as the work's generative core. The imaginary freedom of rock's romanticism included the freedom to make mistakes. Risks taken, even when failure was the result, confirmed the authenticity of all her gestures, however conventional they might have been. Taken together, Smith's reinforcement of rock's art status emphasized and built upon its tendency toward romanticism, suggesting that emotional authenticity was the most important value structuring the field. Lisa Robinson was not the first writer nor was she the last to confirm this when she wrote in March 1974: "What makes Patti Smith special is that when she sings these songs, somehow it rings true. And even in this age of instant and throwaway media, there have to be some things that should remain real to be appreciated."[26] Clearly, Robinson and Smith were working within the same field of cultural production. The rules of the game that they were both playing were so transparent as to approach the imperceptible.

When the members of the trio (supplemented with Tom Verlaine on guitar) entered Electric Ladyland studios early in the summer of 1974, they recorded two songs that document the aesthetic strategies at the core of the group's early performances. The track that garnered the most attention was the B side of the resulting single, which was quickly recorded at the end of the session. "Piss Factory" is a prose poem that Smith chants over a rising chord flourish from Sohl's piano and unobtrusive lead lines from the guitars. The heavily inflected words describe working life on a factory assembly line. The narrator finds life in the factory dull and stupid. The power struggle with the floor boss is inane. The atmosphere is hot and smelly, and the only possibility of any kind of meaningful existence requires that she escape the endless repetitive labor of the assembly line: "It's the monotony that's got to me. Every afternoon like the last one." While the piano keeps the relentless time of the assembly line's flow, Smith's vocal varies, her timing more in tune with human rhythms. Her tempo slows the most dramatically when she fantasizes about the acrid smell of boys in study hall. And it speeds up the most when she proclaims her desire to "get outta here, I'm gonna get on that train and go to New York City and I'm gonna be somebody. . . . I'm gonna be a big star and I will never return no never return."[27]

Smith's romanticism here is almost banal. It could be the story of any aspiring starlet who wants to make it on Broadway. It is the familiar saga of every soul who feels trapped by the machine. But "Piss Factory" is redeemed by the sheer erotic fullness of Smith's presence, which she signifies through such lyrical moments as her references to dicks drooping like lilacs and her quick juxtaposition of nuns in their habits next to "Dot Hook's midwife sweat," and above all by her delivery, that fluid sense of timing that certainly is not free but follows only its own desire. The regularity of the piss factory is not just monotonous; it is oppressive. The lockstep machinery that requires and produces repetitive labor with no variation and no way to succeed, no skills to master and no sense of satisfaction, strips any possibility of beauty from the regularity of everyday life. Against that monotony rises Smith's vocal line that ebbs and flows with its own sense of time, a time that can linger when it wants and race when it needs to.[28]

Smith's interpretation of Gino Valenti's "Hey Joe" was intended to be the A side of the single. It is based on Hendrix's version (which was itself adapted from a version by Tim Rose), taken at a slower tempo than the recordings by the Leaves or the Byrds. Smith's own take begins with her evoking what seems to be an image of Hendrix and a complex sexual relationship between the speaker of the lines and Hendrix's guitar playing. "Honey," she says with a voice of desperate aggression, "the way you play guitar makes me feel so, makes me feel so, masochistic." She emphasizes the *chis* with a stress that suggests a slight wrinkling of the nose and a small forward jut of her chin—yes, with a kiss—and then continues: "The way you go down deep in the neck. And I would do anything, I would do anything." Before spelling out what that anything might be, the narrator abruptly shifts from images of guitars, necks, and submission to an image of Patty Hearst, standing in front of the flag of the Symbionese Liberation Army with her legs spread. The metonymic power of Smith's voice connects the vague fantasy of a union between Smith and Hendrix to an explicit query asked of Hearst: "Were you getting it every night from a black revolutionary man and his women?" Then the narration shifts again, conjuring up images of Hearst's family waiting and worrying about her, only to close this section with a quote from Hearst's father: "Sixty days ago, she was such a lovely child. But now here she is, with a gun in her hand."[29]

During the first thirty seconds of the recording, up to the point where Smith describes Hearst's family at home, no instruments accompany the narration. Only at that moment do the guitars enter the soundscape, with a light *chicka* of pick across muted strings, which establish the pulse. As Smith finishes the line "with a gun in her hand," which not only quotes Hearst's father but is also (almost) a line from the song, Sohl's piano slips in with the song's chords, a five-chord cycle of fifths ending on A major that he calmly repeats for the rest of the recording's five minutes. The guitars then gradually and carefully build an architecture of pulled strings and imprecise picking that first suggests and then insists on the sort of noisy climax appropriate for a song about murdering an unfaithful lover. For most of the song, Smith follows Valenti's verses, speak-singing the words. But at the point when the narrator heads to Mexico "where I can be free," things shift again. Smith speeds up her narration, no longer singing but accelerating through a description of the freedom that Mexico offers with the rapid delivery she relies on to signal intense sincerity. At that point, the various subjects of the enunciation all merge. Patty/Patti/Joe will "go up on a hill and stand there and look at the stars as big as holes in the arms, where the sky is like a backdrop of a flag." In Mexico, on a hill, beneath the flag of rebellion, Smith narrates an imagined identification with both Joe and Hearst. This multiple subject then refuses all the restrictions that have been placed on her. She is nobody's pretty little rich girl, nobody's million-dollar baby, nobody's patsy, just free, that's all, free. And the music fades.[30]

With her version of "Hey Joe," Smith lyrically doubles the romantic image of freedom that rock's generic conventions enact. Although "Hey Joe" builds on and therefore requires the mundane everyday of the backing band, not only for contrast but also for support, the song's freedom is produced as an individualized escape from that context. As with the romanticism of the Symbolists, this freedom is utopian; its possibility is based on an escape from the emotionally restrictive constraints of everyday life. A common feature of rock-song structure is the solo, which carries the musical trace of freedom, as a harshly toned lead instrument contrasts against common triadic harmonies. In the Mexico section of her version of "Hey Joe," Smith's voice takes on the guitar's role as the solo instrument. The grit in her voice grows, and she speaks with the phrasing of a standard guitar lead, verbally imitating the common solo technique of looping back every four or five words in order to repeat that portion of the line and then extend it further up the scale or down the lyric. Smith's vocal timbre and phrasing spiral out from the background and pull together Hearst, Joe, and Smith in a dense palimpsest of splendid isolated individuality, layering verbal and musical images of rock freedom.

This set of lyrics and musical conventions also conveys the racialization of rock's romantic conception of freedom. Smith's version of "Hey Joe" merges her narrating persona with Hearst, but it also merges Hendrix with Cinque Mtume (Donald DeFreeze), the "black revolutionary man" who led the Symbionese Liberation Army. These two black men are the figures who, through their sexual prowess, enable the freedom of Patty/Patti. In building this merger, Smith was surprisingly direct, since the tendency of most rock of the period was to efface the genre's dependence on the legacy of minstrelsy in the development of its conventions. Smith's performative style was too caught up in the history of rock and its origins, however, for her to ignore the metonymic linkage of guns and guitars, freedom and blackness, violence and sexuality built

into the genre's conventions.[31] Neither could she downplay the significance of her recording in the studio that Hendrix built. But to declaim so
forthrightly the connections in the (white) rock imaginary among black
men, guitars, guns, sex, and the danger that so often accompanies freedom was significantly more daring than most rock musicians would have
ventured at the time.[32]

Perhaps surprisingly, no one mentioned this aspect of Smith's work in
print until Dave Marsh discussed her "Maileresque white negro" stylings
in a lengthy article promoting the release of Smith's first album in *Rolling Stone*'s January 1, 1976, issue. In that piece, Marsh quotes Smith directly linking blackness to primitivism and claiming art as the preserve
of whites: "[Hendrix] had to become white because it's a white tradition
to do high art and Jimi was really into poetry." She continues, "And Rimbaud was totally into black people. Rimbaud believed totally that he was
part nigger because of the Ethiopians being a totally relentless physical race."[33] Marsh quickly dismisses this aspect of Smith's persona, but
the quote is important insofar as it renders explicit the racialization of
rock's conventions of freedom and the reinforcement of that racialization through the codification of rock as art. In these words—no doubt
thrown out while she was trying to retain the attention and approval of
one of the writers central to her career—Smith repeats the classic principles of the American racial hierarchy and racial fundamentalism. Hendrix's taste for poetry is evidence of something other than black identity. Rimbaud's sexual desire for black African women suggests that he
is something other than white.

While these cannot have been beliefs that Smith would have endorsed
after reflection or under more thoughtful conditions, the quickness with
which she links together these two heroes of hers as examples of cultural
miscegenation makes it clear that the contradictions of racial identity
were central to that field where her music and her poetry merged. Although she frequently acknowledged with grateful admiration the contributions of black musicians such as Smokey Robinson, James Brown,
Stevie Wonder, and Bob Marley, whenever she spoke of art or poetry, the
references were always to white poets, artists, and musicians.[34] Despite
the fact that black musicians had established many of the musical conventions of the field, they were not legitimated as artists within it. This
contradiction contributed a fundamental racialism to the authenticity
produced in rock.

After the work of the Black Rock Coalition and critics such as Greg

Tate, Kandia Crazy Horse, and Maureen Mahon, there is nothing new about recognizing the invisible centrality of blackness to rock (or the efforts of some to correct this problem).[35] But Smith's unabashed willingness to articulate this invisible centrality in her performances clearly demonstrates the racialization of freedom that the field produced musically and the limits to the constructed authenticity on which the field depended. In this period of rock's generic consolidation, the conventions whereby rock signaled its authenticity were dependent on signaling a desire for an ever-receding blackness as the ultimate unnamable place of freedom. With the solo carrying the musical index of this freedom, always contrasted with the mundane yet solid everydayness of the rhythm section, the musical qualities of the solo instrument tended to carry timbral indicators of black musical styles, whether those timbres come from a saxophone's reeds, an electric guitar's distortion effects, or singer's raspy throat.[36] Even synthesizers, which had no "natural" timbre, were assigned a dirty tone when they began to be featured in solos.[37] Conventionally, distorted tones also functioned as a sign of emotional intensity and sincerity.[38] Describing a performance of Smith's band in the pages of the English music paper *New Musical Express* in 1978, Paul Morley declared that "the power the Patti Smith Group proclaim is: Freedom": "A battered Fender slung sensually over her shoulder, accompanied only by dirge like bass plonking from Kaye, she [Smith] coaxed and implored deathly wails and screeches from the instrument. For five, ten, 15 minutes . . . it was timeless, dreamlike. Smith crouched over her guitar, ripped the strings off, finally leant it against its amp for concluding penetrating feedback. She can't play a note. It was beautiful."[39] Rock's authenticity was built on this romantic connection between freedom and emotional sincerity signaled by antiharmonic tonal distortion. The experience of emotional intensity characteristic of the ecstatic response to the conventionally designed and artfully constructed (even if improvised and ultimately nontonal) solo was an aesthetic confirmation of rock's real. The experience of musical beauty at the core of rock's political agency relied on this set of conventional musical signs that refused its status as signs, insisting instead on its transparent naturalness. This illusio of transparent naturalness at the basis of rock's field of cultural production enabled the construction of artificial authenticities that connected the beauty experienced within the field to an abstract territory outside rock's field of cultural production, resulting in the extension of rock's racialized real to the world outside itself.[40]

Smith was creating her music in an atmosphere of intense engagement with and competition among the work of other musicians (globally: Dylan, David Bowie, post-Exile Stones; locally: Television, Reed, New York Dolls). The work of each was continually reshaping the context within which the work of the entire cohort was produced, and the response of critics and local scene makers shaped how the work was received. So how was it possible that experiences of musical beauty generated in this scene would have any effects at all outside it? One of the central problems in Pierre Bourdieu's theory of fields of cultural production is the absence of a clear connection between the values and standards of judgment that operate inside the field and those that structure the world beyond the field. I have posited that the experience of musical beauty could concretize the value produced within the field as a distillation of this shared experience. Now I want to suggest further that, in its experience of the rightness of relations, the experience of musical beauty can create what Jean-Luc Nancy terms a clining toward the sounding source and that this leaning in could effect a particular abstract experience of community. Although individual listening experiences differ, to the extent that listening results in an experience of beauty, listening involves the effort to make sense of the musical sound, which is manifested in that leaning in that Nancy talks about.[41] By leaning in we find ourselves caught in the resonance of the common, which is produced as an experience in the event of listening, not as a referent to an already preexisting substantive community. As a field, rock legitimated itself and policed itself through regular reference to its authenticity. The authenticity that rock depended on for its legitimacy was an effect of the sensible that rock's performances redistributed and an effect of the sensible that rock operated within; this sensible retained a disappearing center of blackness at its timbral core.

My purpose in reinvoking the conceptual combination of Nancy's sens and Jacques Rancière's distribution of the sensible is to insert here a short formal theoretical description of the means whereby aesthetic effects created within a restricted field of cultural production can have effects outside that field. Where Bourdieu relies on homological similarity between effects produced in culture and those in the field of power, the position I hold is that being-in-common emerges from within the constraints of a particular distribution of the sensible. Rancière's concept of the sensible—the sounds, shapes, feelings, and positions that can be comprehended as part of the shared world of political actors—describes the cultural environment that nurtures any being-in-common. Assuming that Nancy is correct, that the activity of being-in-common is a constantly evolving process of human interconnectedness, then this ongoing production of a never completed community must take place with and through a shared comprehension of the world. The aesthetic pleasure produced within a field of cultural production consolidates an orientation toward the world, a particular distribution of the sensible. This framework of comprehension sets the terms that enable agonistic political action.[42]

Let me clarify a point here. I am not claiming that the field of rock was productive of a white identity. My interest in the political force of music is not focused on identity itself, racial or otherwise. Instead, what I am claiming is that the signs of authenticity that developed in order to legitimate the productions within the field of rock and enable an aesthetic response to that work carried racialized restrictions along with them. That is, there were limits to the possible experiences of beauty that were constructed within the field. These limits were not reducible to the racial identity of the perceivers or the producers; aesthetic experience is not a simple reflection of identity. The limits were an effect of the distribution of the sensible that structured the experiences of those participating in the field. In the case of rock, exemplified by Smith's work, these aesthetic experiences provided the motivating power for its actual political force. The political force of music works by producing the sensible, which enables the experience of the common. The sens of the common constructed through the aesthetic experiences produced by rock was enabled by an almost inaudible comprehension of an always receding blackness as a sign of freedom. This sens limited the range of rock's political community. These limits did not consist of parceled out racialized identities, however. Racial identity did not determine anyone's experience of the beauty of Smith's work. The experience of musical beauty enabled by her work instead enforced a distribution of the sensible that labeled some sensual experiences as obvious common sense while rendering others inaudible. That common sense was not politically unified. It did, however, convey the terms whereby political difference could be articulated.

In order to function as a hidden sign of freedom, the blackness that was deeply encoded in rock's conventions had to be sufficiently deracinated (in the instance I have highlighted, that blackness was reduced to a particular timbral quality of a particular instrumental role—the solo) that its specificity could be almost inaudible as such while still centering the genre. This process also stripped away contextualizing factors that, in genres commonly understood as black, situated musical freedom as a response to violent restrictions. As bell hooks describes this phenomenon: "White folks who do not see black pain never really understand the complexity of black pleasure. And it is no wonder then that when they attempt to imitate the joy in living which they see as the 'essence' of soul and blackness, their cultural productions may have an air of sham and falseness that may titillate and even move white audiences yet leave many black folks cold."[43] While hooks immediately attaches racial identity to this gap between the perception of pain and the enjoyment of pleasurable freedom, I want to insist on the aesthetic disruption of that immediacy. Rock's achievement was to point toward this joy while obscuring its origins. Smith's achievement was to confront rock's listeners with that freedom and point directly at those origins not through a didactic lesson in racial politics but through a full confrontation with the conventions that racialized rock's authenticity and freedom. Political didacticism disrupts the experience of musical beauty. Rock's political force does not follow from its ability to inform its listeners about the social real.[44] Rather, this power is an effect of rock's production of musical beauty. To quote Rancière one more time: "Art is not . . . political because of the messages and sentiments it conveys concerning the state of the world. Neither is it political because of the manner in which it might choose to represent society's structures, or social groups, their conflicts or identities. It is political because of the very distance it takes with respect to these functions, because of the type of space and time that it institutes, and the manner in which it frames this time and peoples this space."[45] The musical beauty of rock works through its internally generated rules of production, which constantly undercut its stabilizing musical structures in search of a freedom that it must efface. The political force of the musical beauty of rock follows from its tendency toward the destruction of its musical conditions of possibility in combination with the way in which this self-destruction negates any immediately indexical political meaning. And yet rock always remains in a specific relation to its historical context. Rock generates an experience of the common that parcels out a commitment to freedom only for those who can sense the freedom that constantly recedes from the center of rock's productions— a freedom coded as disappearing blackness.

Smith's music also contributed to the process of transforming the rigidly masculine sensibility of rock. Legitimated as a poet and, therefore, as a serious artist, Smith was able to command a position in the field of rock that had long been denied to women singers and musicians. In their pathbreaking book *Sex Revolts*, Simon Reynolds and Joy Press include Smith in a category they term "female machisma," a kind of tomboy appropriation of masculine values and subject positions. Sharing this category with Joan Jett and Chrissie Hynde (among others), Smith is said to have begun her work with this simple assimilation into rock's assumed masculinist framework.[46] But by the time of her first full-length album, she and her band had clearly moved well beyond any tomboy mimicry. While art and poetry were coded white for Smith, she continually asserted that true art was somehow beyond gender. In an interview with Amy Gross published in *Mademoiselle* in 1975, Smith insisted: "I was always into art, and you don't have any rules and regulations in art. You don't have any morals or gender in art. . . . You can't worry about gender when you're doing Art on its Highest Level. . . . I'm working on it in popular forms, but the rules in my heart are the rules of art which are almost no rules at all, except to aspire for greatness, aspire to heavenly heights and all that stuff." As an artist, she claimed freedom from the rules (of gender and otherwise) that constrained mere entertainers: "The difference between me and entertainers, say like Helen Reddy, is that maybe they wanted to be entertainers their whole lives and so they fit what they did into the rules and regulations of the entertainment business."[47] Of course, despite her claims to be escaping gender, Smith simply repeats here the gendered ground of the distinction between rock and pop. Reddy is an entertainer who must abide by the rules of pop. Only those greater than entertainers—typically in Smith's world, men—can afford not to worry about gender. Even as she denies the relevance of gender to her desire for artistic greatness, she accedes to the already gendered distinction that distinguishes her chosen field from mere entertainment.[48]

This interview shows Smith at her best, when her self-conscious yet freely flowing words reveal the conditions that generated her contradictions. After confirming her difference from entertainers such as Reddy, who was topping the charts with her anthem "I Am Woman," Smith then precisely details the constructed quality of gender categories. In so doing, she affirms the gendered distinction between rock and pop even as she demonstrates its careful construction:

I'm still a tomboy, old as I am. When I was writing my *Seventh Heaven* book, which has a lot about women and seducing girls, I was in my early twenties and going through this big crisis that I had to learn how to become a girl. Then I was a total boy. I was walking around like "Don't Look Back," I was part Bob Dylan, part Keith Richards, and I figured, fuck guys, I got to learn how to be a girl. So I went totally overboard. I started buying dresses and gold bracelets and going to watch Jeanne Moreau moving over and over and over again. Watching the way she walked, trying to walk in high heels, buying silk stockings, garter belts, sitting around completely self-conscious with all this stuff, trying to figure out how to mingle a garter belt with a Rolling Stone hairdo. I was trying to find out what all this girl stuff meant. I *still* don't know how to put on makeup. I *still* don't know how to walk in shoes higher than sneakers. When all my girlfriends were learning how to pull girl tricks, how to be a girl, I was like "Ah, girls are stupid, girls are dumb." All I cared about was art and being pals with the guys, being tough.[49]

By this point, her evident alertness to the performativity of gender was shaping her work. Rock may be gendered masculine, but that was an effect of its codes, and those codes could be mastered (ahem) by anyone. (See figure 5.2.) As Reynolds and Press point out, female machisma was a strategy shared by multiple female musicians. It worked insofar as one fully embraced rock's conventions and by so doing achieved the (artificially) transparent authenticity that the form's aesthetics demanded. Although Smith did not produce anthemic declarations of feminine power, her music was also not a simple repeat of the traditional and conventionally transparent signs of masculine authenticity. With their first album, the Patti Smith Group used her legitimacy as a poet to twist the conventions of rock by exposing their status as conventions. Fully exploiting her artistic legitimacy, she was able to draw the initial attention of her listeners to her lyrics while using the rhythmic and timbral contrast between her vocal quality and the hyperconventional if roughly delivered backing track created by her band to foreground the constructed qualities of rock's masculinity. In so doing, her work was able to transform the sensible.

FIG. 5.2 Patti Smith, gripping the mic stand, Los Angeles, 1976. Photo courtesy of Michael Ochs Archives/Getty Images.

Horses was hailed at its release as "some kind of definitive essay on the dark night of the American mind," and "an affirmation of life so total that, even in the graphic recognition of death, it sweeps your breath away."[50] But it was also dismissed as "a celebration of the cult of incompetence in rock music," and music "for those who like the idea of rock 'n' roll rather than its perfect execution."[51] Writing for *Crawdaddy*, Susan Shapiro referred to Smith as "an omnisexual high priestess careening freely between the genders, elevating rock 'n' roll into incantation."[52] Charles Shaar Murray remarked in the pages of the *New Musical Express*: "Every woman I played it [*Horses*] to dug it unconditionally. Men tended to get polarized."[53] Greil Marcus framed his review of the album for the *Village Voice* in the context of "the Janis Joplin question," asking whether or not Smith's efforts to record the style she had perfected in performance would result in artificial stylization. He concluded that she had made "an authentic record . . . that captures Smith whole," with the band's sound "much stronger and more pointed." But Marcus also worried that the clarity of this record could expose too fully the concepts behind her work, turning them into a "*schtick*."[54] Twenty years later, Reynolds and Press claimed that the album successfully created a "nonphallic rock, organized around endless crescendos."[55] And in 2008 the literary critic Philip Shaw could simply and directly state: "*Horses* . . . is the greatest rock album of all time: end of story."[56]

How did the Patti Smith Group achieve this level of canonization while challenging the masculinist grounding of the genre's conventions? How could the group have created something called nonphallic rock? What were the musical elements that enabled their first recording to remain recognizably within the genre yet to produce a sensibility recognizably different from what had come before? The transformation starts with the first track. Smith's version of "Gloria" has been analyzed many times.[57] Shaw's discussion of it is nearly definitive, detailing the means whereby the song shows "how desire can lead toward the adoption of unexpected, and often unsettling, identities and attitudes."[58] Shaw's discussion focuses on her lyrical strategies—in particular, the beginning section of the song, which derives from Smith's poem "Oath"—and is also strong on Smith's vocal inflections, her use of portamento (sliding from one note to the next), and the almost careful use of random cracks in her voice. But his discussion leaves out the interaction between her voice and the band. And that is where I want to focus my analysis.

Smith's voice leads the listener through and around the orthodox sounds produced by the band, calling an unconscious attention to the play of these conventions as they are reproduced and transformed.

Written by Van Morrison and first recorded by his band, Them, as a B side, "Gloria" had already become a garage-band classic, with cover versions by Gant and Shadows of Knight receiving regional radio recognition before Smith began to perform the song. Its three chords, cycling endlessly, set up a tonal center that feels ultimately irrelevant, freeing the vocal line from extended melodic demands and allowing the singer to foreground its percussive potential. The power of the original song fully derives from the interplay of Morrison's vocals and the rhythm section. Morrison drives the chorus, growling the letters — G-L-O-R-I-A — while almost swallowing the notes as he pushes and pulls around the heartbeat defined by Bobby Graham's drumming. The drummer's precision contrasts with the splashing rhythm guitar, which, in classic garage-rock fashion, strums down on the beat and up somewhere in the middle — in a different middle each time. The tension in the song, the way it musically signifies lust, comes from Morrison's insistent refusal to line up rhythmically with Graham's heartbeat.[59] Smith learned this lesson well. It is probably the source of the much-discussed rhythm in her poetry. The tension between vocal rhythms and the rhythms of the band lies deep in the roots of the garage tradition. This musical strategy builds upon the groundedness, the simple obviousness, of the beat. Firm and obstinate, this core beat is the opposite of supple. But its stubborn absence of will makes possible a kind of fluidity on the part of the other sounding rhythms. At its most sophisticated, this rhythmic strategy could support a furious sonic assault, like that of the Chicago electric blues masters. But the strategy could also produce an endless redundancy, the fierce unthinking discipline of the assaultive snare. American garage rock, the sounds of the Count Five, the Shadows of Knight, the Standells, and the like, walked the line back and forth between these two extremes, always maintaining its commitment to the beat's capacity to ground any musical deviation.[60]

The Patti Smith Group's approach to the beat in "Gloria" combines the arrogant assertiveness of garage rock with a more encompassing comprehension of alternative rhythmic possibilities, as the heaviness of the garage beat anchors the band's otherwise floating sonorities. They begin their version of "Gloria" with piano and bass only, which softens the opening, quietly coaxing the initial chords out from the piano's keys while the bass passes back and forth between E and D. The guitar enters, barely audible, reinforcing the E–D–C♯ decline of the piano with only a slight bend of the strings destabilizing the pitch. After a few passes around the chords, Smith enters with her most famous line, "Jesus died for somebody's sins but not mine," a line that has distracted almost all her listeners away from the surrounding music. The band continues its quiet support until she reaches the end of the first stanza: "My sins my own, they belong to me." The first full chord from the rhythm guitar lands on that *me*. Slowly the song builds with each instrument carving out a slightly different approach to the central grounding beat. Over the next minute the guitars splash more and more, spreading the core beat across a larger space, with the drums moving from the high hat and kick to include a double smack on the snare. More important, Smith's vocals swoop ahead and fall back, with an approach to time that normally requires a career's worth of achievement and confidence before a singer attempts it. But Smith sounds as if she could not care less whether or not anyone thinks she has earned the right to sing the way she wants. When she looks out the window to see the "sweet young thing, leanin' on the parking meter," she pounds right on the beat. Nothing fancy, nothing subtle. But then she speeds up, with the band following her, all racing to the point where the song fully shifts into the chorus. Here guitars dissolve into strummed multiplicity, each played with a different attack and individual tonal accent, saturating the track with ringing strings. The piano shouts out to Jerry Lee Lewis and then hides again in its supporting role. Smith's shrieks and calls display the entire range of approaches to time that the song can handle. Without chanting, her voice becomes as drumlike as her straight-line melody allows. She sneaks up on the band and then runs away. The band shrugs and chases her, never quite catching up but also not needing to. The song becomes a playground for experiments in the temporality of performance, producing a rhythmic freedom that can be heard right there in the track. This freedom is not a feeling forever disappearing into the distance. The only solo instrument is Smith's voice, her rasp as centering as the snare drum, with none of its stability.

"Land," a triptych of moods and flows that incorporates classic soul lyrics amid a metonymic ordering of horses, waves, drugs, knives, and death, provides the ultimate example of Smith's strategy. Here too the guitars multiply, the drums inflate, and the vocals insert themselves into the crevices between the multitracked instruments, filling up the sonic space with the paradoxical sharp-edged liquidity of her rasp. This recording is most famous for the double tracking of Smith's voice in the middle third of the song where she improvises two different pathways through the breakdown. In this section, Smith's twin voices splash into and around each other, enacting the seas of possibility that she references lyrically. Using her much-loved technique of manipulating the speed of her lines to signal changes in intensity, her two vocal lines stretch and contract as though they are waves being pulled toward the same beach, sometimes crossing over and cancelling each other out, sometimes fully adding to the other's strength. The undercurrent of the band's slowly developing explosion spreads beneath her, contrasting with her modulated ebb and flow. Near the final third of the song, Smith's voice approaches gale force. She seems to care no longer where her voice lands. It hits off this beat and careens around that one while the guitars flail at chords and the piano purely rains down its part. Refusing to be left behind, demanding through their efforts a respect they only just earn, the instruments splash over and around her voices, pushing the impossible drive of the tune as it roils and tumbles toward its end. During the final minute, the song empties out. Guitars drop away; the piano finalizes a dischord; a bass note quiets and stops. In the end, only one of her voices remains, "dancing around to a simple rock 'n' roll song," followed by the drum, the reliable centering drum that echoes into the short fadeout.

Listen to it. That rise and fall, that set of waves crashing, that penetrably full sound. That is what Reynolds and Press meant when they said the piece is "truly like ocean[,] . . . awesomely ambitious."[61] By rendering sonorous so many of the slices between beats, the garage rock of the Patti Smith Group paradoxically opened the conventional centering quality of the beat. In their best work, the crashing of cymbals and frantic strumming of guitar strings rise and fall, splashing the rocks on which they land and leaving behind just a hint of wetness when they recede. This opening of the beat, where precision was not the object but rather a means to greater suggestiveness, had a double effect that bridged the inside and outside of rock's field of cultural production. This was not the precise manipulation of cross-rhythms that characterized the music of Stevie Wonder or the Band or any number of guitar-based soul acts. Anchored in the simplicity of garage rock, this burst of sound revealed the complexity of the beat's drive. The repetition of the beat is never complete. As it varies, it creates possibility. Experienced as beautiful within the field, the splashing rhythms crashing against each other simultaneously reached outside the field as they insisted that anyone could play this music. The artist merged with the amateur through an investment in this beauty that was both carefully felt and apparently free from musical effort.

For both the Patti Smith Group and for Reynolds and Press, the rise and fall of multiple crescendos in "Land," "Gloria," and other songs defined the nonphallic nature of the band's approach.[62] These multiple climaxes certainly marked a significant difference from the bulk of the group's progenitors in garage rock (an important exception of course being the Velvet Underground). But the Patti Smith Group's multiple moments of coordinated tension and release were only one aspect of its larger musical strategy of using concentrated bursts and dispersed tones as a means of creating multiple pathways into the distributed fullness of its sound. Simultaneously full and open, solid and permeable, the sound of the Patti Smith Group created a musical beauty that opened the thrust of rock and produced a sens of the common that held giving and taking as equal partners. The object exchanged in these performances is the gift of the amateur, the one who loves. But producing the gift demands discipline and care; amateurism does not mean sloppiness. Amateurism's love and care must be recognizable as a valuable gift. The care that amateurism takes to produce these sounds is directed toward the concept, drawing attention to the sounding sens that is generated by the openness of the vibrating tissues. And the gift itself is the recognition of the mutuality of desire in the sensing of the common, the shared longing on the part of all who belong.

AFTER *HORSES*

Through this convergence of the artist and the amateur, Smith's *Horses* established the basis for the next decade's reflexive refinement of rock. The album made clear the conventional duality of rock's artistic democracy: the necessary balance of the artist's concept and the amateur's drive. The amateur's unending love for his or her form blended with the artist's clarity of perception, and the form from then on required from its practitioners an equal awareness of these conventions — but this was an awareness that did not eviscerate the drive for a musical beauty now historically grounded. The sounds that had previously seemed natural, inevitable, simply the way that good music was supposed to sound, became specific musical characteristics, particular ways of organizing strums, beats, and vocal lines. This gave way, eventually, to a much wider range of sounds. By mining so deeply the core of rock's legitimacy, Smith was able to turn it inside out, able to force the sounds to function differently. Crashing through some of the differences between beat and nonbeat, redistributing the force of the sound, and creating more openings for different kinds of approaches and different ways into the music, *Horses* functionally filled in the formal transparency of rock. Its critique of masculinism, its nonphallic rock, was a consequence of the band's revelation of rock's conventions. Smith showed that the classic tension and release of rock could be manipulated like any other aspect of its sound. Marcus might have been correct when he worried that the clarity of Smith's concept would lead too quickly to shtick. But her direct confrontation with the generic conventions of the form created the conditions where any succeeding act had, out of necessity, to stake a position vis-à-vis those conventions.

If anything, the form itself was revealed as shtick. Any succeeding act that wanted to be taken seriously within the rock's restricted field of production had to build its sound through a reflexive conversation with those conventions. Examples are many. The Ramones purified the form with a rigor unmatched by any of their contemporaries. The Clash refocused rock's obscured blackness via rhythms abstracted from England's former colonies. Black Flag drew musical power from their ability to link a perverse work ethic with the frustrated desire of the white male laboring body and thereby consolidated and unleashed the form's libertarian anger. Fugazi balanced that anger with a reflexive discipline, refusing to allow their labor to be fully cashed in. Beat Happening created perhaps the most perverse rock beauty of all, channeling their love of the form's possibilities through the authentic performance of imperfection. Each of these bands balanced the clarity of its concepts with gestures that confirmed its amateur standing. But in so doing, the bands delinked authenticity from the musical sounds that had been the basis of rock's transparent musical conventions. Instead, they deliberately explored and exploded those conventions, thereby helping to create the subsequent proliferation of subgenres from hardcore to twee pop in what has been called the era of indie.[63]

While authenticity remained an absolutely necessary value throughout the moment of punk and the following rise of indie, its disarticulation from particular sounds meant that authenticity, like beauty, was clearly revealed as a judgment. Authenticity could no longer be automatically deduced from any individual set of parameters—musical or social. It continued to involve the musical balancing of artistry and amateurism, and it continued to be a means of connecting the value of the music to the extramusical world. But after the revelation of rock's fully conventional construction, the judgment of authenticity could also include a consideration of image, relations with the music industry, even extramusical claims of political or cultural significance. The older form of authenticity did continue to function for some listeners, who relied on the assumption that the earnest enactment of rock's conventions indicated a sincere belief in and commitment to its performance of mastery and freedom. Artists who continued to work this arena—musicians such as Bruce Springsteen, John Mellencamp, Melissa Etheridge, and Toby Keith—could create anthems that reinforced an already existing political unity and the claims of groups within it. These artists could work well within the distribution of the sensible that was currently in force. But their music could not change the shape of the political or create a new awareness of the common. In contrast, the new authenticity that grew out of punk and developed through the rise of indie created its audience and produced its connection outside the restricted field of rock through the production of a new sensibility.

The sensibility inaugurated by Smith and elaborated by what came to be called punk rock drove a belief in open-ended possibility through a narrow channel of musical form. This contrast between the insistence of belief and the constraints of form demanded a creative intelligence to avoid the simple redundant reenactment of its limitations. The contrast promoted the possibility of creative living within brutal conditions as it opened content and forms previously considered unmarketable to the fungible powers of the drive for distinction. With creative destruction and insistent self-determination as core values, punk promised something very similar to the neoliberal belief in individualist freedom and entrepreneurial possibility, where the meritorious would be the victors. Although it may be surprising to think of it in this way, DIY was wholly in line with neoliberal assumptions. An outgrowth of the (somewhat false) assertion that anyone could play the music, DIY insisted that anyone could become a record producer, label owner, booking agent, critic, or publisher. This belief was a source of tremendous productive freedom within punk. It granted permission to anyone to take on the tasks that turned musical desire into sellable commodities and experiences. In itself, this permission released enough generative energy to construct multiple interlocking networks of those initially enmeshed by the sound. The sound itself generated a forceful drive for self-determination that was channeled into and through those networks. While many of punk's practitioners voiced an anticapitalist, or at least an anticorporate, rhetoric, the material base of the form did not escape the discipline of the market, for market relations shaped the exchanges that constituted the networks. Particularly in its most purified form of hardcore, punk's revision of rock paradoxically sang of the destruction of capitalist production while musically performing a set of strategies for survival in a neoliberal world. Let's be clear: hardcore's dream was to use the market in small ways to promote values that contradicted capitalist operations. In some ways, hardcore punk figured the last gasp of egalitarianism— but this figure danced against a background of unrelenting corporate-dominated market discipline. In effect, the mosh pit enacted the clining common of a fiercely reduced possibility. Part of the contradiction of hardcore was this ability to generate a sens of a common where the value of each individual exceeded that of the group. Hardcore achieved this contradiction musically.

THE SENS OF HARDCORE

The first sound you hear is a nicely distorted, fiercely strummed asymmetrical chord change hacked from the overdriven electronics of Dr. Know's guitar. When Earl Hudson kicks in with the drums, the inside-out harmony is pinned down: rolling snares and pumping kick drums mark the bar lines even as the crash cymbal liquefies them. The full change, three slashes at a D major, half a beat on E, then a full beat on the tonic A, takes an entire second to race through. Ten seconds into the track, H.R. (Human Rights) addresses the lyrics, according them the respect they demand, squeezing thirty-two syllables into four seconds of "throat." It is almost incidental that the lyrics spell out the general condition of neoliberal existence: "I came to know with now dismay / That in this world we all must pay / Pay to write, pay to play / Pay to cum, pay to fight." Based on the philosophy of "positive mental attitude" promulgated by the Depression-era businessman Napoleon Hill, the song's words shout a drive for success that is sensed first through the sound.[64] A second verse is followed by a bridge where the final syllables—time, mind, find, hind—are heavily reverbed, echoing the Jamaican dub tradition. This simple production technique is the most prominent sonic indicator on this song of Bad Brains' blackness, which simultaneously distinguished it from any other major hardcore band because this blackness lent fuel to the members' drive to overcome.[65]

Bad Brains initially formed in 1977 in DC as a jazz-fusion group called Mind Power. With musical skills originally oriented toward the twisting harmonic and rhythmic complexities of bands like Return to Forever, Bad Brains retrieved two important skills that had been banished from punk's reflexive reduction of rock's conventions. Performing with the precision of many of the British bands that had inspired Bad Brains, but with tempos at nearly twice the beats per minute, the group restored a meaningful virtuosity to the music. By 1980 they were smoothly integrating reggae elements into their sets. Hudson, the drummer, could shift from the rapid paradiddles that drove most punk to the offbeat bumps of sophisticated reggae, reintroducing a range of approaches to the beat. Dr. Know, the lead guitarist, was never afraid to demonstrate his mastery of the guitar. He could go down deep in the neck whenever the mood struck, thereby retrieving the guitar solo from punk's slag heap. For those with ears so attuned, the rhythmic precision and riffing inventiveness of these instrumentalists set the group apart from most punk speed merchants. For those not paying attention, the effects could be even stronger.

When Hudson hits the crash in "Pay to Cum," as he does every measure, that splashing spray provides the intentional opening of sound that signals the garage-rock tradition. But this openness is quickly countered by the every-other-beat attack he draws from the kick drum and the precise timekeeping of his rolling snare. Invited in by the splash, the not-quite-attending fan is confronted with the insistent discipline of time. "Banned in DC," another track from Bad Brains' first album, demonstrates their ability to shift time, and the song also functions as a showcase for Dr. Know's condensation of the lead guitar role. H.R.'s "throat," the credit he received on the first album, spits words faster than the ear can parse while sustaining a sense of tune and tone. Daryl Jenifer, the bassist, anchors the core beats while looping harmonic suggestions, at a speed that only drew repetitive eighth notes from almost every other punk bass player. The instrumental skill of each musician in Bad Brains contrasted an open invitation to all listeners with an insistent reminder of the extra demand extracted from the socially disadvantaged in a market-driven world: To be good is not enough. Bad Brains were excellent (see figure 5.3).

Their combination of invitation and rigor gathered many followers, among them many of the leading figures of the DC hardcore scene. Ian MacKaye and Jeff Nelson, members of Minor Threat and founders of the independent record label Dischord Records, were astounded by the musicianship of Bad Brains. MacKaye, who first saw Bad Brains while a member of Teen Idles, said their playing "was like another world." Nelson

FIG. 5.3 H.R. and Daryl Jenifer of Bad Brains perform, New York, 1980. Photo © Glen E. Friedman.

testified to their significance: "Bad Brains influenced us incredibly with their speed and frenzied delivery." Henry Garfield, who sang with the DC band SOA and later joined Black Flag as the singer Henry Rollins asserted: "I have never seen anything like 1979–1980 Bad Brains, before or since. You thought they were going to detonate right before your eyes."[66] From 1977 until 1981, Bad Brains were the prime example of the emergent hardcore infatuation with disciplined power.

Their impact on the DC hardcore scene was felt first through their music, which produced and promulgated the sensibility of rigorous intensity that became the signature characteristic of this scene. Bad Brains continued to perform this white-coded music in a very white scene while insisting that this performance choice in no way diminished their racial identity. This insistence required an intense commitment to the demands of the form in the face of multiple forces arranged against their choice. There was no way to escape the fact that these were black musicians playing white-boy punk rock better than any other band at the time. Some of their shows drew the white-supremacy fringe elements of hardcore who were attracted by the music's anger and dumbfounded by Bad Brains' musicianship. According to Jenifer, "Some people just couldn't handle black folks playing rock music." Yet other nights, Bad

Brains could musically transform an audience. Jello Biafra described a performance in San Francisco: "[It was] one of the best shows I've ever seen any band play. . . . They seemed to have the effect of easing a lot of the tension that had been building up in San Francisco. There was a serious racist thug element starting to grow in the scene and some of that really dissipated after the Bad Brains. . . . They had an incredible force to unite so many people."[67]

Yet the band was divided about the proper means to address the race issue. Despite Bad Brains' growing reputation around their city, they could not draw a significant black audience to their shows; the hardcore scene in DC remained overwhelmingly white. As part of an effort to give back to the local black community, they played free shows at housing projects and public parks, where their music was met with bemusement. One possible solution, heavily promoted by H.R., would have been to perform more reggae in an effort to attract a more racially diverse crowd. But that would have meant giving up the band's musical identity, a move the other musicians were reluctant to take. The dominant racial division of musical taste was beyond their ability to transform. Consequently, the Brains' presentation of racial difference remained a disturbance in the distribution of the sensible generated by their music. The intensity produced by that disturbance was central to the legacy of the band; it was the crucial gift that Bad Brains offered to the hardcore scene. That intensity sliced through the traditional concept of authenticity so central to rock. Despite the ferocity of their performances and the skill with which they executed their music—traditionally heard as evidence of authenticity in rock and soul—Bad Brains could not claim to musically represent the black community of DC. Through their performances, therefore, Bad Brains stripped the concept of authenticity of one of its key elements—the belief in a set of links whereby the sounds produced by a particular group of musicians could be said to directly represent the beliefs and values of an identity group to which the musicians belonged. If the music of Bad Brains suggested an ethos, a sensibility, then this ethos could not be judged by virtue of its ability to represent a particular ethnos. The awareness, the sensibility distributed in and through the experience of musical beauty generated by Bad Brains, could not be reduced to an already existing understanding of the world shared by a community outside the field of musical production. Bad Brains had generated something new: a new common, a redistribution of the sensible.

Minor Threat was among the first of the DC bands to adopt the rigorous demands of this musical style and affective sensibility.[68] The source of the style's intensity was evident to those who shared it. As MacKaye put it: "At that time, just being a punk meant you were a magnet for getting shit. . . . You saw how people acted. You kind of understood what it was like to be a black in America, to be just judged by the way you looked. It made us more determined to do what we wanted, to look just the way we wanted."[69] Of course the members of Minor Threat were not black. Neither was the bulk of their audience. White punks were choosing to look the way they did, and they could change their minds when they wanted. Nevertheless, this choice was meaningful. It was an option chosen by some of those who felt outside the normative strictures of everyday American life, those who felt the rightness of the intensity constructed by the contrast between the overwhelming rush of sound and rigorous precision of time. To feel that this contrast constituted the grounds of beautiful relations was not to applaud those restrictive norms. It was simply to recognize the fit between the intensity of feeling generated by that musical contrast and the sens of the world outside the hardcore club. Once again, blackness became a symbolic resource— this time hidden within rock's descendant, hardcore punk. In contrast to rock's construction of blackness as ever-receding freedom, hardcore used blackness to convey the aggressive, nagging rush of insistent surveillance, the feeling of always being watched and judged, and distributed this sense to a different population. In the process of this redistribution, authenticity again became an effect of performance: the ability to generate through feelings of musical intensity a sense of the common that felt right.

Minor Threat's ability to generate that sense can be heard most clearly in three very short songs: "Straight Edge," "Out of Step (With the World)," and "Guilty of Being White." "Straight Edge" gave a name to the orientation toward the world promulgated by many of the band's fans. The lyrics, nearly inaudible during any performance and requiring a lyric sheet to be understood, simply label anyone who takes speed or 'ludes or glue the "living dead." The stripped-down sound of the song, which is a full forty-five seconds long, relies on the interaction between guitar and drum kit to construct its propulsion. Rapid eighth notes on the high hat with quarters on the snare center this version of punk's accelerated polka beat, while the guitar's bursts spread open the spaces between. Prying an entryway into this tightly packed sound, the singer, MacKaye, shouts a pledge to sobriety, to maintaining the competitive advantage of a clear head. "Out of Step (With the World)" directly links bodily purity—"don't smoke, don't drink, don't fuck"—to the need to "keep up" with the world. Faster than "Straight Edge," "Out of Step" dares the guitar to keep up with the drums, a task it fails to accomplish, remaining just behind the ever-so-slightly accelerating beat throughout the song. The vocal separates itself from this singular drive for the song's end, refusing that discipline, constructing its scraped edge from what seems an independent source. Still fast, still racing, but not afraid to be half a step behind, the vocal becomes more audible than it is in most Minor Threat songs. Almost pedantic, the song proclaims that there is no time at all for intoxication; there is no value in sexual pleasure abstracted from social relations. The punk, confronted by a world of intensity, must keep the competitive edge provided by sobriety, even if it means being out of step. "Guilty of Being White" adds one more crucial element to Minor Threat's philosophy: a conflicted awareness of the competitive advantage of whiteness. The singer proclaims his personal innocence even in the face of the historic crimes that created white privilege.

Although the lyrics of these songs may seem to announce an anthemic political unity, forged from an awareness of racial privilege and a recognition of the harsh competitive struggle of everyday life, the hardcore audience was in fact divided about the lyrical meaning of these songs. Within Minor Threat itself there was disagreement over the value of straight-edge living. "Guilty of Being White" was frequently understood by listeners to be a charge of reverse racism. The commons constructed by these songs was not a political unity of like-minded persons. Instead, the commons produced an experience of community without unity, generated through the sound of these songs. This sonic commons was constructed amid a saturated sound space opened up by sharp contrasts between beat and nonbeat, enforced through sudden rhythmic stops, and marked by vocal howls at key moments—in the case of Minor Threat, often at the end of songs—with each instrument contributing its individual musical element almost independently from the others. With their intense fury, their refusal of authority and their adamant individualism, Minor Threat found the difference of their repetition directly embracing conflicting positions among their listeners. With these three songs—each driven by a condensed and intensified reduction of Bad Brains' complexity—Minor Threat performed an authenticity that produced its immediate audience as its referent, not as a political unity but as polis with members who were aware of *being with* those with whom they differed. As Minor Threat's audience slammed in circles, arms swinging and faces pulled inward, hardcore distilled the recognition of itself as divided, agonistic.

The most serious experience of the hardcore real took place in the pit in front of the stage, where dancers reinforced the feel generated by the music. Despite its reputation as a display of unmitigated violence, slamdancing—bodies bent over low, moving in a circle with right arms swinging—incorporated its own ethic of cooperation and mutual care into its ritual of aggression. The circle of dancers typically moved in one direction, counterclockwise, and when one person fell, other dancers stopped to pick him (they were almost exclusively men) up. The violence generated inside the pit was real; fistfights broke out; blood did flow; occasionally bones were broken. But the typical pit was no more violent than line play during a hard-fought high school football game. Of greater importance to the participants than the bruises and cuts was the sense that the violence of the pit was generated by and policed by their own community.[70] The unifying sens of the political produced by hardcore consisted of an intensity of feeling, generated by rhythmic intensity, volume, and speed, reinforced by the physical activity of circling before the stage, bruising into others, falling and being picked up, shouting the key lines in song lyrics that reinforced the temporarily autonomous nature of the club. While the pit generated the greatest intensity of feeling, the physical experience of the real produced in the pit spread throughout the club.[71]

Physically enacted by this swarm of slamming bodies circulating in front of and occasionally on the stage, hardcore's intensity marked the affective charge of an orientation toward the world that derived from the ability to recognize and respond to musical precision (particularly idiosyncratic rhythmic precision) performed at tempos exceeding 160 beats per minute. Hardcore's political force derived from the experience of this intensity as a proper and right set of relations, as beautiful. This experience of musical beauty created a commons based on the felt irritation of constant aggressive contact. The physical contact of the slamdance materialized the awareness of aggressive contact outside the club: constant surveillance, constant judgment, constant demands for submitting to authorities of dubious legitimacy. In his openhearted plea for "revolution without illusion," Mark Andersen, one of the founders of the activist organizations Positive Force DC and We Are Family DC, testifies to the divided commons of the hardcore version of punk. Hardcore consisted of a demand for authenticity "being real [and] . . . unmasking society's illusions and lies," and it was "a kind of misfits club" that saw the world from "the underside of life and history." But hardcore simultaneously declared that the social was built on falsehood as the genre adopted the framework of this artificiality to construct its felt community of opposition.[72] Hardcore insisted that social authority was anti-foundational and arbitrary. Built on illusions and lies, institutionalized power could only be artificial and illegitimate. The commons that hardcore built in opposition to this outside authority was forged from an individualist sense of the authentic, an insistence on independent judgment and self-determination as ends in themselves.

Two opposing conclusions could be and were drawn from this confluence of imperatives. As Andersen points out, hardcore's intense "me-centric" view often turned into a "politics of self-affirmation," where the sense of the common gained strength from a feeling of superiority to the external world. Only inside the punk club could like-minded people be found; only there could the real be experienced; only there could that experience be trusted. On the other hand, the insistence that the world outside hardcore was built on lies and illusions necessarily implied the possibility of change and, perhaps, the obligation to attempt that change. As Andersen puts it: "The punk scene can and does function as a 'free space,' a 'temporary autonomous zone' . . . in which the control of society is weakened enough . . . to allow for seeds to be planted, to germinate, and begin to grow, even blossom."[73] Hardcore drew in its listeners, performed its clining toward community, through a musical sound that, because of its sheer sonic intensity, enacted the refusal of external authority. Inside the scene, each individual judgment of authenticity that reinforced this refusal rested solely on the feeling of the real generated by the experience of musical beauty and the rightness of relations condensed by that experience. Externally, hardcore's refusal of legitimate authority reinforced a libertarian resistance to any widely shared commons.

Among those inspired and intrigued by Minor Threat and the early hardcore days in DC was Calvin Johnson, a high school senior from Olympia, Washington, whose family had recently moved to the DC area. Johnson saw the value of the community that had emerged around these bands, but he was critical of the aggressive masculinity that characterized the scene. "Some people are just using the music as an excuse to wear leather and hit people," he said.[74] Indeed, the level of violence in the scene had begun to bother many long-time participants, including Mac-Kaye. After Minor Threat broke up, MacKaye found himself at a show standing next to H.R. and wondering how the scene had become so ugly. As MacKaye remembered the conversation years later, H.R. turned to him and said, "You want to know who did this? You did."[75] While the

comment took him aback, MacKaye had to admit his complicity in creating a scene where the ultimate value of personal authenticity was displayed through the aggressive insistence on the individual's right to be
where he (advisedly) wanted to be, doing what he wanted to do. In an
interview recorded for the documentary *American Hardcore*, MacKaye
remembered the final punch he threw at a punk show: "The violence was
so stupid and I saw my own role in the stupidity. In 1984, I remember
it was a Minuteman show, it was the last time I punched anybody. A
guy hit my brother and I punched him and I thought, that's the end of
that. I'm done. I felt like the violence had become too central, and it was
clearly alienating to most people. It was ridiculous. And so I thought, 'I'm
out. I'm outta this.'"[76] In effect, the agon that characterized the scene—
the sense of distance from and superiority over the external world that
established the scene as a place of nascent political possibility, along with
the primacy it gave to self-determination—was very easily transformed
into an antagonism that was directed not only at the outside world but
also inward. The divisions within hardcore could have been a source of
strength. But under the pressure of the drive for individual authenticity,
every source of difference posed a question for each participant to consider. While particular qualities of difference had been the motivation
for many to enter the hardcore scene, the persistence of difference inside
the scene challenged each individual judgment of authenticity.

Many of the participants in the hardcore scene believed that the
sense of the real inside the scene ought to be transferable to the world
outside. This could be done through efforts to maintain feelings generated in the scene outside it, in everyday life. In the words of the musician
Brandon Desmet: "Hardcore is an opportunity to satisfy [one's] needs to
live a life outside the lines of what is considered normal." According
to the DIY activist Kent McClard: "The D.C. hardcore scene of the mid to
late eighties was extremely important in that bands . . . were attempting
to redefine that anger . . . and make it more about affecting change both
within and in a person's community." The musician Mike Kirsch puts it
clearly: "People realized it was going to take more than political slogans
to really change stuff. . . . We have to take the elements that feel authentic to us and not worry about the rest of the shit."[77] That shared focus on
the authentic was thoroughly individualistic. MacKaye says: "You are not
as capable of changing politics as you are capable of changing yourself.
If you're able to change yourself, that's for the better. When you get that
one out of the way, then maybe other things will shape up."[78]

Thus, hardcore's performed authenticity, with all of its romantic individualism and all of its intense agon, produced a union of the personal and the political that went both ways. Not only were personal problems understood to be the effects of a multitude of social causes, but political problems and solutions were understood in terms of personal behaviors and beliefs. Here the egalitarian assumption of the value of independent judgment succeeded in transferring the intensity of the hardcore scene outside the punk club, saturating political debates with the affective burden of maintaining personal authenticity. This polis, forced to weigh every choice with the precision and passion more appropriate to existential commitments than to policy decisions, found that the sensibility generated by its music was sharp enough to cleave itself from the surrounding world, but not pointed enough to knit solutions from that world's torn scraps. The best that hardcore could do was to reinforce in its listeners the awareness of an unequally ordered world that was aggressively and violently policed, through which one must navigate according to one's individual strengths and capacities, absent the possibility of a shared general will.[79] Throughout rock's reinvestment in authenticity—even through the removal of rock's transparent connection to musical conventions and its delinking from the requirement of directly representing the values and beliefs of a particular population, and through rock's refinement into punk and hardcore—this central value continued to function as a means of reinforcing the distinction between the field of production within which the music is generated and the field of power outside. Paradoxically, authenticity also functioned as the necessary judgment through which the two fields could be connected.

FROM BEAT HAPPENING'S RIGHTEOUSNESS TO RIOT GRRRL'S AMBIVALENT AUTHORITY

When Johnson moved back to Olympia to attend Evergreen College, he took with him the emphasis on individual authenticity that so powerfully structured the hardcore scene. Somewhat perversely, however, Johnson relied on that value to underwrite the playful reconfiguration of rock conventions that characterized the music of Beat Happening and came to inhabit the subgenre of indie. Inverting nearly every musical rule set down by the DC hardcore scene, Johnson, Heather Lewis, and Brent Lunsford, the members of Beat Happening, worked with the most-rudimentary techniques, switched instruments frequently enough to flout any effects of improvement from practice, and sang as though no one was listening (see figure 5.4). Yet their best songs revealed a deep

FIG. 5.4 Beat Happening. From left: Calvin Johnson, Heather Lewis, and Brent Lunsford. Photo courtesy of Charles Peterson.

familiarity with the secrets of rock while slyly reminding listeners of the significance of tambourines, maracas, and heavily reverbed vocals. The band's overt amateurism confused many listeners. Lyrical references to food, handholding, and pajamas combined with the utter refusal of any suggestion of virtuosity to prompt a too-quick association of innocence with the group's sound and sensibility. But there was nothing innocent about Beat Happening. They were resolutely serious and determined. Although playful and witty, they were rigorous in their grasp of the contradictions that enabled their charm. Beat Happening was firmly aware of the violent edge of desire and the lack of control that lurked behind the gaze of the hungry lover. That authentic discomfort compelled devotion from their listeners who could extract joy from the sonic experience of manifest imperfection.

As the two main songwriters and singers, Johnson and Lewis set up a dialogue of perspectives, an exchange of wary glances that survey the social field before them and pronounce judgments of apprehension and longing. Beat Happening's best songs promise to embrace and protect listeners. Listened to carefully, however, those same songs don't just break their promises; they reject the possibility of a future based on promises. This dialogue was established with Beat Happening's first recording session in 1983 (initially released in 1984). "Our Secret" sets up a repeating guitar figure on an F♯ major barre chord that plays itself out across the entire song. A hint of a harmonic resolution to B major comes when Johnson sings the explanatory line of the song: "That's why we're runnin' away. That's why. I had dinner with her family." But the guitar itself never escapes the riff of a sixteenth note, dotted eighth-note rhythm on a C♯–C♯–B–A♯–B pattern. Beneath the guitar, a tambourine and maracas duet emphasizes the pickup notes that start the riff. The stuttering rhythm those instruments establish starkly contrasts with Johnson's legato baritone and with the simple tom-snare drumbeat. The feel is similar to stubbing your toe every three and a half steps during an otherwise dreamy stroll. The lyrics follow the story of a crush instigated by a glance, followed by a swim in a pond, a walk home, and then dinner with her family. It could be a sweet love song. But it's not. Instead, the dark secret of the song is the suggested antagonism that forces the young couple to run away. And here is the best part of the song: you just know, you can tell from listening, from hearing Johnson's voice and the combination of tones and pulses behind that voice, that the young couple is taking that antagonism with them wherever they run to.

The second song from that first recording session, "What's Important," is sung by Lewis. It could almost be the other side of the same story, told from her viewpoint, and the song more directly and overtly enacts the complexity of personal relationships. Instead of swimming in a pond, she offers a walk by the sea. Instead of the background rhythm instruments stumbling, the rhythm guitar jerks through its chords (which echo Iggy Pop and Bowie's composition "The Passenger"). This guitar's strings are flamboyantly out of tune. Every gesture, every sign seems bigger and more out front in this song, not cast away darkly as in "Our Secret." As Lewis sings the key final line, "we don't have to smile if we don't want to," the drums and guitar both just collapse and stop playing—yet the song continues. Illusions are not dispensed with in this song, because they cannot be lived without. Instead, future happiness is both suggested and denied in the music and lyrics; the imperfect performance of love and friendship centers their absolute necessity. Where both songs from this initial recording session imagine an isolated relationship, protected from the outside world, in each imaginary refuge lives the pain that drives the singers' desires.

Beat Happening's musical and lyrical performance of the darkness inhabiting rock's romanticism and the impermanence of any human connection is most fully enacted in their most famous song, "Indian Summer." By this point in their career, as they were working on their second album, Beat Happening seemed to consciously manipulate the techniques that anchored their simultaneous artistry and amateurism. Recorded in 1988, "Indian Summer" features perfectly tuned guitars, the same chord change as "Heroin," and a drumbeat that both stays in time and conjures the ghost of Moe Tucker's attack with its hollow toms. Thematically, the song captures the compacted sound-image of "Heroin," figuring the need to repeat that follows from the failed promise of redemption. "Indian Summer" makes no effort to convince us that the experience it describes can fully satisfy the needs it addresses. Baked Alaska and French toast with molasses will not eliminate hunger. We'll come back for Indian summer and then simply go our separate ways once more. Instead of speeding up, time is kept relentlessly throughout the song. The acceleration that drove each chorus of "Heroin" has no place in "Indian Summer." Everyone knows that the promise of Indian summer is false. Everyone knows that the promise has to be made anyway, even if the future it proclaims holds no release from the pains of the present. After almost the entire song, when Johnson repeats at the coda, "go our separate ways," only then does he let loose with the familiar flatted pitches that fall away from notes that are completely within his range. By that signature, Beat Happening ensures that we know its promises are permanent and empty.

The amateurism presented through out-of-tune guitars, dropped beats, and cracking voices serves here not simply as an entryway into the sounding depths of the band's songs, but also as a recognition of the value of imperfection itself. As Wendy Fonarow points out, indie values signs of imperfection as emblems of the real. Cotton Seiler firmly states, "Within the indie aesthetic, the tape hiss, dropouts, bungled notes, distortion, and so on are, in fact, the *point*." Indie's authenticity proceeds from the self-conscious rejection of virtuosity and the illusions it fosters. In the place of illusions of mastery and completeness, indie enthrones an authenticity based on displays of the modest, the imperfect, and the emotionally complex.[80] Where hardcore's authenticity retained a vigorous individualism and an insistent equation of personal equals political equals personal, indie instilled incompleteness, contradiction, and an insatiable hunger for constantly deferred meaning. This version of authenticity, which does not provide much of a foundation on which to build a political stance, synthesizes amateurism and artistry and serves instead to allow the music's political community to interrogate its own divisions, to inquire into its ability to produce a chain of equivalences capable of mediating agonistic difference. The community should not resolve difference away but allow it to engender new problems from its momentary incomplete solutions.

Let's stop for a minute to talk about the different distributions of the sensible produced in and through the variant pleasures of hardcore and indie. It must be said that neither genre is monolithic. In fact, each spreads across a spectrum of sounds and embraces a range of differently positioned fans. But if we allow Minor Threat (and its followers) to represent hardcore and Beat Happening (and its followers) to stand in for indie, it is possible to identify aspects of the contrasting sensibilities thrown out by each. Hardcore first uses its sounds and the orientation toward the world that those sounds generate to confirm the distinction between those inside the field and those outside. The judgment of authenticity polices the distinction that defines the field through a concentration on and intensification of the illusio of purity. As the main value that centers the production of capital inside the field, the insistence on purity legitimates the demand for feelings free from contradiction and ambiguity. Only pure feelings can be trusted because only they are direct and relatively unmediated. Within the intense physicality of the hardcore scene, meaningful sounds and legitimate stances are judged to be so to the extent to which they generate unambiguous affective relations. For many participants, the clarity of these feelings derives from their embodied immediacy, an experience that is akin to and grounds the value of work as physical labor and individual integrity as an effect produced by the bodily experience of that work. The mosh pit is the workplace, and the autonomy of the moshing fan is that of the independent worker. The political community generated out of the experience of the scene inclines toward an idealized purification of worker autonomy, based on an imperative of individual truth to self. This imperative carries along with it an element of self-policed violence that emerges from the grounding of individual integrity in the embodied immediacy of emotion. Trusting that a self-organized coordination of differences will emerge from hardcore's toleration of agon, the scene resists a more precise internal definition, and instead solely relies on a commitment to the illusio of purity to mark the borders of its community. The world inside the hardcore scene seems to be a temporary autonomous zone that can aspire to greater purity and integrity than the world outside. Within the scene, the purity of emotional directness is not only the chief value by which sounds are judged. The authenticity of any stance that straddles the scene and the world outside also requires the promise of purity. The distribution of the sensible produced by hardcore, then,

FIG. 5.5 Calvin Johnson of Beat Happening sings indie's imbrication of opposites: attraction paired with repulsion, desire with disgust, serenity with anxiety, and security with fear. Photo courtesy of Charles Peterson.

carries a demand for quickly resolved conflict and a sense of justice anchored in the value of embodied labor.

By contrast, the indie scene distributes an anxious sense of ambiguity, contradiction, and uncertainty that derives from its founding illusio, the primary importance of emotional honesty. Since even the most childlike longings for sweet food and innocent walks carry with them the drive for mastery and the hunger for control, no desires and no feelings can meet the demand for purity. Even the most immediate feelings are interwoven with their contrary: attraction with repulsion, desire with disgust, serenity with anxiety, and security with fear (see figure 5.5). The only response to a world so full of contradiction is an ironic acceptance of ambiguity and uncertainty sustained by the only demand that indie makes of all its participants, emotional honesty. The orientation toward the world that emerges from indie aesthetics accepts the messy complications, the dissatisfying compromises, and the eternal braiding of violence and longing that constitutes desire. In addition to being characteristics of the world outside the scene, they also structure relations inside. In the face of these necessarily impure relations, indie judges the authenticity of its participants by the strength they evince in their displays of emotional honesty. If feelings are always contradictory, imbricated with their contrary, it is better to acknowledge that fact, even if the acknowledgment must come coated in irony. While it does provide a slight prophylactic protection against the astringent emotional demands of the scene, irony does not shield indie participants from the judgment of authenticity. Unlike the hardcore scene where the authentic is rooted in the laboring (usually male) body, the indie scene seeks the authentic in the ability to feel fully and articulate as clearly as possible the contradictions that collaborate in the production of feeling.[81] This is the artistry that is in indie. Within this field, in the face of uncertainty and with the full knowledge of the selfish hunger at the heart of every social desire, the refinement of artistry is necessary to achieve authenticity. Equally, authenticity remains a valid concept for the evaluation of even the most artistically formed surface. For all that authenticity really means is that a well-formed object of cultural production, a musical performance, for example, can be trusted to signify meaningfully and consistently the sensibility from which the performance emerged to the world outside the field in which it was generated.

The worldly orientations of hardcore and indie are not that far apart from each other. In fact, they merged together in the field known as riot grrrl. The riot grrrl movement has been understood as a development of third-wave feminism, an extension of the political significance of the personal. Beth Ditto, of the band the Gossip, gives the movement credit for spreading feminism beyond the academy: "Riot grrrl was by far one of the most undeniably effective feminist movements, turning academia into an accessible down-to-earth language, making feminism a trend for the first time in history. Before the riot grrrls, feminism was only available to kids lucky enough to go to college, but riot grrrl gave a name, a face, a sound to feminist frustration." The movement's use of self-produced fanzines to create a set of forums for the public discussion of private affairs has been the focus of several scholarly works. Other works have foregrounded the tension between the internal vision that riot grrrl had of itself as a movement and the image of it that was spread through mainstream news outlets.[82] Here I want to focus on the musical work that distributed a particular sensible, the orientation toward the world of riot grrrl. In addition to functioning as a vibrant channel for feminist discourse, riot grrrl was also a musical form with its own field of cultural production and flavor of authenticity.

The young women who founded some of the key bands in the Northwest, among them Allison Wolfe, Molly Neuman, Kathleen Hanna, and Tobi Vail, had spent time in DC, where they grasped the value of purity and the guitar-heavy sound of the hardcore scene, even if they were not so enthralled by the overt masculinism of the scene.[83] But they were equally, if not more profoundly, shaped by the attitude and presence of Beat Happening, particularly the bravery of Johnson and Lewis. Cultural critic Julia Downes insists that the sensibility of Beat Happening felt like an opening to the women who went on to start bands in Olympia: "Beat Happening encouraged its audiences to build supportive non-competitive communities, creating an atmosphere and message that opened up creative opportunities and possibilities for many women and girls who were later involved in riot grrrl." Vail clearly ranks Beat Happening as the most important of the early Olympia bands: "When I was 14, Beat Happening were the best band in my town but not everybody knew it." While the boys in town were more caught up with hardcore bands, "the teenage girls were a little more clued in. We knew that punk was about making up your own rules and starting your own thing and Beat Happening showed us the way." According to Vail, she and her friends were in awe of Lewis, of her tough-girl approach and her cool: "Her songs gave expression to stuff we felt in our own lives and her contributions to our scene, via her art, style and attitude inspired the teenage girls to create our own music, poetry and personas on our own terms."[84] It seems important to underline where Vail puts the impetus here—in Lewis's songs. Songs such as "Foggy Eyes" and "What Is Important" carried narratives of emotional complexity on the backs of musical gestures that, through their refusal of virtuosity, demanded an openness to new senses of the musical.

In the late eighties, Vail was performing in Go Team, a band that also included Billy Karren (the soon-to-be guitarist in Bikini Kill), Lois Maffeo, and Johnson. She was also publishing the centrally influential fanzine *Jigsaw*. It was through the fanzine that Vail met Hanna. The band Bikini Kill formed in late 1990, with Vail on drums and vocals, Hanna on vocals, Karren on guitar, and Kathi Wilcox on bass. During the summer of 1991, they recorded their first set of songs, released as an EP on Kill Rock Stars. Throughout their career, Bikini Kill fought the tendency of many writers to treat them, and particularly their charismatic lead singer, Hanna, as the face and the voice of the riot grrrl movement. They consistently struggled to position themselves as simply one band among many, one set of voices within a much larger chorus. But their performances and their recordings were too powerful and too compelling to allow the band to simply blend into its surroundings. It may not be true to the spirit or the intent of the riot grrrl movement to focus on one band. But it is true to the band's significance and to the value of the music it produced. Of the first generation riot grrrl acts (including most notably Heavens to Betsy and Bratmobile), Bikini Kill condensed most forcefully and most musically the separate and conflicting values contributed by indie and hardcore. Much has been written about Hanna's stage presence and the appallingly over-the-top critical reaction that greeted the band's appearance, their stage patter, their insistence on creating a zone in the front for women only, and their lyrics.[85] But very little has been written about their music or about the real political effects of its beauty.

"Double Dare Ya," the first track on their first EP, begins with a buzz. Literally. An ungrounded amplifier or an incompletely plugged-in guitar angrily demands the attention of everyone in the studio. A voice asks, "Is that supposed to be doing that?" After a burst of feedback, the guitar and amp are properly plugged in, and a brief moment of quiet sits there expectantly. Hanna apologizes before shouting the lines that seem to have soaked up all the critical attention that has ever been dropped on this band: "We're Bikini Kill and we want revolution, girl-style now!" Much like Patti Smith's opening line for "Gloria," this declaration of intent has distracted almost everyone who has ever written about the band. Rather than adding yet another slim parsing of that line, I want ears to focus on the rest of the first thirty seconds of that track.

After the noise stops, but before she shouts the riot grrrl slogan, Hanna apologizes. "Okay, sorry. Okay, we're starting now." Apparently spoken to the people operating the tape machines (Ian MacKaye is credited with producing the session), the apology along with the buzz and the question that precede the slogan could have been edited out of the pressed version of the song. Instead, it all remains there for every listener to consider. The noise itself sets up a question—"is that supposed to be doing that?"—the openness of which puts the remainder of the song, the entirety of the production, in question. Is Bikini Kill supposed to be doing this? The apology that follows the cessation of the buzz performs two tasks. It renders evident and audible the frame that edges the song's performance of revolution. But in no way does the apology undermine the performance's intensity. While the deference implied in the apology seems contrary to the song's firm declaration of intent, the tension between the apology and the slogan dramatically illustrates the ambivalent significance of the riot grrrl revolution. Riot grrrl demands access to the structures of power for young women who were taught to be deferent. But at the same time, riot grrrl combines this demand for access to power with a fundamental recognition of the injustice of those very structures. Thus, riot grrrl borrows both hardcore's sonic intensity and indie's musical ambivalence. The demand for revolution is accompanied by an apology.

This ambivalence is carried over into the song proper. The riff, shared by guitar and bass, leaps from the tonic A to the dominant E and then walks down, flatted fifth to fourth (A–E–Eb–D). Underneath the riff, the drums push ahead of the stringed instruments, driving everyone just slightly more furiously than they might have moved if left alone. On top, Hanna's voice shouts the first line—"Hey girlfriend, I gotta proposition goes something like this"—punching each syllable with a precise uplift that shifts the inflection of each note without fully changing its pitch. The ambivalence signaled by the juxtaposition of apology and revolutionary slogan is rhythmically underscored by the contrast between Hanna's vocals and Vail's drums, which pull against Wilcox's and Karren's riffs (both drag just a bit behind). From the second verse on, the vocal notes are held longer and end with the slow flattening that became one of Hanna's signature tricks. This vocal slide sits atop the guitars as together they slip down the end of each phrase in a gesture that reinforces the uncertainty of the song. Throughout, the mad rush of the drums along with the tonality and timbre of the riff insert hardcore intensity and its drive for purity while the vocal line and the slightly off-tempo position of the riff pull the song back from certainty and remind the listeners that maybe they're not really as sure about all of this as they claim to be.

The interruption produced in and through Bikini Kill's musical ambivalence carries over into the first recorded version of the band's best song. "Rebel Girl" was initially recorded in 1992. Again the sense of ambivalence is based on a tension at the core of the performance, which enables this version to enact and articulate the most pressing concern of riot grrrl, which was entry and access. The song is based on an A-major chord that roars constantly throughout the song, marking an ease of entry but also suggesting a necessary determination. This single chord cannot simply be asserted. It must be held; it must be sustained; it must be driven across the full continent of the song. Played with uneven downstrokes, this chord has to hold itself up while the bass beneath it shifts down to the minor seventh (G) once every other bar before returning to the root. On this song, too, the drums complicate matters, pounding out each quarter note on kick, toms, and snare, adding certainty with the tripled hits but taking that certainty away by not hitting them all at precisely the same instant. At the chorus, the emphasis shifts to the crash cymbal. Frustrating the design of the instrument, Vail smashes it on every beat, barely allowing the crash itself to ring out before hitting it again. Hanna's vocal line recapitulates the ambivalence: not with the lyrics, which are straightforward and clear, and not through the melody, which hammers on the tonic A until the chorus. During the chorus, at the title phrase, the vocal line also drops down to the seventh and turns *girl* into a two-syllable word, Instead, the hesitation and slight uncertainty in the voice comes through the exaggeration of the timbral twists and inflective turns that shape the vowels and the notes beneath them. The voice seems not entirely confident that the words match the needs of the sentiment they announce. The vocal turns the words into an opportunity to dance around their meaning, not quite committing itself. That wonderful line about wanting to take her home and try on her clothes is delivered in a singsong voice that cloaks the intensity of the desire in a childish defense. Even the verse that proclaims revolution is undercut by the too-quick screaming drop of the melody. My point is not that these are mistakes. My point is that these gestures of doubt and insecurity covered over by the false bravado of the scream precisely figure the open door that riot grrrl sought to construct. The multiplication of beats, the sparkling splashes from the crash cymbal, the imprecise singing and guitar playing all function to create a sonic openness using gestures drawn from indie that insinuate themselves into and work against hardcore's tonal structures and instrument timbres. The original "Rebel Girl" invites new participants to drop in on this small party and see if they like it. Its political community is exploratory, not fully formed.

Nine months later, the song emerges from its previous intimate party, rerecorded, fully grown, and majestic. Produced by Joan Jett, who also contributes a second guitar, this version of "Rebel Girl" is precise, accurate, and almost polished.[86] The outlines of the individual parts are almost identical to the first version. The drums triple the same quarter notes. The cymbal crashes come in during the chorus. The guitars hammer away at that A chord. But in this recording, every detail is more perfectly attuned to the whole. Each part is played with greater attention to the central pulse. Each part leans in toward this center and pulls the outside of the song tight against its core. The guitars are taut and powerful, building together a muscular fascicle that holds the whole song together. With the bass, they jump up a minor third or down a second (A–C, A–G) at the end of every other measure, just to keep the listener's attention focused on the alloyed strength of guitar, bass, and drum. This rhythm section is leading the march. Throughout most of this recording, Hanna's vocal tone is stronger and more certain. The screams are not isolated, embarrassed moments, but an integrated part of the whole. The singsong voice comes only at the end, after the victory is secured. This "Rebel Girl" knows its musical conventions. There are no unanswered questions here. There are no fuzzy boundaries. This performance, like all well-wrought anthems, sounds its call firmly and proudly. It might seem that this anthemic remake would signal the triumph of hardcore values over those that defined indie, with the assurance of fully known and well-executed parts triumphing over the insecurity of newly discovered possibility. But instead of a disciplined purity dominating insecure emotional honesty, the struggle to articulate an outsider position as the core of the political community comes full circle in "Rebel Girl." Two significant consequences followed from this achievement.

First came the recognition that riot grrrl's political community was not all-embracing. As a network of mostly middle- or upper-middle class white women, with access to musical instruments and photocopy machines, this version of third-wave feminism did not escape all the problems of the second wave. In an article originally published in *Punk Planet*, Mimi Nguyen points out the hegemonic whiteness that continued to structure the assumptions of punk, despite the internal belief that "punk is a quality that's understood as transcending race, gender, sexuality or whatever." Writing five years after the peak of Bikini Kill's career and the high point of riot grrrl, Nguyen shows that within this new community, "differences are seen as potentially divisive. Some—like race or gender—are seen as more divisive than others. The assumption is that 'we'—because punk is so progressive, blah blah—have 'gotten over' such things." She goes on to state: "Now, I truly believe that riot grrrl was—and is—the best thing that ever happened to punk. Please, quote me on that. Riot grrrl critically interrogated how power, and specifically sexism, organized punk. Unfortunately, riot grrrl often reproduced structures of racism, classism, and (less so) heterosexism in privileging a generalized 'we' that primarily described the condition of mostly white, mostly middle-class women and girls."[87]

Nguyen describes the political work of riot grrrl as the production of a we that was limited in terms of race, class, and sexuality, not intentionally but by virtue of the orientation toward the world that it inherited and redistributed. What Nguyen saw was a polis unwilling to recognize its internal differences. It seemed that the foundational openness that was the raison d'etre for riot grrrl could only be maintained when those differences were masked, or at least rendered unthreatening.[88] Nguyen went on to argue that punk's hyperindividualism set up a framework of rights that could be too quickly turned to libertarian concerns, privileging the protection of one's own rights over the consideration of others'. The music of riot grrrl inherited this individualism from hardcore, just as hardcore had incurred the ongoing unspoken privileging of whiteness through the basic timbral formulas of rock. These tendencies were built into the musically produced orientation toward the world into which riot grrl sought to intervene. Riot grrl was a paradoxical intervention. Despite the feminist and antiracist positions clearly stated in the pages of fanzines and in song lyrics, the music itself conveyed something else. In part these musicians sought to deconstruct the categorical privileges that accompanied the mosh-pit celebration of the white male laboring body through the musical assertiveness that had traditionally signaled the entrance of an unencumbered individual. The sens of freedom that the music produced re-created the conditions that the riot grrrl musicians sought to change.

The second consequence of the musical centering of the outsider was a direct result of the musical questioning of these signs of unencumbered freedom by the musicians of riot grrrl. Through their blend of indie and hardcore, these musicians somewhat shifted their musical force away from the hidden but implicit reinforcement of the white male laboring body to a musically compelling questioning of the structures of power that hardcore had performed. The move from the first version of "Rebel Girl," with all its unignorable sounds of ambivalence and questioning, to the second version, where those signs of uncertainty are less audible, was a movement toward the mastery of the musical signals that hid structural privilege within claims of individual independence. The song's conventions, when masterfully performed, successfully claim that independence for (some of) those who had been structurally excluded. In the tighter version, the vocal slide that emphasizes the two-syllable *gi-rl* contrasts more firmly with the precisely executed beats and perfectly targeted chord changes. Within this version of "Rebel Girl," the grrrls are in, and that entrance can be celebrated anthemically: "When she talks, I hear the revolution / in her hips, there's revolution." These musicians used the sounds of rock, as they had been transformed by hardcore and indie, to emphasize an already existing orientation toward the world wherein young middle- and upper-middle class, mostly white mostly heterosexual, women had access to the field of power. This social fact, however, was not an effect of the music. The political force carried by the music of the riot grrrl movement changed little in the campaign for increasing the representation of women in any sphere. This force did not contribute much that was new to identity politics. Instead, riot grrrl's reflection on rock's limitations produced a self-conscious reinvention of the performance of longing, thereby manifesting an ambivalent desire for power. That desire could be performed anthemically, but riot grrrl's contribution was to render that performance with authentic ambivalence. The power of riot grrrl music was much more profoundly enacted through this bold assertion of the troubled nature of authority.

This was the important shifting of the sensible that the music of riot grrrl accomplished. The field of cultural production that these musicians created intervened in the world that hardcore reflected, the neoliberal world of intense competition where success was understood to be wholly the consequence of private effort and the unrestrained judgments of markets. The riot grrrl musicians added something very important to their remapping of this world, the ambivalence inherited through indie. Unlike many indie bands, however, riot grrrl musicians such as Bikini Kill did aspire to a level of performative mastery. The apparent musical mistakes heard on their recordings were no longer *the point* of their music, as Seiler suggests that the mistakes had been for most indie musicians. Instead, the splashing cymbals and off-key vocals proffered a new musical beauty, the sens of a new relation to authority. The difference that riot grrrl music made was to musically undermine the centering force of any rock version of the pop anthem, and in the process create an orientation toward the world that questioned its own foundation. Through its self-reflexive questioning of its own legitimacy, riot grrrl introduced an ineradicable agon into the clining community of the punk club. When a fan jumps onstage and joins the drummer reading critical reviews of her band and then the entire band and its fans mold the force of that criticism into the imperfect performance that follows, this agon is fully internalized into the merger of audience and performer.[89] The purity advocated by hardcore and nearly demanded by the full-force competition of neoliberal society simply could not repel the recognition of ambivalence and contradiction performed by these musicians.

Much in the way that Patti Smith had revealed the conventions of rock and shown how they could be reduced to shtick, the riot grrrl movement showed that the musical conventions of the rock anthem had greater openness than had been previously imagined. This happened once it was performed with the meaningful differences that Charles Keil has termed "participatory discrepancies." Keil introduced this term in 1966 as an analytical descriptive in order to explain the power of the groove in soul and jazz. Over the succeeding decades, he elaborated this concept to the point where he could assert authoritatively: "The power of music lies in its participatory discrepancies, and these are basically of two kinds: processual and textural."[90] By processual and textural, Keil meant time and tune. Steven Feld restates the point with more force: "For Keil, it is the emergent 'edge' created by varieties of out-of-timeness (process) and out-of-tuneness (texture) that generate music's vital force, as well as inviting and guaranteeing the active qualities of participation."[91] This out-of-timeness and out-of-tuneness are the tools, the meaningful musical techniques, that the riot grrrl musicians emphasized in order to create real openness in their anthems of belonging. The ambivalence about legitimate authority that inspired their participatory discrepancies also made it possible for the musicians to leave those splashing cymbals, just-off-the-beat drum hits, and flat vocals in recorded versions of the songs that were not only released to the public but that became classics of the genre. The musical success of riot grrrl derived from the authentic fit between the musical strategy of participatory discrepancies and the political mission of opening the sens within the punk club to the agon of ambivalent authority.

Chapter Six

1969; or, The Performance of Political Melancholy

| | | | |

On March 22, 2008, the new music ensemble Alarm Will Sound work-shopped its concert-length performance piece *1969* at the Kitchen in New York. Not a musical, not a traditional concert, *1969* is a collage of collages, a collection of sonic and visual gestures that orchestrate and illustrate the limits of music's political agency. As a well-conceived yet incomplete whole, the performance evokes a melancholic recognition of connections missed and possibilities lost. The basic premise of the piece is that a missed meeting between Karlheinz Stockhausen and a representative of the Beatles demonstrates the uncontrollable serendipity of musical collaboration. A chance for a shared concert between the most important band in popular music and one of the most highly recognized figures in avant-garde European music slips away, and along with it go the dreams of a musically inspired social transformation. A snowstorm intervenes; Stockhausen spends the afternoon sitting in Lucas Foss's apartment, waiting for Neil Aspinal or Mal Evans or Godot—at any rate, someone who never arrives. Stockhausen returns to composing music for elites while the popular mass audience remains untouched.

This sense of missed possibility animates the entire performance. *1969* is deliberately set in the year after the assassinations of Martin Luther King Jr. and Robert F. Kennedy, the year after the great strikes in Paris, the "Prague Spring," the on-podium black-power salutes from Tommie Smith and John Carlos at the Olympics, student uprisings in Mexico and Poland, and the beginnings of the Cultural Revolution in China. *1969* stands on that year as a moment of puzzlement and, while not quite exhaustion, certainly not despair, but rather a sense of lost possibilities and a collapse of belief in the positive political consequences of a flawlessly conceived work of art. By 1969 it was no longer possible for most people to believe that the will for a more just society could manifest itself through music and art and, in the process, transform the world. As a whole, 1969 registers that sense of loss felt by cultural elites as efforts to form a meaningfully broad-based political alliance through musical beauty failed. 1969 realizes through its performance of complex collages of incompleteness the limits of the political force of musical beauty.

The premise on which the performance is based is itself a fantastic impossibility. By February 1969 the Beatles were barely functioning as a unit. They were in the midst of the agonizing sessions that eventually resulted in *Let It Be*. George Harrison walked out of those sessions after a fight with Paul McCartney over a minor guitar part. As a condition of his return, Harrison insisted that McCartney drop his nascent and incomplete plans for an extravagant large-scale concert. On January 30 of that year the band held its final public performance on the rooftop of 3 Savile Row, and the next day John Lennon made it clear to McCartney that the Beatles would not be performing together in any fashion in the foreseeable future.[1] The evident impossibility of Stockhausen meeting any Beatle or any representative of the Beatles in February 1969 for the purpose of discussing a joint concert only adds to the poignancy of the concept for *1969*.

The idea that such a meeting might have been possible comes from a biography of Stockhausen written by Michael Kurtz. Citing no sources, Kurtz writes: "Stockhausen drove to see Lukas Foss; it was winter and a snow storm was raging over New York. Foss's apartment had been appointed as the meeting-place for discussions about a joint concert with Stockhausen and the Beatles. The other party (either one of the Beatles or a manager) was delayed for hours because of the weather, and finally Stockhausen returned home. A concert that would have united avant-garde and pop music for the first time never even reached the planning stage."[2] This gloomy afternoon of missed opportunity becomes the basis for Alarm Will Sound's extensive meditation not simply on the distance between art music and the popular, between the tastes of elites and the pleasures of the masses, but more directly and firmly on the gap between the musical and the extramusical, between beauty and the social. That felt distance between musical beauty and ostensive meaning is the gap that Lawrence Kramer emphasizes as the animating drive for subjective desire and that Jean-Luc Nancy gestures toward as the motivation for musical listening. It is also the space between the felt sense of a collective and a shared understanding of that collective's purpose, between music and politics. This is the subject of Alarm Will Sound's *1969*—this gap, its multiple dimensions and the multitude of pathways that one can trace through it, driven by musical listening, ever alert to the resonant potential for human connection. *1969* motivates an aesthetic experience of political community as a backward glance at a moment when the production of that community might have carried more than an affective charge of self-recognition. The span of *1969* embraces more than a meeting between Stockhausen and the Beatles. It blends into its mix Leonard Bernstein and Luciano Berio, Yoko Ono and Jimi Hendrix, each of which carries further extramusical connotations and additional social possibilities, none of which is concretely affirmed, all of which sound throughout the hall during the show and continue to echo as the room empties afterward. *1969* is a lament for a lost dream that reproduces through musical beauty the longing that drives those desires. In the process, *1969* also reproduces the absences and blind spots of all such dreams.

STOCKHAUSEN'S DREAM AND THE BEATLES' APPEAL

Let's assume that Kurtz was describing a trip that Stockhausen actually took, and that the composer really was hoping to meet a representative of the Beatles in order to forward some sort of collaborative project. Why might this acknowledged giant of European art-music modernism be interested in working with a pop group? There could be many reasons. But at least one has to do with Stockhausen's desire to reach as large an audience as possible. For years he had been working toward the development of a universal music, toward a set of sounds that he believed would be "a music of the whole world, of all countries and races."[3] He pursued this goal through a series of projects, ranging from *Gesang der Jünglinge* (1956–58) to *Hymnen* (1966–69), *Stimmung* (1968), and *Aus den sieben Tagen* (1968). The precise means whereby this music for the whole world would be realized changed dramatically among these works (and others). But a similar motive drove the composition of each.

Gesang der Jünglinge is an example of Stockhausen's effort to reduce all musical elements to a single variable, that of time. Drawing from his work with the acoustician and information theorist Werner Meyer-Eppler, Stockhausen understood the variability of time relations to underlie his concept of "unity in electronic music." In the electronic-music laboratory, music could be broken down into a set of pulses, a series of on-off relationships. These pulses could be varied in time, ranging from quite slow (circa sixteen pulses per minute) up through quite fast (around sixty thousand pulses per minute). At the slow end, the pulse would be heard simply as a beat. At a faster rate, the pulses would be heard as a pitch. Through patient variation and combination of those patterns of pulses, Stockhausen believed that he could construct all the relationships that constituted musical sound—rhythm, pitch, timbre, attack, and intensity. Following from this electronic reduction and recomposition of sound waves, Stockhausen thought that he had discovered the unity of all music. He was also confident that he had located the unity of music and language, their shared reliance on changes in air pressure.[4]

This unity, the vibratory essence of all sound, becomes the foundation of *Hymnen*, a complex collage of electronically manipulated radio broadcasts, speech sounds, various examples of musique concrète, and the national anthems of more than thirty countries. *Hymnen* operates musically and extramusically on many different levels. As Robin Maconie puts it, the work "may be understood in superficial respects as music with an overriding political message of reflection and reconciliation at a time of student revolution, Vietnam, the Cold War, and other issues of mass protest and mass celebration." Yet, "for any listener the musical meaning of Stockhausen's concrete sounds is not just what they say or signify but what they are acoustically;—indeed, in order to grasp what the sounds are in acoustical reality, the ideal way of listening is to empty one's mind of what the sounds represent."[5] *Hymnen* works in and against itself, always gesturing at the instant political associations conjured by national anthems and then nearly immediately deconstructing the sounds from which the anthems are built and thereby revealing the commonality of their musical processes.

Stimmung extends the examination of speech and music to the interiors of consciousness as a performance of intersubjectivity. A lead singer sounds an initial pitch with a prescribed vowel sound. Resonant singers, or subordinate singers, then execute choices about the accompanying tone and vowel sound that they use to harmonize with the lead voice. Absent any instrumental accompaniment, this piece registers the process of social formation as an internally focused tuning, a harmonizing of interests. Slowly, the resonant singers move through stages of opposition, difference, and sameness. Prescribed barriers and elements of indeterminacy interrupt the tuning process and establish the range of possibilities whereby change and an unpredictable beauty enter the performance. But the harmony that is produced is explicitly focused inward. The most typical performance setup is for the singers to sit in a circle facing each other, leaving the audience outside the harmonic process. This separation not only distinguishes the listener from the performer but also creates a hierarchy of harmonizers. As Maconie tells it, during one performance in Amsterdam in 1969, a group of composers in attendance reacted to this "authoritarian" piece with outrage. Stockhausen's response to their critique was simple and direct: "*Stimmung* will yet reduce the howling wolves to silence."[6]

Finally, *Aus den sieben Tagen* eschews prescribed sound altogether as it puts forward a common intuitive basis for human music making. This work consists of a set of verbal instructions, very similar to pieces previously composed by Yoko Ono, La Monte Young, and others in the Fluxus group. Despite this uncharacteristic echoing of earlier compositions, Stockhausen's ambitions for his intuitive music were quite possibly the most outlandish of all: "Once again we are making a revolution. But this time across the whole globe. Let us now set ourselves the highest possible goal: a gaining of consciousness that puts the whole of humanity at stake."[7] During this decade-plus of compositional efforts, Stockhausen was consistently working to widen the scope of his music in an effort to reach as fully as possible into the human. With that goal in mind, it seems perfectly reasonable that he would be intrigued by the possibilities of working with the Beatles, the most popular musical group in the world.

If Kurtz is to be believed, Stockhausen's favorite Beatle was Lennon. (Everyone does have a favorite, it seems.) After Lennon was assassinated on the streets of New York, Stockhausen claimed that he and Lennon had spoken on the phone a number of times: "He [Lennon] was particularly fond of my *Hymnen* and *Gesang der Jünglinge*, and got many things from them, for example in 'Strawberry Fields Forever,' and his texts also made young people prick up their ears. In my eyes, John Lennon was the most important mediator between popular and serious music of this century."[8] Speaking just after Lennon's death, Stockhausen was paying tribute to the value of the artist's work. A decent argument can be made that Lennon was one of the most important mediators between the world of rock and the world of Western art music. But the first Beatle to be interested in the electronic work of Stockhausen was McCartney, who had been introduced to Stockhausen and Luciano Berio by his friend Barry Miles. Miles was one of the coordinators of the Indica Gallery (where Ono held the exhibit that first caught Lennon's eye), and he was the conduit to a considerable amount of elite cultural works and practices for the entire band.[9] Any influence Stockhausen had on Lennon came well after the composition, arrangement, and recording of "Strawberry Fields Forever." In his exhaustive accounting in *The Beatles as Musi-*

cians, Walter Everett attributes the extensive coda of "Strawberry Fields Forever" to McCartney, as "he was the true avant-gardist at this point." "Tomorrow Never Knows," often considered to be Lennon's first composition with tape loops, also relied on McCartney's handiwork, building on tapes that McCartney had created at home.[10] The meticulous orchestral glissando that mediates between the sections of and ends "A Day in the Life" came out of extensive discussions among McCartney, Lennon, and their producer, George Martin. In fact, Martin scored the glissando using traditional notation that was read by the forty-piece orchestra as the section was recorded.[11] Lennon's serious engagement with Stockhausen's work came only after he had begun to collaborate with Ono. Indeed, "Revolution 9," which is clearly derived from the electronic music that Stockhausen championed, was almost entirely the work of Lennon and Ono (with some contribution from Harrison). By the time of his death, Lennon was widely considered to be the most artistically serious of the Beatles. But this reputation was largely the result of the post-Beatles work of both Lennon and McCartney. Lennon's interest in elite art and culture came after and built upon his furious engagement with beat music, music that moved bodies, a music that owed its most formative conventions and innovations to the work of African American songwriters, musicians, and singers.

Alarm Will Sound's _1969_ is based, then, on misremembered moments and misunderstandings. But these historical errors in no way undermine the premise of the piece. Instead, these misunderstandings generate a fantasy of collaboration between elites and the populace. As with so many fantasies, _1969_ is structured in precise opposition to its proclaimed object of desire. Stockhausen's conception of the popular embraced a united global humanity, a humankind stripped of political difference. Having steeped himself in Japanese gagaku, Balinese Gamelan, and Hindustani musical traditions in addition to Western art music, he was certain that all music was the same and all people of the earth were the same. Yet his approach to music was one of control, of regulation, of precise measurement, sine-wave reductions, and leader-directed tuning. At the opposite side of this staged fantasy was Lennon, who represents not only the Beatles but the entire tradition of rock 'n' roll with all of its complex borrowings, appropriations, and exploitations. Lennon's approach to music, whether his boyhood imitations of Elvis and Little Richard or his post-Beatle immersions in Fluxus-style improvisations and his collaborations with David Bowie, Elton John, and Ono, grew out of his lifelong effort to forge an artistic sensibility in tune with the excitement of possibility and progress, with the post–Civil Rights Movement belief that popular music and social justice were natural dance partners. Like Stockhausen's belief in the universal commonality of humankind, Lennon's belief in the fundamental rightness of the dance-beat impulse eschewed political difference. Perhaps the most significant link between Stockhausen and Lennon was this ambivalence about the relationship between music and politics. For both musicians, the political use of music was abhorrent. Yet each believed that music could unite people across superficial differences. Both musicians articulated their ambivalence from positions of relative privilege that enabled them to believe that their tastes and their political impulses excluded no one. *1969* explores that ambivalence in all its naive hope and precynical wariness.

THE FORMATION OF ALARM WILL SOUND

Alarm Will Sound is a professional musical collective that grew out of the experiences of several graduate students at the Eastman School of Music. The Eastman School of Music was founded in 1921 as part of the University of Rochester. George Eastman of the Eastman Kodak Company donated the initial bequest that began the school, believing that "the life of our communities in the future needs what our schools of music and of other fine arts can give them." Eastman then worked to lure the composer Howard Hanson to the school as its director. Hanson served in this capacity for forty years, establishing Eastman as a leading professional music school.[12] Hanson also set a conservative tone for the school, musically (by eschewing serialism) as well as socially (by overseeing "purges of homosexual faculty and students").[13] This conservative orientation began to fade in the sixties and was certainly gone by the late nineties, when most of the founders of Alarm Will Sound attended Eastman. Nevertheless, a taint of backward-looking academicism remained, even as Eastman was widely recognized as one of the two or three best schools for art-music training.

For many of the students who went on to found Alarm Will Sound, the appeal of Eastman came from its insistence on a professional approach to life as a musician, an approach that included career opportunities outside life as an orchestra member. Courtney Orlando plays violin and sings for Alarm Will Sound. Disillusioned by the experiences of her college violin teacher, she quickly decided that the traditional orchestral position was not for her: "In undergrad my teacher was in the Philadelphia orchestra. I heard him talk about it and learned what his life is like. . . . All he knew was his career, and [in the orchestra] someone is telling you what you to do, like a 9–5 job, under contract, you play your part, very much a part of normal society."[14] Not wanting that kind of relationship to music for herself, Orlando chose Eastman for graduate school and quickly "realized that there was this whole other world of new music."

John Pickford Richards plays viola for Alarm Will Sound. He met Caleb Burhans, a singer and multi-instrumentalist for the ensemble, when they were both high school students at the Interlochen Center for the Arts. The two of them decided on Eastman for undergraduate training at least in part because Richards's viola teacher would recommend no other school. Richards and Burhans were intrigued by the school's "nurturing environment for new music," and its openness to student efforts to organize performances of that music.[15] Payton MacDonald, a percussionist, also made the trek directly from Interlochen to Eastman, after he "did [his] research" and chose "the best school."[16] Jason Price, a trumpeter, was worried that a kid from a small town couldn't get into a "big-deal school" like Eastman. Once he was accepted and enrolled, he found an expanded musical world: "And I think that Eastman really was, probably one of the best decisions that I made. . . . There was at the time a growing student movement to do new music and electronic and jazz. It was a great movement. It was coming from the students, my peers, which makes it a lot more influential. . . . I don't think I would have stayed at Eastman for a doctorate had it not been for that movement."[17]

Each of these musicians describes a student-driven openness to new music that had come relatively recently to Eastman. The student energy was motivated by the perception of two glaring gaps—the absence of minimalism from the standard curriculum and from faculty areas of expertise, and the lack of high-quality large ensembles to perform student compositions. Gavin Chuck, currently the managing director of Alarm Will Sound, was one of those student composers frustrated by the lack of opportunity to hear his own music performed by a stable ensemble. Chuck attended Oberlin as an undergraduate and then moved to Eastman for graduate study in composition and theory. He brought with him an interest in the avant-garde of the sixties and seventies, particularly the work of Earle Brown and Morton Feldman. In the nineties, Eastman's theory and composition programs remained oriented mainly around serialist approaches. Robert Morris's elaboration in *Composition with Pitch Classes* promised a greater emphasis on musical beauty than typically found in serialism, yet his analytical framework grew out of a mathematical approach to the permutations of tone rows and arrays.[18] Morris's approach to teaching composition was open to alternative traditions, and he had an immense influence on many of the composers who have gone on to work with Alarm Will Sound. In the mid-1990s, Chuck met Alan Pierson at a party. A conversation began that would extend for years, as Chuck's interest in developing a more stable performing group met Pierson's desire for more engagement with minimalism. Out of those conversations, which took place over several months, Chuck, Pierson, and four other students established Ossia, a student-run musical organization.[19]

From the start, Ossia was designed to be as professional an organization as possible, challenging the traditional limits for student-run ensembles. A board was established, solely consisting of Eastman students, whose task was to "approve projects and then make them happen," according to Chuck. Specific individuals on the board took responsibility for particular pieces or entire shows as well as for the individual tasks that were necessary for the realization of the group's performances. The first concrete goal was to organize two concerts, the first of which would feature student compositions while the second focused on the music of Steve Reich. But secondary goals were equally important. By insisting that every aspect of this organization be run by students, those involved developed skills and sensibilities that would carry on into their professional post-Eastman lives. The students learned organizing skills and strategies of surveying their peers in order to gauge the interests of their audience and establish the group's musical direction.

The choice of Pierson as the founding conductor of Ossia was fortuitous. Pierson had come to Eastman from MIT, where he had begun his undergraduate studies as a physics major. The summer after his freshman year, Pierson enrolled in a summer music program at Northwestern University, where he heard Steve Reich's *Tehillim* for the first time: "It struck me as being beautiful and powerful and emotionally moving. I remember when I first came [back] to MIT, checking the score out from the library and thinking it would be crazy to perform this. And then thought, why not?"[20] Pierson successfully conducted a performance of *Tehillim* as a sophomore at MIT. Part of the appeal of this project, of conducting a volunteer ensemble performing a complex minimalist work at a university devoted to science and technology, was precisely the outside quality of it: "No one was at MIT to make it as a professional musician, and so everyone there was doing it for fun. It had a tremendous amount of life to it." In this short description of the performers' motivations is the articulation of some of the core values that have remained consistent from Pierson's undergraduate career through his time at Eastman on into his work with Alarm Will Sound. The music performed has to be felt to be beautiful, powerful, and emotionally moving. And the musicians have to be having fun as they inject "a tremendous amount of life" into their performances.

This combination of beautiful music and fun attracted several of the best musicians at Eastman to Ossia. To the credit of Eastman's administration, they understood the value of this. "There was a growing awareness in the late 1990s that there were some problems with the traditional conservatory approach of intensely training players to be soloists, because there were so few opportunities to do this," Pierson told me. The Eastman administration saw Ossia as a chance for young musicians to make their own opportunities. But it was the specific combination of opportunities that inspired musicians such as John Richards to join. According to Richards, Eastman supported Ossia through a "big emphasis on entrepreneurship. Making your dreams come true yourself instead of counting on other preexisting organizations. [They] learned about designing web pages and press releases, and how to give a comprehensive educational presentation." Even more appealing than the development of those skills, however, was the quality of the individuals involved.

Ossia drew musicians who were not interested in simply "sitting still, being invisible, dressed in black," in Chuck's words, nor were the musicians interested in performing the standard repertoire in traditional fashion. As Jason Price put it, "Especially with orchestra playing, some people can start to feel like a cog, a part of a machine. For me, there is definitely a beauty to a perfectly executed machine. Everyone pulls together and it works. I still love to do that. But for me there is an actual love in making something that has no excuse to exist. To play a live transcription of a tape piece or an electronic piece—that is what gets me out of bed." In Orlando's thinking, "What we all have in common is what I said before, we all didn't like the idea of just sitting there and playing. We have that same mind-set and mentality about what it means to play music." That mind-set contains a commitment to fun, where fun is understood as a passionate relationship to the music being performed and a fierce commitment to conveying that passion through one's playing. Stefan Freund studied composition at Eastman, was one of the founding members of Ossia, and currently plays cello for Alarm Will Sound. He underlined the importance of passion in Ossia:

One thing I learned with Ossia was [that] it's much better to do ideas that people are truly passionate about, to do a concert of music that I might not agree 100 percent with, but someone in that group is 100 percent behind it. Because that will be successful. It might not be my thing, but it will be successful. There were programs of Ossia that I would not have programmed. But people were committed to it, and they were some of our best programs. I've really learned that if people are passionate about it, it is going to be impactful and people are going to love it.[21]

At least in part, that relationship among fun, passion, and the injection of life into a piece of music is a consequence of the wide-ranging tastes of many of the musicians who worked with Ossia and have continued on with Alarm Will Sound. Price has played in rock bands and jazz ensembles as well as traditional orchestras and chamber ensembles. Burhans currently performs with experimental rock groups and early music groups, as well as experimental improvisation and new music organizations. Both Burhans and Freund are the children of professional musicians. Burhans's father played with soul, pop, and country figures like Ray Charles and the Everly Brothers.[22] The tunes heard in Freund's musical household included the standard classical music (his father was a professor of music at the University of Memphis and a composer) as well as those sounds of rock and soul that enter the blood as one inhales the thick air of Memphis. Freund describes the impact of that musical context in this way: "My dad, one of the real parts of his style is his integration of popular music. . . . He was highly influenced by Memphis music and that trickled down to me as well." Freund believes that this orientation is widely shared: "The younger generation does not see the boundaries as strict as they were in the past. There's a more egalitarian sense, not an aesthetic judgment based on style but one based on substance. The Beatles are great music and Bach is great music." Every member of Alarm Will Sound whom I spoke with emphasized both this commitment to fun and passionate performance and the importance of the wide stylistic range for the music they perform.

THE INFLUENCE OF STEVE REICH

Alarm Will Sound really began as what Orlando termed "a Reich band," because of its first recording project as Ossia. This was a rendition of the Reich piece that had excited Pierson as an undergraduate, *Tehillim*.

Ossia's approach to this piece provides an early look at many of the core stylistic choices and organizational approaches that characterize the performances of Alarm Will Sound. *Tehillim* is a crucial piece in the development of Reich's oeuvre. Completed in 1981, this work marks the point at which Reich's initial formal interest merged with explicit extramusical content. Two of Reich's early formal concerns were a focus on rhythmic variation, which grew out of his original intervention of phasing, and the interweaving of complex patterns that reveal their organization as they shift and develop, which he first called "music as a gradual process."[23] In *Tehillim* those musical processes meet substantive textual material of great personal significance to the composer. This interaction of formal interests and extramusical cultural associations continues to drive Reich's compositional efforts in the twenty-first century, leading to works like *Different Trains* (1988), *The Cave* (1993), and, most recently, *WTC 9/11* (2011).

In order to understand *Tehillim*'s significance, it helps to place the work in a narrative of Reich's developing interests. Paul Hillier, the conductor and organizer of the Hilliard Ensemble and several other performance groups, edited and introduced a second edition of Reich's writings that was published in 2002. In his introduction, Hillier suggests that Reich's musical innovations produce a set of "self-regulating changes" whereby "apparently simple melodic/rhythmic states yield surprising aural ambiguities, so that our sense of a phrase identity—its beginning and end, or the precise location of its downbeat or principle accents—may suddenly shift as new light is shed on it from within."[24] This description captures the immediate appeal of much of Reich's work. An apparently simple surface beckons to the ear, asking it to come closer, to lean in and pay attention. Once the attention is focused, that surface opens up and reveals a set of interlocking phrases that resist easy or quick closure. The patterns produced by these phrases then interweave again, producing a set of metarelations that can feel like a commentary on the complexity of embodied experience. Reich's earliest and most direct realizations of this compositional strategy, such as *It's Gonna Rain* (1965), *Come Out* (1966), and *Piano Phase* (1967), map out the possibilities that arise from the disarticulation and recombination of relatively simple single phrases. *It's Gonna Rain* and *Come Out* are both tape pieces that chop up and recombine spoken phrases. Reich describes *Piano Phase* as an effort to transfer the compositional strategies of his tape pieces to a more human realm. The piece seems to pose the question of "what it is like to imitate a machine while playing live music."[25] *Piano Phase* seems to almost fall apart in much the same way that the spoken phrase "it's gonna rain" ceases to function as anything like a declarative sentence, becoming instead a set of pulses and formants rhythmically deconstructed and affectively recombined. At that point, when the original sense of the phrase has disappeared, then the process of change generating itself has become the point of the piece. *Come Out* creates almost the same effect. But Sumanth Gopinath points out that the source material of the original phrase ("I had to like open a bruise up and let the blood come out to show them") emerged from and never fully escaped a political context.[26] Despite this context, for Reich the meaning was musical; it emerged from the interactions of the patterns. As he put it in his influential early writing "Music as a Gradual Process," "What I'm interested in is a compositional process and a sounding music that are one and the same thing."[27]

These strategies reached an early apotheosis with the 1971 piece *Drumming*. The first part of the work is scored for four pairs of tuned bongos. The focus of the piece falls on the rhythmic interaction among the drums, and the slightly different timbres of the drums serve as identifying markers that enable the listener to follow the shifting patterns that make up the composition. As one listens, different drums come to the foreground, seeming to lead the group for a while and then fading back away. Reich has said that this particular piece reflects his time spent studying traditional drumming in Ghana the preceding year. And yet the piece sounds nothing like West African drumming. Ghanaian drummers set a dance pulse and then encourage an entire ensemble of fellow drummers to contribute to the elaboration and extension of the rhythmic possibilities created in and through that pulse. Each separate drummer begins with a different downbeat, establishing a different starting point for the phrase. But each drummer is also working toward a commonly built unity of beats that shape a dancing collective. *Drumming*, by contrast, is not interested in a pulse beyond what any drummed phrase might create on its own. The combination of the four parts is not designed to build tension and release around a dance rhythm. In fact, it is almost impossible to imagine dancing to *Drumming*.[28] Reich had other goals for this piece. *Drumming* represents the "final expansion and refinement of the phasing process," along with the introduction of another significant Reichian technique: the gradual replacement of rests by beats, or the reverse, the gradual elimination of beats and replacement by rests. This strategy also results in the merger of composition process and sounding effect.

In an interview that accompanies a filmed performance of several of Reich's works by Alarm Will Sound, Pierson says that a key element that attracts him to the music of Reich is that this music broke down the serialist distinction between "music that was good" and that which was "fun to listen to."[29] This explains at least part of the attraction of *Tehillim*, and this combination of good to think about and fun to play would certainly have been appealing to the young musicians of Ossia. But another very important element of *Tehillim*'s appeal was the synthesis between the music and the extramusical. Reich's earlier work, from the phasing of spoken words in *Come Out* and *It's Gonna Rain* to the reorganization of Ghanaian drumming traditions in *Drumming*, involved the abstraction of sonic material and performance practices from their original social context. But *Tehillim* was not intended to escape its context; it was simply supposed to reorganize its relationship to that context. Similar to Reich's work with Ghanaian drumming traditions, the vocal lines of *Tehillim* are the result of Reich's study of Jewish cantillation but do not use those specific techniques. The emphasis on the vocal line in this piece centers two different stylistic changes in Reich's work. As Antonella Puca has argued, *Tehillim* is the first of Reich's compositions where the semantics of the lyrics are intended to matter.[30] Previously, in works such as *It's Gonna Rain* and *Come Out*, the words were treated more as pure acoustic material. Their phonetics were supposed to matter more than their semantics. Some scholars have noted that the original material of both these early pieces is recorded speech initially articulated by African Americans. In effect, the focus on phased phonetics can be heard as an effort to erase the semantic significance of the source material. Gopinath argues, with respect to *Come Out*, that the manipulation of the original phrase conjures a series of potential meanings, none of which escapes political connotations despite what might have been Reich's intentions.[31] But with *Tehillim*, the full range of semantic denotation and connotation contributes to the meaning of the work. The words themselves were carefully chosen; they were not the result of random selection or tape capture. Selected from the Psalms and sung in Hebrew, the English translation makes clear that these texts praise God, prescribe good actions for people, and sing of music's majestic capacity to glorify God's works.[32] Apparently, Reich was more comfortable affirming the value of religious meanings than he was affirming political ones.

Writing about the change in his life that took place in the mid-1970s, Reich says: "In 1974, I began to miss the fact that my own extremely ancient tradition was one that I had lost touch with. I was brought up with only a superficial exposure to Judaism. I did not learn any Hebrew, any Torah, or any traditional chanting. . . . In 1975, I began to study Hebrew and Torah at Lincoln Square Synagogue in Manhattan."[33] Reich studied Hebrew chanting traditions with Cantor Edward Berman. After these studies and some additional reading, Reich decided that at their roots, all Western chanting traditions—early Christian Gregorian chanting as well as Judaic traditions—were fundamentally the same. Nevertheless, significant differences resided in their precise application to particular texts. In the Jewish tradition, particular inflections, both rhythmic and melodic, leant important emphases to written sources, helping to resolve possible ambiguities carried in the Hebraic alphabet. Reich transferred this traditional interaction between musical form and semantics into *Tehillim*.

But, as he did with *Drumming*, Reich deliberately chose not to copy traditional musical patterns into his own composition. Here the pressure of centuries of tradition weighed on his compositional practice, affecting his choice of texts as well as the particularities of their setting. To have chosen texts from the Torah or Nevi'im (Prophets) would have meant either subsuming his own compositional authority under that of 2,500 years of traditional Jewish practice or confronting and challenging the authority carried by that tradition. Instead, he chose selections from Psalms, because "the oral tradition among Jews in the West for singing Psalms has been lost." He continues, "This meant that I was free to compose the melodies for *Tehillim* without a living oral tradition to either imitate or ignore."[34] This freedom to produce his own melodies enabled the second major contribution that *Tehillim* made to Reich's stylistic development. Previous to this piece, Reich had not concerned himself much with melody. Pitch was simply one means of distinguishing the interweaving parts that composed his patterns. But after years of studying cantillation and coming to understand the contribution that this singing style makes to the disambiguation of sacred texts, Reich found it necessary to rely on the structural imperatives of cantillation in order to convey as clearly as possible the significance of the texts he had chosen. Although "no Jewish themes were used for any of the melodic material," the melodies of the piece directly emerge from the "rhythm of the Hebrew text." In his discussion of the piece, Reich explains how specific pitches and melodic contours were chosen in order to emphasize the textual meanings. Repetition figures less in this work than others because, Reich says, "based on [his] musical intuition, *the text demanded this kind of setting*. . . . The basic reason for avoiding repetition in *Tehillim* was the need to set the text in accordance with its rhythm and meaning."[35] Thus, *Tehillim* became the first of Reich's works that may be considered truly songlike. The entire composition is organized around a unity of word and melody unlike any of his previous works. Throughout the piece, the musical unity constructs a tightly organized setting that is focused on and elaborates devotion to the God of Jewish tradition. Reich's "ethnic and religious background" provided the musical and textual material for a work capable of imploring listeners to lean in closely, compelled by *Tehillim*'s beauty. Composed more consciously as a whole of melodic lines and textual significance, *Tehillim* attempts more than either *Come Out* or *It's Gonna Rain*. It reaches toward the musical elaboration of a particular community.[36]

Ossia's performance of this piece is recorded beautifully. A touch of echo gilding the soprano lines brings out the ringing quality of the upper melodies. A forceful attack from the strings supports those flowing voices, combining an assertive insistence on the entry of their lines with sustained notes that extend the foundation above which the vocals soar. Woven between those sounds are the percussion timbres, which often function as Reich's musical signature, and chordal points from the winds, which solidify the unity of the musical fabric. This performance of *Tehillim* brings out several musical-aesthetic values that Reich has outlined in his writings. It marks a culmination of Reich's move from mechanical sound sources to traditional Western acoustic instruments, which, he argued, "are genuinely richer in sound."[37] The prominence of the vocal lines and the relegation of easily tracked repetitive patterns to the background percussion also reinforce Reich's shift of repetition away from its former position as the primary object of auditory attention. The result is a move toward Western musical traditions that underscores and reinforces the textual move toward religious and ethnic identity. The music is no less complex than earlier Reich compositions. In some ways, its complexity is deeper and more compelling in its architectonic organization. But this new complexity is more immediately linked to tradition than Reich's previous compositions. Ossia's successful recording of the piece brings out its status as "traditional and new at the same time."[38]

CREATING A FUNCTIONAL ORGANIZATION

The organizational clarity of *Tehillim* set the tone for many of the future projects of Alarm Will Sound. When the members of Ossia graduated from Eastman, many of them did not want to lose the camaraderie and the performance opportunities that Ossia had provided. Outside the institutional protection of Eastman, the organization had to develop strategies for economic as well as artistic self-sufficiency. Ossia's governing system that was based on a board of directors that selected pieces for performance was replaced by a managing director (Chuck) and an artistic director (Pierson) who share the responsibility for decision making, yet whose authority is deeply dependent on their ability to inspire and respond to the needs and sensibilities of the musicians in the ensemble. Pierson puts it this way:

> What I was doing in *Tehillim* was coming up with ways of bringing people together to do interesting things. Doing that requires lots of group-management skills. In a way, it's a kind of leadership that is in harmony with what conducting is doing now instead of the way it was before. It is not like working with a group of people who are locked up in a room and have to be there. It is more like coming up with a vision and conveying that vision to people who are under no obligation whatsoever. That became central to the way I started to work. If I wanted to do these big things, I had to find a way to sell this to people who were not being paid or not getting anything concrete out of it to invest in it. I feel like that is a part of what good conducting really is. Communicating that, [while] being open to where things go and what other people are giving. Where their contribution is recognized. That creates a space where people can contribute and will contribute and ultimately it will not be just my project but a project that others will feel ownership of. That's a lot of what Alarm Will Sound is about.

Pierson's leadership style, as it emerges from the group's sense of the value, is dependent on the meaning and the beauty of the project.

Among Chuck's concerns for the organization is the need to make the organization "financially workable, socially and artistically workable, so that people don't have to choose to do something else." His chief concern is will they choose "an Alarm Will Sound show for $250 or a studio gig for $2,000?" Chuck's hope for the organization is that if the "artistic and social goals are right, then the rest will follow." Many of the musicians I interviewed reinforced the success of Chuck and Pierson's approach and shared the sense that the artistic goals of the organization counter the relatively low income. Orlando's articulation of this balance is perhaps the most emphatic: "We all say that all the time. We're not doing this for the money. If someone is doing this for the money, they're not in the right group. Even in our sixth season, it is amazing that we all think of it this way. You know everyone is in it for the right reason. Everyone is feeling pumped about it." For the oboist Jacqueline Leclair, this sense of shared purpose establishes a set of social relations within the ensemble "that comes across in the sound of the music." She says, "I think the members of Alarm Will Sound, we tend to make sure that everyone feels appreciated and understood."[39] Payton MacDonald describes the decision-making process as wholly collective: "People tend to view Alan as a leader, but decisions are made by the group. To Alan's credit, and it is one of his best leadership qualities, when we're trying to figure out whether to accept a gig or anything, he always runs it by the group and if the group doesn't want to do it, then we don't." So a single individual's passion for a particular piece cannot simply trump someone else's equally powerful distaste. For the group to function, a respect for each other's musical taste and personal integrity has to structure all intragroup debates. Pierson sums it up this way: "Although there is a certain level of success now and name recognition for Alarm Will Sound, the individuals are really central to this group, the type of people who are in the group. The fact that Alarm Will Sound has so many people who have such diverse talents and whose thinking is so broad and who bring individuality to the table and are not interested in an orchestra gig and just showing up, playing, and going home—that is the foundation of the group. But still the vision of the group is bigger than any single individual."

For the last several years, the ensemble's performances have been organized around concepts that coordinate and determine the selection of particular musical pieces. When an idea is generated, either for a piece or for an organizing concept, the ensemble vets the idea collectively, typically over e-mail. Price describes the common process: "A couple of people propose ideas and then a committee forms and talks over e-mails or a phone call. Then, if it takes too long, Gavin prods them, and it is presented to the group. The group mulls it over and then gives some suggestions and it becomes a group decision. . . . It is kind of a painful process because it takes so long." However long the process takes, the group itself is responsible for the decision. The most important social fact that emerges from the process is this: the ensemble solidifies itself as a performing community through the choice of music and the identification of the concepts that organize that material into a performance repertoire. The sometimes-painful debates that roar back and forth, up to six hundred e-mails a month while the decision process drags on, result not in perfect unity but in a sense of shared purpose, of the group cohering as an ensemble. While this may sound like a fully democratic process, the members of the group that I spoke with agree that not everyone has an equal voice; the two directors have the final say. They can also shape the direction of the conversation. An initial go-ahead from Pierson or a sharp prod from Chuck can accelerate the process toward completion.

CONCEPTUALIZING THE PROJECTS

The group's concerts are typically centered on an organizing concept. A project from 2006, *Odd Couples*, paired works by unlikely composers, such as John Adams and Wolfgang Rihm. The simple point of the program was that careful listening, encouraged by the particular performative emphases insinuated by the musicians, would reveal the fundamental underlying commonalities between apparently disparate compositional styles. Although not a particularly strong idea, it was relatively straightforward, and it enabled the group to perform a number of pieces that had support from several musicians. Orlando told me, "With *Odd Couples*, by the time we got it to Carnegie Hall, it felt really good. We were convinced of what we were doing. We knew the pieces and felt good about it and we all had a lot of enthusiasm about it." This is an important payoff for the musicians, reinforcing the entire decision-making process through the reward of successful performance.

An earlier concept had aroused more debate. Burhans suggested that the group could develop acoustic arrangements of computer-based pieces composed and recorded by Richard James, who records and performs as Aphex Twin. While many of the musicians in Alarm Will Sound were familiar with this music, some had never heard any of it before. The idea raised significant questions about the range of musical concepts that fit within the group's purview. The resulting concept, termed *Acoustica* (in an obvious nod to the electronica genre of the Aphex Twin originals), conjoined the interests of several of the musicians and composers in Alarm Will Sound as it demonstrated the musical similarities between ambient electronica and minimalism. Perhaps unsurprisingly, several of the reworked Aphex Twin pieces (see, for example, "Fingerbib") sound as though they could have been Reich works—especially from the period after *Tehillim*, after Reich's move toward melody and a "more human" sound. Indeed, the *Acoustica* project moves in a similar direction as the acoustic arrangements of these songs shift some of the extramusical resonances of the material. For example, when played on a drum, the opening pulse of "Blue Calx" carries an echo that suggests a physical depth beyond that heard in the original. When the opening chords sound, the materiality of the strings cannot be ignored. To play these chords on strings requires a community of performers. The strings' unmistakable timbre prompts a mental image of arms slowly bowing, commanding attention with their august presence. It is not difficult to imagine musical circumstances where the sound of strings would not produce this kind of image and accompanying associations. But the whole point of this project—to perform electronic sounds on acoustic instruments—is to demonstrate the arrangers' abilities to reimagine the means of production for these sounds and the musicians' abilities to realize these transcriptions on traditional instruments. The concept demonstrates these multiple forms of virtuosity at the same time that it slyly suggests a reshaping of the Western musical tradition. It is not insignificant that the Aphex Twin pieces carry with them a considerable amount of subcultural capital. It is possible to hear *Acoustica* as simply about the subsumption of this value back into traditions of conservatories and orchestras. But that would be a one-sided interpretation. The willingness as well as the ability of these musicians to manipulate wooden boxes and metal tubes, steel strings and tightly stretched leather, to produce sounds initially generated through digital codes and electronic speakers also marks the reinvigoration of those old art-music traditions. Musical meaning and musical possibility have changed as a result of electronic composition. The possibilities of minimalism and new music change when the value of ambient electronica is recognized.

The musicologist Robert Fink has described this new set of possibilities as a "recombinant mutation . . . of desiring production." Fink argues that minimalism shares with disco (and it is not too much of a stretch to add ambient electronica) a constantly changing set of interweaving patterns that the listeners can allow to wash over themselves or upon which they can focus their attention. Fink's point is that the pleasures of minimalist and related musics share the structures of late-capitalist consumer desire, a similar intermingling of fast and slow, a similar responsiveness to both attention and inattention, aimed at a similar flow of objects that are both unique and identical, and all presented in shifting layers of foreground and background. This is not to say that this music is nothing but the soundtrack to the advertising spectacle nor that the music represents an unthinking acceptance of consumer society's voracious demands. Fink does argue that this group of genres creates in sound the structure of feeling produced by the flow of goods, each with its own nonnegligible nugget of intelligible craving. But he goes further to suggest that although it seems as though nothing really happens in this music, the real changes in harmonic structures, in rhythmic orientation, and in timbral relations produce palpable moments of tension that are rarely fully released. The pleasures produced in and through the changing patterns of repeating phrases not only attune the listener to this constant flow of objects but also establish through their cascading cadences, harmonic ascensions, and incomplete resolutions the possibility of self-recognition. When structures of feeling turn back on themselves in reflexive awareness, pleasure does not solely mark the moment of capitulation; pleasure can also generate critique through changing one's awareness of the formal conditioning of the sensible.[40]

This is one of the results of Alarm Will Sound's acoustic performances of Aphex Twin—what seems to be new is old *and* that which is old must be transformed by the new. In line with Reich's use of the old in the new through his reconfiguration of Hebrew cantillation in *Tehillim*, the transformation of ambient electronica by means of the timbres of traditional orchestral instruments reforms that tradition. This music does not simply rehumanize the machine (as Reich described *Piano Phase*). Instead the music reopens the relationship between the human and the machine. What is actually added when multiple bodies act in concert to bow strings, blow winds, and pound mallets in order to reproduce and audibly reshape sounds composed for and initially generated by electronic sources? Violins, clarinets, and marimbas are revealed as machines in their own right, machines manipulated by multiple bodies organized around a communal human intention for the purposes of sound production. Once considered in that way, the different patterns that fingers must trace in order to operate these different machines imply a different intelligence, alternative forms of awareness, perception, and apperception. These gestures encourage the recognition of collective possibilities that extend beyond individualist resistance as they generate musical relations that were first imagined as electro-mechanical movements.

During the 2006–7 academic year, Alarm Will Sound were musical artists in residence at Dickinson College in Carlisle, Pennsylvania. For a performance in November 2006, they presented a range of material, including pieces from the *Odd Couples* project and an early glimpse of some of the work that they would develop into a later project, *a/rhythmia*. The program ranged from Edgard Varese's *Dance for Burgess*, *Octandre*, and *Poeme electronique* to John Adams's *Scratch Band*, Wolfgang Rihm's *Will Sound* (composed for the ensemble), and Giacinto Scelsi's *Pranam II* to several of the studies for player piano composed by Conlon Nancarrow.

Of the Varese material, *Poeme electronique* featured Alarm Will Sound's interests in and abilities to translate electronic music into acoustic performances. Composed for chamber orchestra by Evan Hause (who was in attendance for rehearsals as well as the performance), this piece demanded and demonstrated the ensemble's ability to work together to shape electronic music for tape into a virtuoso performance.

Most of the afternoon rehearsal on November 10 was devoted to working through *Poeme electronique*. Hause sat in the middle of the hall, score in hand, as the musicians worked with the materiality of their instruments, relying on the *sawari* embodied in each acoustic machine to generate sounds that both evoked the original tape piece and gestured beyond it. Near the beginning of the run-through, Pierson asked Mike Harley, who generally plays bassoon but on this piece was singing, to make his sound "more flautier," as he slid through a glissando. John Orfe threw keys onto the strings of his piano. Dennis DeSantis bowed his marimba. And Jacqueline Leclair blew directly through the double reed that she had freed from the body of her oboe. Bags of plastic and paper were squashed and rattled. A three-foot-long block of wood stood by the grand piano, waiting to smash clusters from the keyboard. As Miles Brown stretched to bow beneath the bridge of his double bass, he asked Hause about the desired sound quality. The composer replied, "Less pitch, even. As ugly as possible." Yet pitch was not insignificant. Vocal lines are oriented by pitch with beginning and end points notated. At one moment, Mike Harley found himself unmoored in the surrounding noises and asked Pierson where he might find a C to locate himself. Pierson pointed out that Orlando, whose head was stuck under a piano lid, happened to be singing a D against which Harley could pitch his note. Many of the musicians changed instruments during the piece, which added to the difficulty of the performance. Questions arose about the best possible route from the strings in the front row back to the piano, or from one percussion instrument to another.

As I listened from the back right of the hall, I was most struck by the calm and matter-of-fact manner by which the musicians approached this organization of seeming chaos. Hause evidently had precise intentions for the dynamics, section play, and articulation issues for every nontraditional sound wrung from the instruments. Surprisingly to me, Pierson appeared to have a very good grasp of those intentions. He checked with the composer to ensure that his intuitions were correct, but only rarely did Hause voice an alternate interpretation of the score. At one point, Pierson directed the ensemble to accelerate through a phrase independently of each other, so individually in fact that they risked the phrase falling apart. He paused to double-check with Hause, who quickly nodded his confirmation. By this point, even the rehearsal seemed to be a display of communal virtuosity. It was not simply a virtuosity of individual musicianship but a highly skilled ability to interact meaningfully and sensitively with each other in the group, oriented toward the joint performance of complex innovation. While some listeners may find the acoustic performance of electronic music to be somewhat gimmicky, or may find it a travesty of both the original tape piece and the orchestral tradition, those interpretations miss the key quality of communal interaction that is necessary for the construction of the piece and that becomes a central aspect of its performance. Unlike the performance of traditional orchestral pieces and even most twentieth-century works, this rehearsal manifested a collaboration among twenty musicians, a music director, and a composer-arranger who were all reaching for something beyond what any of them could construct alone as they worked toward the realization of a set of imagined sounds that had not before been heard.[41]

It is important, however, not to paint a picture of easy, conflict-free rehearsals. No one who has been a part of a vital performing group would recognize such a scene. The morning's rehearsal of Varese's *Octandre* provoked intense questioning of the score and considerable disagreement about the meanings of particular dynamics markings and tempo. Even more contentious were the rehearsals for Nancarrow's *Studies for Player Piano*. These studies were composed for a mechanical player piano because of their extreme rhythmic difficulty. They work radically separate meters against each other, and for most of his life, Nancarrow was unable to find musicians who could play them. In the twenty-first century, however, the ability to perform these pieces has become a mark of rhythmic virtuosity among highly trained young musicians. Professional ensembles such as Calefax and student groups from Juilliard upload their successful realization of these pieces to YouTube.[42] But the sheer difficulty of performing these pieces remains undiminished. At this rehearsal, however, rhythmic complexity was not the source of the tension. For their performance at Dickinson, Alarm Will Sound had added to the already existing difficulty of the piece by choreographing a set of movements for the musicians to enact as they performed.

"Player Piano Study 6" begins with an odd metered riff that continues throughout, conjuring the image of an old drunk in a weathered suit hobbling down the street. After a few repetitions, a differently measured line rises across the top. The two parts strain against each other rhythmically, pulling further apart during the first minute of the piece. Alarm Will Sound played Yvar Mikhashoff's arrangement of the work, which spreads the top lines of the piece across the woodwinds, with clarinet, oboe, flute, and piccolo sharing parts that imaginary multiple right hands would have played on the piano. The different timbres of these instruments highlight the distance between the two lines, lending an intensely lyrical quality that brightens the piece. During the rehearsal an additional gloss was given to that difference by the staging. All the musicians began with their backs to the audience. The oboist Leclaire turned and began walking forward as she began her line. The clarinetist, Elisabeth Stimpert, initiated her line while standing by the piano, and then she too walked forward. After about a minute and a half, as a rising wave of winds flowed in to support the top lines above the piano riff, the remaining musicians turned to face first Leclair and then the audience. This seemed unnatural to some of the musicians. Stimpert complained that she felt as if she were back in marching band. Brown argued that turning around was actually a difficult maneuver for the bass and cello. Despite the vehemence with which each concern was voiced, there was never any doubt that the group supported the general idea of the staging, ensuring that the criticisms were not heard as harsh dismissals. But they forced the staging director, Nigel Maister, to articulate the basic concept behind the movement. Imagining this performance as a conversation among the different instruments, Maister had staged the musicians as though their parts led them toward one another. Although he did not state this overtly, the point of the movement then seemed to approach a reintegration of the parts that had been dispersed from a single mechanical player piano to multiple instruments. Again the production of a kind of collective coherence seemed to be the aim of this transformation of a piece originally written for machine into a musical work for an acoustic ensemble. The staging contributed a visual and gestural element to the arrangement's ability to reanimate the world as the group brought this music to life.

A year later, Alarm Will Sound performed their *Arrhythmia* concert at Otterbein College in Westerville, Ohio. Among the featured works were the *Player Piano Studies*. This time, however, there were no staged movements choreographed into the performance. The Nancarrow pieces were integrated into a concert that was organized around the concept of straining meters, "where a basic pulse . . . is disturbed either by distortions in the flow of time . . . or by juxtaposition with other conflicting pulses." The point of these rhythmic disturbances is to create a musical space "where regularity and irregularity meet."[43] This concept arose after George Steel (then the director of Miller Theater at Columbia University) suggested that the group work up some of the Nancarrow studies. In Pierson's words, "I wasn't all that thrilled by the idea, but some of it was interesting, and so I came back with the idea of what if we came back with Nancarrow in the context of a project, we would juxtapose his music with other pieces that used similar ideas." The resulting concert and recording (*a/rhythmia* on Nonesuch) capture this sense of clashing times, of a stumble that reorganizes your perception of the sidewalk rising up to meet your face. This was a case where not all of Alarm Will Sound was fully in favor of the project and all of its component parts, and there was a considerable amount of discussion and disagreement among the musicians. The concept organizes a wide range of material, from Johannes Ciconia (fourteenth century) and Josquin des Prez (fifteenth century) to Nancarrow, György Ligeti, and Harrison Birtwistle (mid-twentieth century), up to Benedict Mason, Michael Gordon, and Mochipet (late twentieth and twenty-first centuries). In its concert form, the concept even included a rock piece whose disruptions might even have challenged its basic authority.

For the concert at Otterbein College, the disagreements within the ensemble were thematized as evidence of the disruptive capacity of the music being presented. The horn player Matt Marks introduced Gordon's "Yo Shakespeare," saying that he hated it the first time he heard it. In his words, the three contrasting rhythms of the piece gave him a "Michael Gordon headache," although it was music you could ultimately "learn to like."[44] Similarly, when Price introduced the Shaggs' "Philosophy of the World," he acknowledged that not all the members of the ensemble were thrilled by the piece. During our conversation, Pierson acknowledged that he had never heard of the Shaggs before Price suggested the song, calling it "a classic example of an idea that . . . depends on the kind of eclectic knowledge of the group[,] . . . an encyclopedic knowledge of weird music." He assured me that the inclusion of the song was "pretty intensely debated." Some of the terms of that debate can be gleaned from the program notes for the concert.

Unlike the rest of the material organized by the concept of arrhythmia, the Shaggs' piece would most likely not be described as a purposeful exploration of contrasting pulses. The program notes compare "Philosophy of the World" to songs by Aphex Twin and Mochipet, but it also remarks that the complexity of the Shaggs' piece "may not be the result of intelligence." The original version of the song can be heard on the group's only album, also titled *Philosophy of the World*, which was a virtually unknown vanity recording for the first thirty years of its existence, and even now it has little more than a tiny cult following. Characterized as "outsider music," the Shaggs' album was rereleased in the nineties and has since earned some critical acclaim for its unpretentious honesty and authentic ambition. The band was made up of three sisters who were lovingly encouraged to record by their father. The *Arrhythmia* program notes included the story of the father's love for his daughters and repeated an often-told story about the girls seeming to know exactly what they wanted in the studio, despite the auditory evidence of chaos. The resulting recording is a miraculous document of desire transcending ability, of vision exceeding execution, of charm emerging from that chaos. Heard in those terms, *Philosopy of the World* has been termed a masterpiece of youthful longing, akin to the best work of Daniel Johnston. Yet for those who are unaware of the backstory, listening to the Shaggs can often provoke derision. For first-time listeners, the rhythmic complexity of "Philosophy of the World" is most typically heard as nothing more than incompetence. Whereas Gordon's piece demands to be heard as a serious investigation of clashing time signatures, "Philosophy of the World" risks being dismissed as a joke. One of the concerns raised during the debate within Alarm Will Sound was whether or not "Philosophy of the World" truly fit into the concert's concept. Were the Shaggs, in Pierson's words, "artistically meaningful"? Conversely, would the ensemble's replication of the missed beats and colliding cadences result in little more than a mocking of their guileless intentions? Again, Pierson put it succinctly: "Is it only charming in that it was haphazard, and will that charm be decimated by having it meticulously transcribed and debated?" If the point of *Arrhythmia* was to create a space where musical regularity and irregularity met, where was the regularity in the music of the Shaggs?[45]

When Price introduced the piece during the concert at Otterbein, he noted these concerns and restated the story of the Shaggs. He spoke of the "hopes and the dreams built up in the Shaggs' beautiful music that is sometimes hard to listen to." Price also announced that in order to perform the piece, individual musicians had to be put on their own individual click tracks, in order not to be pulled back toward each other's beat. As the members of Alarm Will Sound put on their headphones and Pierson bent over a single snare drum, the piece began. In this concert the performance was beautiful. The beauty of the song, arranged by

Chuck, with divergent lines spread across the ensemble, was an effect of the complete surprise that erupts at the moment when all the shattered efforts at timekeeping merge with the astoundingly affirmative final line of the chorus. Alarm Will Sound did not sing the words when performing, but the lyrics were printed in the notes for all to follow. "Philosophy of the World" is a song about desire, about the obstacles to desire, and about the longing for what one does not have, regardless of the bounty one might possess. Reflecting the intensity of that desire, the imprecise performance of the music emerges as a longing for mastery, which is only briefly achieved at the very end of the chorus. The full phrase, "you can never please anybody in this world," ends with three solid beats, three affirmative notes ("in this world"), on which the band achieves unity, rising up to the tonic in a gesture of resonant community. The instant the song continues, however, the immediate loss of that mastery echoes tragically, seeming to confirm the lyrical assertion that you really cannot please anyone. In performance that night at Otterbein, Alarm Will Sound made evident this moment of dramatic regularity and astounding beauty in the Shaggs' "Philosophy of the World" as the swaying bodies of the ensemble enacted the divergence and convergence of the song's multiple rhythms, pulling the audience with them into the transcendent disappearing unity of that chorus.

Alarm Will Sound's recorded version of "Philosophy of the World" did not make it onto the *a/rhythmia* CD. It is available online, however. Heard in isolation from the performance context, Alarm Will Sound's version conveys little of the tension and transcendence that emerges from the Shaggs' recording and none of the mysterious commonality produced at Otterbein. In the recorded instance, two factors work against the arrangement, musical factors that had worked positively for Alarm Will Sound in other cases. Like "Player Piano Study 6," "Philosophy of the World" distributes lines that had been produced by a chordal instrument (here guitars instead of piano) across a range of winds and strings. But where the arrangement of the Nancarrow piece plotted those different lines as truly independent forces, which maintained their independence when shifted to the more traditional instruments, the rhythmic unity that the strings must sound in order to replicate the force of one human's pick across guitar strings creates a unified block of sound. Against this block, the woodwinds and brass heighten their differences, producing lines more intricate than heard on the original. The resulting tension consequently feels more deliberate, more intentional. Where the transcription of electronic and mechanically produced rhythmic complexity (e.g., Nancarrow, Aphex Twin, and Mochipet) to orchestral instruments adds a sonic depth that feels more human, this transfer of desire and longing out from the coded significance of guitars and basic drum kit stabilizes the pull of each section, reducing its capacity to resonate the boundless quality of desire. The participatory discrepancies that conveyed the humanity of the Shaggs had been carefully transcribed in order to be performed precisely.[46] As Pierson worried, it does strip away the haphazard nature of the Shaggs' original and, in so doing, collapses the sense of musical longing. Although no rhythmic complexity has been lost—indeed, in places it has been heightened in the chamber-ensemble arrangement—the chorus does not provide the seemingly miraculous release one hears in the Shaggs' recording. Supplemented by the moving bodies of the performers, echoed by the movements of the audience, this same arrangement worked in concert. Absent that moving community, almost-the-same sounds cannot generate the same lure, the same regularity of its longing to be.[47]

1969; OR, POLITICAL MELANCHOLY

Alarm Will Sound's concert concept, 1969, addresses music's capacity to generate shared political longing. Directly and indirectly, 1969 also exposes the limits of that capacity. Using staged gestures from the musicians, slides and short film clips, audiotape, actors with lines, and musical performances of rock classics and avant-garde experiments, the concert produces a collective sense of loss among its audience as well as an inkling of possibility. Listeners leave the hall speaking about what could have been and wondering about what might be. On the evening of March 21, 2009, the lobby of Murch Auditorium at the Cleveland Museum of Natural History echoed with quiet whispers while very well-dressed patrons examined each other's costumes of privilege. The night before, at the New Hazlett Theater in Pittsburgh, the audience was younger, more energetic, and a bit more rowdy, shouting plans for late-night activities across the room while gesturing vigorously with their wine glasses. The cellist Eric Edberg attended a performance of 1969 at Zankel Hall in New York on March 4, 2011, and wrote this for his blog: "Since I left the performance, I've been asking myself what a musician's responsibility to society is in times like these, in times like those. And what does that have to do with how people like me teach and train young musicians? An evening that produces a shift like that is an evening more than well spent." Arthur Leonard, a law professor at New York

Law School, responded to the same performance this way: "There are different kinds of beauty—poetic truth can be at once ugly and beautiful for its very depth and truthfulness—and I heard beauty last night."[48] Indeed, 1969 addresses the relationships between music and society, between poetic truth and musical beauty, through performances that refuse to be reduced to simplistic stances or tender sentiments.

Where *Arrhythmia* is organized by the concept of clashing pulses, 1969's performance of political longing is structured by three relations. The entire work, as well as each piece chosen for inclusion, engages the relationships between (1) collage and composition; (2) art and the popular; and (3) the musical and the extramusical. The central figures—John Lennon and Karlheinz Stockhausen—stake out important positions on each of these themes, and they are explored in detail. Supporting characters, all of whom are historical figures, supplement these positions. Some, like Martin Luther King Jr. and Daniel Berrigan, stand outside music, helping instead to ground the political tensions of the period. But all the musicians—Berio, Bernstein, Ono, McCartney, Hendrix, even the composers for the off-Broadway musical *Oh! Calcutta!*—contribute works that extend and elaborate the multidimensional matrix of forces encompassed by the three structuring oppositions. At the center of this matrix stands "Revolution 9," in an arrangement by Marks, the horn player. During the performances in the spring of 2009, this virtuoso rendition of the Beatles' most infamous track came at the end of the concert, bringing together all the tensions and themes of the piece and sending the audience out of the hall contemplating the conundrum of music's relation to the political.[49]

On March 20, 2009, at the New Hazlett Theater, Christopher Evan Welch played the part of Karlheinz Stockhausen. Dressed in a suit, standing stiffly and speaking with what was not quite a German accent, this character represented a more formal and analytical approach to the tensions structuring the evening's performance. Stockhausen's oeuvre was represented by taped and live performances. Selections from *Hymnen*, *Gesang der Jünglinge*, *Stimmung*, and *Aus den sieben Tagen* demonstrated the precision with which the composer had rethought the basic principles of music. Each of the pieces musicalized material that began as found sounds or abstract principles, using electronic techniques or collage approaches. Even the pieces that allowed the performers some freedom included strict prescriptions about the manner of producing their sounds. Every one of these excerpts had been arranged by individual members of Alarm Will Sound, giving the ensemble ample opportunity to exhibit its ability to give life to the most difficult-to-execute instructions and the most obscure musical concepts. *Hymnen*'s juxtaposition of banal extramusical content with avant-garde electronic techniques appeared as a set of beautifully suggestive evocations of incomplete national unity amid dissonant splinters of antagonism. *Stimmung*'s internally focused tuning emerged from its small onstage community to embrace the audience, helped at least in part by the fact that the piece was not performed in a closed circle. "Set Sail for the Sun" from *Aus den sieben Tagen* instructs the musicians to "play a tone for so long until you hear the individual vibrations," and then slowly move toward a harmony with the tones played by other musicians, "and the whole sound turns to gold, to pure, gently shimmering fire."[50] Alarm Will Sound's version brought out the intensity of the piece's ambitions. *Gesang der Jünglinge*'s transformation of electronic impulses merged with "Tomorrow Never Knows," making the tightest link between the music of the two lead characters.

The role of Lennon was played by John Walker. This Lennon carried a beer bottle with him throughout the performance, occasionally appearing to sip from it. While Stockhausen stood stiff and analytic, Lennon slumped, sat, and spoke with elliptical intuitive grace. Alarm Will Sound's transformations of Lennon's Beatles material was not as illuminating as their revivifying of the Stockhausen works. Chamber-ensemble arrangements of "A Day in the Life," and "Tomorrow Never Knows" lessened the impact of the Beatles' use of musical forms and timbres from outside the beat-group tradition. This made it more difficult to hear the musical means whereby these pieces pointed beyond musical meaning. "A Day in the Life" began the show, providing a comfortable and straightforward introduction to the concert's structuring tensions. While the orchestral climax of the song lost some of its force when preceded by the same instrumentation, John Orfe's arrangement highlighted the differences between the Lennon-composed section and McCartney's contribution. In this way, a sense of both collaboration and collage came through the performance. Furthermore, the association of each part with its famous author pointed listeners beyond the sounds, paradoxically establishing the historical setting through a song from 1967. Although "Tomorrow Never Knows" was well played, with an electric bass complementing the strings and the trombone's ability to slide the backward-taped sounds particularly prominent, the magnificent final track on *Revolver* became little more than a musical puzzle in its chamber-ensemble arrangement, losing its references to ego death and the collapse of the individual. Yet the juxtaposition with *Gesang der Jünglinge* created its own meaningful collage, again focusing the listener's attention on the deeper similarities beneath the different approaches of Lennon and Stockhausen.

Performed together, the two pieces contrasted the different public personae of the central figures. Lennon's status as a *popular* artist who relied on an intuitive grasp of his musical experiments carried with it a seeming commitment to the world beyond music and the social changes of the time. According to Ian MacDonald, however, Lennon was the most internally focused of the Beatles during this period of his work. Counter to Lennon's later reputation as the more overtly political Beatle, Mac-Donald points out that Lennon and Ono took "a particularly dim view of the Chicago riots of August 1968."[51] Stockhausen's status as one of the intellectual leaders of the European avant-garde seemed to situate him outside the social struggles of the sixties, leading some critics to declare him a servant of imperialism. In fact, Stockhausen tried to avoid any overt political resonances for his music, telling Jonathan Cott: "I can have a political opinion as a composer, but I shouldn't try to limit the music that comes about through me to what I think politically. That would be the worst thing in the world, because it immediately cuts out all the people who have intellectually different opinions." And yet, Stockhausen also expressed the view that one of the goals of his music was to plant seeds that would come to fruit one hundred years later, by touching the consciousness of his listeners.[52] Neither musician denied his music's capacity to affect the world. Both chose to work through music first. Alarm Will Sound's transformative collage of "Tomorrow Never Knows" and *Gesang der Jünglinge* then shows how closely positioned these supposedly opposed musicians were.

Luciano Berio is another European composer firmly situated within the structuring matrix of the show. Berio had met Stockhausen during seminars in Darmstadt, Germany. He had worked on radio and tape collages similar to the works that Stockhausen was producing in the sixties. Furthermore, Berio had been one of Steve Reich's composition teachers. Berio was intrigued by possibilities he heard in popular music. He was not immune to the flattering attention he received from McCartney, and Berio had arranged a set of Beatles' songs for his then wife, Catherine Berberian. He acknowledged the determining power of the market even if only as a negative force operating on art-music composers.[53] As with both Stockhausen and Lennon, Berio was unimpressed by most arguments for the political uses of music. The direct identification of particular melodies or rhythms with specific class fractions made little sense to him, as it seemed to deny music's intellectual autonomy.[54] Despite this, the extramusical, indeed the political, was not outside Berio's concerns. He composed an opera about the Civil Rights Movement, and "O King," a song that was later incorporated into his longer work *Sinfonia*, was dedicated to the memory of Martin Luther King Jr. Berio's work was never simply about music itself, yet extramusical materials could only enter his work once they had been translated and transformed into music. Berio recognized that the experience of listening elicited associations and contextual knowledge that inevitably became part of the musical experience. Composition, therefore, required "a delicate balance" between technical musical concerns and the chief task of "giving a new life to an object of knowledge."[55]

One of Berio's favorite techniques for achieving this balance was the use of collage. Through quoting outside sources—texts and also the music of other composers—Berio's music was able to gesture beyond itself and even outside the limits of music. *Sinfonia* includes words from Claude Lévi-Strauss's *The Raw and the Cooked*. *Sinfonia* also quotes snippets of music from a range of late nineteenth- and early twentieth-century composers. It extensively reforms and reshapes material from Gustav Mahler's second symphony. Through this set of musical gestures, *Sinfonia* references not only the contemporary issues that concerned Mahler but also Leonard Bernstein, who had been leading the revival of interest in Mahler's work. *1969* positions Berio in its matrix of forces by presenting his arrangement of "Michelle," "O King," and portions of *Sinfonia* along with words that Berio had spoken. These quotations ask simple yet profound questions about music's ability to affect the price of bread or to end war, further complicating any direct relationship between music and politics. In the context of *1969*, then, these pieces of music and words present another particularly nuanced understanding of the relationships among collage and composition, art music and popular music, and the musical and the extramusical.[56]

Even more firmly planted in the middle of these conflicts was the figure of Leonard Bernstein, who emerges as the emotional heart of *1969*. More than any other figure of the sixties, Bernstein was publicly known for his efforts to bridge the worlds of (white) art music and pop music.[57] He wrote for musical theater and scored movies. In 1966 he claimed, somewhat notoriously: "[I can find] far more pleasure in following the musical adventures of Simon and Garfunkel or of the Association singing 'Along Comes Mary' than I have with most of what is being written now by the whole community of 'avant garde' composers."[58] He consistently praised the songwriting of the Beatles; during one of his *Young People's Concerts* he used the example of "And I Love Her" to illustrate the sonata form.[59] He even hosted a special CBS news program titled *Inside Pop: The Rock Revolution*, which first aired in April 1967.[60] One of his biographers has claimed: "The idea that music could be—ought to be—fun is a recurrent theme in Bernstein's life."[61] At the same time though, he was the music director of the New York Philharmonic, where he led the revival of interest in the works of Gustav Mahler even while promoting twentieth-century composers such as Takemitsu Toru, György Ligeti, and, of course, Karlheinz Stockhausen. Bernstein was also a highly visible member of the New York liberal intelligentsia, which meant that he was a strong supporter of Robert Kennedy, was actively against the war in Vietnam, and hosted a cocktail party fundraiser in support of the Black Panther Party that became notorious through the mocking journalism of Tom Wolfe. Yet Bernstein remained committed to music as his most effective means of engaging with social turmoil, having said after the assassination of John F. Kennedy: "This will be our reply to violence: to make music more intensely, more beautifully, more devotedly than ever before."[62]

Bernstein is a central character in 1969; words of his are spoken by the bassoonist and vocalist Michael Harley (including the quotation about President Kennedy). Moments from Bernstein's biography are used to situate the social turmoil of the era. The historical events of 1967–70, the moments of political loss that are so central to the affective charge of the whole work, are imagined through the lens of the typical New York intellectual. Daniel Berrigan's arrest for antiwar activism is conveyed through a press photograph. Martin Luther King Jr.'s final "I've Been to the Mountaintop" speech is heard via a tape of the radio broadcast. Similarly, King's assassination is announced through a speech by Robert Kennedy. The increasingly hostile and polarized political environment is suggested by quotations from the famously cynical social observer Wolfe, whose satire of the Bernstein family's cocktail party in honor of the Black Panther Party was widely read in *New York Magazine*. Coining the term *radical chic*, Wolfe contrasted "Roquefort cheese morsels rolled in crushed nuts" with the aura of violent masculinity that Wolfe stereotypically located in the Panthers. He found hypocrisy in the spectacle of servants delivering drinks and hors d'oeuvres at an event dedicated to the promotion of equality.[63] Such potshots were less common in 1970 than they have become in the twenty-first century; their sting was even sharper then. Alarm Will Sound uses these events to theatrically establish a world where the aesthetic and the political were mixing uneasily, where the first neoconservatives were beginning to gleefully expose the contradictions of cultural power, and where taste no longer seemed to be a clear sign of progressive virtue.

It was in this milieu of intensifying political oppositions and cultural contradictions that Bernstein composed *Mass*, his ambitious attempt to explore the relationships among religious belief, individual personal development, social transformation, and music as a powerful cultural force. Bernstein composed *Mass* for the opening of the John F. Kennedy Center for the Performing Arts in 1971. The work lies somewhere between an opera and a musical and draws from an even broader range of musical sources as it borrows the format of the Catholic Mass to structure the narrative. The work throws together disparate song styles in collage fashion—almost making its case for the musical unity *Mass* just fails to achieve. The event was important enough for the *New York Times* to assign two different reviewers to cover it—Nan Robertson reported on the social aspect of the evening, while Harold Schonberg reviewed the performance. The *New York Times* also published a review of the premiere recording only a few months later. Neither of the music reviews is positive. Don Heckman noted: "The very arrogance of his self-assumed familiarity with all these idioms—rock, jazz, blues, 'classical' orchestrations, choral scoring, Broadway-style melody writing—is enchanting, even though [Bernstein's] reach exceeds his grasp."[64] Schonberg is more dismissive, calling the performance "a sentimental response to great problems of our time," advocating nothing more than "the thin watery liberalism of . . . the brotherhood of man."[65] Heard through the filtering reviews of these two gatekeepers, *Mass* seems to violate hard rules about boundaries—genre boundaries and political boundaries, boundaries that separate religious issues from musical ones, issues of identity from those of power, "serious" music and that which is fun.

Mass directly refuses those distinctions, and insofar as its reach does exceed its grasp, to the extent that *Mass* insists on the legitimacy of its ambitions even in the face of its incomplete achievement, this work is the musical and theatrical ancestor of *1969*. Alarm Will Sound integrates three selections from *Mass* into its own take on the same issues. At the performance in Pittsburgh, those three pieces *rocked*. Most impressive was Alarm Will Sound's take on "Agnus Dei," with its nearly shouted chorus of "Dona Nobis Pacem" sung to a dramatically descending, abruptly terminated melodic line. The ensemble's vocals swirled about the stage, filling the air with outrage but also with precision and a commitment to the quality of the sound, thereby creating the feeling of making music more intensely in the face of crisis. By ending the first act with "Agnus Dei," Alarm Will Sound emphasizes the connection between its work and Bernstein's. *Mass* is about the loss of faith, both religious faith and faith in the ability of beauty to transform the world. Somewhere near the end of the first act, Pierson turns around, faces the audience and states: "We all know that music can't stop war, right?" Harley, in his role as Bernstein, raises the issue of a global food crisis and asks why the West insists on eating at the expense of the rest of the world. *1969* produces that same sense of loss in its audience at least in part through its inclusion of Bernstein's sense of loss after the collapse of progressive political opportunity that took place from 1967 to 1970.

By this moment in the performance, it has become clear that the crises confronted in *1969* are centered in 1968, the King and Kennedy assassinations, the riots that spread across the nation and the world that summer, and the election of Richard Nixon. Alarm Will Sound's title references the year after those crises of 1968, and the most intense musical moments in the performance come from a work that did not premier until two years later. Through this expansive approach to time, *1969* suggests the slippery temporality of music's extramusical effects as it reopens the question of music's ability to reshape the world. Alarm Will Sound's decision to include so much of Bernstein, the expansive ambitions of *Mass* and incidents from his life and his words, ensures that Bernstein's loss of faith is not the end of the story. Instead, the possibility of extramusical effects reemerges through the recontextualizing effects of collage and the performed hope that music's political force endures.

Intensely aware of the limitations of music, of the way in which its performance of freedom works against any pedantic message, Bernstein could only hope to produce a longing for unity amid difference. The public display of this conscious intention brought him ridicule. Music critics such as Schonberg and cultural critics such as Wolfe saw the contradictions and mocked the absence of specific and direct steps to take. But Bernstein understood, as did Lennon and even Stockhausen and Berio, that the promotion of policy and even the identification of policy alternatives were not within the domain of music. Although none of these musicians was overtly concerned with this question, it is clear that they shared an inchoate and intuitive understanding that music's political force lies in its ability to encourage an audience to lean together, to listen carefully and musically to a set of sensibilities encoded in sound, and consequently, perhaps, have their sense of the world around them transformed, in common. In the end, the central action of 1969 moves through this effort to create moments of musical beauty that carry an extramusical force into the world.

Central to the exploration of these themes is the piece that ended the performances in 2009: Matt Marks's transcription of the Beatles' "Revolution 9." This song was originally a tape piece built from audio scraps found in the closets at Abbey Road. For decades, the song has been the least-listened-to track from *The Beatles* (aka *The White Album*). Lennon and Ono, with help from Harrison and George Martin, constructed the Beatles' version on top of an extended coda that had been cut from the first version of "Revolution 1." "Revolution 9" is a significant advance over their first electronic collaboration, *Unfinished Music No. 1: Two Virgins*, which evidenced none of the attention to detail and form that characterizes "Revolution 9."[66] One hundred fifty-four samples taken from forty-five different sources were layered atop more than six minutes of guitars shifting from D major to A major and Lennon shouting "all right" and Ono reciting short lines of her own verse. With the exception of a few of Lennon's shouts and Ono saying, "if you become naked," this base is nearly inaudible in the final mix.[67] Ian MacDonald's somewhat dismissive interpretation argues that "the actual experience of listening to this track, where not merely boring or baffling, often inclines to the sinister, an effect ascribable to the twin driving forces behind it: chance determination and drugs."[68] Lennon's relationship to the piece changed from an initial claim that the track was "painting in sound a picture of revolution" to the counterclaim that it was nothing but "anti-revolution."[69] Akin to Lennon's famous declaration of ambivalence in "Revolution 1," (out/in), whatever overt political intentions might be behind "Revolution 9" are buried beneath what are clearly achieved musical goals. Rather than a random assortment of found sounds disorganized by a drugged consciousness, "Revolution 9" displays a sensitivity to musical morphology that shapes the song's overt references to crowd behavior (football chants and popular dances), mass feeling (choral hymns and nearly hysterical laughter), and music's ability to direct those actions and feelings toward a particular goal. The song's concern with the shape of sound has much more in common with Stockhausen's tape pieces than most heard at the time, as they share a willingness to engage sonic material that is susceptible to transformation, yet which carry their extramusical associations with it in the new form. This suggests that an intensive investigation of transformation itself lies at the heart of "Revolution 9." The question really is, what can musical listening do? This focus on transformation centers Alarm Will Sound's acoustic performance of the piece on the boundary between the musical and the extramusical. In a process now familiar, the ensemble reconfigures backward-taped guitars and orchestral crescendos, voices of crowds and individuals, an isolated crinkling sound, and the gunshots and whoops from a western movie among other material into sounds produced by strings, percussion, piano, trumpet, trombone, clarinet, flute, oboe, and voices. Quite probably the most stunning achievement of all Alarm Will Sound's transformations from the electronic, this version of "Revolution 9" captures the thwarted ambition that 1969 inherits from *Mass* even as it vividly displays the mastery of form that can follow from the deformation of inherited concepts. Marks's rearrangement highlights the musicality of the original, calling the attention of the audience to the piece's existence as a composed musical work. With our attention directed in this fashion, we hear the relationships of parts as they grow and diminish, building and releasing tension in just the way we expect from music. Yet this musicality never loses touch with its origins as a tape piece. In performance that relationship extends forward to the audience, connecting their memories of the impossible sense of the Beatles' track to their current experience of its emotive potential. This potential emerges from the astonishing virtuosity of the transformation but is reinforced by the impassioned agility imputed into the music through the sheer physicality of Alarm Will Sound's playing.

A video of Alarm Will Sound's version of "Revolution 9" has been uploaded to YouTube.[70] When you watch it, you will probably be struck first by the apparent incongruity of Alan Pierson standing before the ensemble and conducting this piece in a traditional fashion: beating time, marking out dynamic changes, and signaling the entry of specific instruments at particular moments. You might even stop to consider the musicians dressed in traditional black, sitting in the standard formation, with their music stands and orchestral instruments before them. Just as you wonder, why do they look like this, the piece begins with Orfe's quiet piano layering beneath Chuck's stolid intoning of the familiar phrase "number nine, number nine." Gradually the music builds, for music it irrefutably is. Before the first minute has passed, the winds have conspired with the strings to generate a tonal block that sounds as if it is going backward. The horns climb atop a rousing clash of percussion and Chuck's reading of the vocal lines accelerates to a rapid peak that quickly fades down again to that backwards sound—which has instantly become iconic. That sound, the sound of taped music moving backward performed on winds and strings, is the acoustic connection between the memories of the audience and its current experience. Together with the title phrase, that backward sound functions like any icon, standing in for itself, locating the audience in relation to its history. That history leaps to life in a pattern of rising and falling waves of sound that grow a bit longer with each iteration as it incorporates a wider variety of sounds. About halfway through the performance, the musicians begin to play their bodies, either clapping hands or slapping thighs. More vocals enter; furious shouts replace nervous laughter. The horns repeat a two-note announcement that they had hinted at earlier, and the strings whirl behind them. During this crescendo, the musicians' bodies materialize the music's pulse. The violins' fierce precision, the cello's commanding certainty, and the trombone's liquid coil are all buttressed by the movements of their players. Abruptly, this peak halts, sharply replaced with more clapping and shouting, which, in turn, give way to the first football chant. (See figure 6.1.)

"Hold that line" assumes a delicious ambiguity here. Yes, it is obviously a direct reference to crowds and the barely controlled violence of American football. But the lyric also suggests the struggle between musical sounds and the physicality of the musicians. The line between the musical and extramusical disappears in "Revolution 9" insofar as the extramusical references of the piece have been integrated into its performance *as part of the music*. After about five and a half minutes, an apparent shouting match erupts between percussion and piano on one hand and the rest of the musicians on the other. The football game and its opposing fans have apparently entered the music itself in what turns out to be the loudest climax of the piece. When the quiet returns, spoken word moves to the fore. Orlando whispers the few recognizable words uttered by Ono on the original. Marks and Chuck recite their final lines. Then in a brief reprise of forced passion, "Revolution 9" ends with the musicians leaning together and shouting the football chants at each other. "Hold that line. Block that kick. Hold that line."

The beauty and the power of Alarm Will Sound's "Revolution 9" precisely derive from its refusal to hold that line between the musical and the extramusical. The dissolution of that line is thematized in the work, but the resulting merger also invades the performers' consciousness. Stefan Freund told me, "'Revolution 9' is so exciting, dramatic, passionate, and riveting for the audience. I am so riveted in performing that piece that I can't imagine the audience isn't." The word choice is impor-

FIG. 6.1 Alarm Will Sound performing *1969* at Le Poisson Rouge, New York.
Photo courtesy of David Goldman, *New York Times*, and Redux Pictures.

tant here. To be riveted is to be fixed in part of a structure, to be held still, incapable of movement. Yet Freund's experience of being riveted materializes precisely as movement—movement in playing his instrument with passion and vigor, movement in gesturing at the wild climaxes. Still, *riveted* is the correct word. The riveting passion of the performance anchors the extravagant rush of feelings produced through this music, tightening its hold on the impossible-to-resolve question of the relationship between the music and what stands outside it. The audience is held in place just as the musicians are, suspended between the opposing positions of music as an internal revolutionary force, demanding change only for music's own forms, and music as an external drive, capable of commanding its auditors to shift the way we understand the world and our place in it. That suspension results from the interaction of concrete sounds and active aural attention. That is what musical listening can do. We lean in, wanting more.

Through its articulation of the musical and the extramusical, achieved through the fusion of collage and composition and the merger of art music and popular music, *1969* compels its audience to listen. That clining attention hears through the moments of musical beauty, through the collage of border-crossing works, to perceive a carefully produced emptiness at the center of the performance, a space absent of action, explicitly emptied of political possibility by the narrative in which it is encased. Around that space circulates a classic melancholia, the refusal to give up the possible force of musical beauty that each individual piece suggests. The selections from Bernstein's *Mass* thread a strand of sad recognition through the thwarted universalist ambitions presented in Stockhausen's and Lennon's music, weaving a paradoxical yearning for a community of belonging motivated by a shared experience of beauty. At the center of this melancholic community lies a lost object, the absent force of the political. Performing this circuit of frustrated desire for an object that it cannot attain, *1969* creates a *sens* of a polis minus the fundamental contradiction that generates all political drive. *1969*'s beauty therefore risks evoking the familiar destructive desire for a universal community without politics, a community that cannot exist.[71]

Any sens of the polis constructed in this fashion runs the risk of reproducing what already is by not seeing, or rather not hearing, what has been left out. The fundamental contradiction of aesthetics, that it feels objective when it is rooted in one's inescapably subjective history, renders any community built from its pleasures susceptible to an unthinking reproduction of the same. Nancy warns against this possibility, and

Rancière bases his entire concept of the aesthetic on the importance of new voices, new sounds erupting into and reshaping the common. Any actualization of being-in-common in this historical moment, therefore, must bring with it an attitude of self-critique, a self-reflexive interrogation of what has not been constructed in this moment of political longing.[72] The affective intensity that seems to affirm the significance of joint longing carries the potential power to lull an audience into an exercise in self-affirmation. All the work that led up to 1969—the collective communal effort that transformed electronically produced sounds into humanly performed tones, all the work that transformed concepts of musical transcendence into embodied enactments of collective coherence, all of that musicalization of political desire—risks collapsing into nostalgic longing for a community of the same, a whitewashed memory of lost possibility.

1969 indirectly performs a set of limits to music's ability to forge political community. This is why it is necessary to remember some of the other art music that was being made in the period covered in 1969. That year, the Art Ensemble of Chicago arrived in Paris, performed across Europe to great acclaim, and released its first recordings. The group's use of collage and montage techniques was well received at festivals and nightclubs alike, drawing comparison to European composers such as Iannis Xenakis and Stockhausen. Other representatives of the Chicago-based Association for the Advancement of Creative Musicians were also regularly performing in Paris, challenging European audiences' conceptions of black music. George Lewis writes about the Chicago musicians' performances in France: "No sound was excluded and no tradition was sacrosanct, and French audiences and the jazz press quickly fell in love with the ruptures and surprises."[73] The day after Woodstock ended, Miles Davis entered the studio and began the process of recording his landmark fusion album, *Bitches Brew*. This recording was Davis's most commercially successful effort to crack the walls between rock and jazz and expand the realm of popular music. Produced via multiple takes and extensive editing, *Bitches Brew* openly broke with jazz orthodoxy. Featuring some of the most evil bass clarinet ever recorded and some astonishingly discordant interplay among the multiple keyboards, the album opened the ears of those raised on rock's incorporation of the blues. Davis insisted that the genre of fusion was something new; it could not be reduced to any preexisting forms. Even more pertinently, he believed fusion had the potential to, in Kevin Fellezs's words, "cut across generational as well as racial borders." Fellezs quotes Davis saying: "I started thinking about building a new audience for the future. . . . I thought it would be good if I could get all these young people together listening to my music and digging the groove."[74] Davis wanted to incite the clining.

As Lewis has shown, the experimental music community in New York was segregated in terms of venues, of journalists assigned to cover the different music, and most of all in terms of the assumed racial identity of the categories into which the music was sorted. The genres themselves were racialized. Even though there were individual musicians who crossed these boundaries—a few black artists working in the white-majority avant-garde scene, more white musicians working in the black-majority jazz scene—once the music of a group or an individual musician had been labeled, it could only rarely be performed in other venues. However experimental or artistic their music, groups led by black musicians or made up mostly of black musicians were prima facie sorted into the jazz category. Black music could only find coverage in the jazz pages of the press, written by critics whose focus was jazz. As Lewis puts it, "Race itself was assumed to overdetermine the identity of the black creative artist."[75] This segregation was undeniably a component of the musical world of 1969. To that extent, Alarm Will Sound's representation of that historical moment is simply accurate. But it is very important that the group's audience in the twenty-first century, those captured by the musical beauty and the political lure of this program, recognize its limits. It would be even better for all to listen to "A Brain for the Seine," or "Pharaoh's Dance," or even "November Steps" (which was premiered by the New York Philharmonic in 1967) upon arriving home. To this day, these works by the Art Ensemble of Chicago, Davis, and Takemitsu create an alternate version of the architectonics of tradition, power, and belonging, one that might have been able to locate some hope and sound some newly resonating difference among the audiences for 1969. Another political lay just outside the concert's white melancholy.

Just as this book has not mentioned many important moments of the musical performance of political longing, no concert can or should include every style. Alarm Will Sound should not be expected to perform every genre of music at the highest level. The 2011 version of 1969 did expand to include an arrangement of Hendrix's version of "The Star-Spangled Banner," adding a black musical creator to the group's representation of the time period and referencing one of the few well-known moments of hope from that troubled year. Even with that inclusion, 1969's performance of melancholy and loss accurately captures the dismay that white elites felt when attempting to shape and direct the emergence of the postcolonial world. Let me be clear: I do not mean that Alarm Will Sound directly intends this set of implications for its piece. Nor do I mean that Bernstein, Stockhausen, Lennon, and the rest had a sense of the interaction between their music and the global process of decolonization. Instead, I believe that the collage of their music constructed by Alarm Will Sound takes on the air of melancholy when placed in the context of iconic events from the sixties that demonstrated the impossibility of the peaceful progressive transformation of society. The assassinations, the riots, and the use of state power to quash antiwar demonstrations exemplify the violence that erupted in response to the global transformations that the world was just beginning to experience. The music of 1969 rejects those moments of antagonism but finds no other response equal to that force. The music produced from 1967 to 1970 is an overwhelmingly vast cultural resource that resonates a world in utter transformation. Some of this music captures that violence, finds beauty in the extremes reinforced by it. 1969 focuses the attention of its audiences on the collapse of a cultural-political bridge between white elites and the popular audience for rock. 1969's white melancholy cannot register the fact that musicians around the world were creating other echoes of a reformed sensible.

Chantal Mouffe's correction of Carl Schmitt's formulation of the political recognizes the necessity for fundamental difference and contradiction in any political community.[76] The irresolvable tension between the conflicting goods of equality and liberty ensures that a democratic community must respond to the disruptions generated at any single historical moment when these competing imperatives clash. No outcome is ever guaranteed, but the mutual recognition of joint belonging is necessary for the tensions to be approached in an agonistic rather than antagonistic fashion. The tragedy presented in 1969 is not the failure of past political projects. Rather, its tragic commentary refers to the present, this moment in time when we seem incapable of comprehending a political community inclusive of meaningful difference, an agonistic polis clining toward the future.

Coda

Listening through the Aural Imaginary

||||

Compassion . . . is the disturbance of violent relatedness.

—Jean-Luc Nancy, *Being Singular Plural*

Music entrains us with sonic patterns of engaging with the world. Musical listening brings to our awareness patterns of tension and release, a tolerance for dissonance, the pleasures of delayed resolution, the relative independence of multiple layers that twine the knots of our experience, and the differential power of timbral resonance for enabling our ears to follow those layers. Music's ability to focus our attention on those patterns, on the production of those patterns and the disruption of those patterns, encourages us to sharpen our perceptions of the intricate relations of difference that constitute our world. In so doing, music provides us with embodied experiences of the abstraction of the social.

Music provides us with primary evidence that we are not solitary beings, that our innermost selves are interwoven with others. As Jean-Luc Nancy says in his little book *Listening*, "Musical listening seems, then, to be . . . a relationship to meaning, a tension toward it, but toward it completely ahead of signification."[1] Elsewhere Nancy argues that this tension or clining toward meaning is necessarily social. "Meaning is the name of our being-with one another," he says.[2] Musical listening, then, induces a set of experiences that link together our inner awareness of ourselves reaching toward meaning with our sense of the groups to which we belong. This clining, this leaning toward the awareness of our coexistence, is how music provides experiential evidence of what Nancy terms "being singular plural." Groups themselves are always plural, always constructed of relations of difference. Music's presentation of multiple interlocking patterns of physical experiences built from vibrations of difference produce an awareness of self that is always an awareness of the plurality of ourselves and of others, as well as an awareness of our dependence on others even to recognize the existence of our selves.

Music begins to produce these effects just before the moment we recognize that what we are listening to is music. Once that awareness captures our attention and we begin to listen musically, we begin a process of interpretation that engages what Lawrence Kramer calls our "structures of prejudgment." Acts of interpretation take place at the point where prejudgment collapses, and music's lack of semantic solidity places musical listening right on this edge.[3] Paradoxically, in order to listen musically, which means to engage the sounds we are hearing as feelingfully meaningful in their own right, we must project into the interpretive process our understanding of the social conditions out of which that music has emerged. These conditions are an ineradicable component of music. Our judgment of whether or not the sounds we are listening to are music is nearly instantaneous, even if that judgment remains open to revision. But in order to interpret that music, in order to truly listen musically, we must assess, however tentatively, the music's characteristics. In so doing, we organize our responses around a sense of genre.

Genres are shared organizations of patterns, sets of conventions. Among those conventions that coalesce into genres are social associations. These social associations are not secondary considerations, except in the nearly instantaneous temporal sense that I have just described. The social aspects of genre are not simply the context that surrounds the text of music. Rather, the social aspects of genre immediately shape and direct our interpretation of musical sound. Conversely, the impact of the social does not deny or limit the power of musical form. Instead, the instantaneous intermediation of sound and the social is part of the interpretation of the formal conventions of any genre. We always listen socially, with a constant tracking back and forth between sounds and imagined others. We can never not do that. Even if we hear something that fits no genre we know, we apply the conventions of what we do know until the lack of fit forces us to reconsider. If and when we reconsider the musical terms, we begin to feel our way into a new understanding of social conventions as well. Listening musically is something more than assessing the abilities of the producers of music to manipulate sound and create intriguing beacons of sensibility. Through attention to music, we assess our degree of relatedness to and distance from other people.

These effects are the consequence of the experience of musical beauty, of musical strangeness, perhaps even of musical banality and vulgarity.

The feeling of musical beauty is common and everyday, yet extraordinary and sublime. We confront our own bodies through the experience of patterned sounds, and we confront the bodies of others through our interpretations of those patterned sounds. In the recognition of musical beauty, we acknowledge the connectedness of bodies, the irreducible plurality of being. In the immediate experience of musical beauty, an architectonic arrangement develops, equally constructed from the sonic and the social, and extends its way into our sense of right relations. In the encounter with musical beauty, our sense of the social is necessarily affected.

The problem that I heard in Alarm Will Sound's 1969 is a general one. It is the problem that results from staying within the music we already know, the music that already pleases us, whose beauty is familiar. If our listening is so restricted, the music we hear can only anthemically reinforce our already present awareness of the way things should be, confirming the well-worn pathways frequently traveled by our senses. Anthems celebrate already existing political communities. Functioning as sonic mirrors, anthems merely reflect the surfaces shown to them. The historical convergence of the Civil Rights Movement, the folk revival, and the emergence of soul music created a peak moment in our historical awareness of the political force of music, establishing the standard for music's transformative possibilities. But "We Shall Overcome" should not be allowed to stand alone as our marker of politically productive music. Initial politically agentive work had been performed by songs such as "This Little Light of Mine" in a context of congregational singing, and later a national alliance formed around the popular spread of soul and its compelling insistence on the proper blend of dignity and embodied pleasure. Rock's ability to approach the pleasures of soul, while accelerating its pace, flattening its rhythms, and eschewing dignity for defiance ensured that the political community that rock formed would encircle itself with a series of ever-more restrictive gestures of refusal. The longed-for purity of punk quickly found the hardcore limits of this strategy, and the more humble and less ambitious strand of indie delineated an ambiguous and tentative assertion of emotional authority. Each of these developments had its moment of political expansion; each has faded into sonic evidence of a past formation. Listening to old favorites can be comforting. But this is not the time for reassurance. The old sensibilities are ill prepared for today's complexities. They must be reimagined. That is what both Takemitsu Toru and Yoko Ono recognized when they turned inward and reoriented the significance of the most traditional Japanese musical sounds, opening up the physical tensions of *sawari* and the fully connective emptiness of *ma*.

Yet it is no simple project to search out new sounds and listen for alternative distributions of the sensible. Because another problem arises when we encounter new sounds, unfamiliar sounds from an unfamiliar context, and feel something of music's ability to shift our sensibilities. Roshanak Kheshti calls this the problem of the "aural imaginary" and defines it as "the symbolic realm in which the listener engages in an imagined relation, often affective, with an other that is elicited in sound."[4] Kheshti uses this concept to critique the world-music market, making use of online consumer reviews of an album by a female Brazilian singer to demonstrate the persistence of gendered and racialized assumptions that position the singer as a willing supplicant performing for the North American listener. According to Kheshti, the aural imaginary is always structured by relations of dominance. The experience of musical pleasure, perhaps even of all forms of musical beauty, is necessarily shaped by power relations. In the world-music market, these relations situate the performer as exotic and other. The shaping power of the aural imaginary is exacerbated by the probability that the listener will not have had extensive exposure to the genre and its conventions. Even more likely is the probability that the world-music consumer will know little about the social qualities of the genre beyond what is included in the marketing of the music. As a consequence, the listener's structure of prejudgment can project fantasies that reinforce the listener's desire for mastery, a desire frequently catered to in commodity relations. Although she develops the concept in and through a critique of the world-music market, Kheshti's concept of the aural imaginary has significant implications for all forms of listening, perhaps especially the kind of listening that might enable the emergence of new political communities.[5]

For example, let's look again at the interaction between Alan Lomax and Vera Hall. Throughout his career, Alan Lomax saw himself as a defender, a celebrator, a champion of human populations who for a while had seemed to escape the worst ravages of capitalist modernity. His chief approach to the celebration and defense of these populations was to listen as carefully as he could to their music, for he believed, as do I, that music provides a way of feeling your way into and coming to know human differences and commonalities. In his ambitious but incomplete project of cantometrics, Lomax documented the music of South American peasants, Spanish shepherds, Italian dockworkers, Scottish farmers, Russians, North Africans, Caribbean islanders, and, probably most famously, singers black, brown, and beige from the American South. Throughout his career, he argued that song is a way for people to know that they belong somehow to the same community, the same interacting group.[6]

Alan Lomax was determined to hear the coarticulation of the social and musical. He was open and generous in his listening, firmly committed to the Boasian position that all cultures, all peoples, and all musical styles—so long as those styles were authentically expressive of a people's values—were equally significant and equally valuable. Nevertheless, despite his commendable personal intentions and professional goals, Lomax's work reproduced the relations of dominance that put the desires and needs of his immediate community over those of the people he studied. His approach to recording and documenting the music of the world's peoples carried assumptions about social relations that he could not reflect upon, and these assumptions (most significantly, assumptions about the "naturalness" of non-Western cultures) limited his capacity to hear the complexity and multivoiced quality of the musical samples he collected. When Hall sang for Lomax and when she told him stories about growing up in Jim Crow America, Lomax heard only songs and stories about the way things used to be in a different culture called the American South. He could not hear the challenges that were coded in her words, challenges to the conditions within which their own exchange took place, challenges that are much easier for us to hear today. When Hall described her strategies for keeping white folks at bay, Lomax paradoxically felt closer to her.

Lomax was working at the vanguard of white musical listeners from the late 1930s through the 1950s. His ears and his corporeal habitus recognized commonalities and dining possibilities where so many of his contemporaries heard the inarticulate hollering of nature. The distance he felt and described between his own conditions of being and the life of Hall, her golden voice and her steely calm, was the distance between a black, female domestic worker living in Jim Crow Alabama and a white, male song collector and folklorist making his home in New York. His inability to hear the full complexity of her message does not undercut the value of the beauty he felt or the tension toward meaning that this beauty produced—even if a profound distance remained.

It would be disingenuous not to acknowledge the similarities between Lomax's approach and my own. I certainly share his belief that music lays bare the interconnectedness of humans, and recognize in his work some of my own methodological focus on feels, tensions, and tempos.

For listeners such as myself, the Alan Lomax problem, the likelihood that I am not hearing the same sounds in the same way as others toward whom I lean, is inescapable. The truth is that musical listening cannot escape the dangers of the aural imaginary.

Not even the methodological requirements of ethnomusicology can provide a safe haven. Based on the recognition of the inextricable intertwining of the musical and the social, ethnomusicology supplements musical analyses with ethnographic investigations of the lives and social conditions of a particular musical community. The ethnographic focus does have the capacity to illuminate the musical meanings shared within a defined locality. But in our current world of coexistence, it is no longer possible to fully determine the extent or reach of "the community." The porousness of community boundaries in our time is a consequence of the interconnectedness of the fate of all humans. Any grounding of musical belonging in a bounded interior of like-thinking individuals cannot grasp the complexity of our current predicament. Nor does it provide us with a way to listen for the political force of musical beauty. Ethnography is an important yet limited method for connecting musical meanings and the social. Ethnography is an effort, finally, to control the meanings of music, to limit in advance the acts of interpretation that are at the core of musical listening by grounding them in the needs and already existing patterns of a particular subgroup, a locality, a constrained system of exchange and communication. Ethnomusicology cannot anchor the drift of music as it is driven by the currents of an increasingly connected world. Innocent listening is impossible. A listening purified of preexisting judgments is impossible. Yet to remain trapped in the conservatory of known sounds and already understood social formations is to fail to hear the prefiguring harmonics that signal global political transformations; it is to cut oneself off from the rhythmic dynamism of the world. Instead, we must keep listening for the previously unheard.

In *Darker Than Blue*, Paul Gilroy simultaneously celebrates and worries about the role that black music has played in the construction of global power relations. Critical of the vapidly sentimental assumption of equality based on shared pleasure, Gilroy still suggests that the experience of sentimental attachment can initiate the drive for an interrogative listening, one that recognizes the adamant responsibility incumbent upon the members of a shared political community. Evoking, as he often does, the ghost of Bob Marley, Gilroy traces the reception of Marley's music to a convergence of marketing strategies and redistributed sensibilities: "An aura of rebel authenticity was projected, not to validate his complex parapolitical aspirations or demotic intransigence, but to invest the arresting music with a mood of carefully calculated transgression designed to make it salable and appealing. A thrilling and exotic racial otherness was invoked and contained where that music was made to supply an affecting background to essentially boring and empty activities like shopping and getting stoned."[7] As Jason Toynbee has documented, Chris Blackwell, the owner of Island Records, carefully and deliberately shaped the sentimental conditions of reception for Marley's music so that it could appear both dangerous and safe for white rock fans.[8] Using Kheshti's terms, the meaning of Marley's music in North America echoed in and through the aural imaginary of these fans, reinforcing their feelings of comfort with global political relations. But Gilroy takes a longer-term view of this event in global stardom, insisting that Marley's "interventions actually helped to bring a novel solidarity network into being" when global geopolitics shifted its axis from an East-West to a North-South orientation.[9] The sentimental Anglo-American attachment to the sounds of reggae was only one step in Marley's redistribution of the sensible.

Even listened to as a background to mindless activities, Marley's music could establish an "affective soundscape" capable of producing "attachments to and investments in a sense of political and social mutuality." Indeed, the shared enjoyment of music can be a primary force in the construction of "intimate publics," Lauren Berlant's term for juxtapolitical communities of feeling.[10] Gilroy's insistence on the long-term effectiveness of Marley's music underscores an aspect of black music that Jayna Brown identifies as its "utopian impulse . . . that is as momentary, ephemeral, and elusive as it is physically, historically, and politically placed."[11] This utopian impulse is what enables black music to center the clining, the subtle leaning together, that produces so many communities of feeling around the globe.

World music is a particularly troublesome category of music. Not a genre per se, yet not fully reducible to a marketing strategy, world music can most easily be thought of as non-Western popular music marketed to Western consumers. At the end of 2011, the National Academy of Recording Arts and Sciences collapsed the distinction between best traditional and best contemporary world-music album and returned to having a single category for the best world-music album for the Grammy Awards.[12] On February 12, 2012, that award was given to Tinariwen's *Tassili*. Tinariwen was perfectly placed to capitalize on the collapse of the distinction between contemporary and traditional. For

FIG. C.1 Tinariwen's extension of the polis, Cincinnati, 2013.
Photo by Ricky Crano.

more than a decade, the group of Tuareg musicians had toured heavily
and recorded frequently, creating a body of music that sounded contemporary while signifying an exotic tradition (see figure C.1). In a review
of their 2007 album, *Aman Iman*, Joe Tangari described their music this
way: "The music of Tinariwen is at once exotic and familiar—the scales
and arrangements are as strange to our ears as the language they sing
in, but there's a force operating on a more subliminal level that unites
it to something rattling around inside anyone who was brought up on
blues or rock & roll. It's music of longing and rebellion, weary wisdom
and restless energy, and it sounds so, so good."[13] That subliminal level
is structured by the aural imaginary. Tinariwen's droning guitars and
deep masculine voices reverberate off ear canals trained by decades of
rock's romanticization of the blues impulse and stimulate the longing
for political music that haunts the aural imaginary of many American
listeners. When describing Tinariwen's 2009 album, *Imidiwan*, Tangari
outlined the context for its production, describing the "intermittent violence and displacement" the Tuareg people experience "as they've fought
to maintain their culture and lifestyle in a world that isn't built to accom-

modate it." He then declared, "There is a unique magic to the sounds of the Sahara. *Imidiwan* captures that magic with skillful grace."[14] Listening to these recordings, the disproportionately young white male readers of these *Pitchfork* reviews could imagine a soundscape that integrated tones both familiar and exotic, guitar drones amid North African scales, non-English lyrics repeated with strophic phrasing, within a contemporary geopolitical struggle, conjuring the associations of black music with the drive for human emancipation. "The blues is present," says Tangari, "as a sense of intense longing and defiance in the face of despair that hums in sympathetic vibration with its trans-Atlantic cousin."[15] Writing for the *Village Voice*, Robert Christgau, among the most thoughtful of all rock critics, calmly acknowledges: "The spiritual gravity of their melodies and grooves demands your attention without offering to reward it— what's sought isn't your affection but your respect."[16]

Of course, the differences between the African and the American historical and political contexts are immense. The musicians of Tinariwen are not inheritors of the legacy of the trans-Atlantic slave trade. They are Tuareg, an ethnic group often included among the Berbers but distinguished by their language, Tamashek. When France's North African colonies achieved independence in the 1960s, the Tuareg found their traditional territory divided among the nations of Mali, Niger, and Libya. At the time of decolonization, the Tuareg were a mostly nomadic people, whose way of life was increasingly threatened by the modernizing projects transforming the region's economy. In addition a long drought period greatly reduced the landscape's ability to support nomadic groups and their animal herds. One of the results of these environmental and economic pressures was the Tuareg rebellion, a decades-long conflict that has gone through periods of greater and lesser violence. Despite the uneven nature of the fighting, with extended periods where few casualties occurred, the Tuareg social world has been fundamentally transformed. The traditional self-sufficient way of life has been nearly completely eradicated, and the concept of unemployment is now a lived reality.[17]

Like all ethnic groups, however, the Tuareg are divided within themselves politically. Not all are united in their opposition to national governments or modern life. The Tuareg rebellion calmed down considerably in the mid-1990s, when peace accords were issued and a momentary reconciliation with the Mali government was achieved. The Malian state made overtures to the Tuareg, creating positions for them in the government. Even before then, some Tuaregs had fought in the Malian Army, and there were political divisions that split families. A growing percentage of this ethnic group has come to live in the cities of Mali, particularly the northern cities of Kidal and Timbuktu but also Bamako in the Southwest.[18] Despite this accommodation to modernity by many Tuareg, armed struggle has broken out again. Now the Tuareg find themselves combating an insurgent Islamic radical group, Ansar Dine, who have taken control of much of the territory, banned secular music, and destroyed old shrines. In 2012 Tuareg nationalists were battling to retain cultural autonomy within Azawad (as they refer to this area), not to wrest it from the Malian state.[19] As the anthropologist Susan Rasmussen argues, the idea of the nation is a relatively recent import that remains ambiguous among the Tuareg, often more cultural than political, more geographical than tribal. An unstable concept, Tuareg nationalism and its complexities within this struggle are not easily conveyed through music.[20]

Several of the musicians in Tinariwen, including Ibrahim Ag Alhabib, the most senior member of the band, and the fellow founder, Abdallah Ag Alhousseyni, met during the 1980s in camps in Libya while undergoing military training conducted by Qaddafi's army. This camp encounter is a central node in the narrative that links the sounds of Tinariwen to the romantic image of the camel-riding rebel. The melodies and rhythms that sound exotic to Tangari emerged from a tradition of guitar-accompanied warrior praise songs called *ichumar* or *alguitara*. It is an adaptation of a slightly (but only slightly) older traditional style called *teherdent*. According to the ethnomusicologist Nadia Belalimat, the teherdent style features both male and female singers, the women alternating ululations with the men's chants. The instrumentation is sparse, featuring rhythms beat out on a *tinde* drum reinforced by handclaps, while the melodies are echoed on the three-string lute from which the style takes its name. Originally a style that was performed only by local musicians for an audience of extended family and friends, its orientation shifted outward during the 1960s. Belalimat notes, "Many musician-artisans started performing outside their own lineage affiliations in order to provide for themselves, since their former employers could no longer support them."[21] The teherdent style adapted to the guitar when that instrument spread across the region. The guitar could be both louder and more percussive than the teherdent, and it was just as easy to carry. When the Tuareg resistance began, the instrument quickly became metonymically linked to weapons of rebellion. Another of the founding members of Tinariwen, Keddou Ag Ossad, was praised for riding into battle with a rifle in one hand, a traditional saber in the other, and his guitar on his back.[22] As Rasmussen explains, "In the early ichumar music, the composers, performers, and audience all were combatants. . . . Early ichumar songs were composed by one rebel to praise another and were performed by the composer or the subject of praise in a tightly knit 'circle' of mutual support."[23] As the alguitara or ichumar style developed, recordings of this music were banned by the Malian government and circulated only via underground cassette copies.

After the mid-1990s peace accords, however, Tuareg popular music came aboveground. Belalimat argues that during the period of reconciliation, a tamed and modernized version of teherdent became "the urban dance music for a cosmopolitan and multi-ethnic public."[24] As Rasmussen points out, "There is pressure now, for many musicians, to comply with the requests and tastes of diverse governments and audiences, with different viewpoints and agendas. The music and songs of the ichumar have become submerged in changing uses of guitar performance."[25] In Mali there is no longer a direct, immediate link between alguitara and armed rebellion. It is now one musical style among many.

This is the complicated musical-political context out of which developed the sounds of Tinariwen. The band carefully nurtures its reputation as a group formed of rebel fighters, although they insist that their fighting days are over (see figure C.2). They do not enjoy a large following in Mali. Their audience is mainly elsewhere, largely in France, the United States, and the United Kingdom. Their first internationally released recording, *The Radio Tisdas Sessions*, establishes the basic outlines of their sound. Characteristics shared with teherdent music include a regular and unvarying tinde drum pattern that reinforces the feeling of uneven constancy, while a sense of musical movement comes from melodies that rise chant-like as far as the fifth note of the scale and then sway down to a flatted seventh before returning to the tonic. Texture is provided by a variation in voices that suggests antiphony. But in the alguitara of Tinariwen, these echoing voices do not always achieve the full effect of call-and-response, as guitars repeat the melodies beneath all the lines. Multiple guitar lines interweave across a modal background that remains nearly static throughout each song. Indeed, guitars simply dominate the sound. Their slightly varying timbres—some acoustic, some electric—and shifting styles—some featuring Garcia-like doodlings, others droning the bottom E string—underline and entangle the alternating voices. In their intertwining, they model a weaving of slight differences, a hammering on and pulling off that carries the voices, spreading their drones and chants across an array of vibrating strings

FIG. C.2 Tinariwen chanting the wild, Cincinnati, 2013. Photo by Ricky Crano.

and vocal chords, then pulling the entire ensemble together and tying it up neatly into one communal sound. Its closest melodic and rhythmic cousin is the Malian blues of Ali Farka Touré, but Tinariwen transforms Touré's lonesome qualities into sounds that don't celebrate community but rather manifest its practice. While Tinariwen sounds nothing like Skip James, nothing like Bessie Smith, nothing like Muddy Waters, it does extend musical invitations to strangers, in a fashion much like those masters of the African American musical tradition, asking them to lean closer.

Tassili, the 2011 Best World Music award winner, was clearly and obviously produced for the U.S. market. There is no ethnomusicology that makes sense of this album. Traditional notions of authenticity are just not relevant here. This is not a traditional sound rooted in established lifeways. The album is a response to ongoing disruption that merges feelings of loss with relentless determination, tied together by global listening practices. Like much world music, the sound is derived at least as much from musical strategies developed in the United States as those that emerged elsewhere—in this case, in the Sahara.[26] The recording features the American indie rock musicians Nels Cline, Kyp Malone, and

Tunde Adebempe, as well as the New Orleans avant-rootists the Dirty Dozen Brass Band, each of whom add their signature sonic qualities to the tracks on which they appear. Cline's background guitar hum is familiar from the last several Wilco albums. The Dirty Dozen Brass Band works its harmonic magic spreading triads across the range of horns as well as supplying a twisted sax solo. But the most successful trans-Atlantic blend can be heard on the tracks shared with the musicians from TV on the Radio.

Of those, "Tenere Taqqim Tossam" received the most promotional attention. It is the first song that plays when you visit Tinariwen's Anti-Records website. An accompanying video re-creates the condition of the song's production, alternating shots of musicians sitting around a fire, sharing tea, picking up guitars, beating on drums, clapping hands, and singing with not-quite trite shots of blowing sand, night-blue skies, and tensely patterned tapestries. The visual narrative ends with a concert scene that reestablishes Tinariwen as the song's ultimate authors. The video produces the fantasy of the musical encounter, a fantasy central to the appeal and also to the latent political possibility heard in world music. As Paul Gilroy puts it: "[The encounter is] where world music cease[s] to be a marketing label and [becomes] an ethically infused aspiration, [and] it can also help to identify a uniquely cosmopolitan space where musicians from all sorts of places and backgrounds could begin — once again in opposition to the hierarchies of race and logics of empire — to meet one another as equals. In that utopian location, they could imagine what it might mean to create together on the singular foundation of common human creativity — in real time and face to face."[27] When you listen to "Tenere Taqqim Tossam," you will note some key differences between this track and earlier Tinariwen recordings. First, this song has a bridge. Sung by Adebempe over a recognizable chord progression played by Kyp Malone, the chorus interrupts the classic Tinariwen arrangement. Where earlier songs such as "Les Chants des Fauves" worked the melodic territory sketched out by a classic modal drone, "Tenere Taqqim Tossam" forges its drone atop shifting harmonies. Malone's guitar maps the chord patterns, but the guitar chords are mixed down while the lead lines that characterize the sound of Tinariwen are pushed to the front. These interlocking guitar lines have to do more in this song, maintaining its continuity across the uncommon verse-bridge divide. The vocal line in the bridge, though, presents the most striking difference. Here a shift to Adebempe's falsetto is matched by the novel appearance of English lyrics. The encounter between Tinariwen and TV on the Radio could not be more clearly foregrounded than it is here during the bridge. Rising higher than any other male voice on the album (or any previous Tinariwen recording I know), Adebempe's voice tracks an arc both melodic and lyrical, conforming to the tinde beat while articulating a longing for the anthropomorphized place of the encounter—the jealous desert:

> O Tenere!
> A jealous desert!
> Why can't you see?
> You are a treasure
> I've seen the world,
> I love you better
> Oh Tenere!
> You are the treasure
> Of my soul.

The melodic arc of that last line—"Of my soul"—creates a soft landing for Adebempe's voice and sends the song back into the more Tinariwen-like section of the song. The falsetto voice, common to both West African singing styles and a range of African American popular genres, sings the unity momentarily fantasized in the song. Moving vocally to a higher place and then returning to the gruff masculinity of Tinariwen's singers, the two different parts weave together a newer, more expansive, and more complicated unity created on the scene of a desert fantasy. Any effort to anchor the affective resonances of this performance solely in the sands of the Sahara would simply miss the key encounters at the heart of the performance. This is not teherdent music. It is not blues. It is not rock, indie or otherwise. Its beauty forces a re-cognition, a reordering of the relations that inscribe genre.

Before I rush too quickly into a celebration of the potential of this performance, it is important to recall Jayna Brown's caution about the fantasy of the encounter:

> In terms of time, the fantasy of the first encounter is a foundational process in the construction of world music and remains a site of intense utopian fantasy. There remains a belief that at the heart of any encounter is a moment powerful enough to transcend even its own politics of inequality. In terms of space, and less laden with troublesome history, is the concept of contact zones, spaces within the music where forms, symbolic of the bodies they represent, crisscross each other, their touch producing new forms of personal fulfillment. But

this concept can be just as misleading as the first, as it takes social inequalities, the material conditions of the music's creation, as purely aesthetic "differences."[28]

While Brown's caution is well taken, I want to emphasize the political potential of the encounter between such aesthetic differences. It is in this space where musical beauty exerts its power. Here, in the encounter between aural imaginaries forced to acknowledge the rightness of new relations, the redistribution of the sensible is possible. Through an encounter that demands and enables recognition of a previously unimaginable commonality, the high voices of the American indie-rock band merge with the low voices of the Tuareg alguitara musicians, not to create a utopia of equality but to stage an exchange of articulate voices — the necessary first step in truly aesthetic work, the redistribution of the sensible.[29]

The encounter between TV on the Radio and Tinariwen does not generate knowledge of the decades-long armed struggle in northern Mali. Instead, this encounter functions as a meeting of equals who recognize each other in the act of musicking. Listeners can hear that encounter, the sounds of that recognition. But they do not hear the truth of the Tuareg or the history of their struggles. To hear the beauty of "Tenere Taqqim Tossam" is not to align oneself with a resistance movement. It is, instead, to experience the echo of that musical recognition, to come to a felt awareness of the Tuareg's existence as political beings (see figure C.3).

If music is a way of knowing others, and if sharing experiences of musical beauty is a means of developing the extended sensibilities out of which emergent political communities can grow, then there is no escape from the fantasies generated through the aural imaginary. The musical encounter between TV on the Radio and Tinariwen stages a potential encounter for their listeners, one that at first, at the moment of encounter, is experienced aesthetically. The problem is not that the listeners who hear and imagine this encounter do not have full knowledge of the communities from which this new musical beauty arises. Such full knowledge is both impossible to achieve and not the necessary grounds for a clining toward a new commons. The real difficulty comes from the fact that the understanding of others means, as Nancy puts it, "in every sense, understanding others through 'me' and understanding 'me' through others."[30] This means of knowing is fraught with danger. It constantly tempts the listener to clothe new sounds in familiar and nonthreatening social rai-

FIG. C.3 Tinariwen performing musical interplay in Cincinnati, 2013.
Photo by Ricky Crano.

ment. Listening for the political force of musical beauty risks the reduction of new relations of difference to a natural and trouble-free evolution from the old, maintaining in the process the long-standing hierarchies of power and value.

Rather than attempt to escape this danger, those listening for the political should simply confront it head on. The political force of musical beauty derives from its ability to intervene in the audible relations that preexist the encounter, to cause a reorganization of internally sensed relations of difference so that the singular plural of the listener's being has been touched and transformed. The danger here is not that listeners cannot escape their own social conditions or transcend their particular subjectivities. The social grounding of one's ears, and the aural imaginary that necessarily results, are the conditions of possibility for musical listening. When Tinariwen and TV on the Radio perform on the *Colbert Report* (as they did in February 2012), their music does not produce a newly unified political community. But the musical beauty they generate establishes the shared feelings required for an intimate public to form. While an intimate public is only ever juxtapolitical, it can lay the affective groundwork necessary for the difficulties of real political work.

The danger that derives from the aural imaginary is this: there is no necessary political trajectory that results from musical listening. At best, the experience of musical beauty does redistribute the sensible, and in so doing, it does demand a deeper interrogative listening to any political claims made. But the political force of music stops at that point. The clining that follows from a redistribution of an audible sensible does not guarantee justice. The particular political direction of a renewed and redefined community is contingent. The political community that emerges from the experience of musical beauty might not be open to new relations. The Tuareg rebellion is not a stable object for the political longings of young Westerners, but the music of Tinariwen can elicit a clining toward others who hear its musicality.

There must always be a moment of doubt, a moment of self-questioning that permeates all efforts to listen to the music of others. Communities built on the juxtapolitical ground of musical listening are only communities of listeners oriented toward an object of musical beauty. The shared musical meanings toward which they incline cannot be rooted purely and totally in the social grounds experienced by the artists, the performers, the producers of the musical sounds, nor should these shared musical meanings be understood as the confirmation of the

listener's comfort. There is, moreover, no guarantee of a positive political outcome; there is no guarantee of a fundamental equality among the
participants. There is only listening, only listening to the musical beauty
of a world remaking itself, and clining toward the meanings that beauty
suggests.

Notes

INTRODUCTION. A PRELUDE

In most cases, Asian names are listed with the family name first. A few artists (such as Yoko Ono) rose to international attention using the Western order of their names. In those cases, Western order will be used.

1. S. Craig Werner, *A Change Is Gonna Come: Music, Race, and the Soul of America*, revised ed. (Ann Arbor: University of Michigan Press, 2006); Marc Anthony Neal, *What the Music Said: Black Popular Music and Black Public Culture* (New York: Routledge, 1999); Robert Cantwell, *When We Were Good: The Folk Revival* (Cambridge, MA: Harvard University Press, 1996).

2. Theodor Adorno, "Late Style in Beethoven" and "Alienated Masterpiece: *The Missa Solemnis*," in Theodor Adorno, *Essays on Music*, ed. Richard Leppert and trans. Susan H. Gillespie (Berkeley: University of California Press, 2002).

3. Dave Hickey, *The Invisible Dragon: Essays on Beauty*, revised and expanded ed. (Chicago: University of Chicago Press, 2009), 71. The ellipses take the place of the qualifier *American* in the original. I do not find a national limit to this sentiment.

4. Jacques Rancière, *The Politics of Aesthetics*, trans. Gabriel Rockhill (New York: Continuum Books, 2004); see esp. 12–19.

5. "Tonally moving forms" is the phrase that Eduard Hanslick used to describe music's effects in the absence of any referential content. Eduard Hanslick, *On the Musically Beautiful: A Contribution towards the Revision of the Aesthetics of Music*, trans. Geoffrey Payzant (New York: Hackett, 1986).

6. For a critique of the concept of structural listening, see Theodore Gracyk, *Listening to Popular Music; Or, How I Learned to Stop Worrying and Love Led Zeppelin* (Ann Arbor: University of Michigan Press, 2007).

7. Lauren Berlant, *The Female Complaint: The Unfinished Business of Sentimentality in American Culture* (Durham, NC: Duke University Press, 2008), viii; see esp. vii–x and 5–13.

8. Pierre Bourdieu, *The Field of Cultural Production: Essays on Art and Literature* (New York: Columbia University Press, 1993).

CHAPTER ONE. LISTENING TO THE POLITICAL

1. Brent DiCrescenzo, review of *Play*, by Moby, *Pitchfork*, December 31, 1999, accessed January 21, 2009, http://pitchfork.com/reviews/albums/5344 -play; Frank Owen, "Blues for Jesus: Review of *Play*," *Village Voice*, June 8, 1999; Scott Marc Becker, "Sharps and Flats: Moby Draws a Bold Line Straight from the Mississippi Delta to the South Bronx, Connecting the Dots of Black Music in a Search for the Roots of His Electronic Craft," *Salon*, June 8, 1999, accessed June 8, 2009, http://www.salon.com/ent /music/review/1999/06/08/moby/index.html; "luxnigra," "Moby, Black Appropriation and White Electronics," *The Last Angel of History* (blog), May 6, 2007, accessed June 8, 2009, http://lastangelofhistory.wordpress .com/2007/05/06/moby-black-appropriation-and-white-electronics/. A big thank you to my research assistant, Ricky Crano, who located many of these early reviews.

2. Karl Hagstrom Miller, *Segregating Sound: Inventing Folk and Pop Music in the Age of Jim Crow* (Durham, NC: Duke University Press, 2010).

3. Ronald Radano, *Lying up a Nation: Race and Black Music* (Chicago: University of Chicago Press, 2003); Marybeth Hamilton, *In Search of the Blues* (New York: Basic Books, 2008); W. E. B. Du Bois, *The Souls of Black Folk* (New York: Oxford University Press, 2007); Portia Maultsby, "Africanisms in African-American Music," in *Africanisms in American Culture*, ed. Joseph Holloway (Bloomington: Indiana University Press, 1990); Samuel Floyd, *The Power of Black Music: Interpreting Its History from Africa to the United States* (New York: Oxford University Press, 1995); Mark Anthony Neal, *What the Music Said: Black Popular Music and Black Popular Culture* (New York: Routledge, 1999).

4. Maureen Mahon, *The Right to Rock: The Black Rock Coalition and the Cultural Politics of Race* (Durham, NC: Duke University Press, 2004); Greg Tate, *Flyboy in the Buttermilk: Essays on Contemporary America* (New York: Simon and Schuster, 1992); Kandia Crazy Horse, ed., *Rip It Up: The Black Experience in Rock 'n' Roll* (New York: Palgrave, 2004).

5. George Lipsitz, *Dangerous Crossroads: Popular Music, Postmodernism and the Poetics of Place* (London: Verso, 1994); Rafael Pérez Torres, "Mestizaje in the Mix: Chicano Identity, Cultural Politics, and Postmodern Music," in *Music and the Racial Imagination*, ed. Ronald Radano and Philip V. Bohlman (Chicago: University of Chicago Press, 2000); Frances Aparicio, "Ethnifying Rhythms, Feminizing Cultures," in *Music and the Racial Imagination*, ed. Ronald Radano and Philip V. Bohlman (Chicago: University of Chicago Press, 2000); Josh Kun, *Audiotopia: Music, Race, and America* (Berkeley: University of California Press, 2005); Deborah Wong, *Speak It Louder: Asian*

Americans Making Music (New York: Routledge, 2004); E. Taylor Atkins, *Blue Nippon: Authenticating Jazz in Japan* (Durham, NC: Duke University Press, 2001).

6. Roshanak Kheshti, "Musical Miscegenation and the Logic of Rock and Roll: Homosocial Desire and Racial Productivity in 'A Paler Shade of White,'" *American Quarterly* 60, no. 4 (December 2008).

7. See Ted Gioia, *Delta Blues: The Life and Times of the Mississippi Masters Who Revolutionized American Music* (New York: W. W. Norton, 2009).

8. John Blacking, *How Musical Is Man?* (Seattle: University of Washington Press, 1973), 22.

9. Blacking, *How Musical Is Man?*, 28.

10. Blacking, *How Musical Is Man?*, 107–8.

11. Steven Feld, "Aesthetics as Iconicity of Style (Uptown Title); Or, 'Lift-Up-Over Sounding': Getting into the Kaluli Groove," in *Music Grooves: Essays and Dialogues*, 2nd ed., ed. Charles Keil and Steven Feld (Tucson, AZ: Fenestra Books, 2005).

12. Paul Gilroy, *The Black Atlantic: Modernity and Double Consciousness* (Cambridge, MA: Harvard University Press, 1993), 76.

13. Ronald Radano and Philip Bohlman, "Introduction: Music and Race, Their Past, Their Presence," in *Music and the Racial Imagination*, ed. Ronald Radano and Philip Bohlman (Chicago: University of Chicago Press, 2000), 9, 8. See also the other chapters from this volume: Deborah Wong, "The Asian American Body in Performance," 57–94; Brian Currid, "'Ain't I People?': Voicing National Fantasy," 113–44; Christopher Waterman, "Race Music: Bo Chatmon, 'Corrine Corrina,' and the Excluded Middle," 167–205; Zoila Mendoza, "Performing Decency: Ethnicity and Race in Andean 'Mestizo' Ritual Dance," 231–70; Margaret J. Kartomi, "Indonesian-Chinese Oppression and the Musical Outcomes in the Netherlands East Indies," 271–317; and Peter Manuel, "Ethnic Identity, National Identity, and Music in Indo-Trinidadian Culture," 318–45.

14. Helena Simonett, *Banda: Mexican Musical Life across Borders* (Middletown, CT: Wesleyan University Press, 2001), 78–96.

15. Aaron Fox, *Real Country: Music and Language in Working-Class Culture* (Durham, NC: Duke University Press, 2004), 319.

16. Louise Meintjes, *Sound of Africa! Making Music Zulu in a South African Studio* (Durham, NC: Duke University Press, 2003), 149.

17. The concept of anthems used here incorporates the common understanding of national anthems but extends it to include musical examples that confirm and reinforce any political or ethnic identity. For examples see John Blacking, *How Musical Is Man?* (Seattle: University of Washington Press, 1973); and Steven Feld, "Aesthetics as Iconicity of Style (Uptown Title); Or, 'Lift-Up-Over Sounding': Getting into the Kaluli Groove," in Keil and Feld, *Music Grooves*. I also address this point in chapter 2.

18. Georgina Born, section 4, "Music and the Representation/Articulation of

Sociocultural Identities," in "Introduction: On Difference, Representation and Appropriation in Music," in *Western Music and Its Others: Difference, Representation, and Appropriation in Music*, ed. Georgina Born and David Hesmondhalgh (Berkeley: University of California Press, 2000), 35.

19. "Sens" is a term derived from the work of Jean-Luc Nancy. It refers to an active engagement with the world prior to meaning. See note 26 below.

20. On one level, Cage wanted to argue against the special category of music, insisting that his goal was to enable sounds to be themselves. On the other hand, he was insistent that performers follow the instructions for his pieces with concentration and precision. His insistence on the integrity of the work suggests that the proper frame for the comprehension of his pieces remains that of music. See John Cage, "Composition as Process," in John Cage, *Silence: Lectures and Writings* (Middletown, CT: Wesleyan University Press, 1961); John Cage, "Happy New Ears," in John Cage, *A Year from Monday: New Lectures and Writings* (Middletown, CT: Wesleyan University Press, 1969); and James Pritchett, *The Music of John Cage* (New York: Cambridge University Press, 1996). See also the discussion of happenings in Richard Kostelanetz, *Conversing with Cage*, 2nd ed. (New York: Routledge, 2003), 117–20.

21. Cage discusses the beauty of traffic sounds in a clip from a French documentary; see "John Cage about Silence," posted to YouTube by "jdavidm," July 14, 2007, accessed March 24, 2011, http://www.youtube.com/watch?v=pcHnL7aS64Y.

22. Jacques Attali, *Noise: The Political Economy of Music*, trans. Brian Massumi (Minneapolis: University of Minnesota Press, 1985), 6.

23. The classic statement of purely musical meaning is Eduard Hanslick, *The Beautiful in Music*, trans. Gustav Cohen (New York: Liberal Arts Press, 1957).

24. Lawrence Kramer, "Subjectivity Rampant! Music, Hermeneutics, and History," in *The Cultural Study of Music: A Critical Introduction*, ed. Martin Clayton, Trevor Herbert, and Richard Middleton (New York: Routledge, 2003), 130, 131.

25. Jean-Luc Nancy, *Listening*, trans. Charlotte Mandell (New York: Fordham University Press, 2007), 26–27.

26. Nancy, *Listening*, 7. Nancy uses the French word *sens* to indicate a precognitive yearning apprehension of the world. It is an active engagement prior to meaning. Charlotte Mandell translates the word here as "sense," which is not quite right. I retain the French, therefore, in my discussion of this concept.

27. Theodor Adorno, *Aesthetic Theory*, trans. Robert Hullot-Kentor (Minneapolis: University of Minnesota Press, 1997), 6.

28. Clarissa Rile Hayward, "Democracy's Identity Problem: Is 'Constitutional Patriotism' the Answer?," *Constellations* 14, no. 2 (2007): 182.

29. For a detailed discussion of this set of problems, see Amy Gutman, *Identity*

in *Democracy* (Princeton, NJ: Princeton University Press, 2003). This set of issues is also at the center of Jürgen Habermas's *Between Facts and Norms: Contributions to a Discourse Theory of Law and Democracy*, trans. William Rehg (Cambridge, MA: MIT Press, 1996).

30. Chantall Mouffe, *The Return of the Political* (London: Verso Books, 1993), 110, 114. See also Ernesto Laclau and Chantall Mouffe, *Hegemony and Socialist Strategy: Towards a Radical Democratic Politics* (New York: Verso Books, 1985).

31. For some theorists, such as Carl Schmitt, it is only the eruption into violence and the concomitant rise to significance of the friend-enemy distinction that brings political considerations into effect. Schmitt wants to fully distinguish between cultural concerns and political concerns. Such a distinction, however, too quickly militarizes all conflict. Mouffe, Paul Hirst, Slavoj Žižek, and Jacques Derrida, among others, have shown how every politically salient group is constituted by and of difference and that the state's intervention into any dispute can only be the result of a decision that, in its nonrational nature, voids any effort to delineate clear distinctions between the internal identity of the polis and the external identity of the enemy. That is, the friend-enemy distinction is no simple matter. While Mouffe builds her argument on Schmitt's thought, she insists: "The great strength of liberal democracy *pace* Schmitt, is precisely that it provides the institutions that, if properly understood, can shape the element of hostility in a way that defuses its potential." Mouffe, *Return of the Political*, 5. See also Chantal Mouffe, ed., *The Challenge of Carl Schmitt* (London: Verso Books, 1999), which includes essays by Hirst, Žižek, and others; and Jacques Derrida, *The Politics of Friendship*, trans. George Collins (New York: Verso Books, 1997).

32. Jean-Luc Nancy, *The Inoperative Community*, trans. Peter Connor (Minneapolis: University of Minnesota Press, 1991). My understanding of Nancy's key concepts is deeply indebted to the generosity of my colleague, Philip Armstrong, whose book *Reticulations: Jean-Luc Nancy and the Networks of the Political* (Minneapolis University of Minnesota Press, 2009), unpacks many of Nancy's most difficult concepts. All misunderstandings are of course my own responsibility. "Society must be defended" is a political slogan taken as a title for a series of lectures by Michel Foucault that attempt to demonstrate the origins of modern racist thought. Michel Foucault, *"Society Must Be Defended": Lectures at the College de France, 1975–76*, trans. David Macey (New York: Picador Press, 2003).

33. Tommie Shelby, *We Who Are Dark: Philosophical Foundations of Black Solidarity* (Cambridge, MA: Harvard University Press, 2005), 11–12. Robert Gooding-Williams says something very similar: "Generally speaking, to be black (in America) is, simply to be subject to a practice of racial classification that counts one as black. Corresponding to being black, however, are numerous ways of being a black person—that is, numerous ways of inter-

preting and assigning significance to being black." See Robert Gooding-Williams, *Look, a Negro! Philosophical Essays on Race, Culture and Politics* (New York: Routledge, 2006), 95.

34. James Baldwin, "The Black Boy Looks at the White Boy" and "The Price of the Ticket," in James Baldwin, *Collected Essays* (New York: Library of America, 1998).

35. Jacques Rancière, *The Politics of Aesthetics*, trans. Gabriel Rockhill (New York: Continuum, 2004), 12.

36. Jacques Rancière, "The Paradoxes of Political Art," in Jacques Rancière, *Dissensus: On Politics and Aesthetics*, ed. and trans. Steven Corcoran (New York: Continuum, 2010), 139.

37. Rancière, "The Paradoxes of Political Art," 139.

38. Gabriel Greenberg, "Speech for Vera Hall's Induction to the Alabama Women's Hall of Fame," delivered March 3, 2005, accessed September 3, 2008, http://www.awhf.org/hall.html.

39. Gabriel Greenberg, "Speech for Vera Hall's Induction to the Alabama Women's Hall of Fame." As of June 3, 2009, the Vera Hall Project is no longer online.

40. Nolan Porterfield has this recording trip taking place in the spring 1937. Nolan Porterfield, *Last Cavalier: The Life and Times of John A. Lomax, 1867–1948* (Urbana: University of Illinois Press, 1996), 404. John Lomax is equally vague about the precise date. See John Lomax, *Adventures of a Ballad Hunter* (New York: Macmillan, 1947), 190–203. The biographers of Ruby Pickens Tartt follow suit. Virginia Pounds Brown and Laurella Owens, *Toting the Lead Row: Ruby Pickens Tartt, Alabama Folklorist* (Tuscaloosa: University of Alabama Press, 1981). But the Archive of Folk Culture at the Library of Congress card catalogue lists the earliest recordings for Vera Hall as July 1937. Regardless, these were the first recordings of Hall and her cousin, Dock Reed, that Lomax made under the auspices of the Archive of American Folk Song.

41. Brown and Owens, *Toting the Lead Row*, 12–16. Tartt's complicated relationship to white Southern privilege, Jim Crow segregation, and Southern black culture was not totally idiosyncratic. See Marybeth Hamilton's description of Dorothy Scarborough's similar position in *In Search of the Blues* (New York: Basic Books, 2008), 73–83.

42. Porterfield, *Last Cavalier*, 170. See also Hazel Carby, *Race Men* (Cambridge, MA: Harvard University Press, 2000); Benjamin Filene, *Romancing the Folk: Public Memory and American Roots Music* (Chapel Hill: University of North Carolina Press, 2000); and Marybeth Hamilton, *In Search of the Blues* (New York: Basic Books, 2008).

43. John Lomax, *Adventures of a Ballad Hunter*, 190.

44. Dock Reed and Vera Hall, "Trouble So Hard," *Afro-American Spirituals, Work Songs, and Ballads*, Rounder Records, Library of Congress Archive of Folk Culture, CD reissue 1998, originally released in 1942.

45. The *New York Times* covered every night of 1948's festival except the folk-music night. Two years later, the paper reluctantly covered the "Program of Folk Music," remarking that the music "was contemporary only in that some of the music was still being sung in rural areas." C. H. "Program of Folk Music," *New York Times*, May 22, 1950, PDF downloaded from www .nytimes.com on June 1, 2009.

46. The names of performers and of the evening's event can be found at the bottom of the sheet listing the track numbers for the digitized version of the recording tapes in Alan Lomax Collection, Archive of Folk Culture, Library of Congress, Washington, DC.

47. Alan Lomax, *The Rainbow Sign: A Southern Documentary* (New York: Duell, Sloan and Pearce, 1959), 70.

48. Lomax, *The Rainbow Sign*, 21–22.

49. Typescript of interview, reel 11, pages 2–3, box 3, 1, folder 12, Alan Lomax Collection, Archive of Folk Culture, Library of Congress, Washington, DC.

50. Ralph Ellison, "Change the Joke and Slip the Yoke," in Ralph Ellison, *The Collected Essays of Ralph Ellison* (New York: Modern Library, 1995).

51. Lomax, *The Rainbow Sign*, 105.

52. Charlie Gillett, *Making Tracks: Atlantic Records and the Growth of a Multi-billion Dollar Industry* (New York: E. P. Dutton, 1974).

53. Shirley Collins, *America over the Water* (London: SAF Publishing, 2005), 60.

54. Recording logs for the trip are reprinted as an appendix to Collins, *America over the Water*.

55. Ann Powers, "Pop Review: Fighting Fire with Fire; Moby's Agenda," *New York Times*, July 31, 1999, accessed October 10, 2008, http://www.nytimes .com/1999/07/31/arts/pop-review-fighting-fire-with-fire-moby-s-agenda .html.

CHAPTER TWO. THE ANTHEM

1. Jefferson Cowie and Lauren Boehm, "Dead Man's Town: 'Born in the USA,' Social History, and Working-Class Identity," *American Quarterly* 58, no. 2 (June 2006).

2. Lauren Berlant, *The Female Complaint: The Unfinished Business of Sentimentality in American Culture* (Durham, NC: Duke University Press, 2008).

3. Ronald Eyerman, "Music in Movement: Cultural Politics and New Social Movements," *Qualitative Sociology* 25, no. 3 (Fall 2002); S. Craig Werner, *A Change Is Gonna Come: Music, Race and the Soul of America* (New York: Plume Books, 1999).

4. Mark Anthony Neal, *What the Music Said: Black Popular Music and Black Public Culture* (New York: Routledge, 1999).

5. The reference is to antiphonal singing, the alternation between choirs in a church service. Thanks to Ronald Radano for this point.

6. Joseph Otten, "Antiphon," *Catholic Encyclopedia*, vol. 1, 1913, accessed Sep-

tember 4, 2012, http://en.wikisource.org/wiki/Catholic_Encyclopedia_%
281913%29/Antiphon.

7. Nicholas Temperley, "Anthem," in *The Oxford Companion to Music*, ed.
Alison Latham (Oxford: Oxford University Press, 2002), 48.

8. Temperley, "Anthem," 48.

9. Owen Chadwick, *The Reformation* (New York: Penguin Books, 1972), 434.

10. For examples of both styles see Peter Phillips and the Tallis Scholars, *The
Tallis Scholars Sing William Byrd*, Gimell Records, CDGIM 208, CD, originally
released in 2007. Phillips discusses this difference in the liner notes to this
set of recordings.

11. John Harley, *William Byrd: Gentleman of the Chapel Royal* (Brookfield, VT:
Ashgate Publishing, 1997), 177–87, 299–306.

12. Anthony Hicks, *Handel's Coronation Anthems*, Choir of King's College, Cambridge and Academy of Ancient Music, EMI Classics, 724355714022, CD,
originally released in 2001, liner notes.

13. Nicholas Temperley, "Nationalism," in *The Oxford Companion to Music*,
ed. Alison Latham (Oxford: Oxford University Press, 2002), 826–29; Paul
Nettl, *National Anthems*, 2nd ed., trans. Alexander Gode (New York: Frederick Ungar Publishing, 1967), 45. See also F. Gunther Eyck, *The Voice of Nations: European National Anthems and Their Authors* (Westport, CT: Greenwood Press, 1995).

14. Benedict Anderson, *Imagined Communities* (London: Verso, 1983), 145.

15. Robert J. Branham, "'Of Thee I Sing': Contesting America," *American Quarterly* 48, no. 4 (1996): 625.

16. Holmes quoted in Branham, "'Of Thee I Sing,'" 626.

17. See Anderson, *Imagined Communities*.

18. Carl Schmitt, *Political Theology*, trans. George Schwab (Chicago: University
of Chicago Press, 2005), 36.

19. Sean Wilentz, *The Rise of American Democracy: Jefferson to Lincoln* (New
York: W. W. Norton and Co., 2005), 791.

20. Branham, 624.

21. Drew Gilpin Faust, *The Creation of Confederate Nationalism* (Baton Rouge:
Louisiana State University Press, 1989), 18, 67–69.

22. Coleman Hutchison, "Whistling 'Dixie' for the Union (Nation, Anthem,
Revision)," *American Literary History* 19 (Fall 2007).

23. Berlant, *The Female Complaint*, 7.

24. Berlant, *The Female Complaint*, 5.

25. Berlant, *The Female Complaint*, 10.

26. The second half of the nineteenth century saw the most prolific production
of national anthems. Nettl, *National Anthems*, vii.

27. Quoted in Branham, "'Of Thee I Sing,'" 626. See also James H. Stone, "Mid-
Nineteenth-Century American Beliefs in the Social Values of Music," *The
Musical Quarterly* 43, no. 1 (1957).

28. Nettl, *National Anthems*, 64, 69, 205.

29. James Weldon Johnson, *Along This Way* (New York: The Viking Press, 1968), 154–55.
30. Brooke quoted in Julian Bond and Sondra Kathryn Wilson, *Lift Every Voice and Sing: A Celebration of the Negro National Anthem; 100 Years, 100 Voices* (New York: Random House, 2000), 36.
31. Baraka quoted in Bond and Wilson, 16.
32. Eddie S. Glaude, Jr., *Exodus! Religion, Race, and Nation in Early Nineteenth-Century Black America* (Chicago: University of Chicago Press, 2000), 21.
33. Evelyn Brooks Higginbotham, *Righteous Discontent: The Women's Movement in the Black Baptist Church, 1880–1920* (Cambridge, MA: Harvard University Press, 1993), 186.
34. Tommie Shelby, *We Who Are Dark: The Philosophical Foundations of Black Solidarity* (Cambridge, MA: Harvard University Press, 2005).
35. Bond and Wilson, *Lift Every Voice and Sing*, 185.
36. Juan Williams quoted in Bond and Wilson, *Lift Every Voice and Sing*, 254.
37. Shelby, *We Who Are Dark*, 252, 11–12. On July 1, 2008, the jazz singer Renee Marie sang before a state-of-the-city address given by the mayor of Denver, Colorado, John Hickenlooper. Expected to sing the national anthem, Marie surprised the seven hundred in attendance by adapting the words of James Weldon Johnson's "Lift Every Voice and Sing" to the melody of "The Star-Spangled Banner." According to the *Rocky Mountain News*, this mash-up of two anthems caused an outpouring of hate mail from local citizens. By singing the words of "Lift Every Voice and Sing" to the melody of "The Star-Spangled Banner," Renee Marie brought into immediate awareness the possible antagonism between those hailed by the two different anthems. See Daniel Chacon, "'Black National Anthem' Brings City Council President Hate Mail," *Rocky Mountain News*, July 2, 2008, accessed, July 20, 2009, http://www.rockymountainnews.com/news/2008/jul/01/singing-black-national-anthem-hits-sour-note/.
38. Bernice Johnson Reagon, *If You Don't Go, Don't Hinder Me: The African American Sacred Song Tradition* (Lincoln: University of Nebraska Press, 2001), 47.
39. Charles Keil, "Participatory Discrepancies and the Power of Music," in *Music Grooves*, 2nd ed., ed. Charles Keil and Steven Feld (Tucson, AZ: Fenestra, 2005), 96.
40. Jones quoted in Bernice Johnson Reagon, "African American Music as Resistance: The Civil Rights Movement," in *African American Music: An Introduction*, ed. Melonee V. Burnim and Portia K. Maultsby (New York: Routledge, 2006), 602.
41. Kay Mills, *This Little Light of Mine: The Life of Fannie Lou Hamer* (Lexington: University Press of Kentucky, 2007), 85.
42. Cheryl Lynn Greenberg, ed., *A Circle of Trust: Remembering SNCC* (New Brunswick, NJ: Rutgers University Press, 1998), 122.
43. Greenberg, *A Circle of Trust*, 112.

44. Keil, "Participatory Discrepancies and the Power of Music," 96.
45. Guy Carawan and Candie Carawan, eds., *We Shall Overcome! Songs of the Southern Freedom Movement* (New York: Oak Publications, 1963), 18.
46. Carawan and Carawan, *We Shall Overcome!* 8.
47. Robert Shelton, "Civil Rights Songs," *New York Times*, August 20, 1962, 1, 14.
48. Reagon, "African American Music as Resistance," 602.
49. Julius Lester, *Search for the New Land: History as Subjective Experience* (New York: Dial Press, 1969), 56.
50. See, for example, Ron Eyerman and Andrew Jamison, *Music and Social Movements: Mobilizing Traditions in the Twentieth Century* (New York: Cambridge University Press, 1998).
51. Nancy S. Love, *Musical Democracy* (Albany, NY: SUNY Press, 2006).
52. Albert Burkhardt and Rudolf Telling, *Let's Sing Together: Britische und Amerikanische Lieder* (Berlin: Volk und Wissen Volkseigener Verlag, 1973), 3.
53. Ronald D. Cohen, *Rainbow Quest: The Folk Music Revival and American Society, 1940–1970* (Amherst: University of Massachusetts Press, 2002).
54. Pete Seeger and Bob Reiser, *Everybody Says Freedom* (New York: W. W. Norton and Co. 1989), 8. See also Pete Seeger, *The Incompleat Folksinger*, ed. Jo Metcalf Schwartz (New York: Simon and Schuster, 1972). Carawan adds that he also reintroduced "We Shall Not Be Moved" and "Keep Your Eyes on the Prize" to the repertoire of the movement when he sang at "conferences in Nashville, Raleigh, Atlanta and at Highlander." Carawan and Carawan, *We Shall Overcome!*, 5.
55. Seeger, *The Incompleat Folksinger*, 112.
56. Quoted in Greenberg, *A Circle of Trust*, 122.
57. See Robert Darden, *People Get Ready! A New History of Black Gospel Music* (New York: Continuum, 2004); Gerald Early, *One Nation under a Groove: Motown and American Culture* (Hopewell, NJ: Ecco Press, 1995); Peter Guralnick, *Sweet Soul Music: Rhythm and Blues and the Southern Dream of Freedom* (New York: Harper and Row, 1986); LeRoi Jones, *Blues People: Negro Music in White America* (New York: Morrow and Co. 1963); Neal, *What the Music Said*; and Werner, *A Change Is Gonna Come*.
58. Brian Ward, *Just My Soul Responding: Rhythm and Blues, Black Consciousness, and Race Relations* (Berkeley: University of California Press, 1998).
59. LeRoi Jones, *Black Music* (New York: Da Capo, 1998). While Jones focused on gospel as a way of pointing backward toward what he considered to be the roots of black music, Guthrie Ramsey understands gospel as one of the birthing grounds for Afro-modernism. See Guthrie Ramsey Jr., *Race Music: Black Cultures from Bebop to Hip-Hop* (Berkeley: University of California Press, 2003).
60. Anthony Heilburt, *The Gospel Sound: Good News and Bad Times* (New York: Simon and Schuster, 1971); Darden, *People Get Ready!*, 165–80.
61. Darden, *People Get Ready!*, 197–203; Gayle Wald, *Shout, Sister, Shout! The*

Untold Story of Rock-and-Roll Trailblazer Sister Rosetta Tharpe (Boston, MA: Beacon Press, 2007).

62. Albert Murray, *Stomping the Blues* (New York: Da Capo, 1989), 24–27.

63. This story is told with compelling detail in Peter Guralnick's *Dream Boogie: The Triumph of Sam Cooke* (New York: Back Bay Books, 2005), 65–129.

64. My thanks to Ronald Radano for emphasizing the significance of this aspect of Cooke's sound.

65. For the details of these shows and of the struggles that Cooke and other musicians faced while touring the South during the Civil Rights era, see Guralnick, *Dream Boogie*, esp. 228, 259, 327, and 368–71.

66. Guralnick, *Dream Boogie*, 540–41.

67. Michelle Arrow, "'It Has Become My Personal Anthem': 'I Am Woman,' Popular Culture and 1970s Feminism," *Australian Cultural Studies* 22, no. 53 (July 2007); Aaron Fox, "'Alternative' to What? *O Brother*, September 11, and the Politics of Country Music," in *Country Music Goes to War*, ed. Charles Wolfe and James Akenson (Lexington: University of Kentucky Press, 2005); Nadine Hubbs, "'I Will Survive': Musical Mappings of Queer Social Space in a Disco Song," *Popular Music* 26, no. 2 (2007).

CHAPTER THREE. TURNING INWARD, INSIDE OUT

1. Peter Burt, *The Music of Toru Takemitsu* (New York: Columbia University Press, 2006), 22–23.

2. Alan Clayson, with Barb Jungr and Robb Johnson, *Woman: The Incredible Life of Yoko Ono* (New Malden, UK: Chrome Dreams, 2004), 12–20.

3. Harry Harootunian, *Overcome by Modernity: History, Culture, and Community in Interwar Japan* (Princeton, NJ: Princeton University Press, 2000), xxv, xxvi.

4. Bonnie Wade, *Music in Japan: Experiencing Music, Expressing Culture* (New York: Oxford University Press, 2005), 14. See also Dan Ikuma, "The Influence of Japanese Traditional Music on the Development of Western Music in Japan," *Transactions of the Asiatic Society of Japan* 8, no. 3 (1961), for a discussion of the social meanings attached to traditional Japanese genres. (This was translated and delivered to Asiatic Society on April 20, 1959, by Dorothy G. Britton.)

5. Christine Yano, *Tears of Longing: Nostalgia and the Nation in Japanese Popular Song* (Cambridge, MA: Harvard University Press, 2002).

6. Luciana Galliano, *Yōgaku: Japanese Music in the Twentieth Century*, trans. Martin Mayes (Lanham, MD: Scarecrow Press, 2002), 33.

7. Mara Miller, "Art and the Construction of Self and Subject in Japan," in *Self as Image in Asian Theory and Practice*, ed. Roger Ames, Thomas Kasulis, and Wimal Dissanayake (Albany, NY: SUNY Press, 1998), 422.

8. Harold Bloom, *The Anxiety of Influence: A Theory of Poetry* (New York: Oxford University Press, 1973). Bloom's concepts have been applied to Western

art music in Joseph N. Strauss, "'The Anxiety of Influence' in Twentieth-Century Music," *Journal of Musicology* 9, no. 4 (1991).

9. Dan, "The Influence of Japanese Traditional Music on the Development of Western Music in Japan," 201.

10. Dan, "The Influence of Japanese Traditional Music on the Development of Western Music in Japan," 202. For a discussion of the khora as the space of meaning generation, see Julia Kristeva, "The System and the Speaking Subject," in *The Kristeva Reader*, ed. Toril Moi (New York: Columbia University Press, 1986), 24–33.

11. Galliano, *Yogaku*, 65–89.

12. Watsuji Tetsuro, *Watsuji Tetsuro's Rinrigaku*, trans. Yamamoto Seisaku and Robert E. Carter (Albany, NY: SUNY Press, 1996). My understanding of Watsuji's philosophy is influenced by essays by Robert E. Carter. See Carter, "Interpretive Essay: Strands of Influence," in *Watsuji Tetsuro's Rinrigaku*. See also Robert E. Carter, "Watsuji Tetsuro," *Stanford Encyclopedia of Philosophy*, online edition, updated December 17, 2009, accessed May 3, 2010, http://plato.stanford.edu/entries/watsuji-tetsuro/.

13. Nishida Kitaro, *An Inquiry into the Good*, trans. Masao Abe and Christopher Ives (New Haven, CT: Yale University Press, 1990), 139–41.

14. For a full discussion of the progressive potential that can be found in Nishida's thought, see Christopher S. Goto-Jones, *Political Philosophy in Japan: Nishida, the Kyoto School, and Co-prosperity* (New York: Routledge, 2005).

15. "Imperial Rescript on Education" (the official translation) was published as appendix V to Japan Ministry of Education, *Kokutai no Hongi: Cardinal Principles of the National Entity of Japan*, ed. Robert King Hall and trans. John Owen Gauntlett (Cambridge, MA: Harvard University Press, 1949).

16. See Goto-Jones, *Political Philosophy in Japan*.

17. Japan Ministry of Education, *Kokutai no Hongi*, 52.

18. Japan Ministry of Education, *Kokutai no Hongi*, 83.

19. On musical composition between the wars, see Yayoi Uno Everett, "Intercultural Synthesis in Postwar Western Art Music: Historical Contexts, Perspectives, and Taxonomy," in *Locating East Asia in Western Art Music*, ed. Yayoi Uno Everett and Frederick Lau (Middletown, CT: Wesleyan University Press, 2004); and Judith Herd, "The Cultural Politics of Japan's Modern Music: Nostalgia, Nationalism, and Identity in the Interwar Years," in Everett and Lau, *Locating East Asia in Western Art Music*. On the significance of the work of Tanabe Hajime, see Himi Kiyoshi, "Tanabe Hajime," in *Routledge Encyclopedia of Philosophy*, ed. Edward Craig Online version: http://www.rep.routledge.com.proxy.lib.ohio-state.edu/article/G123?ssid =1001537474&n=3#, last accessed August 4, 2013.

20. Matsudaira simply says that during the war he could not concentrate on composing. See Joaquim M. Benitez and Kondo Jo, "Serialism in a Japa-

nese Context: A Conversation with Matsudaira Yoritsune," *Contemporary Music Review* 17, no. 4 (1998): 88.

21. Galliano, *Yogaku*, 115, 116; see also 113–21.

22. Galliano, *Yogaku*, 130.

23. Judith Herd, "The Neonationalist Movement: Origins of Contemporary Japanese Music," *Perspectives of New Music* 27, no. 2 (1989): 121.

24. Edward Lockspeiser, *Debussy: His Life and Mind*, vol. 2, *1902–1918* (New York: Cambridge University Press, 1978), 23–26.

25. Wade, *Music in Japan*, 134; Galliano, *Yogaku*, 77.

26. See Herd, "The Neonationalist Movement." See in particular her discussion of two main groups of composers, Yagi no Kai and Sannin no Kai. The latter group included Dan and Mayuzumi, both of whom were overtly concerned with maintaining strong Japanese national feelings and extending the sphere of Japanese musical influence.

27. Herd, "The Neonationalist Movement," 133.

28. Herd, "The Neonationalist Movement," 137; Mayuzumi Toshiro, *Nirvana Symphonie*, NHK Symphony Orchestra, conducted by Wilhelm Schuchter, Mainstream Records, MS 5012, 1970 (originally released 1962) LP.

29. A more recently recorded version of *Nirvana Symphony* features the Tokyo Metropolitan Symphony Orchestra. On this version, the vocal lines are more melodic and the singers sound more operatic. I vastly prefer the NKH version, and my discussion of this piece is based on its recording. Tokyo Metropolitan Symphony Orchestra and Monks of Yakushiji Temple, *Nirvana Symphony and Buddhist Chants*, conducted by Hiroyuki Iwaki, Denon Records, B0000043 WF, CD, originally released in 1996.

30. Mayuzumi Toshiro, *Nirvana Symphonie*, liner notes. Curiously, the cover art for this recording was created by Ono, and the A&R director was Earle Brown.

31. Mayuzumi's personal politics grew increasingly reactionary as he grew older. His nationalism became intensely essentialist and patriarchal. His opera, *Kinkakuji* (*Temple of the Golden Pavillion*) was based on a novel by Mishima and included reactionary elements and overt misogyny. See the brief discussion in Galliano, *Yogaku*, 186.

32. Benitez and Kondo, "Serialism in a Japanese Context," 95.

33. Matsudaira Yoritsune, *Bugaku Dance Suite*, Osaka Century Orchestra, conducted by Ken Takaseki, Naxos 8.555882, CD originally released in 2005.

34. Benitez and Kondo, "Serialism in a Japanese Context," 95; Shiina Ryosuke, "Contradictions of Modernism: Reading Matsudaira Yoritsune's Articles," *Contemporary Music Review* 17, no. 4 (1998): 21; Takemitsu Toru, "Contemporary Music in Japan," *Perspectives of New Music* 27, no. 2 (Summer 1989): 201.

35. Benitez and Kondo, "Serialism in a Japanese Context," 95.

36. "It is a totally ceremonial music. That is, this music has no feeling. . . .

What is interesting for me is its formal side." Matsudaira quoted in Shiina, "Contradictions of Modernism," 25.

37. See Benitez and Kondo, "Serialism in a Japanese Context"; Galliano, *Yogaku*; and Herd, "The Neonationalist Movement."

38. For an extensive discussion of the physical limitations on the sounds produced by traditional Japanese lutes (including the *biwa*) see Rolf Klein, "Aspects of Some Recent Works by Matsudaira Yoritsune," *Contemporary Music Review* 17, no. 4 (1998).

39. Wade, *Music in Japan*, 138.

40. Raymond Ericson, "Ozawa Conducts at Philharmonic," *New York Times*, November 10, 1967, 57; Raymond Ericson, "18 Works Sought by Philharmonic," *New York Times*, April 6, 1967, 45; Takemitsu Toru, "Sound of East, Sound of West," in *Confronting Silence: Collected Writings* (Berkeley, CA: Fallen Leaf Press, 1995), 59–66. See also Ozawa's foreword to *Confronting Silence*.

41. From the moment of its publication in 1978, Edward Said's *Orientalism* (New York: Pantheon Books) has provoked much debate and inspired considerable new research into the cultural interactions between peoples and nations of the East and West. Criticized for relying too heavily on a limited set of textual evidence and for focusing his investigation of Orientalism too closely on the Middle East, Said nevertheless named a framework of analysis that has shaped and continues to shape knowledge production in the West about Asian cultures, histories, politics, and social structures. Consistently, Orientalist discourse presents the Westerner as vigorous, masculine, mature, rational, and normal, while the Easterner is represented as passive, feminine, childlike, emotional, and Other. For Said, such representations have material effects. Subjectivity is shaped in part by such oppositions, especially as they became increasingly instrumentalized through the workings of governmental institutions. Within Asian American studies, the restriction these oppositions placed on the possibilities of Asian American masculinity has been examined as part of a project of *racial castration* that produces its own reaction formation. David Eng argues that the Asian or Asian American male is trapped between a feminized passivity and a hypermasculine aggressivity. For Eng, only a set of queer strategies can escape this trap. See David Eng, *Racial Castration: Managing Masculinity in Asian America* (Durham, NC: Duke University Press, 2001). For Sheng-Mei Ma, rather than being mutually exclusionary, Orientalism and Asian American identity share a symbiotic relationship: "Orientalist misrepresentations conceivably become self representations." Such a statement is simply an extrapolation from the Foucauldian understanding of discourse that underlies Said's analysis. But the statement illuminates the complex productivity of Orientalist exchanges. Sheng-Mei Ma, *The Deathly Embrace: Orientalism and Asian American Identity* (Minneapolis: University of Minnesota Press, 2000), xii. For a review of the cri-

tiques of Said's work, see Lata Mani and Ruth Frankenberg, "The Challenge of *Orientalism,*" *Economy and Society* 14 (1985). Eng's literary examples of feminized passivity and hypermasculinity include such works as David H. Hwang's *M. Butterfly* (New York: Plume, 1989) and Frank Chinn's *Donald Duk* (Minneapolis, MN: Coffee House Press, 1991).

42. Donald Henahan, "Ozawa Conducts the Philadelphia," *New York Times,* November 13, 1968, 37; Said, *Orientalism.*

43. In her introduction to an important book on East-West musical blends, Yayoi Everett created a useful taxonomy that distinguishes the major strategies for integrating these different musical worlds. Her largest categories are "transference," where simple content elements from one tradition are borrowed by the other; "syncretism," whereby more-structural aspects such as timbre, tuning, and scales become the basis for the blend; and finally "synthesis," which she privileges as a more profound achievement in musical integration. Among the works that she cites approvingly as examples of synthesis are Mayazumi's *Nirvana Symphony,* and Matsudaira's *Bugaku.* Takemitsu's *November Steps* is described as a syncretic work and nothing of Ono's appears at all. Everett, "Intercultural Synthesis in Postwar Western Art Music," in Everett and Lau, *Locating East Asia in Western Music.*

44. Takemitsu, "Contemporary Music in Japan," 199.

45. John Cage, "History of Experimental Music in the United States," in John Cage, *Silence: Lectures and Writings by John Cage* (Middletown, CT: Wesleyan University Press, 1961), 70; John Cage, "Happy New Ears!," in John Cage, *A Year from Monday: New Lectures and Writings by John Cage* (Middletown, CT: Wesleyan University Press, 1969), 33–34. For further discussions of Cage's Orientalism, see John Corbett, "Experimental Oriental: New Music and Other Others," in *Western Music and Its Others: Difference, Representation, and Appropriation in Music,* ed. Georgina Born and David Hesmondhalgh (Berkeley: University of California Press, 2000), 163–86; Barry Shank, "Productive Orientalisms: Imagining Noise and Silence across the Pacific, 1957–1967," in *Postnational Musical Identities: Cultural Production, Distribution and Consumption in a Globalized Scenario,* ed. Alejandro Madrid and Ignacio Corona (Lexington, MA: Lexington Books, 2007).

46. Takemitsu, "Nature and Music," in *Confronting Silence,* 7–8. For discussion of Takemitsu's emphases on timbre and stream of sound organization as well as the critical reception of Takemitsu as a tonal colorist, see Burt, *The Music of Toru Takemitsu,* 236–53. For attempts to identify structural principles of formal development and pitch organization, see Lewis Cornwell, "Toru Takemitsu's *November Steps,*" *Journal of New Music Research* 31, no. 3 (2002); Steven Nuss, "Hearing Japanese, Hearing Takemitsu," *Contemporary Music Review* 21, no. 4 (2002); and Edward Smaldone, "Japanese and Western Confluences in Large-Scale Pitch Organization of Toru Take-

mitsu's *November Steps* and *Autumn,*" *Perspectives of New Music* 27, no. 2
(Summer 1989); Takemitsu, "Nature and Music," in Takemitsu, *Confronting
Silence*. Alexandra Munroe describes the effects of Cage and Tudor's 1961
tour of Japan as "the Cage-Ichiyanagi shock." Alexandra Munroe, "A Box
of Smile: Tokyo Fluxus, Conceptual Art and the School of Metaphysics," in
Scream against the Sky: Japanese Art after 1945, ed. Alexandra Munroe (New
York: Harry Abrams, 1994), 218.

47. Burt, *The Music of Toru Takemitsu*, 110–11.
48. Takemitsu, "Sound of East, Sound of West," in *Confronting Silence*, 62.
49. Joji Yuasa, "Music as a Reflection of a Composer's Cosmology," *Perspectives of New Music* 27, no. 2 (Summer 1989): 192. For more on Japanese instruments and the relationship between pitch and noise, see Smaldone, "Japanese and Western Confluences in Large-Scale Pitch Organization of Toru Takemitsu's *November Steps* and *Autumn*"; and Takemitsu, "Toru Takemitsu on *Sawari*," in Everett and Lau, *Locating East Asia in Western Art Music*.
50. Henry Cowell, "The Joys of Noise," *The New Republic*, July 31, 1929, 287–88. The concepts of sawari and ma have inspired a large literature. Among the most useful articles are Smaldone, "Japanese and Western Confluences in Large-Scale Pitch Organization of Toru Takemitsu's *November Steps* and *Autumn*"; Takemitsu, "Sound of East, Sound of West"; Takemitsu, "Takemitsu on *Sawari*," in Everett and Lau, *Locating East Asia in Western Art Music*; and Yuasa, "Music as a Reflection of a Composer's Cosmology."
51. Yuasa, "Music as a Reflection of a Composer's Cosmology," 183; Takemitsu, "Takemitsu on *Sawari*," in Everett and Lau, *Locating East Asia in Western Art Music*, 203; Burt, *The Music of Toru Takemitsu*, 237; Miller, "Art and the Construction of Self and Subject in Japan."
52. Takemitsu Toru, "November Steps" (New York: C. F. Peters Corporation, 1967); Cornwell, "Toru Takemitsu's *November Steps*," 211–14.
53. Takemitsu, "November Steps," in *Confronting Silence*, 83–90.
54. Tsuruta Kinshi, Yokoyama Katsuya, and the Music Department of the Imperial Household, "November Steps (10th Step), *Takemitsu in an Autumn Garden*, Deutsche Grammaphon, CD reissue #471 590–2, 2002 (original recordings from 1974 and 1977).
55. Attali, *Noise*, 135.
56. Jacques Rancière, *Dissensus: On Politics and Aesthetics*, ed. and trans. Steven Corcoran (New York: Continuum, 2010). See also Jacques Rancière, *The Politics of Aesthetics*, trans. Gabriel Rockhill (New York: Continuum, 2004).
57. Yuasa, "Music as a Reflection of a Composer's Cosmology," 177. See also Attali, *Noise*, 6. There Attali says, "All music . . . is . . . a tool for the creation or consolidation of community or a totality."
58. Takemitsu, "Sound of East, Sound of West," in *Confronting Silence*, 65.
59. Takemitsu, "Sound of East, Sound of West," in *Confronting Silence*, 64–65.

60. For discussions of women's roles in Japanese society during this period, see Harootunian, *Overcome by Modernity*; Sharon H. Nolte and Sally Ann Hastings, "The Meiji State's Policy Toward Women, 1890–1910," in *Recreating Japanese Women, 1600–1945*, ed. Gail Lee Bernstein (Berkeley: University of California Press, 1991); Barbara Sato, *The New Japanese Woman: Modernity, Media, and Women in Interwar Japan* (Durham, NC: Duke University Press, 2003); and Miriam Silverberg, "The Modern Girl as Militant," in Bernstein, *Recreating Japanese Women, 1600–1945*.

61. Ono quoted in Melody Sumner, Kathleen Burch, Michael Sumner, "Interview [with Yoko Ono]," in Melody Sumner, Kathleen Burch, Michael Sumner, eds., *The Guests Go in to Supper* (Santa Fe, NM: Burning Books, 1986), 171–84, quote p. 173; Clayson, Jungr, and Johnson, *Woman*, 25. For other discussions of Ono's youth, see Jerry Hopkins, *Yoko Ono* (New York: Macmillan Books, 1986); Donald Kirk, "In Tokyo," in Editors of *Rolling Stone*, *The Ballad of John and Yoko* (Garden City, NY: Doubleday Books, 1982); and Alexandra Munroe and Jon Hendricks, eds., *Yes Yoko Ono* (New York: Japan Society and Harry Abrams, Inc., 2000).

62. For discussions of the Ono family, particularly in the context of social history in Japan, see Kirk, "In Tokyo," in Editors of *Rolling Stone*, *The Ballad of John and Yoko*; Hopkins, *Yoko Ono*; Tamara Levitz, "Yoko Ono and the Unfinished Music of 'John & Yoko': Imagining Gender and Racial Equality in the late 1960s," in *Impossible to Hold: Women and Culture in the 1960s*, ed. Avital Bloch and Lauri Umanksy (New York: New York University Press, 2005); and Sumner, Burch, and Sumner, *The Guests Go in to Supper*.

63. See Burt, *The Music of Toru Takemitsu*; Hugh De Ferranti, *Japanese Musical Instruments* (Oxford: Oxford University Press, 2000); Takemitsu, *Confronting Silence*; Yuasa, "Music as a Reflection of a Composer's Cosmology."

64. Jonathan Cott, "Yoko Ono and Her Sixteen-Track Voice," *Rolling Stone*, March 18, 1971, 116.

65. Clayson, *Woman*, 25–30; Midori Yoshimoto, *Into Performance: Japanese Women Artists in New York* (Piscataway, NJ: Rutgers University Press, 2005), 79–86; Yoko Ono, *Grapefruit: A Book of Instructions and Drawings* (New York: Simon and Schuster, 2000), n.p.

66. Yoshimoto, *Into Performance*, 86. For an account of the significance of Ono's work with instruction pieces, see Munroe, "A Box of Smile."

67. Munroe, "A Box of Smile," 221.

68. Ono, *Grapefruit*, n.p. For discussions of this piece, see Helen Molesworth, ed., *Work Ethic* (University Park: Pennsylvania State University Press, 2003), 175; Joan Rothfuss and Midori Yoshimoto, "Works," in Munroe and Hendricks, *Yes Yoko Ono*, 104.

69. Barbara Haskell and John G. Hanhardt, *Yoko Ono: Arias and Objects* (Salt Lake City, UT: Peregrine Smith Books, 1991), 28.

70. Munroe, "A Box of Smile," 217; Haskell and Hanhardt, *Yoko Ono*, 35.

71. Henry Burnett, "Minezaki Koto's *Zangetsu*: An Analysis of a Traditional

Japanese Chamber Music Composition," *Perspectives of New Music* 27, no. 2 (Summer 1989): 80; Robert Palmer, "On Thin Ice," Onobox, Rykodisc CD, originally released in 1992, liner notes; William Malm, "Music in the Kabuki Theater," in *Studies in Kabuki: Its Acting, Music and Historical Context*, ed. James Brandon, William P. Malm, and Donald H. Shively (East-West Center: University of Hawai'i, 1978).

72. For these comparisons see Jody Denberg, "Interview with Yoko Ono," accessed April 21, 2002, http://www.a-i-u.net/ryko97.html As of August 7, 2013 this website is no longer available.; Levitz, "Yoko Ono and the Unfinished Music of 'John and Yoko'"; Robert Palmer, "The Other Half of the Sky: The Songs of Yoko Ono," in Editors of *Rolling Stone, The Ballad of John and Yoko*.

73. Levitz, "Yoko Ono and the Unfinished Music of 'John and Yoko,'" 223.

74. The only preserved performances by the Dirty Mac are found in the television program *The Rolling Stones Rock and Roll Circus*, which was rereleased on DVD in 2004.

75. Tamara Levitz has written beautifully about the gendered interplay here, emphasizing the model of equal collaboration that the two musicians construct. See Levitz, "Yoko Ono and the Unfinished Music of 'John and Yoko,'" 224–28.

76. Ono quoted in Sumner, Burch, and Sumner, *The Guests Go in to Supper*, 176.

77. Ono, *Grapefruit*, n.p.; Yoko Ono, "What Did I Do," *Approximately Infinite Universe*, Apple Records, SVBB 3399, CD, originally released in 1972.

CHAPTER FOUR. "HEROIN"

1. See Steve Chapple and Reebee Garofalo, *Rock and Roll Is Here to Pay* (Chicago: Nelson Hall, 1977); and Marc Eliot, *Rockonomics: The Money behind the Music* (New York: Franklin Watts, 1989).

2. Pierre Bourdieu, "The Market of Symbolic Goods," in Pierre Bourdieu, *The Field of Cultural Production*, trans. Richard Nice (New York: Columbia University Press, 1993).

3. Pierre Bourdieu, "The Field of Cultural Production, or the Economic World Reversed," in Bourdieu, *The Field of Cultural Production*.

4. See Simon Frith and Howard Horne, *Art into Pop* (London: Methuen Press, 1987); and Bernard Gendron, *Between Montmartre and the Mudd Club: Popular Music and the Avant-Garde* (Chicago: University of Chicago Press, 2002).

5. As early as 1950, David Riesman had demonstrated that the audience for jazz had developed an antipop critique. However, this critique was about the aesthetic borderline between pop and jazz. The argument of this chapter is that the antimarket critique did not enter the realm of popular music until after the critical recognition of the Velvet Underground. David Ries-

man, "Listening to Popular Music," *American Quarterly* 2, no. 4 (Winter 1950).

6. As recorded by Branden Joseph, Conrad believes that this unit of musical experimentation played a founding role in the development of musical minimalism. A fair argument can be made that the Theatre of Eternal Music's focus on the interaction of pitch and rhythm set the terms from which the genre developed. Joseph labels this a "metaphysical" argument, and, for the purposes of this chapter there is no reason to delve into the argument any further. What is important for me is that here Young, Conrad, Zazeela, and Cale developed an intense focus on long sustained tones that sharpened Cale's sound. Branden Joseph, *Beyond the Dream Syndicate: Tony Conrad and the Arts after Cage* (Cambridge, MA: Zone Books, 2008), 27.

7. Keith Potter, *Four Musical Minimalists* (Cambridge, UK: Cambridge University Press, 2000), 27.

8. Joseph, *Beyond the Dream Syndicate*, 154.

9. Peter Lavezzoli, *The Dawn of Indian Music in the West, Bhairavi* (New York: Continuum Press, 2006), 57.

10. Lavezzoli, *The Dawn of Indian Music in the West, Bhairavi*, 1.

11. Daniel Neuman, *The Life of Music in North India: The Organization of an Artistic Tradition* (Detroit, MI: Wayne State University Press, 1980), 173–75.

12. Neumann, *The Life of Music in North India*, 22. See also Lavezzoli, *The Dawn of Indian Music in the West, Bhairavi*, 57.

13. Anupam Mahajan, *Ragas in Indian Classical Music* (New Delhi: Gian Publishing House, 1989); Fox Strangways is quoted on page 6, and Mahajan is quoted on page 10.

14. Yehudi Menuin speaking during the introduction of the musicians on Ali Akbar Khan, *Music of India*. Prestige B00000oZES, 1995 CD.

15. Richard Kostelanetz, *Theatre of Mixed Means*, 2nd ed. (New York: Routledge, 2003), 195.

16. La Monte Young and Jackson Mac Low, *An Anthology of Chance Operations* (Bronx, NY: Young and Mac Low, 1963).

17. Potter, *Four Musical Minimalists*, 52.

18. Tony Conrad, *Early Minimalism*, Table of the Elements Records, 1997, "Lyssophobia: On Four Violins," liner notes, 14.

19. For a clear, accessible explanation of just intonation, see Kyle Gann, "Just Intonation Explained," KyleGann.com, accessed June 10, 2009, http://www.kylegann.com/tuning.html.

20. Kostelanetz, *Theatre of Mixed Means*, 201.

21. Gann, "Just Intonation Explained."

22. Conrad, "Lyssophobia," 16; see also 8–28.

23. Joseph, *Beyond the Dream Syndicate*, 105.

24. John Cale with Victor Bockris, *What's Welsh for Zen? The Autobiography of John Cale* (New York: Bloomsbury Press, 1999), 58, 60.

25. A controversy over the authorship of the music captured by recordings of the Theatre of Eternal Music has kept their recordings unreleased for forty years. The only released version is a tape of one performance titled "Day of Niagara." Young's comment about directing the Theatre of Eternal Music is "La Monte Young," MelaFoundation.org, accessed July 21, 2008, http://www.melafoundation.org/ly1para8.htm.
26. La Monte Young, "On Table of Elements CD 74 'Day of Niagara' April 25, 1965." http://melafoundation.org/statemen.htm. Accessed August 7, 2013.
27. Kostelanetz, *Theatre of Mixed Means*, 201.
28. These are approximate pitches, determined with the aid of a guitar and tuner. My focus on pitches here is intended to help the reader grasp something of the sounds of this recording. In Hindustani music and in the music of Theatre of Eternal Music, the actual musical focus is on scale degrees, which are expressions of relationships, not pitches, which are positions in a spectrum of frequencies. My thanks to Benjamin Piekut for this nuance.
29. The success of Theatre of Eternal Music's efforts to sustain notes and maintain an ambiguity of tonal center becomes more clear when this recording is listened to in juxtaposition to the recordings that Tony Conrad released as part of the *Early Minimalism* project. The recording that Conrad titles "April, 1965" shows much more evident bow strokes, more frequently sounded. And the tonal center is not so ambiguous, retaining a pretty steady G.
30. Cale and Bockris, *What's Welsh for Zen?*, 65. For discussions of this moment on Ludlow Street, see Cale and Bockris, *What's Welsh for Zen?*, 64–65; and Joseph, *Beyond the Dream Syndicate*, 226.
31. Victor Bockris and Gerard Malanga, *Uptight: The Velvet Underground Story* (New York: Omnibus Press, 1983), 14.
32. Bockris and Malanga, *Uptight*, 14.
33. Victor Bockris, *Transformer: The Lou Reed Story* (New York: Da Capo Press, 1997), 84.
34. For a particularly egregious example of this version of the Velvets' criticism, see Richard Witts, *The Velvet Underground* (Bloomington: Indiana University Press, 2007).
35. Bockris and Malanga, *Uptight*, 17.
36. Quoted in Bockris, *Transformer*, 78.
37. Bockris and Malanga, *Uptight*, 17. And yes, the pitch mentioned is specifically A♯ not B♭.
38. Joseph, *Beyond the Dream Syndicate*, 224.
39. Bockris, *Transformer*, 79.
40. The Roughnecks (Reed, Philips, Vance, Sims), "You're Driving Me Insane," available on YouTube, posted by Vespa202, https://www.youtube.com/watch?v=BS272WD14t8 last accessed August 7, 2013.

41. "The Ostrich" is the song for which Reed and his Pickwick cohorts tuned all the strings on their guitars to A♯, the key in which the song is played.
42. The Primitives (Reed, Sims, Vance, Philips), "The Ostrich" (originally released Pickwick PC 9001), available on YouTube, posted by Pan Lecslav, https://www.youtube.com/watch?v=vxcP4jsal8o, last accessed August 7, 2013.
43. Bockris and Malanga, *Uptight*, 18.
44. Lou Reed, "A View from the Bandstand," *Aspen*, no. 3 (1966), accessed July 25, 2008, http://www.ubu.com/aspen/aspen3/index.html.
45. Philip Milstein, M. C. Kostek, and Katherine Messer, "The Maureen Tucker Interview (1980-90)," in *The Velvet Underground Companion*, ed. Albin Zak III (New York: Schirmer Books, 1996), 154.
46. Ignacio Julia, "Feedback: The Legend of the Velvet Underground, the Fully Revised Version (1986-1996)," in Zak, *The Velvet Underground Companion*, 214; ellipsis in original.
47. Julia, "Feedback," 187.
48. Milstein, Kostek, and Messer, "The Maureen Tucker Interview," 129, 167; Julia, "Feedback," 202.
49. In addition to Milstein, Kostek, and Messer, "The Maureen Tucker Interview," see the extensive interview on the DVD documentary of *The Velvet Underground: Under Review* (New York: Sexy Intellectual, 2006).
50. Milstein, Kostek, and Messer, "The Maureen Tucker Interview," 154.
51. Milstein, Kostek, and Messer, "The Maureen Tucker Interview," 164.
52. B. Michael Williams, "Babatunde Olatunji," Percussive Arts Society Hall of Fame, accessed July 11, 2013, http://www.pas.org/experience/halloffame/OlatunjiBabatunde.aspx.
53. Bockris and Malanga, *Uptight*, 22.
54. Julia, "Feedback," 190. Angus MacLise was the first drummer for the Velvet Underground. MacLise had worked with Cale in the Theatre of Eternal Music, where he played a style based on Indian tabla drumming. His work can be heard faintly and intermittently on the "Day of Niagara" recording.
55. Julia, "Feedback," 185. Like many white rock 'n' roll musicians of the period, there is little self-consciousness here about the origins of this practice of finding fun for white folks in black music. The awareness of the long historical reach of blackface minstrelsy did not extend to practicing rock 'n' roll musicians for several more years.
56. Robert Mortifoglio, "*White Light/White Heat*," in Zak, *The Velvet Underground Companion*, 63.
57. Robert Mortifoglio, "*White Light/White Heat*," 63.
58. Julia, "Feedback," 187.
59. Julia, "Feedback," 187.
60. Quoted in Bockris, *Transformer*, 125.
61. Immanuel Kant, *Critique of Judgment*, trans. J. H. Bernard (New York:

Hafner Press, 1951), 27–28. While Kant may seem an extraordinarily ideal-ist philosopher for the grounding of any concept of embodied pleasure, his aesthetics is based in an attempt to harmonize the faculties of reason and understanding in a subjective experience that feels objective. As Jonathan Loesberg explains, pleasure is a sign that this harmony has been felt. Plea-sure is not the goal of judgment, but it is a phenomenological consequence of judgment. Jonathan Loesberg, *A Return to Aesthetics: Autonomy, Indiffer-ence, and Postmodernism* (Stanford, CA: Stanford University Press, 2005), 74–144, esp. 100.

62. Milstein, Kostek, and Messer, "The Maureen Tucker Interview," 154.

63. Julia, "Feedback," 198.

64. Bockris, *Transformer*, 94.

65. Robert Somma, "Problems in Urban Living," in *All Yesterday's Parties: The Velvet Underground in Print, 1966–1971*, ed. Clinton Heylin (New York: Da Capo Press, 2005), 92. Historically, the terminology begins to shift at pre-cisely this moment. *Rock* becomes the name given to rock 'n' roll music made in self-conscious awareness of its aesthetics.

66. Ellen Willis, "Velvet Underground," in Zak, *The Velvet Underground Compan-ion*, 72.

67. The literature on Andy Warhol is too voluminous to list here. Some of the major works include Thierry De Duve, *Kant after Duchamp* (Cambridge, MA: MIT Press, 1996); Douglas Fogle, ed., *Andy Warhol/Supernova: Stars, Deaths and Disasters, 1962–1964* (Minneapolis, MN: Walker Art Center, 2005); Hal Foster, *The Return of the Real: The Avant-Garde at the End of the Century* (Cambridge, MA: MIT Press, 1996); and Annette Michelson, ed., *Andy Warhol* (Cambridge, MA: MIT Press, 2001). A valuable collection of shorter pieces can be found in Alan R. Pratt, ed., *The Critical Response to Warhol* (Westport, CT: Greenwood Press, 1997). Valuable biographical efforts include Victor Bockris, *Warhol: The Biography*, 2nd ed. (New York: Da Capo Press, 2003); and Wayne Koestenbaum, *Andy Warhol: A Penguin Life* (New York: Penguin Books, 2001).

68. Bockris, *Transformer*, 111.

69. The Velvet Underground, "Heroin," demo version, *Peel Slowly and See*, disc 1, Polydor Records, CD, originally released in 1995.

70. Although the released version is in D♭, everyone—and I mean every-one—plays the song in D natural. Whether the tape was slowed down after recording or the guitars were tuned down a step makes no real dif-ference. "Heroin" is in D, even if its most famous version sounds to be in D♭. Throughout the discussion of the commercially released version, I will refer to the song as if it is played in and sounds in the key of D major. The Velvet Underground, "Heroin," *Peel Slowly and See*, disc 2, Polydor Records, CD, originally released in 1995.

71. Morrison quoted in Bockris and Malanga, *Uptight*, 74. In an interview

years later, Tucker complained: "'Heroin' drives me nuts. That's such a good song, I remember getting chills whenever we played it, and to listen to it on the album, it's really depressing. Especially to think of someone who listens to that, and never heard us play live. And they think that that's 'Heroin,' and they say, 'What's the big deal?' It's a pile of garbage on the record. Because on that one, for instance, the guys plugged straight into the board. They didn't have their amps up loud in the studio, so of course, I couldn't hear anything. Anything. And when we got to the part where you speed up, you gotta speed up together, or it's not really right. And it just became this mountain of drum noise in front of me. I couldn't hear shit. I couldn't see Lou, to watch his mouth to see where he was in the song. And I just stopped. I was saying, 'This is no good, this isn't gonna work, we need phones or something.' So I stopped, and being a little wacky, they just kept going, and that's the one we took. And it's infuriating because . . . that's a bitch, that song. I consider that our greatest triumph. Lou's greatest triumph, too, maybe songwriting-wise." Milstein, Kostek, and Messer, "The Maureen Tucker Interview," 133.

72. Gendron has identified an antiauthentic aesthetic that developed in the pop-music criticism at the same time. This aesthetic applauds the supposedly superficial qualities of mass culture and pop. This separate aesthetic, a kind of "pop-ism," has figured in popular-music studies since the mid-1980s work of Simon Frith. The standard understanding of this pop aesthetic is based, however, on a fundamental misreading of the rhetoric employed at the time. Gendron identifies Richard Goldstein as the leading critic of pop in the late sixties, celebrating the superficialities of the pop song. But he also acknowledges that Goldstein claims to be articulating values that are believed to be important for the music's fans. In Goldstein's work, the values of relatively instant gratification and disposability are opposed to high-culture values in order to establish a separate field of criticism, not one beholden to the critical standards of European classical music. This desire for an independent field of critical judgment is not in any way inauthentic, and it is not intended to evaluate a music produced for its own pleasures apart from the needs or desires of its audience. See Gendron, *Between Montmartre and the Mudd Club*, 213–15. Frith's conceptualization of a pop aesthetic can be found in Simon Frith, *Music for Pleasure: Essays in the Sociology of Pop* (New York: Routledge, 1988).

73. Gendron, *Between Montmartre and the Mudd Club*, 199–215.

74. Gendron, *Between Montmartre and the Mudd Club*, 233–47.

75. Lester Bangs, "Of Pop and Pies and Fun: A Program for Mass Liberation in the Form of a Stooges Review or, Who's the Fool?," in *Psychotic Reactions and Carburetor Dung*, ed. Greil Marcus (New York: Vintage Books, 1988), 39, 44, 42.

76. Bangs, "Of Pop and Pies and Fun," 43.

77. Lester Bangs, "Dead Lie the Velvets, Underground," in *All Yesterdays' Parties: The Velvet Underground in Print 1966–1971*, ed. Clinton Heylin (New York: Da Capo Press, 2005), 222, 220.

78. Bourdieu, *The Field of Cultural Production*, 44.

CHAPTER FIVE. THE CONUNDRUM OF AUTHENTICITY

1. Marshall Berman, *The Politics of Authenticity: Radical Individualism and the Emergence of Modern Society* (London: Verso, 2009).

2. Regina Bendix, *In Search of Authenticity: The Formation of Folklore Studies* (Madison: University of Wisconsin Press, 1997). A more current form of the question about selves and groups would, of course, pluralize both.

3. Theodor Adorno, *The Jargon of Authenticity*, trans. Knut Tarnowski and Frederic Will (Evanston, IL: Northwestern University Press, 1973), 59.

4. See Robert Cantwell, *When We Were Good: The Folk Revival* (Cambridge, MA: Harvard University Press, 1996); Ronald D. Cohen, *Rainbow Quest: The Folk Music Revival and American Society, 1940–1970* (Amherst: University of Massachusetts Press, 2002); Benjamin Filene, *Romancing the Folk: Public Memory and American Roots Music* (Chapel Hill: University of North Carolina Press, 2000).

5. See Eric Lott, *Love and Theft: Blackface Minstrelsy and the American Working Class* (New York: Oxford University Press, 1995); Robert Toll, *Blacking Up: The Minstrel Show in Nineteenth Century America* (New York: Oxford University Press, 1977).

6. The literature on nineteenth-century musical practice is continually expanding. For examples of some of the best work, see Robert C. Allen, *Horrible Prettiness: Burlesque and American Culture* (Chapel Hill: University of North Carolina Press, 1991); Daphne Brooks, *Bodies in Dissent: Spectacular Performances of Race and Freedom, 1850–1910* (Durham, NC: Duke University Press, 2006); Dale Cockrell, *Demons of Disorder: Early Blackface Minstrels and Their World* (New York: Cambridge University Press, 1997); Hilary Poriss, *Changing the Score: Arias, Prima Donnas, and the Authority of Performance* (New York: Oxford University Press, 2009); and Ronald Radano, *Lying up a Nation: Race and Black Music* (Chicago: University of Chicago Press, 2003).

7. Karl Hagstrom Miller, *Segregating Sound: Inventing Folk and Pop Music in the Age of Jim Crow* (Durham, NC: Duke University Press, 2010).

8. See Marybeth Hamilton, *In Search of the Blues* (New York: Basic Books, 2008); and Richard Peterson, *Creating Country Music: Fabricating Authenticity* (Chicago: University of Chicago Press, 1999).

9. This was the critical orientation that has recently been deemed "rockist." See Kelefa Sanneh, "The Rap against Rockism," *New York Times*, October 31, 2004, accessed June 22, 2010, http://www.nytimes.com/2004/10/31/arts/music/31sann.html.

10. Keir Keightley, "Reconsidering Rock," in *The Cambridge Companion to Pop and Rock*, ed. Simon Frith, William Straw, and John Street (New York: Cambridge University Press, 2001), 131.
11. Other valuable discussions of authenticity include Philip Auslander, *Liveness: Performance in a Mediatized Culture* (New York: Routledge, 2008), esp. 81–85; and Simon Frith, "The Real Thing," in Simon Frith, *Music for Pleasure: Essays in the Sociology of Pop* (New York: Routledge, 1988).
12. Carl Schmitt, *The Concept of the Political*, trans. George Schwab (Chicago: Chicago University Press, 1996), 45. See also Jacques Derrida, *The Politics of Friendship*, trans. George Collins (New York: Verso, 1997); and Slavoj Žižek, "Carl Schmitt and the Age of Post-politics," in *The Challenge of Carl Schmitt*, ed. Chantal Mouffe (London: Verso, 1999).
13. Patti Smith, *Just Kids* (New York: HarperCollins, 2010), 126.
14. Brigid Berlin quoted in John Hagleston's liner notes to The Velvet Underground, *The Velvet Underground Live at Max's Kansas City*, Atlantic Records, CD reissue, originally released in 2004.
15. Bernard Gendron, *Between Montmartre and the Mudd Club: Popular Music and the Avant-Garde* (Chicago: University of Chicago Press, 2002), 199–215, 233–47.
16. Gendron, *Between Montmartre and the Mudd Club*, 199–215, 233–47; Lester Bangs, *Psychotic Reactions and Carburetor Dung* (New York: Anchor Books, 1988), 43.
17. Childers quoted in Victor Bockris and Roberta Bayley, *Patti Smith: An Unauthorized Biography* (New York: Simon and Schuster, 1999), 16–17.
18. For details of Smith's early life, see Bockris and Bayley, *Patti Smith*; Clinton Heylin, *From the Velvets to the Voidoids: The Birth of American Punk Rock* (Chicago: A Cappella Books, 2005); Mark Paytress, *Break It Up: Patti Smith's Horses and the Remaking of Rock 'n' Roll* (London: Portrait Books, 2006); Philip Shaw, *Horses* (New York: Continuum, 2008); and Smith, *Just Kids*.
19. Patti Smith, *Seventh Heaven* (New York: Telegraph Books, 1972). Andrew Wylie published a book of poetry that same year that featured even shorter lines, more overt sex, and significantly less rhythmic interest. Andrew Wylie, *Yellow Flowers* (New York: Dot Books, 1972).
20. Bockris and Bayley, *Patti Smith*, 84.
21. Smith's poetry first appeared in *Creem* in September 1971. Tony Glover, review of *7th Heaven* by Patti Smith, *Creem*, October 1972, 52; Lester Bangs and Jaan Uhelszki, "Sulky Angel: The Poetry of Patti Smith," *Creem*, February 1974, 30.
22. Bockris and Bayley, *Patti Smith*, 82.
23. Susan Shapiro, "Patti Smith: Somewhere, over the Rimbaud," in *Rock She Wrote: Women Write about Rock, Pop, and Rap*, ed. Evelyn McDonnell and Ann Powers (New York: Cooper Square Press, 1999), 282.
24. Smith, *Just Kids*, 238.
25. While it is true that Reed's song "Rock and Roll" (let alone Chuck Berry's

"Rock and Roll Music" and the dozens of that song's imitators) preceded Smith's evocation of the field, these songs appealed to the genre as a whole. Smith's naming of names specified the tradition and presented the aura of preceding artists who were active in the field.

26. Lisa Robinson, "Human Dignity Is Where It's At," *Creem*, March 1974, 78.

27. Patti Smith, "Piss Factory," Mer Records, 45 originally released in 1974. The words are reprinted in Patti Smith, *Early Work: 1970–1979* (New York: W. W. Norton and Co. 1994), 38–40.

28. For a nearly contemporaneous discussion of authenticity, freedom, and the Enlightenment origins of romanticism, see Marshall Berman, *The Politics of Authenticity: Radical Individualism and the Emergence of Modern Society* (London: Verso, 2009).

29. Patti Smith, recorded intro to "Hey Joe," Mer Records, 45 originally released in 1974. Patty Hearst was the granddaughter of William Randolph Hearst. She had disappeared from her family's home and been missing for weeks when she showed up on a bank surveillance video, holding a rifle during a robbery organized by a fringe radical group called the Symbionese Liberation Army.

30. It is probably not surprising that this layering of the relations between freedom and race had to be placed elsewhere, beyond the borders of the United States. See Josh Kun, *Audiotopias: Music, Race, and America* (Berkeley: University of California Press, 2005), for more discussion of the displacement of U.S. racial categories and conflict onto Mexican space, where new resolutions of the problem can be imagined.

31. See Greil Marcus, *Mystery Train: Images of America in Rock 'n' Roll Music* (New York: E. P. Dutton, 1975); Barry Shank, "'That Wild Mercury Sound': Bob Dylan and the Illusion of American Culture," *boundary 2* 29, no. 1 (Spring 2002).

32. Reed's "colored girls" were going "doo-de-doo" in "Walk on the Wild Side" by 1972, and the Rolling Stones had sung about the sexual relations of slavery in "Brown Sugar" in 1971. Both were narrated in the third person and neither captured the full panoply of allusions connecting sex, rock, freedom, and danger to the extent that Smith's "Hey Joe" did.

33. Dave Marsh, "Her Horses Got Wings, They Can Fly: Factory Girl, Coal Stove Visionary, Scion of Rimbaud and the Ronnettes, Patti Smith Now Challenges the Assembly Line of Rock & Roll," *Rolling Stone*, January 1, 1976, 40. See also Norman Mailer, *Advertisements for Myself* (New York: Putnam Books, 1959), 337–58. Graham Robb briefly discusses Rimbaud's affair with "Mariam," an Abyssinian woman he "kept" during his time in Ethiopia, in *Rimbaud* (New York: W. W. Norton and Co. 2000), 357–58.

34. For an example of Smith's name checking of soul singers, see Shapiro, "Patti Smith," 279–83. In the same essay, she discusses the artists who moved her early in life: Brancusi and Picasso.

35. Greg Tate, *Flyboy in the Buttermilk: Essays on Contemporary America* (New

York: Simon and Schuster, 1992); Kandia Crazy Horse, *Rip It Up: The Black Experience in Rock 'n' Roll* (New York: Palgrave, 2004); Maureen Mahon, *Right to Rock: The Black Rock Coalition and the Cultural Politics of Race* (Durham, NC: Duke University Press, 2004).

36. For an in-depth discussion of the timbral qualities associated with black music, see Samuel Floyd, *The Power of Black Music: Interpreting Its History from Africa to the United States* (New York: Oxford University Press, 1995).

37. For an almost humorous example, listen to any Yes recording from the early seventies.

38. When the writers who confirmed and articulated the rock aesthetic turned their ears to jazz, the soloists they admired most were those like John Coltrane and Albert Ayler, not Ben Webster or Grover Washington. Their ears were attuned to the rasp as the sound of authentic freedom.

39. Paul Morely, "Patti Smith: A Woman's Place," *New Musical Express*, April 1, 1978, accessed June 30, 2010, http://www.rocksbackpages.com/article.ht ml?ArticleID=12198.

40. For the most concise discussion of Bourdieu's theory of fields, see Pierre Bourdieu, *The Field of Cultural Production: Essays on Art and Literature*, trans. Richard Nice (New York: Columbia University Press, 1993).

41. Jean-Luc Nancy, *The Inoperative Community*, trans. Peter Connor (Minneapolis: University of Minnesota Press, 1991); Jean-Luc Nancy, *Listening*, trans. Charlotte Mandell (New York: Fordham University Press, 2007).

42. See chapter 1 of this volume; Jacques Rancière, *Dissensus: On Politics and Aesthetics*, ed. and trans. Steven Corcoran (New York: Continuum 2010); Nancy, *The Inoperative Community*.

43. bell hooks, "Madonna: Plantation Mistress or Soul Sister?," in McDonnell and Powers, *Rock She Wrote*, 319.

44. Rancière, *Dissensus*, 63.

45. Rancière, *Dissensus*, 23. This understanding of the relationship between art and the political neatly fits with that of Theodor Adorno. See his *Aesthetic Theory*, trans. Robert Hullot-Kentor (Minneapolis: University of Minnesota Press, 1997).

46. Simon Reynolds and Joy Press, *The Sex Revolts: Gender, Rebellion, and Rock 'n' Roll* (Cambridge, MA: Harvard University Press, 1995), 236–38. *Sex Revolts* has been critiqued for its borderline essentialism. But its standing as the first full textual analysis of gender difference in rock remains. For more on Smith and the gendering of rock, see Norma Coates, "(R)evolution Now? Rock and the Political Potential of Gender," in *Sexing the Groove: Popular Music and Gender*, ed. Sheila Whitely (New York: Routledge, 1997). For a detailed discussion of the ongoing reproduction of rock's masculinist tendencies, see Marion Leonard, *Gender in the Music Industry: Rock, Discourse and Girl Power* (Aldershot, UK: Ashgate Publishing, 2007), 23–42.

47. Amy Gross, "I'm Doing a Revenge for Bad Skin: Introducing Rock 'n' Roll's Lady Raunch, Patti Smith," *Mademoiselle*, September 1975.

48. On the distinction between rock and pop, see Keightley, "Reconsidering Rock"; and Diane Railton, "The Gendered Carnival of Pop," *Popular Music* 20, no. 3 (2001).

49. Gross, "I'm Doing a Revenge for Bad Skin." Republished online: http://www.oceanstar.com/patti/intervus/7509made.htm. Accessed August 8, 2013.

50. Charles Shaar Murray, "Weird Scenes inside Gasoline Alley," *The Penguin Book of Rock & Roll Writing*, ed. Clinton Heylin (London: Penguin Books, 1993), 230; Lester Bangs, "Patti Smith: *Horses*," in *Mainlines, Blood Feasts, and Bad Taste: A Lester Bangs Reader*, ed. John Morthland (New York: Anchor Books, 2003), 103.

51. Steve Lake quoted in Paytress, *Break It Up*, 19; Mike Watts quoted in Paytress, *Break It Up*, 196.

52. Shapiro, "Patti Smith," 280.

53. Charles Shaar Murray, "Patti Smith: *Radio Ethiopia*," *New Musical Express*, October 23, 1976, accessed June 30, 2010, http://www.rocksbackpages.com/article.html?ArticleID=12614.

54. Greil Marcus, "*Horses*: Patti Smith Exposes Herself," *Village Voice*, November 24, 1975, accessed June 30, 2010, http://www.rocksbackpages.com/article.html?ArticleID=665.

55. Reynolds and Press, *The Sex Revolts*, 356.

56. Philip Shaw, *Horses* (New York: Continuum Books, 2008), 12.

57. Every review cited in notes 49–54 includes a discussion of this song, as does every biography of Patti Smith.

58. Shaw, *Horses*, 103.

59. This is an example of what Charles Keil terms "participatory discrepancies." See Charles Keil, "Participatory Discrepancies and the Power of Music," in Charles Keil and Steven Feld, *Music Grooves: Essays and Dialogue* (Tucson, AZ: Fenestra, 2005).

60. Lenny Kaye was the first serious archivist of this tradition, codifying its conventions through the choices he made for the first *Nuggets* collection, issued on Elektra Records in 1972.

61. Reynolds and Press, *The Sex Revolts*, 357.

62. Reynolds and Press quote Smith from a 1978 interview: "We're a feminine band, we'll go so far and peak and then we'll start again and peak, over and over" (*The Sex Revolts*, 356).

63. For examples of these achievements, listen to the Ramones, "Jackie Is a Punk," on *The Ramones* (Sire Records, 1976); The Clash, "(White Man) In Hammersmith Palais" 45 (Columbia Records, 1978); Black Flag, "Rise Above," *Damaged* (Unicorn Records, 1982); Fugazi, "Burnin'," *7 Songs* (Dischord Records, 1988); and Beat Happening, "Indian Summer," *Jamboree* (K Records, 1988). For a discussion of American indie music, see Michael Azerrad, *Our Band Could Be Your Life: Scenes from the American Indie Underground 1981–1991* (Boston: Little, Brown and Co., 2001). Cotton Seiler con-

tributes an insightful discussion of the indie scene in Louisville, Kentucky, in "Have You Ever Been to the Pleasure Inn? The Transformation of Indie Rock in Louisville, Kentucky," *Journal of Popular Music Studies* 13 (2001).

64. Bad Brains, "Pay to Come," *Bad Brains*, ROIR, cassette tape, originally released in 1981. According to Mark Andersen and Mark Jenkins, these words were inspired by the "positive mental attitude" articulated in two early self-help books by Napoleon Hill. Hill's first book was apparently a major inspiration for H.R.'s initial plan for the band. See Napoleon Hill, *Think and Grow Rich, Original 1937 Classic Edition* (New York: Soho Books, 2010). Mark Andersen and Mark Jenkins, *Dance of Days: Two Decades of Punk in the Nation's Capital* (New York: Akashic Books, 2009), 28–29.

65. For more on Bad Brains and the politics of identity, see Shayna Maskell, "Performing Punk: Bad Brains and the Construction of Identity," *Journal of Popular Music Studies* 21, no. 4 (2009).

66. Andersen and Jenkins, *Dance of Days*, 28–30, 37–38, 40–43, 54–55, 67–69, 104–111. Garfield is quoted on page 43; MacKaye and Nelson are quoted on page 55.

67. Andersen and Jenkins, *Dance of Days*, 38, 106.

68. According to the journalist and musician Howard Wuelfling, "the difference between Teen Idles and Minor Threat was Bad Brains. They set the example of how to play extremely fast but with extreme precision." Quoted in Andersen and Jenkins, *Dance of Days*, 73.

69. MacKaye quoted in Andersen and Jenkins, *Dance of Days*, 63.

70. William Tsitsos, "Rules of Rebellion: Slamdancing, Moshing and the American Alternative Scene," in *The Popular Music Studies Reader*, ed. Andy Bennett, Barry Shank, and Jason Toynbee (New York: Routledge, 2006).

71. For a helpful discussion of the different viewing positions inside the music club and their different contributions to the overall experience of live music, see Wendy Fonorow, *Empire of Dirt: The Aesthetics and Rituals of British Indie Music* (Middletown, CT: Wesleyan University Press, 2006).

72. Mark Andersen, *All the Power: Revolution without Illusion* (Chicago: Punk Planet Books, 2004), 37.

73. Andersen, *All the Power*, 38.

74. Johnson quoted in Andersen and Jenkins, *Dance of Days*, 74.

75. MacKaye quoted in Andersen and Jenkins, *Dance of Days*, 157.

76. Ian MacKaye, interview from *American Hardcore*, directed by Paul Rauchman, written by Steve Blush, Sony Pictures Classics, 2006.

77. These quotes are from Brian Peterson's monumental documentation of the nineties hardcore scene, *Burning Fight: The Nineties Hardcore Revolution in Ethics, Politics, Spirit and Sound* (Huntington Beach, CA: Revelation Records, 2009), 12, 14, 16.

78. MacKaye quoted in Andersen and Jenkins, *Dance of Days*, 80.

79. For an extensive discussion of the power and limits of hardcore's political stances, see Peterson, *Burning Fight*.

80. Fonorow, *Empire of Dirt*, 187–202; and Seiler, "Have You Ever Been to the Pleasure Inn?," 191.

81. Joshua Clover discusses the inward turn of grunge (one form of indie) away from the outward political thrust of seventies punk in *1989: Bob Dylan Didn't Have This to Sing About* (Berkeley: University of California Press, 2009), 73–89.

82. Beth Ditto, "Foreward," in *Riot Grrrl: Revolution Girl Style Now!*, ed. Nadine Monem (London: Blackdog Publishing, 2007), 8. Fanzines are analyzed in detail in Leonard, *Gender in the Music Industry*. The tension between the news media and fanzine images of riot grrrl is discussed in Joanne Gottlieb and Gayle Wald, "Smells Like Teen Spirit: Riot Grrrls, Revolution, and Women in Independent Rock," in *Microphone Fiends: Youth Music and Youth Culture*, ed. Andrew Ross and Tricia Rose (New York: Routledge, 1994); Kristen Schilt, "'Riot Grrrl Is . . .': Contestation over Meaning in a Music Scene," in Andrew Bennett and Richard Peterson, *Music Scenes: Local, Translocal and Virtual* (Nashville, TN: Vanderbilt University Press, 2004); also see Leonard, *Gender in the Music Industry*; and Monem, *Riot Grrrl*. There is a rapidly growing group of books that discuss the movement, including Sara Marcus, *Girls to the Front: The True Story of the Riot Grrrl Revolution* (New York: Harper Perennial, 2010); Marisa Meltzer, *Girl Power: Nineties Revolution in Music* (New York: Faber and Faber, 2010); and Maria Raha, *Cinderella's Big Score: Women of the Punk and Indie Underground* (Emeryville, CA: Seal Press, 2005). Of these, Marcus's discussion of the riot grrrl movement as a national political event is the most comprehensive. Andersen and Jenkins, *Dance of Days*, also have a very useful discussion of the movement's beginnings in DC.

83. Julia Downes cites a 1988 meeting of Sharon Cheslow, Amy Pickering, Lydia Ely, and Cynthia Connelly where sexism in the DC scene was discussed as an early spark for what became riot grrrl. Julia Downes, "Riot Grrrl: The Legacy and Contemporary Landscape of DIY Feminist Cultural Activism," in Monem, *Riot Grrrl*, 17.

84. Vail quoted in Lois Maffeo's liner notes, "Crashing Through," for Beat Happening, *Crashing Through*, K Records, CD box set, originally released in 2002.

85. Raha provides a concise review of this response in her discussion of Bikini Kill in *Cinderella's Big Score*, 203–8.

86. Joan Jett was a founding member of the Runaways. The Runaways were an "all-girl band" formed in Los Angeles in 1975. One of their signature achievements was to lay the groundwork for enough female musicians to enter the rock field that the designation "all-girl band" became outmoded. After the Runaways broke up, Jett produced the only album by the LA punk legends the Germs, and she had an international hit as a solo artist in 1982 with "I Love Rock and Roll." The tight professional sound of that record presaged the second version of "Rebel Girl." Jett joins Patti Smith as an im-

portant precursor, helping to pave the way for the bands associated with riot grrrl.

87. Mimi Nguyen, "It's Not a White World: Looking for Race in Punk," *Punk Planet*, November/December 1998, accessed July 6, 2010, http://thread andcircuits.wordpress.com/2010/03/14/its-not-a-white-world-looking -for-race-in-punk-1998/.

88. For a brief yet careful discussion of this problem, see S. Marcus, *Girls to the Front*, 250–52.

89. See Sara Marcus's discussion of this famous moment from a Bikini Kill show in *Girls to the Front*, 17–18.

90. Charles Keil, "Participatory Discrepancies and the Power of Music," in Keil and Feld, *Music Grooves*, 96.

91. Steve Feld, "Aesthetics as Iconicity of Style," in Keil and Feld, *Music Grooves*, 120.

CHAPTER 6. 1969

1. This period is well documented in the massive Beatles literature. Two relatively recent sources are Jonathan Gould, *Can't Buy Me Love: The Beatles, Britain, and America* (New York: Three Rivers Press, 2007); and Philip Norman, *John Lennon: The Life* (New York: HarperCollins ebooks), 2011.

2. Michael Kurtz, *Stockhausen: A Biography*, trans. Richard Toop (London: Faber and Faber, 1992), 170. Even had this concert gone forward, it would not have been the first performance shared by the avant-garde and pop. The *Exploding Plastic Inevitable* concerts of the Velvet Underground certainly preceded this, as well as various other collaborations among individuals such as Henry Flynt, Tony Conrad, John Lennon, Yoko Ono, and others. See earlier chapters of this book as well as Benjamin Piekut, *Experimentalism Otherwise: The New York Avant-Garde and Its Limits* (Berkeley: University of California Press, 2011).

3. Stockhausen quoted in Kurtz, *Stockhausen*, 141.

4. For discussions of Stockhausen's work with Meyer-Eppler, see Robin Maconie, *Other Planets: The Music of Karlheinz Stockhausen* (Oxford: Scarecrow Press, 2005), 124–38. Stockhausen discusses his approach to the unity of all music in Karlheinz Stockhausen and Elaine Barkin, "The Concept of Unity in Electronic Music," *Perspectives in New Music* 1, no. 1 (Autumn 1962). See also Gunter Peters, *Holy Seriousness in the Play: Essays on the Music of Karlheinz Stockhausen* (Kurten, Germany: Stockhausen-Verlag, 2003).

5. Maconie, *Other Planets*, 275.

6. Maconie, *Other Planets*, 301.

7. Quoted in Kurtz, *Stockhausen*, 163.

8. Quoted in Kurtz, *Stockhausen*, 171.

9. Gould, *Can't Buy Me Love*, 313–15; Barry Miles, *In the Sixties* (London:

Jonathan Cape, 2002); Walter Everett, *The Beatles as Musicians: Revolver through the Anthology* (New York: Oxford University Press, 1999), 32–33.

10. Everett, *The Beatles as Musicians*, 34–38, 78–83.
11. Everett, *The Beatles as Musicians*, 116–22. Everett describes this glissando as a "Pederecki-like aleatoric counterpoint," 118.
12. For a brief official history of the Eastman School of Music, see its website, http://www.esm.rochester.edu/about/history/ (accessed July 28, 2011).
13. Nadine Hubbs, *The Queer Composition of America's Sound: Gay Modernists, American Music, and National Identity* (Berkeley: University of California Press, 2004), 127.
14. Courtney Orlando, phone interview with author, July 26, 2008. All further quotes from Orlando are from this interview.
15. John Pickford Richards, phone interview with author, January 5, 2009. All further quotes from Richards are from this interview.
16. Payton MacDonald, phone interview with author, June 19, 2008 All further quotes from MacDonald are from this interview.
17. Jason Price, phone interview with the author, October 2, 2008. All further quotes from Price are from this interview.
18. Robert E. Morris, *Composition with Pitch-Classes: A Theory of Compositional Design* (New Haven, CT: Yale University Press, 1987). See also Andrew Mead, review of *Composition with Pitch-Classes*, by Robert Morris, *Perspectives of New Music* 29, no. 1 (1991).
19. Gavin Chuck, interview with the author, November 11, 2006. Carlisle, PA. All further quotes from Chuck are from this interview. See also Gavin Chuck, "Our Story," AlarmWillSound.com, accessed May 25, 2012, http://www.alarmwillsound.com/about.php.
20. Alan Pierson, phone interview with the author, August 18, 2008. All further quotes from Pierson are from this interview.
21. Stefan Freund, phone interview with the author, February 3, 2009. All further quotes from Freund are from this interview.
22. The biographical information about Caleb Burhans came from his personal website, CalebBurhans.com: http://www.calebburhans.com/bio/ (accessed July 29, 2011).
23. Steve Reich, "Music as a Gradual Process," in Steve Reich, *Writings on Music, 1965–2000*, ed. Paul Hillier (New York: Oxford University Press, 2002), 34–35.
24. Paul Hillier, "Introduction," in Steve Reich, *Writings on Music*, 4–5. See also Steve Reich, "Music as a Gradual Process," 34–35, in Reich, *Writings on Music*.
25. Steve Reich, "Piano Phase," in Reich, *Writings on Music*, 24.
26. Sumanth Gopinath, "The Problem of the Political in Steve Reich's *Come Out*," in *Sound Commitments: Avant-Garde Music and the Sixties*, ed. Robert Adlington (New York: Oxford University Press, 2009), 127.
27. Steve Reich, "Music as a Gradual Process," in Reich, *Writings on Music*,

35. That sentence and the efforts it represents only make sense after the nearly absolute separation of composition and sound produced by serialist composition strategies. Luciano Berio once looked at an early score and told Reich that if he wanted to write tonal music, he ought to go ahead and do so.

28. Which only makes Jiri Kylian's "Falling Angels" such an amazing achievement in modern dance.

29. Alarm Will Sound, *Reich at the Roxy: Alarm Will Sound Performs Steve Reich Live in New York*, Sweetspot Music, SSSRCD001, DVD and CD, originally released in 2005 and recorded in 2004.

30. Antonella Puca, "Steve Reich and Hebrew Cantillation," *The Musical Quarterly* 81, no. 4 (Winter 1997).

31. Gopinath, "The Problem of the Political in Steve Reich's *Come Out*." See also Lloyd Whitesell, "White Noise: Race and Erasure in the Cultural Avant-Garde," *American Music* 19, no. 2 (Summer 2001).

32. The lyrics are presented in both Hebrew and English inside the cover booklet for Alarm Will Sound and Ossia, *Steve Reich: Tehillim, the Desert Music*, conducted by Alan Pierson, Cantaloupe Music CA, 21009, originally released in 2002.

33. Steve Reich, "Hebrew Cantillation as an Influence on Composition," in Reich, *Writings on Music*, 107.

34. Steve Reich, "*Tehillim*," in Reich, *Writings on Music*, 101.

35. Reich, "*Tehillim*," 101, 104.

36. Reich, "Hebrew Cantillation as an Influence on Composition," 107.

37. Reich, "Music as a Gradual Process," 67.

38. Reich, "*Tehillim*," 101.

39. Jackie Leclair, phone interview with the author, June 20, 2008. All further quotes from Leclair are from this interview.

40. Robert Fink, *Repeating Ourselves: American Minimal Music as Cultural Practice* (Berkeley: University of California Press, 2005), 89. See also the discussion of Steve Reich's *Octet*, Terry Riley's *In C*, Louis Andriessen's *Hoketus*, and the "media sublime" on pages 150–57.

41. Details of the rehearsal are taken from my field notes of November 10, 2006, at the Rubendall Recital Hall at Dickinson College.

42. For Calefax's performance of "Study 2," see "Studies on Nancarrow (1/3) #2" uploaded to YouTube by "albanw," December 8, 2008, accessed August 11, 2013, https://www.youtube.com/watch?v=F-SMX64UYeo. For the Juilliard students' rendition of "Study 21," see "Nancarrow: Study No. 21 @ Juilliard," uploaded to YouTube by "dmuniz513," April 9, 2008, accessed August 12, 2011, http://www.youtube.com/watch?v=q5bJcMoQRcM&feature=related.

43. Alarm Will Sound, *a/rhythmia*, Nonesuch Records, 467708–2, CD, originally released in 2009, Alan Pierson, "Arrhythmia," liner notes.

44. The quote by Marks is from my notes taken during the concert: Alarm Will

Sound, *Arrhythmia*, Riley Auditorium, Battelle Fine Arts Center, Otterbein College, September 29, 2007.

45. It is true that the Shaggs were not the most competent of rock musicians. When they recorded their music, furthermore, the conventions of rock had no room for their imprecise approach to the beat and the niceties of chord changes. Their gender also contributes to the tendency to dismiss them as unworthy of serious listening. But with generous and open ears, a kind of beauty can be heard. The Shaggs, *Philosophy of the World*, RCA Victor (BMG Classics), 09026 63371–2, CD reissued in 1999 (originally released in 1969).

46. Charles Keil, "Participatory Discrepancies and the Power of Music," in Charles Keil and Steven Feld, *Music Grooves: Essays and Dialogue* (Tucson, AZ: Fenestra, 2005).

47. Alarm Will Sound's recording of "Philosophy of the World" is available on their website. http://www.alarmwillsound.com/recordings.php. Last accessed August 18, 2011.

48. Eric Edberg, Alarm Will Sound's 1969 at Zankel: What Is a Musician's Responsibilty [sic] to Society?," *Eric Edberg* (blog), March 14, 2011, accessed May 4, 2011, http://ericedberg.wordpress.com/2011/03/14/alarm-will-sounds-1969-at-zankel-what-is-a-musicians-responsibilty-to-society/; Arthur Leonard, "Alarm Will Sound's '1969' Show at Zankel Hall," http://www.artleonardobservations.com/category/music/page/16/, accessed August 11, 2013.

49. *1969* has been performed in at least three versions. The most recent performances, from the spring of 2011, added two pieces, a new composition by Stefan Freund, "Swimming," and an arrangement of Jimi Hendrix's version of "The Star-Spangled Banner." I have not been able to hear these works. While I will address some of the symbolic significance of the inclusion of Hendrix as a supporting figure, I cannot write about Freund's contribution. My discussion will be based on the version that was performed in the spring of 2009, focusing in particular on the show in Pittsburgh on March 20, 2009, and in Cleveland on March 21, 2009. "Revolution 9" was the final work performed during that pair of performances.

50. Karlheinz Stockhausen, *From the Seven Days/Aus den Sieben Tagen*, Universal Edition 14790, nr.26, composed in May 1968, 21.

51. Ian MacDonald, *Revolution in the Head: The Beatles' Records and the Sixties*, 3rd. ed. (Chicago: Chicago Review Press, 2007), 289. See MacDonald's discussion of Lennon's LSD use on pages 186–93, 217, 228, and 265.

52. Cornelius Cardew, *Stockhausen Serves Imperialism, and Other Articles* (London: Latimer New Dimensions Limited, 1974); Jonathan Cott, *Stockhausen: Conversations with the Composer* (New York: Simon and Schuster, 1973), 119–20.

53. Luciano Berio with Rossana Dalmonte and Balint Andras Varga, *Two Inter-*

views, ed. and trans. David Osmond-Smith (New York: Marion Boyars, 1985), 55.

54. Berio, Dalmonte, and Varga, *Two Interviews*, 80.

55. Luciano Berio, *Remembering the Future* (Cambridge, MA: Harvard University Press, 2006), 5.

56. Davis Osmond-Smith, *Playing on Words: A Guide to Luciano Berio's* Sinfonia (London: Royal Music Association, 1985).

57. The segregation of art music in the late sixties is discussed in George Lewis, *A Power Stronger Than Itself: The AACM and American Experimental Music* (Chicago: University of Chicago Press, 2008). Alarm Will Sound does little to challenge the historical segregation of the time. The nod to Hendrix carries an unfortunate air of tokenism. Curiously, Bernstein himself had commented on the racism of the orchestral concert scene in an article published in the *New York Times* in 1947. He wrote, "The prejudice which exists against the Negro everywhere becomes a double-barreled load in music." See Leonard Bernstein, "The Negro in Music: Problems He Has to Face in Getting a Start," *New York Times*, November 2, 1947, accessed August 23, 2011, http://select.nytimes.com/gst/abstract.html?res=F50A10F F3B5E17738DDDAB0894D9415B8788F1D3&scp=1&sq=Bernstein+Negro+ in+Music&st=p.

58. Bernstein quoted in Michael Freedland, *Leonard Bernstein* (London: Harrap, 1987), 208.

59. Leonard Bernstein, "Young People's Concert: What Is Sonata Form," accessed August 22, 2011, http://www.leonardbernstein.com/ypc_script_wh at_is_sonata_form.htm.

60. See "Inside Pop: The Rock Revolution," uploaded to YouTube by drksrfr, March 16, 2012. https://www.youtube.com/watch?v=afU76JJcquI, accessed August 11, 2013.

61. Meryle Secrest, *Leonard Bernstein: A Life* (New York: Alfred A. Knopf, 1994), 248.

62. This Bernstein quote can be found in many places. One is the website for Carnegie Hall's program on Bernstein the social activist. See http://www .carnegiehall.org/bernstein/leonardbernstein/socialactivist.aspx (accessed August 22, 2011).

63. Tom Wolfe, "These Radical Chic Evenings," in Tom Wolfe, *The Purple Decades: A Reader* (New York: Berkley Books, 1983), 182.

64. Don Heckman, "Its Reach Exceeds Its Grasp," *New York Times*, November 21, 1971.

65. Harold Schonberg, "Bernstein's New Work Reflects His Background on Broadway," *New York Times*, September 9, 1971, accessed August 22, 2011, http://select.nytimes.com/gst/abstract.html?res=F50A1EFF345B1A7493C BA91782D85F458785F9. See also Nan Robertson, "Glittering Audience Attends Kennedy Center's Opening," *New York Times*. September 9, 1971, ac-

cessed August 23, 2011, http://select.nytimes.com/gst/abstract.html?res
=F10D11FF345B1A7493CBA91782D85F458785F9&scp=3&sq=Nan+Roberts
on+Kennedy+Center+Bernstein&st=p.

66. Yoko Ono and John Lennon, *Unfinished Music I: Two Virgins*, Rykodisc RCD
10411, CD reissue 1997, originally released in 1969); The Beatles, "Revolution 9," *The Beatles*, EMI/Apple Records, digital remaster, CD reissue 2009,
originally released in 1968.

67. Everett, *The Beatles as Musicians*, 174–75.

68. MacDonald, *Revolution in the Head*, 289.

69. Everett, *The Beatles as Musicians*, 174; MacDonald, *Revolution in the Head*,
288.

70. "Revolution 9 live by Alarm Will Sound," uploaded to YouTube by
"AlarmWillSound," October 16, 2010, accessed August 18, 2011, http://
www.youtube.com/watch?v=_WjfQSxcqoc.

71. Freud's classic discussion of melancholia is "Mourning and Melancholia,"
in his *General Psychological Theory: Papers on Metapsychology*, ed. Philip
Rieff (New York: Collier Books, 1963).

72. Jean-Luc Nancy, *The Inoperative Community*, trans. Peter Connor (Minneapolis: University of Minnesota Press, 1991), xl; Jacques Rancière, "The
Ethical Turn of Aesthetics and Politics," in *Dissensus: On Politics and Aesthetics*, ed. and trans. Steven Corcoran (New York: Continuum, 2010).

73. Art Ensemble of Chicago, *A Jackson in Your House/Message to Our Folks*,
Charly Licensing, ANSP 066 CD, CD reissue 2001, originally released in
1970; Lewis, *A Power Stronger Than Itself*, 226; see also pages 220–30.

74. Miles Davis, *Bitches Brew*, Sony Music, C2K 65774, CD reissue 1999, originally released in 1970; Kevin Fellezs, *Birds of Fire: Jazz, Rock, Funk, and the
Creation of Fusion* (Durham, NC: Duke University Press, 2011), 66.

75. Lewis, *A Power Stronger Than Itself*, 33. Fred Moten links this artistic segregation to the legacy of Hegelian thought, where the avant-garde is one
form of the surplus made possible through forced labor. As a consequence
of this historical development, the very "idea of a black avant-garde exists
. . . oxymoronically." Fred Moten, *In the Break: The Aesthetics of the Black
Radical Tradition* (Minneapolis: University of Minnesota Press, 2003), 32.

76. Chantal Mouffe, *The Return of the Political* (London: Verso Books, 1993).

CODA. THE AURAL IMAGINARY

1. Jean-Luc Nancy, *Listening*, trans. Charlotte Mandell (New York: Fordham
University Press, 2007), 26–27.

2. Jean-Luc Nancy, *Being Singular Plural*, trans. Robert D. Richardson and
Anne E. O'Brien (Stanford, CA: Stanford University Press, 2000), 1.

3. Lawrence Kramer, *Interpreting Music* (Berkeley: University of California
Press, 2011), 55–60; and Lawrence Kramer, "Subjectivity Rampant! Music,
Hermeneutics, and History," in *The Cultural Study of Music: A Critical Intro-*

duction, ed. Clayton, Martin, Trevor Herbert, and Richard Middleton (New York: Routledge, 2003).

4. Roshanak Kheshti, "Touching Listening: The Aural Imaginary in the World Music Culture," *American Quarterly* 63, no. 3 (October 2011): 724.

5. Bob White makes a similar point when he asserts that consuming world music often leads to essentialist assumptions about the culture that produced the music. His analysis of the problem is less subtle than Kheshti's, however, relying as it does on an unnecessary one-to-one link between musical style and cultural identity for his own position as well as the listening practices he critiques. But his list of strategies for avoiding essentialist listening is useful. Bob White, "The Promise of World Music: Strategies for Non-essentialist Listening," in *Music and Globalization: Critical Encounters*, ed. Bob White (Bloomington: Indiana University Press, 2012).

6. John Szwed, *Alan Lomax: The Man Who Recorded the World* (New York: Penguin, 2011); see also Alan Lomax, *Folksong Style and Culture* (Washington, DC: American Association for the Advancement of Science, 1968).

7. Paul Gilroy, *Deeper Than Blue: On the Moral Economies of Black Atlantic Culture* (Cambridge, MA: Belknap and Harvard University Press, 2010), 89.

8. For a more detailed discussion of Blackwell's musical and image manipulation, see Jason Toynbee, *Bob Marley: Herald of a Postcolonial World* (New York: Polity Press, 2007).

9. Gilroy, *Deeper Than Blue*, 92.

10. Lauren Berlant, *Cruel Optimism* (Durham, NC: Duke University Press, 2011), 224. In this passage, Berlant is quoting from the important work of Charles Hirschkind, *The Ethical Soundscape: Cassette Sermons and Islamic Counterpublics* (New York: Columbia University Press, 2006). See also Lauren Berlant, *The Female Complaint: The Unfinished Business of Sentimentality in American Culture* (Durham, NC: Duke University Press, 2008).

11. Jayna Brown, "Buzz and Rumble: Global Pop Music and Utopian Impulse," *Social Text* 28, no. 1 (Spring 2010): 127.

12. From 1996 to 2002, there was only a single award. This changed in 2003, when the Traditional/Contemporary division was initiated. See Timothy D. Taylor, "World Music Today," in White, *Music and Globalization*.

13. Joe Tangari, "Aman Iman: Water Is Life," *Pitchfork*, April 4, 2007, accessed September 13, 2012, http://pitchfork.com/reviews/albums/10055-aman-iman-water-is-life/.

14. Joe Tangari, "Imidiwan: Companions," *Pitchfork*, October 13, 2009, accessed September 13, 2012, http://pitchfork.com/reviews/albums/13549-imidiwan-companions/.

15. Tangari, "Aman Iman."

16. Robert Christgau, "Consumer Guides: Tinariwen," Robertchristgau.com, accessed November 21, 2012, http://www.robertchristgau.com/get_artist.php?id=5036&name=Tinariwen.

17. Baz Lecocq, "Unemployed Intellectuals in the Sahara: The Teshumara

Nationalist Movement and the Revolutions in Tuareg Society," supplement, *International Review of Social History* 49, no. S12 (2004), 94–98.

18. Lecocq, "Unemployed Intellectuals in the Sahara." 94–98.

19. David Zoumenou, "West Africa: The Sahel—Is There a Solution to the Tuareg Insurgency?," Institute for Security Studies, March 20, 2012, accessed September 20, 2012, http://allafrica.com/stories/201203201295 .html. See also Banning Eyre, "Tinariwen's Abdullah Ag Alhoussein Talks about Mali," Afropop Worldwide, July 3, 2012, accessed November 21, 2012, http://www.afropop.org/wp/3616/tinariwens-abdallah-ag-alhousseini -talks-about-mali/; and Afua Hirsch, "Islamic Extremists Face Citizen Uprising in Mali," *Guardian* (UK), July 17, 2012, accessed November 21, 2012, http://www.guardian.co.uk/world/2012/jul/17/islamist-extremists -alqaida-uprising-mali. Thanks go to Ryan Skinner for pointing me toward these sources.

20. Susan Rasmussen, "Moving beyond Protest in Tuareg Ichumar Performance," *Ethnohistory* 53, no. 4 (Fall 2006).

21. Nadia Belalimat, "The *Ishumar* Guitar: Emergence, Circulation and Evolution from Diasporic Performances to the World Scene," in *Tuareg Society within a Globalized World*, ed. Fischer and Kohl (London: Tauris, 2010), 160.

22. Rasmussen, "Moving beyond Protest in Tuareg Ichumar Performance," 643.

23. Rasmussen, "Moving beyond Protest in Tuareg Ichumar Performance," 635, 639.

24. Belalimat, "The *Ishumar* Guitar," 160. An example of teherdent style is the music of Tartit, whose first international release, *Ichichila*, came out in 2000.

25. Rasmussen, "Moving beyond Protest in Tuareg Ichumar Performance," 646.

26. Taylor, "World Music Today," 178.

27. Gilroy, *Deeper Than Blue*, 94.

28. Brown, "Buzz and Rumble," 131.

29. Jacques Rancière, *The Politics of Aesthetics: The Distribution of the Sensible*, trans. Gabriel Rockhill (New York: Continuum, 2004).

30. Nancy, *Being Singular Plural*, 27.

| | | | |

Adorno, Theodor. *Aesthetic Theory*. Trans. Robert Hullot-Kentor. Minneapolis: University of Minnesota Press, 1997.

———. *Essays on Music*. Ed. Richard Leppert and trans. Susan H. Gillespie. Berkeley: University of California Press, 2002.

———. *The Jargon of Authenticity*. Trans. Knut Tarnowski and Frederic Will. Evanston, IL: Northwestern University Press, 1973.

Allen, Robert C. *Horrible Prettiness: Burlesque and American Culture*. Chapel Hill: University of North Carolina Press, 1991.

Andersen, Mark. *All the Power: Revolution without Illusion*. Chicago: Punk Planet Books, 2004.

Andersen, Mark, and Mark Jenkins. *Dance of Days: Two Decades of Punk in the Nation's Capital*. New York: Akashic Books, 2009.

Anderson, Benedict. *Imagined Communities*. London: Verso, 1983.

Armstrong, Philip. *Reticulations: Jean-Luc Nancy and the Networks of the Political*. Minneapolis: University of Minnesota Press, 2009.

Arrow, Michelle. "'It Has Become My Personal Anthem': 'I Am Woman,' Popular Culture and 1970s Feminism." *Australian Cultural Studies* 22, no. 53 (July 2007): 213–31.

Atkins, E. Taylor. *Blue Nippon: Authenticating Jazz in Japan*. Durham, NC: Duke University Press, 2001.

Attali, Jacques. *Noise: The Political Economy of Music*. Trans. Brian Massumi. Minneapolis: University of Minnesota Press, 1985.

Auslander, Philip. *Liveness: Performance in a Mediatized Culture*. New York: Routledge, 2008.

Azerrad, Michael. *Our Band Could Be Your Life: Scenes from the American Indie Underground 1981–1991*. Boston: Little, Brown and Co., 2001.

Baldwin, James. *Collected Essays*. New York: Library of America, 1998.

Bangs, Lester. "Patti Smith: *Horses*." In *Mainlines, Blood Feasts, and Bad Taste: A Lester Bangs Reader*, ed. John Morthland, 101–3. New York: Anchor Books, 2003.

Bangs, Lester, and Jaan Uhelszki. "Sulky Angel: The Poetry of Patti Smith." *Creem*, February 1974, 30–31.

Becker, Scott Marc. "Sharps and Flats: Moby Draws a Bold Line Straight from the Mississippi Delta to the South Bronx, Connecting the Dots of Black Music in a Search for the Roots of His Electronic Craft." *Salon*, June 8, 1999. Accessed June 8, 2009. http://www.salon.com/ent/music /review/1999/06/08/moby/index.html.

Belalimat, Nadia. "The *Ishumar* Guitar: Emergence, Circulation and Evolution from Diasporic Performances to the World Scene." In *Tuareg Society within a Globalized World*, ed. Ines Kohl and Anja Fischer, 155–70. London: Tauris, 2010.

Bendix, Regina. *In Search of Authenticity: The Formation of Folklore Studies*. Madison: University of Wisconsin Press, 1997.

Benitez, Joaquim M., and Kondo Jo. "Serialism in a Japanese Context: A Conversation with Matsudaira Yoritsune." *Contemporary Music Review* 17, no. 4 (1998): 87–96.

Berio, Luciano. *Remembering the Future*. Cambridge, MA: Harvard University Press, 2006.

Berio, Luciano, with Rossana Dalmonte and Balint Andras Varga. *Two Interviews*. Ed. and trans. David Osmond-Smith. New York: Marion Boyars, 1985.

Berlant, Lauren. *Cruel Optimism*. Durham, NC: Duke University Press, 2011.

———. *The Female Complaint: The Unfinished Business of Sentimentality in American Culture*. Durham, NC: Duke University Press, 2008.

Berman, Marshall. *The Politics of Authenticity: Radical Individualism and the Emergence of Modern Society*. London: Verso, 2009.

Bernstein, Gail Lee, ed. *Recreating Japanese Women, 1600–1945*. Berkeley: University of California Press, 1991.

Bernstein, Leonard. "The Negro in Music: Problems He Has to Face in Getting a Start." *New York Times*, November 2, 1947. Accessed August 23, 2011. http:// select.nytimes.com/gst/abstract.html?res=F50A10FF3B5E17738DDDAB0 894D9415B8788F1D3&scp=1&sq=Bernstein+Negro+in+Music&st=p.

Blacking, John. *How Musical Is Man?* Seattle: University of Washington Press, 1973.

Bloom, Harold. *The Anxiety of Influence: A Theory of Poetry*. New York: Oxford University Press, 1973.

Bockris, Victor. *Transformer: The Lou Reed Story*. New York: Da Capo Press, 1997.

———. *Warhol: The Biography*. 2nd ed. New York: Da Capo Press, 2003.

Bockris, Victor, and Roberta Bayley. *Patti Smith: An Unauthorized Biography*. New York: Simon and Schuster, 1999.

Bockris, Victor, and Gerard Malanga. *Uptight: The Velvet Underground Story*. New York: Omnibus Press, 1983.

Bond, Julian and Sondra Kathryn Wilson. *Lift Every Voice and Sing: A Celebra-*

tion of the Negro National Anthem; 100 Years, 100 Voices. New York: Random House, 2000.

Born, Georgina, and David Hesmondhalgh, eds. *Western Music and Its Others: Difference, Representation, and Appropriation in Music*. Berkeley: University of California Press, 2000.

Bourdieu, Pierre. *The Field of Cultural Production: Essays on Art and Literature*. Trans. Richard Nice. New York: Columbia University Press, 1993.

Branham, Robert J. "'Of Thee I Sing': Contesting America." *American Quarterly* 48, no. 4 (1996): 623–52.

Brooks, Daphne. *Bodies in Dissent: Spectacular Performances of Race and Freedom, 1850–1910*. Durham, NC; Duke University Press, 2006.

Brown, Jayna. "Buzz and Rumble: Global Pop Music and Utopian Impulse." *Social Text* 28, no. 1 (Spring 2010): 125–46.

Brown, Virginia Pounds, and Laurella Owens. *Toting the Lead Row: Ruby Pickens Tartt, Alabama Folklorist*. Tuscaloosa: University of Alabama Press, 1981.

Burkhardt, Albert, and Rudolf Telling. *Let's Sing Together: Britische und Amerikanische Lieder*. Berlin: Volk und Wissen Volkseigener Verlag, 1973.

Burnett, Henry. "Minezaki Koto's *Zangetsu*: An Analysis of a Traditional Japanese Chamber Music Compositio." *Perspectives of New Music* 27, no. 2 (Summer 1989): 78–117.

Burt, Peter. *The Music of Toru Takemitsu*. New York: Columbia University Press, 2006.

Cage, John. *A Year from Monday: New Lectures and Writings*. Middletown, CT: Wesleyan University Press, 1969.

——. *Silence: Lectures and Writings*. Middletown, CT: Wesleyan University Press, 1961.

Cale, John, with Victor Bockris. *What's Welsh for Zen? The Autobiography of John Cale*. New York: Bloomsbury Press, 1999.

Cantwell, Robert. *When We Were Good: The Folk Revival*. Cambridge, MA: Harvard University Press, 1996.

Carawan, Guy, and Candie Carawan, eds. *We Shall Overcome! Songs of the Southern Freedom Movement*. New York: Oak Publications, 1963.

Carby, Hazel. *Race Men*. Cambridge, MA: Harvard University Press, 2000.

Cardew, Cornelius. *Stockhausen Serves Imperialism, and Other Articles*. London: Latimer New Dimensions Limited, 1974.

Chacon, Daniel. "'Black National Anthem' Brings City Council President Hate Mail." *Rocky Mountain News*, July 2, 2008. Accessed July 20, 2009. http://www.rockymountainnews.com/news/2008/jul/01/singing-black-national-anthem-hits-sour-note/.

Chadwick, Owen. *The Reformation*. New York: Penguin Books, 1972.

Chapple, Steve, and Reebee Garofalo. *Rock and Roll Is Here to Pay*. Chicago: Nelson Hall, 1977.

Clayson, Alan, with Barb Jungr and Rob Johnson. *Woman: The Incredible Life of Yoko Ono*. New Malden, UK: Chrome Dreams, 2004.

Clover, Joshua. *1989: Bob Dylan Didn't Have This to Sing About*. Berkeley: University of California Press, 2009.

Coates, Norma. "(R)evolution Now? Rock and the Political Potential of Gender." In *Sexing the Groove: Popular Music and Gender*, ed. Sheila Whitely, 50–64. New York: Routledge, 1997.

Cockrell, Dale. *Demons of Disorder: Early Blackface Minstrels and Their World*. New York: Cambridge University Press, 1997.

Cohen, Ronald D. *Rainbow Quest: The Folk Music Revival and American Society, 1940–1970*. Amherst: University of Massachusetts Press, 2002.

Collins, Shirley. *America over the Water*. London: SAF Publishing, 2005.

Corbett, John. "Experimental Oriental: New Music and Other Others," in *Western Music and Its Others: Difference, Representation, and Appropriation in Music*, ed. Georgina Born and David Hesmondhalgh, 163–86. Berkeley: University of California Press, 2000.

Cornwell, Lewis. "Toru Takemitsu's *November Steps*." *Journal of New Music Research* 31, no. 3 (2002): 211–20.

Cott, Jonathan. *Stockhausen: Conversations with the Composer*. New York: Simon and Schuster, 1973.

———. "Yoko Ono and Her Sixteen-Track Voice." *Rolling Stone*, March 18, 1971, 113–25.

Cowell, Henry. "The Joys of Noise." *The New Republic*, July 31, 1929, 287–88.

Cowie, Jefferson, and Lauren Boehm. "Dead Man's Town: 'Born in the USA,' Social History, and Working-Class Identity." *American Quarterly* 58, no. 2 (June 2006): 353–78.

Crazy Horse, Kandia, ed. *Rip It Up: The Black Experience in Rock 'n' Roll*. New York: Palgrave, 2004.

Dan Ikuma. "The Influence of Japanese Traditional Music on the Development of Western Music in Japan." *Transactions of the Asiatic Society of Japan* 3, no. 8 (1961): 201–17.

Darden, Robert. *People Get Ready! A New History of Black Gospel Music*. New York: Continuum, 2004.

De Duve, Thierry. *Kant after Duchamp*. Cambridge, MA: MIT Press, 1996.

De Ferranti, Hugh. *Japanese Musical Instruments*. Oxford: Oxford University Press, 2000.

Derrida, Jacques. *The Politics of Friendship*. Trans. George Collins. New York: Verso, 1997.

DiCrescenzo, Brent. Review of *Play*, by Moby. *Pitchfork*, December 31, 1999. Accessed January 21, 2009. http://pitchfork.com/reviews/albums/5344-play/.

Du Bois, W. E. B. *The Souls of Black Folk*. New York: Oxford University Press, 2007.

Duckworth, William. *Talking Music: Conversations with John Cage, Philip Glass, Laurie Anderson and Five Generations of American Experimental Composers*. New York: Schirmer Books, 1995.

Early, Gerald. *One Nation under a Groove: Motown and American Culture.* Hopewell, NJ: Ecco Press, 1995.

Editors of *Rolling Stone. The Ballad of John and Yoko.* Garden City, NY: Doubleday Books, 1982.

Eliot, Marc. *Rockonomics: The Money behind the Music.* New York: Franklin Watts, 1989.

Ellison, Ralph. *The Collected Essays of Ralph Ellison.* New York: Modern Library, 1995.

Eng, David. *Racial Castration: Managing Masculinity in Asian America.* Durham, NC: Duke University Press, 2001.

Ericson, Raymond. "18 Works Sought by Philharmonic." *New York Times,* April 6, 1967, 45.

————. "Ozawa Conducts at Philharmonic." *New York Times,* November 10, 1967, 57.

Everett, Walter. *The Beatles as Musicians: Revolver through the Anthology.* New York: Oxford University Press, 1999.

Everett, Yayoi, and Frederick Lau, eds. *Locating East Asia in Western Art Music.* Middletown, CT: Wesleyan University Press, 2004.

Eyck, F. Gunther. *The Voice of Nations: European National Anthems and Their Authors.* Westport, CT: Greenwood Press, 1995.

Eyerman, Ronald. "Music in Movement: Cultural Politics and New Social Movements." *Qualitative Sociology* 25, no. 3 (Fall 2002): 443–58.

Eyerman, Ronald, and Andrew Jamison. *Music and Social Movements: Mobilizing Traditions in the Twentieth Century.* New York: Cambridge University Press, 1998.

Eyre, Banning. "Tinariwen's Abdallah Ag Alhoussein Talks about Mali." Afropop Worldwide, July 3, 2012. Accessed November 21, 2012. http://www.afropop.org/wp/3616/tinariwens-abdallah-ag-alhousseini-talks-about-mali/.

Faust, Drew Gilpin. *The Creation of Confederate Nationalism.* Baton Rouge: Louisiana State University Press, 1989.

Fellezs, Kevin. *Birds of Fire: Jazz, Rock, Funk, and the Creation of Fusion.* Durham, NC: Duke University Press, 2011.

Filene, Benjamin. *Romancing the Folk: Public Memory and American Roots Music.* Chapel Hill: University of North Carolina Press, 2000.

Fink, Robert. *Repeating Ourselves: American Minimal Music as Cultural Practice.* Berkeley: University of California Press, 2005.

Floyd, Samuel. *The Power of Black Music: Interpreting Its History from Africa to the United States.* New York: Oxford University Press, 1995.

Fogle, Douglas, ed. *Andy Warhol/Supernova: Stars, Deaths, and Disasters, 1962–1964.* Minneapolis, MN: Walker Art Center, 2005.

Fonorow, Wendy. *Empire of Dirt: The Aesthetics and Rituals of British Indie Music.* Middletown, CT: Wesleyan University Press, 2006.

Foster, Hal. *The Return of the Real: The Avant-Garde at the End of the Century*. Cambridge, MA: MIT Press, 1996.

Foucault, Michel. *"Society Must Be Defended": Lectures at the College de France, 1975–76*. Trans. David Macey. New York: Picador Press, 2003.

Fox, Aaron. "'Alternative' to What? *O Brother*, September 11, and the Politics of Country Music." In *Country Music Goes to War*, ed. Charles Wolfe and James Akenson, 164–91. Lexington: University of Kentucky Press, 2005.

———. *Real Country: Music and Language in Working-Class Culture*. Durham, NC: Duke University Press, 2004.

Freedland, Michael. *Leonard Bernstein*. London: Harrap, 1987.

Freud, Sigmund. "Mourning and Melancholia," in his *General Psychological Theory: Papers on Metapsychology*, ed. Philip Rieff. New York: Collier Books, 1963.

Frith, Simon. *Music for Pleasure: Essays in the Sociology of Pop*. New York: Routledge, 1988.

Frith, Simon, and Howard Horne. *Art into Pop*. London: Methuen Press, 1987.

Frith, Simon, Will Straw, and John Street, eds. *The Cambridge Companion to Rock and Pop*. New York: Cambridge University Press, 2001.

Galliano, Luciana. *Yogaku: Japanese Music in the Twentieth Century*. Lanham, MD: Scarecrow Press, 2002.

Gendron, Bernard. *Between Montmartre and the Mudd Club: Popular Music and the Avant-Garde*. Chicago: University of Chicago Press, 2002.

Gillett, Charlie. *Making Tracks: Atlantic Records and the Growth of a Multi-billion Dollar Industry*. New York: E. P. Dutton, 1974.

Gilroy, Paul. *The Black Atlantic: Modernity and Double Consciousness*. Cambridge, MA: Harvard University Press, 1993.

———. *Darker Than Blue: On the Moral Economies of Black Atlantic Culture*. Cambridge, MA: Belknap Press and Harvard University Press, 2010.

Gioia, Ted. *Delta Blues: The Life and Times of the Mississippi Masters Who Revolutionized American Music*. New York: W. W. Norton, 2009.

Glaude, Eddie S., Jr. *Exodus! Religion, Race, and Nation in Early Nineteenth-Century Black America*. Chicago: University of Chicago Press, 2000.

Glover, Tony. "Review of *7th Heaven* by Patti Smith," *Creem*, October 1972, 52.

Gooding-Williams, Robert. *Look, a Negro! Philosophical Essays on Race, Culture and Politics*. New York: Routledge, 2006.

Gopinath, Sumanth. "The Problem of the Political in Steve Reich's *Come Out*." In *Sound Commitments: Avant-Garde Music and the Sixties*, ed. Robert Adlington, 121–44. New York: Oxford University Press, 2009.

Goto-Jones, Christopher S. *Political Philosophy in Japan: Nishida, the Kyoto School, and Co-Prosperity*. New York: Routledge, 2005.

Gottlieb, Joanne, and Gayle Wald. "Smells Like Teen Spirit: Riot Grrrls, Revolution, and Women in Independent Rock." In *Microphone Fiends: Youth Music and Youth Culture*, ed. Andrew Ross and Tricia Rose, 250–74. New York: Routledge, 1994.

Gould, Jonathan. *Can't Buy Me Love: The Beatles, Britain, and America*. New York: Three Rivers Press, 2007.

Gracyk, Theodore. *Listening to Popular Music; Or, How I Learned to Stop Worrying and Love Led Zeppelin*. Ann Arbor: University of Michigan Press, 2007.

Greenberg, Cheryl Lynn, ed. *A Circle of Trust: Remembering SNCC*. New Brunswick, NJ: Rutgers University Press, 1998.

Gross, Amy. "I'm Doing a Revenge for Bad Skin: Introducing Rock 'n' Roll's Lady Raunch, Patti Smith." *Mademoiselle*, September 1975. Republished online: http://www.oceanstar.com/patti/intervus/7509made.htm. Accessed August 8, 2013.

Guralnick, Peter. *Dream Boogie: The Triumph of Sam Cooke*. New York: Back Bay Books, 2005.

———. *Sweet Soul Music: Rhythm and Blues and the Southern Dream of Freedom*. New York: Harper and Row, 1986.

Gutman, Amy. *Identity in Democracy*. Princeton, NJ: Princeton University Press, 2003.

Habermas, Jürgen. *Between Facts and Norms: Contributions to a Discourse Theory of Law and Democracy*. Trans. William Rehg. Cambridge, MA: MIT Press, 1996.

Hamilton, Marybeth. *In Search of the Blues*. New York: Basic Books, 2008.

Hanslick, Eduard. *The Beautiful in Music*. Trans. Gustav Cohen. New York: Liberal Arts Press, 1957.

———. *On the Musically Beautiful: A Contribution towards the Revision of the Aesthetics of Music*. Trans. Geoffrey Payzant. New York: Hackett, 1986.

Hardt, Michael, and Antonio Negri. *Empire*. Cambridge, MA: Harvard University Press, 2000.

Harley, John. *William Byrd: Gentleman of the Chapel Royal*. Brookfield, VT: Ashgate Publishing, 1997.

Harootunian, Harry. *Overcome by Modernity: History, Culture, and Community in Interwar Japan*. Princeton, NJ: Princeton University Press, 2000.

Haskell, Barbara, and John G. Hanhardt. *Yoko Ono: Arias and Objects*. Salt Lake City, UT: Peregrine Smith Books, 1991.

Hayward, Clarissa Rile. "Democracy's Identity Problem: Is 'Constitutional Patriotism' the Answer?" *Constellations* 14, no. 2 (2007): 182–96.

Heckman, Don. "Its Reach Exceeds Its Grasp." *New York Times*, November 21, 1971, 1, 10.

Heilburt, Anthony. *The Gospel Sound: Good News and Bad Times*. New York: Simon and Schuster, 1971.

Henahan, Donald. "Ozawa Conducts the Philadelphia." *New York Times*, November 13, 1968, 37.

Herd, Judith. "The Neonationalist Movement: Origins of Contemporary Japanese Music." *Perspectives of New Music* 27, no. 2 (1989): 119–63.

Heylin, Clinton, ed. *All Yesterday's Parties: The Velvet Underground in Print, 1966–1971*. New York: Da Capo Press, 2005.

————. *From the Velvets to the Voidoids: The Birth of American Punk Rock*. Chicago: A Cappella Books, 2005.

Hickey, Dave. *The Invisible Dragon: Essays on Beauty*. Revised and expanded ed. Chicago: University of Chicago Press, 2009.

Higginbotham, Evelyn Brooks. *Righteous Discontent: The Women's Movement in the Black Baptist Church, 1880–1920*. Cambridge, MA: Harvard University Press, 1993.

Hill, Napoleon. *Think and Grow Rich, Original 1937 Classic Edition*. NY: Soho Books, 2010.

Hirsch, Afua. "Islamic Extremists Face Citizen Uprising in Mali." *Guardian* (UK), July 17, 2012. Accessed November 21, 2012. http://www.guardian.co.uk/world/2012/jul/17/islamist-extremists-alqaida-uprising-mali.

Hirschkind, Charles. *The Ethical Soundscape: Cassette Sermons and Islamic Counterpublics*. New York: Columbia University Press, 2006.

Hopkins, Jerry. *Yoko Ono*. New York: Macmillan Books, 1986.

Hubbs, Nadine. "'I Will Survive': Musical Mappings of Queer Social Space in a Disco Song." *Popular Music* 26, no. 2 (2007): 231–44.

————. *The Queer Composition of America's Sound: Gay Modernists, American Music, and National Identity*. Berkeley: University of California Press, 2004.

Hutchison, Coleman. "Whistling 'Dixie' for the Union (Nation, Anthem, Revision)." *American Literary History* 19, no. 3 (Fall 2007): 603–29.

Japan Ministry of Education. *Kokutai no Hongi: Cardinal Principles of the National Entity of Japan*. Ed. Robert King Hall and trans. John Owen Gauntlett. Cambridge, MA: Harvard University Press, 1949.

Johnson, James Weldon. *Along This Way*. New York: The Viking Press, 1968.

Jones, LeRoi. *Black Music*. New York: Da Capo, 1998.

————. *Blues People: Negro Music in White America*. New York: Morrow and Co., 1963.

Joseph, Branden. *Beyond the Dream Syndicate: Tony Conrad and the Arts after Cage*. Cambridge, MA: Zone Books, 2008.

Julia, Ignacio. "Feedback: The Legend of the Velvet Underground, the Fully Revised Version, (1986–1996)." In Zak, *The Velvet Underground Companion*, 214.

Kant, Immanuel. *Critique of Judgment*. Trans. J. H. Bernard. New York: Hafner Press, 1951.

Keil, Charles, and Steven Feld. *Music Grooves: Essays and Dialogue*. Tucson, AZ: Fenestra, 2005.

Kheshti, Roshanak. "Musical Miscegenation and the Logic of Rock and Roll: Homosocial Desire and Racial Productivity in 'A Paler Shade of White.'" *American Quarterly* 60, no. 4 (December 2008): 1037–55.

————. "Touching Listening: The Aural Imaginary in the World Music Culture." *American Quarterly* 63, no. 3 (October 2011): 711–31.

Klein, Rolf. "Aspects of Some Recent Works by Matsudaira Yoritsune." *Contemporary Music Review* 17, no. 4 (1998): 33–84.

Koestenbaum, Wayne. *Andy Warhol: A Penguin Life*. New York: Penguin Books, 2001.

Kostelanetz, Richard. *Conversing with Cage*. 2nd ed. New York: Routledge, 2003.

Kramer, Lawrence. *Interpreting Music*. Berkeley: University of California Press, 2011.

———. "Subjectivity Rampant! Music, Hermeneutics, and History." In *The Cultural Study of Music: A Critical Introduction*, ed. Martin Clayton, Trevor Herbert, and Richard Middleton. New York: Routledge, 2003.

Kristeva, Julia. "The System and the Speaking Subject." In *The Kristeva Reader*, ed. Toril Moi, 24–33. New York: Columbia University Press, 1986.

Kun, Josh. *Audiotopia: Music, Race, and America*. Berkeley: University of California Press, 2005.

Kurtz, Michael. *Stockhausen: A Biography*. Trans. by Richard Toop. London: Faber and Faber, 1992.

Laclau, Ernesto, and Chantal Mouffe. *Hegemony and Socialist Strategy: Towards a Radical Democratic Politics*. New York: Verso Books, 1985.

Latham, Alison, ed. *The Oxford Companion to Music*. Oxford: Oxford University Press, 2002.

Lavezzoli, Peter. *The Dawn of Indian Music in the West, Bhairavi*. New York: Continuum Press, 2006.

Lecocq, Baz. "Unemployed Intellectuals in the Sahara: The Teshumara Nationalist Movement and the Revolutions in Tuareg Society." Supplement, *International Review of Social History* 49, no. S12 (2004): S87–S109.

Leonard, Marion. *Gender in the Music Industry: Rock, Discourse and Girl Power*. Aldershot, UK: Ashgate Publishing, 2007.

Lester, Julius. *Search for the New Land: History as Subjective Experience*. New York: Dial Press, 1969.

Levitz, Tamara. "Yoko Ono and the Unfinished Music of 'John and Yoko': Imagining Gender and Racial Equality in the late 1960s." In *Impossible to Hold: Women and Culture in the 1960s*, ed. Avital Bloch and Lauri Umansky, 217–39. New York: New York University Press, 2005.

Lewis, George. *A Power Stronger Than Itself: The AACM and American Experimental Music*. Chicago: University of Chicago Press, 2008.

Lipsitz, George. *Dangerous Crossroads: Popular Music, Postmodernism and the Poetics of Place*. London: Verso, 1994.

Lockspeiser, Edward. *Debussy: His Life and Mind*. Vol. 2, *1902–1918*. New York: Cambridge University Press, 1978.

Loesberg, Jonathan. *A Return to Aesthetics: Autonomy, Indifference, and Postmodernism*. Stanford, CA: Stanford University Press, 2005.

Lomax, Alan. *Folksong Style and Culture*. Washington, DC: American Association for the Advancement of Science, 1968.

———. *The Rainbow Sign: A Southern Documentary*. New York: Duell, Sloan and Pearce, 1959.

Lomax, John. *Adventures of a Ballad Hunter.* New York: Macmillan, 1947.

Lott, Eric. *Love and Theft: Blackface Minstrelsy and the American Working Class.* New York: Oxford University Press, 1995.

Love, Nancy S. *Musical Democracy.* Albany, NY: SUNY Press, 2006.

"luxnigra." "Moby, Black Appropriation and White Electronics." *The Last Angel of History* (blog), May 6, 2007. Accessed June 8, 2009. http://lastangel ofhistory.wordpress.com/2007/05/06/moby-black-appropriation-and -white-electronics/.

Ma, Sheng-Mei. *The Deathly Embrace: Orientalism and Asian American Identity.* Minneapolis: University of Minnesota Press, 2000.

MacDonald, Ian. *Revolution in the Head: The Beatles' Records and the Sixties.* 3rd ed. Chicago: Chicago Review Press, 2007.

Maconie, Robin. *Other Planets: The Music of Karlheinz Stockhausen.* Oxford: Scarecrow Press, 2005.

Maffeo, Lois. "Crashing Through." Beat Happening, *Crashing Through.* K Records, CD. Originally released in 2002.

Mahajan, Anupam. *Ragas in Indian Classical Music.* New Delhi: Gian Publishing House, 1989.

Mahon, Maureen. *Right to Rock: The Black Rock Coalition and the Cultural Politics of Race.* Durham, NC: Duke University Press, 2004.

Mailer, Norman. *Advertisements for Myself.* New York: Putnam Books, 1959.

Malm, William. "Music in the Kabuki Theater." In *Studies in Kabuki: Its Acting, Music and Historical Context,* ed. James Brandon, William P. Malm, and Donald H. Shively. East-West Center: University of Hawai'i, 1978.

Mani, Lata, and Ruth Frankenberg. "The Challenge of *Orientalism.*" *Economy and Society* 14 (1985): 174–92.

Marcus, Greil. "*Horses*: Patti Smith Exposes Herself." *Village Voice,* November 24, 1975.

———. *Mystery Train: Images of America in Rock 'n' Roll Music.* New York: E. P. Dutton, 1975.

———, ed. *Psychotic Reactions and Carburetor Dung.* New York: Vintage Books, 1988.

Marcus, Sara. *Girls to the Front: The True Story of the Riot Grrrl Revolution.* New York: Harper Perennial, 2010.

Marsh, Dave. "Her Horses Got Wings, They Can Fly: Factory Girl, Coal Stove Visionary, Scion of Rimbaud and the Ronnettes; Patti Smith Now Challenges the Assembly Line of Rock & Roll." *Rolling Stone,* January 1, 1976, 39–42, 64.

Maskell, Shayna. "Performing Punk: Bad Brains and the Construction of Identity." *Journal of Popular Music Studies* 21, no. 4 (2009): 411–26.

Maultsby, Portia. "Africanisms in African-American Music." In *Africanisms in American Culture,* ed. Joseph Holloway, 185–210. Bloomington: Indiana University Press, 1990.

McDonnell, Evelyn, and Ann Powers, eds. *Rock She Wrote: Women Write about Rock, Pop, and Rap*. New York: Cooper Square Press, 1999.

Mead, Andrew. Review of *Composition with Pitch-Classes*, by Robert Morris. *Perspectives of New Music* 29, no. 1 (1991): 264–310.

Meintjes, Louise. *Sound of Africa! Making Music Zulu in a South African Studio*. Durham, NC: Duke University Press, 2003.

Meltzer, Marisa. *Girl Power: Nineties Revolution in Music*. New York: Faber and Faber, 2010.

Michelson, Annette, ed. *Andy Warhol*. Cambridge, MA: MIT Press, 2001.

Miles, Barry. *In the Sixties*. London: Jonathan Cape, 2002.

Miller, Karl Hagstrom. *Segregating Sound: Inventing Folk and Pop Music in the Age of Jim Crow*. Durham, NC: Duke University Press, 2010.

Miller, Mara. "Art and the Construction of Self and Subject in Japan." In *Self as Image in Asian Theory and Practice*, ed. Roger Ames, Thomas Kasulis, and Wimal Dissanayake, 421–59. Albany: SUNY Press, 1998.

Mills, Kay. *This Little Light of Mine: The Life of Fannie Lou Hamer*. Lexington: University Press of Kentucky, 2007.

Milstein, Philip, M. C. Kostek, and Katherine Messer, "The Maureen Tucker Interview (1980–90)." In Zak, *The Velvet Underground Companion*, 154.

Molesworth, Helen, ed. *Work Ethic*. University Park: Pennsylvania State University Press, 2003.

Monem, Nadine, ed. *Riot Grrrl: Revolution Girl Style Now!* London: Blackdog Publishing, 2007.

Morely, Paul. "Patti Smith: A Woman's Place." *New Musical Express*, April 1, 1978. Accessed June 30, 2010. http://www.rocksbackpages.com/article .html?ArticleID=12198.

Morris, Robert E. *Composition with Pitch-Classes: A Theory of Compositional Design*. New Haven, CT: Yale University Press, 1987.

Moten, Fred. *In the Break: The Aesthetics of the Black Radical Tradition*. Minneapolis: University of Minnesota Press, 2003.

Mouffe, Chantal, ed. *The Challenge of Carl Schmitt*. London: Verso, 1999.

———. *The Return of the Political*. London: Verso, 1993.

Munroe, Alexandra. "A Box of Smile: Tokyo Fluxus, Conceptual Art and the School of Metaphysics." In *Scream against the Sky: Japanese Art after 1945*, ed. Alexandra Munroe, 215–25. New York: Harry Abrams, 1994.

Munroe, Alexandra, and Jon Hendricks, eds. *Yes Yoko Ono*. New York: Japan Society and Harry Abrams, Inc., 2000.

Murray, Albert. *Stomping the Blues*. New York: Da Capo, 1989.

Murray, Charles Shaar. "Patti Smith: *Radio Ethiopia*." *New Musical Express*, October 23, 1976.

———. "Weird Scenes inside Gasoline Alley." In *The Penguin Book of Rock & Roll Writing*, ed. Clinton Heylin, 228–33. London: Penguin Books, 1993.

Nancy, Jean-Luc. *Being Singular Plural*. Trans Robert D. Richardson and Anne E. O'Brien. Stanford, CA: Stanford University Press, 2000.

———. *The Inoperative Community*. Trans. Peter Connor. Minneapolis: University of Minnesota Press, 1991.

———. *Listening*. Trans. Charlotte Mandell. New York: Fordham University Press, 2007.

Neal, Mark Anthony. *What the Music Said: Black Popular Music and Black Popular Culture*. New York: Routledge, 1999.

Nettl, Paul. *National Anthems*. 2nd ed. Trans. Alexander Gode. New York: Frederick Ungar Publishing, 1967.

Neuman, Daniel. *The Life of Music in North India: The Organization of an Artistic Tradition*. Detroit, MI: Wayne State University Press, 1980.

Nguyen, Mimi. "It's Not a White World: Looking for Race in Punk." *Punk Planet* (November/December 1998).

Nishida Kitaro. *An Inquiry into the Good*. Trans. Masao Abe and Christopher Ives. New Haven, CT: Yale University Press, 1990.

Norman, Philip. *John Lennon: The Life*. New York: Harper Collins ebooks, 2011.

Nuss, Steven. "Hearing Japanese, Hearing Takemitsu." *Contemporary Music Review* 21, no. 4 (2002): 35–71.

Ono, Yoko. *Grapefruit: A Book of Instructions and Drawings*. New York: Simon and Schuster, 2000.

Osmond-Smith, Davis. *Playing on Words: A Guide to Luciano Berio's* Sinfonia. London: Royal Music Association, 1985.

Owen, Frank. "Blues for Jesus: Review of *Play*." *Village Voice*, June 8, 1999.

Paytress, Mark. *Break It Up: Patti Smith's* Horses *and the Remaking of Rock 'n' Roll*. London: Portrait Books, 2006.

Peters, Gunter. *Holy Seriousness in the Play: Essays on the Music of Karlheinz Stockhausen*. Kurten, Germany: Stockhausen-Verlag, 2003.

Peterson, Brian. *Burning Fight: The Nineties Hardcore Revolution in Ethics, Politics, Spirit and Sound*. Huntington Beach, CA: Revelation Records, 2009.

Peterson, Richard. *Creating Country Music: Fabricating Authenticity*. Chicago: University of Chicago Press, 1999.

Piekut, Benjamin. *Experimentalism Otherwise: The New York Avant-Garde and Its Limits*. Berkeley: University of California Press, 2011.

Poriss, Hilary. *Changing the Score: Arias, Prima Donnas, and the Authority of Performance*. New York: Oxford University Press, 2009.

Porterfield, Nolan. *Last Cavalier: The Life and Times of John A. Lomax, 1867–1948*. Urbana: University of Illinois Press, 1996.

Potter, Keith. *Four Musical Minimalists*. Cambridge, UK: Cambridge University Press, 2000.

Powers, Ann. "Pop Review: Fighting Fire with Fire; Moby's Agenda." *New York Times*, July 31, 1999. Accessed October 10, 2008.

Pratt, Alan R., ed. *The Critical Response to Warhol*. Westport, CT: Greenwood Press, 1997.

Pritchett, James. *The Music of John Cage*. New York: Cambridge University Press, 1996.

Puca, Antonella. "Steve Reich and Hebrew Cantillation." *The Musical Quarterly* 81, no. 4 (Winter 1997): 537–55.

Radano, Ronald. *Lying up a Nation: Race and Black Music.* Chicago: University of Chicago Press, 2003.

Radano, Ronald, and Philip V. Bohlman. *Music and the Racial Imagination.* Chicago: University of Chicago Press, 2000.

Raha, Maria. *Cinderella's Big Score: Women of the Punk and Indie Underground.* Emeryville, CA: Seal Press, 2005.

Railton, Diane. "The Gendered Carnival of Pop." *Popular Music* 20, no. 3 (2001): 321–31.

Ramsey, Guthrie, Jr. *Race Music: Black Cultures from Bebop to Hip-Hop.* Berkeley: University of California Press, 2003.

Rancière, Jacques. *Dissensus: On Politics and Aesthetics.* Ed. and trans. Steven Corcoran. New York: Continuum, 2010.

———. *The Politics of Aesthetics: The Distribution of the Sensible.* Trans. Gabriel Rockhill. New York: Continuum, 2004.

Rasmussen, Susan. "Moving beyond Protest in Tuareg Ichumar Performance." *Ethnohistory* 53, no. 4 (Fall 2006): 633–55.

Reagon, Bernice Johnson. "African American Music as Resistance: The Civil Rights Movement." In *African American Music: An Introduction*, ed. Melonee V. Burnim and Portia K. Maultsby, 598–623. New York: Routledge, 2006.

———. *If You Don't Go, Don't Hinder Me: The African American Sacred Song Tradition.* Lincoln: University of Nebraska Press, 2001.

Reed, Lou. "A View from the Bandstand." *Aspen* no. 3. Accessed July 25, 2008. http://www.ubu.com/aspen/aspen3/index.html.

Reich, Steve. *Writings on Music, 1965–2000.* Ed. Paul Hillier. New York: Oxford University Press, 2002.

Reynolds, Simon, and Joy Press. *The Sex Revolts: Gender, Rebellion, and Rock 'n' Roll.* Cambridge, MA: Harvard University Press, 1995.

Riesman, David. "Listening to Popular Music." *American Quarterly* 2, no. 4 (Winter 1950): 359–71.

Robb, Graham. *Rimbaud.* New York: W. W. Norton and Co., 2000.

Robertson, Nan. "Glittering Audience Attends Kennedy Center's Opening." *New York Times*, September 9, 1971, 1, 51.

Robinson, Lisa. "Human Dignity Is Where It's At," *Creem*, March 1974, 78.

Said, Edward. *Orientalism.* New York: Pantheon Books, 1978.

Sanneh, Kelefa. "The Rap against Rockism." *New York Times*, October 31, 2004. Accessed June 22, 2010. http://www.nytimes.com/2004/10/31/arts/music/31sann.html.

Sato, Barbara. *The New Japanese Woman: Modernity, Media, and Women in Interwar Japan.* Durham, NC: Duke University Press, 2003.

Scarborough, Dorothy. *In Search of the Blues.* New York: Basic Books, 2008.

Schilt, Kristen. "'Riot Grrrl Is . . .': Contestation over Meaning in a Music

Scene." In *Music Scenes: Local, Translocal and Virtual*, ed. Andrew Bennett and Richard Peterson, 115–30. Nashville, TN: Vanderbilt University Press, 2004.

Schmitt, Carl. *The Concept of the Political*, trans. George Schwab. Chicago: Chicago University Press, 1996.

———. *Political Theology*. Trans. George Schwab. Chicago: University of Chicago Press, 2005.

Schonberg, Harold. "Bernstein's New Work Reflects His Background on Broadway." *New York Times*, September 9, 1971.

Secrest, Meryle. *Leonard Bernstein: A Life*. New York: Alfred A. Knopf, 1994.

Seeger, Pete. *The Incompleat Folksinger*. Ed. Jo Metcalf Schwartz. New York: Simon and Schuster, 1972.

Seeger, Pete, and Bob Reiser. *Everybody Says Freedom*. New York: W. W. Norton and Co., 1989.

Seiler, Cotton. "Have You Ever Been to the Pleasure Inn? The Transformation of Indie Rock in Louisville, Kentucky." *Journal of Popular Music Studies* 13 (2001): 189–205.

Shank, Barry. "Productive Orientalisms: Imagining Noise and Silence across the Pacific, 1957–1967." In *Postnational Musical Identities: Cultural Production, Distribution and Consumption in a Globalized Scenario*, ed. Alejandro Madrid and Ignacio Corona. Lexington, MA: Lexington Books, 2007.

———. " 'That Wild Mercury Sound': Bob Dylan and the Illusion of American Culture." *boundary 2* 29, no. 1 (Spring, 2002): 97–124.

Shaw, Philip. *Horses*. New York: Continuum, 2008.

Shelby, Tommie. *We Who Are Dark: Philosophical Foundations of Black Solidarity*. Cambridge, MA: Harvard University Press, 2005.

Shelton, Robert. "Civil Rights Songs." *New York Times*, August 20, 1962, 1, 14.

Shiina Ryosuke. "Contradictions of Modernism: Reading Matsudaira Yoritsune's Articles." *Contemporary Music Review* 17, no. 4 (1998): 17–30.

Simonett, Helena. *Banda: Mexican Musical Life across Borders*. Middletown, CT: Wesleyan University Press, 2001.

Smaldone, Edward. "Japanese and Western Confluences in Large-Scale Pitch Organization of Toru Takemitsu's *November Steps* and *Autumn*." *Perspectives of New Music* 27, no. 2 (Summer 1989): 216–31.

Smith, Patti. *Early Work: 1970–1979*. New York: W. W. Norton and Co., 1994.

———. *Just Kids*. New York: HarperCollins, 2010.

———. *Seventh Heaven*. New York: Telegraph Books, 1972.

Stockhausen, Karlheinz. *From the Seven Days/Aus den Sieben Tagen*. Universal Edition 14790, nr.26, 1968.

Stockhausen, Karlheinz, and Elaine Barkin. "The Concept of Unity in Electronic Music." *Perspectives in New Music* 1, no. 1 (Autumn 1962): 39–48.

Stone, James H. "Mid-Nineteenth-Century American Beliefs in the Social Values of Music." *The Musical Quarterly* 43, no. 1 (1957): 38–49.

Strauss, Joseph N. "'The Anxiety of Influence' in Twentieth-Century Music." *Journal of Musicology* 9, no. 4 (1991): 430–47.

Sumner, Melody, Kathleen Burch, and Michael Sumner, eds. *The Guests Go in to Supper*. Santa Fe, NM: Burning Books, 1986.

Szwed, John. *Alan Lomax: The Man Who Recorded the World*. New York: Penguin, 2011.

Takemitsu Toru. *Confronting Silence: Collected Writings*. Berkeley, CA: Fallen Leaf Press, 1995.

———. "Contemporary Music in Japan." *Perspectives of New Music* 27, no. 2 (Summer 1989): 198–204.

———. "November Steps." New York: C. F. Peters Corporation, 1967.

Tangari, Joe. "Aman Iman: Water Is Life." *Pitchfork*, April 4, 2007. Accessed September 13, 2012. http://pitchfork.com/reviews/albums/10055-aman -iman-water-is-life/.

———. "Imidiwan: Companions." *Pitchfork*, October 13, 2009. Accessed September 13, 2012. http://pitchfork.com/reviews/albums/13549-imidiwan -companions/.

Tate, Greg. *Flyboy in the Buttermilk: Essays on Contemporary America*. New York: Simon and Schuster, 1992.

Toll, Robert. *Blacking Up: The Minstrel Show in Nineteenth Century America*. New York: Oxford University Press, 1974.

Toynbee, Jason. *Bob Marley: Herald of a Postcolonial World*. New York: Polity Press, 2007.

Tsitsos, William. "Rules of Rebellion: Slamdancing, Moshing and the American Alternative Scene." In *The Popular Music Studies Reader*, ed. Andy Bennett, Barry Shank, and Jason Toynbee, 121–27. New York: Routledge, 2006.

Wade, Bonnie. *Music in Japan: Experiencing Music, Expressing Culture*. New York: Oxford University Press, 2005.

Wald, Gayle. *Shout, Sister, Shout! The Untold Story of Rock-and-Roll Trailblazer Sister Rosetta Tharpe*. Boston: Beacon Press, 2007.

Ward, Brian. *Just My Soul Responding: Rhythm and Blues, Black Consciousness, and Race Relations*. Berkeley: University of California Press, 1998.

Watsuji Tetsuro. *Watsuji Tetsuro's Rinrigaku*. Trans. Yamamoto Seisaku and Robert E. Carter. Albany, NY: SUNY Press, 1996.

Werner, Craig. *A Change Is Gonna Come: Music, Race and the Soul of America*. Ann Arbor: University of Michigan Press, 2006.

White, Bob. "The Promise of World Music: Strategies for Non-essentialist Listening." In *Music and Globalization: Critical Encounters*, ed. Bob White, 189–217. Bloomington: Indiana University Press, 2012.

Whitesell, Lloyd. "White Noise: Race and Erasure in the Cultural Avant-Garde." *American Music* 19, no. 2 (Summer 2001): 168–89.

Wilentz, Sean. *The Rise of American Democracy: Jefferson to Lincoln*. New York: W. W. Norton and Co., 2005.

Witts, Richard. *The Velvet Underground*. Bloomington: Indiana University Press, 2007.

Wolfe, Tom. "These Radical Chic Evenings." In Tom Wolfe, *The Purple Decades: A Reader*, 181–97. New York: Berkley Books, 1983.

Wong, Deborah. *Speak It Louder: Asian Americans Making Music*. New York: Routledge, 2004.

Wylie, Andrew. *Yellow Flowers*. New York: Dot Books, 1972.

Yano, Christine. *Tears of Longing: Nostalgia and the Nation in Japanese Popular Song*. Cambridge, MA: Harvard University Press, 2002.

Yoshimoto, Midori. *Into Performance: Japanese Women Artists in New York*. Piscataway, NJ: Rutgers University Press, 2005.

Young, La Monte, and Jackson Mac Low. *An Anthology of Chance Operations*. Bronx, NY: Young and Mac Low, 1963.

Young, La Monte, and Marian Zazeela. *Selected Writings*. Munich: Heiner Friedrich, 1969.

Yuasa Joji. "Music as a Reflection of a Composer's Cosmology." *Perspectives of New Music* 27, no. 2 (Summer 1989): 176–97.

Zak, Albin, III, ed. *The Velvet Underground Companion*. New York: Schirmer Books, 1996.

Zoumenou, David. "West Africa: The Sahel—Is There a Solution to the Tuareg Insurgency?" Institute for Security Studies. Accessed September 20, 2012. http://allafrica.com/stories/201203201295.html.

| | | | |

Alarm Will Sound. *Reich at the Roxy: Alarm Will Sound Performs Steve Reich Live in New York*. Sweetspot Music, SSSRCD001, DVD and CD. Originally released in 2005.

Alarm Will Sound and Ossia. *Steve Reich: Tehillim, the Desert Music*. Cantaloupe Music CA 21009, CD. Originally released in 2002.

Art Ensemble of Chicago. *A Jackson in Your House/Message to Our Folks*. Charly Licensing ANSP 066, CD. CD reissue, 2001.

Bad Brains. "Pay to Come." *Bad Brains*. ROIR, cassette tapes. Originally released in 1981.

Beat Happening. "Indian Summer." *Jamboree*. K Records, CD. Originally released in 1988.

The Beatles. "Revolution 9." *The Beatles*. EMI/Apple Records, CD. CD reissue, 2009 (originally released in 1968).

Black Flag. "Rise Above." *Damaged*. Unicorn Records, CD. Originally released in 1982.

The Clash. "(White Man) In Hammersmith Palais." Columbia Records, CD. Originally released in 1978.

Conrad, Tony. *Early Minimalism*. Table of the Elements Records, CD. Originally released in 1997.

Davis, Miles. *Bitches Brew*. Sony Music C2K 65774. CD reissue, 1999 (originally released in 1970).

Fugazi. "Burnin.'" *7 Songs*. Dischord Records, CD. Originally released in 1988.

Hicks, Anthony. *Handel's Coronation Anthems*. Choir of King's College, Cambridge, and Academy of Ancient Music. EMI Classics 724355714022, CD. 2001.

Mayuzumi Toshiro. *Nirvana Symphonie*. NHK Symphony Orchestra, conducted by Wilhelm Schuchter. Mainstream Records MS 5012.

Ono, Yoko. "What Did I Do." *Approximately Infinite Universe*. Apple Records, SVBB 3399. LP Originally released in 1972.

Ono, Yoko, and John Lennon. *Unfinished Music I: Two Virgins*. Rykodisc, RCD 10411. CD reissue, 1997 (originally released in 1969).

Palmer, Robert. "On Thin Ice." *ONObox*. Rykodisc, CD. Originally released in 1992. Liner notes.

Phillips, Peter, and the Tallis Scholars. *The Tallis Scholars Sing William Byrd*. Gimell Records, CDGIM 208, CD. Originally released in 2007.

Pierson, Alan. "Arrhythmia." Alarm Will Sound, *a/rhythmia*. Nonesuch Records, 467708–2, CD. Originally released in 2009.

The Primitives. "The Ostrich." Pickwick PC 9001. 45 Originally released in 1964.

Ramones, "Jackie Is a Punk." *The Ramones*. Sire Records, LP. Originally released in 1976.

Reed, Dock, and Vera Hall. "Trouble So Hard." *Afro-American Spirituals, Work Songs, and Ballads*. Rounder Records, Library of Congress Archive of Folk Culture. CD reissue 1998 (originally released in 1942).

The Shaggs. *Philosophy of the World*. RCA Victor (BMG Classics), 09026 63371–2. CD Reissue 1999 (originally released in 1969).

Smith, Patti. "Piss Factory." Mer Records. 45 Originally released in 1974.

Tokyo Metropolitan Symphony Orchestra and Monks of Yakushiji Temple. *Nirvana Symphony and Buddhist Chants*, conducted by Hiroyuki Iwaki. Denon Records, B0000043 WF, CD. Originally released in 1996.

Tsuruta Kinshi, Yokoyama Katsuya, and the Music Department of the Imperial Household. "November Steps (10th Step)." *Takemitsu in an Autumn Garden*. Deutsche Grammaphon, CD reissue no. 471 590–2, 2002. Original recordings from 1974 and 1977.

The Velvet Underground. "Heroin" (demo version). *Peel Slowly and See*. Polydor Records, CD. Originally released in 1995.

————. *The Velvet Underground Live at Max's Kansas City*. Atlantic Records. CD reissue, 2004.

Yoritsune, Matsudaira. *Bugaku Dance Suite*. Osaka Century Orchestra, conducted by Ken Takaseki. Naxos 8.555882, CD. Originally released in 2005.

Note: Italics indicate figures, footnoted items are denoted by "n" preceding the number.

Archive of American Folk Song, 30, 31, 268n40, 269n46

a/rhythmia (and *Arrhythmia*), 221, 224–26, 229

art music: as a Westernizing tool in post-World War II Japan, 75, 81, 82, 277n43; European tradition of, 31, 207, 220, 231, 232; influence of on rock 'n' roll, 143, 202, 203, 205; Twentieth-Century innovations in, 240, 241; Twentieth-Century segregation of, 297n57

aural imaginary: and the achievement of human equality, 260–61; the Alan Lomax problem, 8, 249; importance of the contact zone, 257–58; psychosocial implications of expanding the, 8–9, 249

Aus den sieben Tagen, 203, 205, 229, 230

authenticity: as a political concept, 147–48; artistic amateurism as, 6; as a subjective perception, 15, 150, 165, 175–76; as an effect of performance, 181, 182; and freedom, 158; hard core punk rock concept of, 183–84, 185–86, 189, 192; indie rock concept of, 189; musical, 148–51, 157, 163–64, 175

Bad Brains, 6, 177–80, 182, 291n64, 291n68

Bangs, Lester, 143–45, 153, 155, 158

Beach Boys, The, 143, 149

Beat Happening: embrace of imperfection by, 7, 175, 186–87, 189; "Indian Summer," 188–89; influence of on indie rock, 190–91, 193; lyrical commentaries of on impermanence, 186–88

Beatles, The: Alarm Will Sound rendering of, 211, 229–30, 236–37; commercial success of, 4, 111, 124, 143, 149,

205; Karlheinz Stockhausen's dream collaboration with, 202–7; music of, 132, 211, 233; "Revolution" series, 8, 229, 236

beauty. *See* musical beauty

Berio, Luciano, 203, 205, 229, 231–32, 235, 295–96n27

Berlant, Lauren, 5, 48

Bernstein, Leonard: *Mass*, 234–35, 237, 240; socio-political and musical activism of, 232–34, 235, 243, 297n57

Bikini Kill, 193–95, 197, 199

biwa (Japanese lute): and Japanese musical tradition, 85; unique compositional requirements of, 92–94, 97, 276n38; use of in compositions by Takemitsu, 87, 91, 93, 95–96, 98, 107; use of the *sawari* attachment to the by musicians, 91–94, 99

blues music: as an ethnomusical political statement, 12, 33–34, 149, 252, 255; influence of on rock 'n' roll music, 132, 241; "Natural Blues," 5, 10, 11, 35–37; overlap of with gospel, 66–67; tonalities of, 12, 31, 68, 126, 251; "Yer Blues" performance, 104–5. *See also* R&B music

Bourdieu, Pierre, 6, 110, 142, 145, 164

Burhans, Caleb, 208, 211, 219

Byrd, William, 42, 65, 84

Cage, John: on Japanese music, 89–90; promotion of avant-garde music by, 88–89, 97, 101–3; on sound, silence, and music, 17, 89, 93, 266n20, 266n21

Cale, John: experiments of with the North Indian drone, 112, 122, 124, 281n6; interest of in rock 'n' roll, 123–25; prior to the Velvet Underground, 111, 125–26, 129; and the Theatre of Eternal Music, 112, 119, 120–22; and the Velvet Underground, 110, 137–39; work of with Patti Smith, 152

"Change is Gonna Come, A," 5, 67, 68–70

chants: Buddhist, 82, 83–84; as employed by Patti Smith, 153, 158, 159, 172; experimentation with by Dream Syndicate, 121–22; football, 236, 238; Reich's study of Hebrew cantillation, 214–15, 221; *teherdent*, 253–55; traditional Hebrew, 215; use of in combination with drones, 122, 254

Chuck, Gavin: in Alarm Will Sound, 217, 219, 227, 237, 238; in Ossia, 208–10

church: as the locus for black communal music, 35, 54–56, 57–58, 66; as procreator of the anthem, 39–43

church music. *See* anthem; Civil Rights Movement; congregational-style singing; gospel music; spiritual music

Civil Rights Movement: redefinition of the concept of equality within the, 59–60, 66–67; role of anthemic music in the, 39, 53–64; use of congregational-style singing in the, 39, 41, 56–57, 59, 246. *See also* racist attitudes

collages: concert and mixed-media, 7, 201–2, 204, 229–32, 235, 240–41; sound, 8, 229, 234

community: the anthem as a means of preserving a sense of, 16, 38–39, 43, 63–64; citizenship and the sense of, 44, 46; collective identity versus bonding to create a, 25, 64; collective longing for the egalitarian, 8, 228, 240; and the concept of being-in-common, 24–25, 26, 164–65, 241; ephemeral as a product of group clining, 40; the ethnomusical, 12; formation of the around aesthetic

judgment, 23–26, 156, 202; the function of *sens* in the formation of, 28–29, 151, 164–65; need of new aesthetics for growth, 240–41; self-affirmation as a stagnating effect on the, 240–41; and the sense of boundaries, 24

composers: limitations of in controlling musical sound, 91–93, 96–98; responses of Japanese to Western influences, 5, 75–76, 81–84, 86

congregational-style singing, 56–58

Conrad, Tony: interests of in rock 'n' roll, 123–26; and the North Indian drone, 112–13, 115, 117, 281n6; and the Theatre of Eternal Music, 119–23, 282n29; and the Velvet Underground, 111, 112, 126, 293n2; work of on "just intonation," 120–21, 124

Cooke, Sam, 67–70

country music: and the concept of authenticity, 15, 149; harmony singing style in, 124; influence of on rock music, 6; tones of country blues in, 12

critical commentaries: on the aesthetics of pop music, 285n72; on the aesthetics of rock 'n' roll, 143–44, 149–50, 152–53; on Bernstein's *Mass*, 235; on black influences in rock music, 162–63; on the guitar work of Sterling Morrison, 132; on jazz versus pop, 280–81n5; on Moby's *Play* album, 10–11; on the music of Lou Reed, 126–27; on the music of Patti Smith, 154–55, 164, 170; on the music of Takemitsu, 277n46; on the music of the Velvet Underground, 125; on the music of Tinariwen, 252; on Olatunji's *Drums of Passion*, 131; on Ono's *Painting to Hammer a Nail*, 102–3; on Ono's use of hetai singing in rock music, 106–7; on the per-

Exploding Plastic Inevitable, The, 130, 137, 139, 140, 293n2

extramusical meaning: and the concept of authenticity, 6, 147, 150, 151, 175–76; as the experience gap between object and listener, 19, 212, 214, 219, 230, 238; group identification through, 16, 19; the political character of, 65, 202, 203, 204, 232, 235–37; in rock music, 7; the subjective character of, 19

fanzines, 126, 192, 193, 198, 292n82

folk music: black American, 28, 31, 35, 58, 66; and the concept of authenticity, 148; ethnomusicologic analyses of, 13, 74, 82; folk revival, 60, 65, 126, 148, 246; influence of on rock music, 6, 109, 111, 138, 139; Japanese, 80, 82, 83; use of in Civil Rights Movement, 39, 60, 61, 65, 246

freedom: anthemic music as a promise of, 52; audible creativity versus commercial constraints on, 144, 167; as an audible experience, 146, 153, 154, 172; blackness as a musical metonym for lack of, 161, 163, 165–66, 181; as conceptualized in hardcore punk rock, 181; response of riot grrrl music to, 198; romanticization of in rock 'n' roll music, 134, 158, 161–62, 163, 176; songs of the Civil Rights Movement, 56–57, 59–60

Freund, Stefan (of Alarm Will Sound), 210, 211, 238, 240

fun: as an aesthetic value of music, 133–34, 214, 233, 234; as a value of musical performers, 130, 132–33, 209–11, 283n55; used for musical statement, 66

gender: as a consideration in creating art, 167, 292n83, 292–93n86; musical

associations with, 168, 197, 289n46, 296n45

Gesang der Jünglinge, 203, 205, 229, 230, 231

"Gloria," 4, 170–71, 174, 194

"God Save the King," 38, 39, 42–43, 51, 55, 58

gospel music: influence of on soul and R&B music, 65–70, 272n59; as an outgrowth of church-centered black communities, 36, 65–66; role of in the Civil Rights Movement, 60–61; as social commentary, 35–36, 57

Hall, Vera, 5, 10, 28–37, 247–48, 268n40

hardcore punk rock music: emphasis of on authenticity, 183–84, 185–86, 192; emphasis of on individualism, 6–7, 177; emphasis of on the struggle for freedom, 161, 164, 165–66, 181, 186; role of DC music scene in developing, 6, 151, 177–80, 184, 186; on the *sens* of, 177–86, 198; violence associated with, 183–85, 186

Harrison, George, 202, 206, 236

Hause, Evan, 222–23

Hendrix, Jimi, 153, 160–62, 203, 229, 242, 296n49

"Heroin," 6, 109, 131, 137–45, 284n70, 284–85n71

"Hey Joe," 4, 160–61, 288n29, 288n32

Horses, 152, 170–74, 175

Hymnen, 203, 204, 205, 229, 230

hymns: antiphons, 40, 254, 269n5; as predecessors to anthems, 41, 43, 53

Ichiyanagi, Toshi, 89, 101, 102, 103

illusio, 142, 157, 163, 190–91

Indian music: hierarchical playing tradition of, 114; Hindustani employment of the drone, 109, 114, 116, 282n28; *Music of India, The* album, 113–14, 115, 116, 131; the raga, 112,

just intonation, 119–20, 122, 124, 142, 281n19
juxtapolitical. *See* intimate public

Kabuki performance style, 99, 104, 105, 106
Kramer, Lawrence on extramusical meaning, 19, 202, 245

Leclair, Jacqueline (of Alarm Will Sound), 218, 222, 224
Lennon, John: collaborations of with Yoko Ono, 104–7, 231, 236; Karlheinz Stockhausen's dream collaboration with, 8, 202, 205–7, 229, 240; musical interests of, 205–7, 231; rejection of political differences by, 207, 231, 235–36, 240, 243
Lewis, Heather, 186–88, 193
"Lift Every Voice and Sing," 52–56, 58, 271n37
Lomax, Alan, 8, 10, 31–36, 247–48
Lomax, John, 29–31, 36, 37

ma: concept of in Japanese music, 72, 73, 85, 92–95, 97, 246–47; defined, 76, 278n50; use of the *shakuhachi* to communicate, 92; versus silence, 76, 92–93, 97. See also *sawari*
MacDonald, Payton (of Alarm Will Sound), 208, 218
MacLise, Angus (of Velvet Underground), 112, 120, 122, 283n54
Marley, Bob, 162, 249–50
Mass, 234–35, 237, 240
materiality: as a meeting point between music and instrument, 92, 106, 120, 222; capacity of the drone to highlight instrumental, 109; timbre as a product of instrumental, 117, 145, 220; use of the vibration to highlight instrumental, 120

Matsudaira, Yoritsune, 80, 84–86, 87, 88, 89, 274n20
Mayuzumi, Toshiro, 82–84, 86, 87, 88, 103, 275n26
McCartney, Paul, 202, 205, 206, 229, 230, 231
Meintjes, Louise, 15–16
Menuhin, Yehudi, 113–14, 115, 116
Minor Threat, 178, 180–82, 184, 190
Moby, 5, 10–11, 29, 35–37
Morrison, Sterling: as a rhythm guitarist, 112, 132–33; contribution of to the drone, 132–33; and the Velvet Underground, 110, 111, 129–30, 131–34, 137, 140
music: as a basis for ethnic identity, 12, 14–15, 216, 265n17; ability of to alert listeners to Otherness, 8, 98, 107, 250; as a challenge of self-redefinition, 98, 258, 261; as a means of globalizing human equality, 206, 235, 243, 249, 250, 255; appropriations in, 10–11, 36, 61, 167, 206; as auditory symbolism, 15–16, 70; capacity of to create a shared sense of the world, 2, 17, 19, 79, 243; capacity of to transform the polis into experience, 16; concept of pan-African, 15–16; concepts of authenticity and sincerity in, 148–51, 157, 158, 175–76, 180, 189–92; concepts of hierarchy in, 14, 93, 114, 141, 205; the disruptive power of, 17, 38; evocative power of, 34, 182; inability of to force political equality, 13, 28, 67–68, 70, 257–58; instructional approach to composition, 94, 99, 101–3, 106, 118, 205; as the juncture of private and collective feelings, 19; overlap of sonic and material elements in, 91, 92; performance of instructional compositions, 99, 102, 103, 230, 266n20; power of to promote a sense

209–12, 214, 216–17. *See also* Alarm
Will Sound
overtones, 83, 92, 105, 107, 122
Ozawa, Seiji, 87, 91, 95

participatory discrepancies concept,
199–200
"Pay to Cum," 177–78
"Philosophy of the World" (and *Philosophy of the World*), 225–27, 296n45
Pickwick Records, 125–27, 128
Pierson, Alan: in Alarm Will Sound,
211, 214, 217–19, 235, 237; on Alarm
Will Sound experiments with arrhythmia, 225–26, 228; and Ossia,
209–10 *Poeme electronique* rehearsal,
222
Play, 5, 11, 29, 35, 36
polis: as a musical experience, 16, 182,
186; and the concept of citizenship,
22, 64; and the concept of communal insiders and outsiders, 21, 24–25,
86, 146, 151, 267n31; as an inherently
political community, 27–28, 40, 197;
music as a means of re-envisioning
the, 88, 97–98, 107, 109, 240, 243
political community: as an aesthetic
experience, 18, 23–28; the anthem
as a means of preserving the, 39, 50,
63–64, 69, 72, 265n17; as a product of
musical listening, 107, 251, 255–56,
257; assumption of equality among
members of a, 39; beauty as a basis
for formation of the, 3; concept
of as preexisting and fixed, 15, 24;
concepts of "I" versus "we" in the,
44–45, 63; disagreement as a natural element of the, 3, 189–90, 243,
267n31; diversity as inherent to the,
2–3, 22; and the goal of a globalized
humanity, 206, 235, 243, 249, 250,
255; inequality as a defining force for
the, 25, 45; the juxtapolitical, 64–65;

Kaluli ethnomusicologic example
of the, 13–14; power of ephemeral
unions to change the, 25, 26, 60, 165,
260; responsible listening as a key to
forming the, 249–50; sentimentality
as a basis for the, 15
political values: expressed by hardcore rock music, 183–84, 186, 190;
expressed by indie music, 187–92;
expressed by punk rock music, 176,
183–86, 193–95, 197–98; expressed
by riot grrrl music, 7, 192, 197–98;
expressed by rock 'n' roll music, 143;
influence of aesthetic judgment on,
23–24, 28
pop (popular) anthem music: as compared to religious and political anthems, 64, 69; and the concept of
the intimate public, 5, 40, 65; contributions of Sam Cook to, 66–71; and
the distortions of the marketplace,
108–9; origins of, 64–66; on the
power of, 39–40; power to promote
a sense of equality among listeners,
69; riot grrrl anthems of belonging,
197, 198, 199, 200; within the rock
music tradition, 167, 168, 176, 182.
See also anthem
Price, Jason (of Alarm Will Sound),
208, 210, 211, 218, 225, 226
punk rock music, 127–28, 175–86, 193,
197–98, 246, 292–9386

R&B music, 6, 65–66, 67, 130. *See also*
blues music
racial diversity: among listeners of
musical genres, 67, 180; crossover
music stars, 67–68, 162, 273n65; race
as a subjectifying practice, 14–15,
165; within musical groups, 65
racist attitudes: as a separator in the
music industry, 11, 149, 197, 242,
297n57, 298n95; of false liberals,

ment, 36, 37; as used in experimental music, 89, 91, 93; versus the Japanese concept of *ma*, 76, 92–93, 97

singing: anthems, 43; antiphonal, 269n5; blues, 33–34; choir in anthems, 41, 55; collective as a means of promoting unity, 50, 51, 54, 57–58; processual, 58; styles of Vera Hall versus Dock Reed, 31; *teherdent* and *alguitara*, 253–54, 258; unisonance, 43, 46, 49–50, 55, 57–58, 72

slavery: as a hindrance to formation of the intimate public, 45, 46, 47; impact of on American musical traditions, 12, 49, 53, 59, 69, 148

Smith, Patti: on black influences on the music industry, 162–63; connections of to the Velvet Underground, 151–53, 158, 174; "Gloria" version, 170–72; "Hey Joe" version, 160–61, 288n29; *Horses* album, 170–74; impact of on rock 'n' roll music, 6, 151–55, 158–59, 164, 174–76, 287–88n25; performances of, 6, 154–57, 161–62, 163, 169; "Piss Factory," 159–60; poetry of, 153–55, 287n21; and the promotion of female machisma, 167–68, 289n46, 290n62, 292–93n86; reiterations of concerning freedom, 165–66

soul music: as a product of black pain and joy, 166; and the concept of participatory discrepancy, 199–200; and congregational singing style, 39; influence of on rock music, 6, 130; origins of, 65–67, 246; as secularized gospel music, 67, 70

sound: capacity of to be inherently beautiful, 17; Japanese versus Western concepts of sound and pitch, 92; musical vibrations, 20, 26, 94, 109, 120, 125; noise as musical, 3, 4, 17, 20–21, 91–92, 96–98; the physicality

of, 18, 99, 101, 105, 109; thinking in versus thinking accompanied by, 75; and volume, 120, 122

spiritual music: performance of, 31, 66; role of in the Civil Rights Movement, 39, 56–61; as socio-political commentary, 35

"Star-Spangled Banner, The," 38, 47, 50–52, 242, 271n37, 296n49

Stimmung, 203, 204, 205, 229, 230

Stockhausen, Karlheinz: as a champion of electronic music, 206; Alarm Will Sound rendering of, 229–31, 243; dream collaboration of with the Beatles, 8, 201–7, 293n2; dream of a universal music, 203–5, 206, 207, 231, 240; on music and politics, 207, 231, 235; music of, 203, 205

Takemitsu, Toro: on the concept of *ma*, 93; on the concept of *sawari*, 99; early life of, 73, 86; integration of Japanese musical traditions and Western instrumentation by, 91, 93–95, 97, 246–47; Jikken Kobo (Experimental Workshop), 86, 88, 98, 100; musical challenges of to Orientalist biases, 88–89, 98, 110, 242; *November Steps*, 86–88, 89, 93–98, 107, 242; other orchestral works of, 87–88, 91, 95; reappropriation of traditional Japanese musical sounds by, 5, 72–73, 86, 88–90, 99, 107

Tartt, Ruby Pickens, 29–30, 33, 37, 268n41

teherdent and *alguitara* singing, 253–54, 258

Tehillim, 209, 211–12, 214–17, 219, 221

Theatre of Eternal Music: collaborations of with John Cale, 111, 112, 125, 139; musical experimentations of, 119, 123–25, 142, 281n6, 282n28,

Theatre of Eternal Music (*continued*)
282n29; performances and record-
ings by, *121*, 122, 282n25
"This Little Light of Mine," 57–58, 60,
63, 246
Tinariwen, 8, 250–60
"Trouble So Hard," 5, 31, 35
Tuareg: culture and politics of the, 251–
53; music and musicians, 8, 250–60
Tucker, Maureen (Moe): drumming
techniques of, 110, 112, 130–32; and
Velvet Underground, 111, 129–32,
133, 137–39, 141, 284–85n71
TV on the Radio, 256–57, 258, 260

unisonance, 43, 46, 49–50, 55, 57–58,
72

Velvet Underground, The: and Andy
Warhol, 108, 135–37; employment
of the North Indian drone, 109–10,
112, 122, 124, 132–33; "Heroin," 6,
109, 131, 137–45, 284n70, 284–85n71;
influence of on Patti Smith, 151–53,
158, 174; influence of on rock 'n' roll
music, 109–12, 125, 129–35, 143–45,
149, 280–81n5; musical experimentation of, 6, 109

Venda people, 13
virtuosity: as a requirement for marginalized groups, 6, 178; as a value to
be rejected, 7, 187, 189, 193; communal musical, 220, 223, 237

Warhol, Andy: art activism of, 6, 128,
151–52; support of Velvet Underground by, 135–38
Washington, DC musical scene, 6, 151,
177–80, 184, 186, 192
Watsuji, Tetsuro, 77, 78, 79
"We Shall Overcome," 38, 57, 58, 60–61,
63–64, 246

Young, La Monte: and the Theatre of
Eternal Music, 111, 119, 122, 282n25;
and the Velvet Underground, 125,
129, 137, 141–42; work of in experimental music, 102, 108, 116–19, 205;
work of on "just intonation," 120–
21; work of with the North Indian
drone, 112–13, 115–18, 119, 123,
141–42, 281n6
Yuasa, Joji, 89, 91, 93, 98

Zazeela, Marian, 112, 119, 120–22, 123,
281n6